For Katie,
The Girl of My Dreams

Fourth Edition

Mental Health and Social Policy

The Emergence of Managed Care

David Mechanic
Institute for Health, Health Care Policy, and Aging Research
Rutgers University

Allyn and Bacon
Boston • London • Toronto • Sydney • Tokyo • Singapore

Editor-in-Chief, Social Sciences: Karen Hanson
Series Editor: Judy Fifer
Editorial Assistant: Jennifer Muroff
Marketing Manager: Susan E. Brown
Editorial-Production Administrator: Donna Simons
Editorial-Production Service: Shepherd, Inc.
Composition and Prepress Buyer: Linda Cox
Manufacturing Buyer: Suzanne Lareau
Cover Administrator: Jenny Hart
Electronic Composition: Shepherd, Inc.

Library of Congress Cataloging-in-Publication Data
Mechanic, David
    Mental health and social policy : the emergence of managed care /
David Mechanic. — 4th ed.
        p.   cm.
    Includes bibliographical references and index.
    ISBN 0-205-26993-1 (pbk.)
    1. Mental health services—United States.   2. Mental health
policy—United States.   I. Title.
RA790.6.M37   1998
362.2'0942—dc21   97-32789
                                                              CIP

Printed in the United States of America
10 9 8 7 6 5 4 3 2   03 02 01 00 99

Contents

Preface

It is almost a decade since the last edition, a period in which the seeds of innovation in the prior two decades found fertile ground; many experimental practices are now established as usual care. For the serious and persistently mentally ill, assertive community treatment has become fairly commonplace although large gaps and deficiencies of care remain. Community mental health programs now routinely concern themselves with a broad range of issues, including housing, medication education, psychosocial skills training, and work rehabilitation. Families, often seen as a source of mental illness in earlier eras, increasingly have become partners in the therapeutic alliance, and there is much greater recognition of their contributions and the burdens they bear. For the broader community of persons with psychiatric disorders, treatment has become less stigmatized and more acceptable, and better drugs and more targeted psychotherapeutic approaches have improved treatment effectiveness and moderated adverse side effects from treatment. Insurance for coverage of mental illness and substance abuse for the employed population and their dependents has grown. Medicaid, Medicare, and other government programs have substantially improved care for people with serious psychiatric disabilities. Long-term care in public mental hospitals has continued to decrease, with only about 80,000 patients in public mental hospitals. Although the number of admissions to hospital beds for psychiatric problems remains quite large, stays in the hospital tend to be short, and most care now takes place in community settings. Psychiatry as a profession has moved closer to medicine, and general physicians are now more aware and responsive to psychiatric problems.

Other important changes have taken place as well. Attention is increasingly focused on children with mental disorders, and many new efforts have been initiated to provide appropriate care. Services for children are particularly complicated because of the need to bring together participants from many different systems with different objectives, philosophies, and orientations. Appropriate care requires addressing not only family issues but also those involving the educational, social services, and juvenile justice systems. Adjudicating the boundaries of these involved sectors can be extremely challenging. With increasing numbers of children in single-parent families and greater proportions of U.S. children growing up in poverty, vulnerability to mental health problems increases. Related problems, such as teen-age pregnancy, inadequate parenting, and high levels of drug and alcohol abuse, exacerbate mental health problems.

Predominant forms of treatment have also been changing. With improved drugs and the medicalization of psychiatric problems, therapy increasingly is focused on medication. Psychotherapy is still common, but psychoanalysis and long-term psychotherapy continue their decline. Psychotherapy is now most commonly brief and directed, less oriented to uncovering unconscious patterns than to addressing current life problems. Older psychotherapies have given way to cognitive and interpersonal therapies that attempt to modify more directly how people define their life situations and how they cope with them. As psychiatrists shift to more medical and management roles, the major providers of psychotherapy are increasingly psychologists, social workers, and nurses. Research shows that combining medication and psychotherapy is often more effective than either alone; and in the care of persons with serious illness, involving families in patient management and psychoeducational programs adds to the quality of outcomes. Family and patients groups have become important advocates in the mental health arena, and they increasingly have a strong voice in how services are organized.

Given these developments, one might surmise that psychiatry and mental health services have reached a point of maturity, confidence, and public support comparable to other important disease sectors. Certainly there are indications of substantial progress, from the growth of insurance coverage to inclusion of mental health services as an important part of the health reform debate in the 1990s. Many major political figures now support parity of mental health coverage with other major illnesses. Despite these obvious gains, psychiatry and mental health services now face challenges to almost every aspect of their endeavors by the growth of managed care. The future definition of mental health services, assessments of who needs care, standards for appropriateness of care, and definitions of appropriate providers are all up for grabs. Nor is it clear to what extent the power of decisions will be with professionals who provide services as compared with insurance plan personnel, both medical and nonmedical, who manage the mental health insurance benefit. These changes will not only bear importantly on everyday practice, but also will significantly affect future recruitment into the mental health professions and mental health professional training.

In its most simple sense, managed care consists of a variety of organizational arrangements for the purpose of changing treatment practices to achieve good quality care at lower cost. Historically, the availability of mental health services was limited by state budgets for mental hospitals and the ability and willingness of patients to cover the costs of outpatient treatment. With the growth of private and public health insurance, patients who had coverage could receive whatever covered services the psychiatrist thought necessary. Although insurance coverage was limited typically to a specified number of days of care, number of outpatient visits, or maximum dollar allowances, within these constraints there were no other limits on how psychiatric services could be used. Patterns of insurance coverage and psychiatric practices resulted in high rates of hospital admission, long lengths of inpatient stays, and long and intensive outpatient treatments. These patterns of care were based more on professional habits than on established evidence of effectiveness. Managed care seeks to impose a much tougher standard on expensive decisions of mental health professionals by requiring them to justify hospitalization, length of stay, use of expensive diagnostic and treatment interventions, and the length and intensity of care.

Managed care organizations use two basic approaches to induce more careful decision making. Plans and professional groups may be paid by some form of capitation, a fixed payment per person over some period of time for a defined range of services. Such organizations and providers are at financial risk should they spend more for services than the aggregated capitation payments allow. This induces them to think carefully about how they provide services, since if they are prudent they may have a budget surplus, while if they overspend they earn less money or even lose money. Alternatively, utilization management, another form of managed care, reviews professional decisions within a plan, requiring professionals to seek permission to put a patient in the hospital, extend a hospital length of stay, or make other specified expensive care decisions. Capitation and utilization review can be combined in various ways, which we will discuss later. Here it is only necessary to understand the basic mechanisms used to reduce the costs of care. Managed care programs may offer more extensive and flexible benefits than traditional insurance with fixed benefits because gatekeepers watch over and control the cost of decisions.

In principle, it is difficult to quarrel with the underlying notion of managing care, since everyone would agree with the importance of using mental health resources as effectively and efficiently as possible. Many of the traditional model programs for caring for persons with serious mental illness, such as the Program of Assertive Community Treatment (PACT), were in essence efforts to organize and plan care within a fixed but flexible budget. So why are mental health professionals, and particularly psychiatrists, so upset? The problem is largely one of trust. Many managed care organizations who sell their services to employers and health insurance programs are for-profit firms who earn money for themselves and their stockholders when they reduce the costs of providing care. Many mental health professionals suspect that their primary motivation is to reduce costs and earn profits rather than ensure high-quality care. Even nonprofit HMOs organized around capitation usually have a general physician gatekeeper who decides whether a mental health referral is needed, and often there are financial incentives for such physicians to make fewer referrals. Some experts believe that keeping more treatment within the general medical sector results in less adequate mental health treatment. Managed care firms also look over the professionals' shoulders, limiting their autonomy and decision making. Some of the personnel who make such decisions have less training and experience than the treating clinicians, and professionals resent having to account to reviewers and case managers for their treatment decisions. Moreover, the process of utilization review is time-consuming and frustrating, and many professionals dislike the hassle. Managed care firms also often substitute less expensive and less intensive care for more expensive types of services, or negotiate tough prices, and many mental health professionals are concerned about their livelihoods.

Nevertheless, managed care is here to stay. We are early in this development, however, and the structures for managing care are likely to change over time. It is essential to understand how different forms of managing care affect mental health practice and its likely impact on various types of patients. Managed care is now ubiquitous in the private mental health sector, and public programs are moving quite rapidly as well into a managed care framework. From a public policy viewpoint, decisions must be made on which types of managed care to promote and which ones need careful regulation. What income incentives to providers are appropriate, and when do those incentives become so powerful that they encourage underutilization and poor treatment? What are the rights and responsibilities of government, managed care organizations, professionals, and patients and families? What provisions are required to ensure the quality of care, to make it possible for patients and families to have their grievances heard, and to allow consumers a voice in the future systems of care? These and many other such issues need to be addressed in the context of our knowledge about psychiatric disorders and the functioning of mental health services.

Just a few years ago, many were optimistic that the U.S. health care system would be replaced with a system of universal insurance entitlement, with few people uninsured. Treatment options for mental illness received a lot of exposure in this debate, and initially there was considerable support for ending discrimination in mental health insurance coverage and putting mental health services on a par with services for other conditions. When actuaries calculated the costs of open-ended mental health services, however, policy makers became concerned and limited proposed coverage to control growth in expenditures. The final Clinton proposal did not include parity for mental health coverage immediately, but proposed parity once an adequate structure for managed care was in place in the year 2001. The demise of the Clinton health plan is now part of history, but the realization that full mental health benefits would only be financially acceptable within a managed care framework suggests the importance of managed care as an instrument for achieving broader coverage at acceptable cost.

It remains to be seen to what extent the marketplace will direct the future development of managed care and what role professional associations, government, and consumer organizations will have in making managed care organizations accountable to the public. It is impossible to predict how the managed care sector will look ten or twenty years from now, but we can be sure that it will have profound effects on mental health work and the mental health professions. The picture of the lone therapist, working with patients independent of all other parties, is a thing of the past except perhaps for the very rich. The new context of care requires more information to pass among members of the mental health team and between therapists and managers. It makes confidentiality issues particularly salient and the need for careful protections essential.

Managed care is simply a framework. What takes place within this framework will continue to be affected by our economic and social philosophies and values and by our conceptions about the nature of mental health and mental illness. In the chapters that follow, I will present our current understanding about how people define and respond to psychiatric disorders and the evolution of professional thinking and practice around these matters.

Acknowledgments

In this book, I define the major issues and questions that the mental health planner, practitioner, advocate, and researcher must face. I explore the ambiguities surrounding these issues and the research studies that help clarify at least some of them. Although this book is written to be informative to the general reader as well as to students in the areas related to mental health, it is based on more than forty years of active involvement in the mental health field as teacher, researcher, and policy consultant.

Much of my own research discussed throughout the book has been supported by the National Institute of Mental Health and by the Robert Wood Johnson Foundation, and I am grateful for their support over many years. I direct the NIMH Center for Research on the Organization and Financing of Care for the Severely Mentally Ill at Rutgers, and have benefited from a wonderful group of colleagues and postdoctoral students. Allan Horwitz, who co-directs the Rutgers Postdoctoral Training Program with me, and Gerald Grob, one of the world's experts on the history of mental health, deserve a special mention.

Some of the thinking in the book about managed care has been helped by an Investigator Award in Health Policy from the Robert Wood Johnson Foundation, and some sections of the book were published elsewhere. I thank the *American Journal of Public Health,* the *Journal of Nervous and Mental Disease,* the *Journal of Health and Social Behavior,* and the *Journal of Human Stress* for permission to integrate parts of these discussions into the book. Also, some sections have appeared in the *Milbank Quarterly, Health Affairs,* and the fourth edition of the *Handbook of Medical Sociology* (Prentice Hall).

LaVonne Mansur was helpful in typing parts of the manuscript and in assisting in details of its preparation for publication. Trish Prossick and Donna McAlpine ably checked references, pulled together the revised references, and proofread the manuscript. I am grateful for their assistance. Thanks are also due to reviewers of previous editions of the text, including Creigs Beverly, Wayne State University; Madeleine R. Stoner, University of Southern California; and Richard C. Tessler, University of Massachusetts at Amherst.

David Mechanic
Rutgers University

$$Chapter \quad 1$$

Mental Health and the Mental Health Professions

Human feelings and behavior are extremely variable. The same people may be happy or sad, energetic or lethargic, anxious or calm depending on their environment and personal lives at the time. Many emotions and reactions fall within the normal range because everyday events evoke varying responses from us. To be sad when a loved one dies or to be anxious about an important but difficult examination is a normal response because such feelings fit the situation. Feelings of sadness, depression, or anxiety in themselves do not constitute abnormal responses unless they are dissonant with social and personal circumstances.

We usually recognize deviations from "normal" mental health in two ways. Persons sometimes engage in behavior that is strikingly discordant with their social circumstances and life situation; their behavior or expressed feelings at such a time is so bizarre and difficult to interpret that we infer illness. It should be emphasized that the context of behavior is critical in making such assessments. Although a person from a cultural background characterized by a belief system based on witchcraft might understandably be fearful of being poisoned or harmed by magic, a similar reaction from a person born and raised in Akron, Ohio, might leave us puzzled and concerned. Such an incongruity might suggest mental illness.

Another major way of identifying deviations from mental health is through recognition of personal suffering that is not justified by the circumstances of the individual's life. Although it may be normal for an unemployed person who cannot adequately provide for his or her children and who is objectively deprived and discriminated against to feel frustrated and angry, we infer that a person showing a similar reaction under favorable life circumstances and in the absence of any provocation may be psychiatrically disordered.

Bizarre behavior or profound suffering is not difficult to recognize. Much of our social behavior and most of our life circumstances, however, are not so clear-cut, and it is not always easy to ascertain whether a particular pattern of behavior or feelings is inappropriate to or discordant with the social circumstances. Because extensive subgroup differences

1

in value orientations and behavior characterize community life, it is often impossible to decide whether a person's behavior is bizarre or whether he or she is responding to a set of values characteristic of some subgroup rather than to the dominant or supposedly dominant cultural norm. Persons with counter-cultural life styles may appear bizarre to older and more conventional persons, but their patterns of dress and action are not necessarily discordant with the social scene. Similarly, many aspects of a person's life may lead to sadness or anxiety, but these circumstances are not always apparent unless we explore in some detail that person's real-life situation.

Attempts to define mental illness is some precise fashion have been disappointing. Although it is usually defined in terms of some deviation from normality, defining normality is not a simple matter. From a practical standpoint the persons themselves often become aware that something is not quite right and that their feelings, outlook, or state of mind is unusual or aberrant compared with their own previous experience or that of other persons. On other occasions, people define another's behavior as bizarre because it appears to be inconsistent with usual standards of normality or departs from that person's previous behavior. Because early definitions of mental illness depend on lay judgments involving varying criteria (Mechanic 1962a), many behavior patterns are perceived as mental illness by laypersons.

All of us may sometimes digress from usual standards of behavior and expression in a manner that appears strange to others, but these digressions do not lead to a diagnosis of mental illness. Such a diagnosis is ordinarily not considered unless the behavior is persistent or is so bizarre as to be unexplainable in any other terms. The definition of mental illness extends beyond aberrant acts and expressions to implicate the person's entire identity and personality. When we define such behavior, we not only say that the person is behaving in a manner discordant with circumstances, but also that he or she is mentally ill or suffering from a mental disorder. This inference that the person suffers from some condition that permeates his or her whole being rather than from a more specific defect in learning or interpersonal relations has many consequences, which we shall discuss later.

From the perspective of particular value systems, the definition of mental illness in terms of failures in social adjustment or of lack of conformity to social expectations is inappropriate. Some psychologists have argued, for example, that neurotic persons who struggle psychologically and socially against the patterns of their society and may appear to be misfits in one way or another are more healthy than those who conform easily to all the mandates of their community (Fromm 1955). In this view, a person who conforms to a "sick" society rather than struggling against it, such as the Germans who obeyed Nazi mandates, cannot be said to have a high level of mental health.

In trying to describe the characteristics of people with positive mental health, some clinicians and investigators have sought to define various persistent aspects of social character or personality that could be viewed independent of the social context. They emphasize such themes as social sensitivity, the capacity for environmental mastery, a unifying outlook on life, self-actualization, and self-acceptance (Jahoda 1958). However, such themes do not help us identify in any specific way patterns of behavior or feelings that indicate health. Social values and social expectations determine who is socially sensitive or who is achieving self-actualization, and the application of varying sets of values leads to different assessments. Although the concept of positive mental health is one worth keeping in mind, it is not very helpful in classifying different persons, groups, or populations.

Mental health professions have specific conceptions of mental health and mental disorder; we shall describe these in some detail in Chapter 2. At this point, however, a variety of concepts frequently used in a confusing manner in the mental health field must be defined.

Symptoms, Diseases, and Reaction Patterns

Those in the mental health field do not always make a distinction between symptoms and conditions. A *symptom* is a specific deviation from normality, such as high fever, lower-back pain, or apathy and depression. A *condition* is a constellation of symptoms believed to be typical of a particular underlying disorder. Such symptoms as fever, depression, apathy, and loss of appetite may be characteristic of a variety of different conditions; thus information on a particular symptom is usually inadequate for specifying the condition believed to be responsible for it. At times the same word is used to refer to both the symptom and the condition. The word *depression* describes a particular feeling state on the one hand and a general psychiatric condition on the other. Psychiatrists often find themselves in verbal binds, for example, when they maintain that a patient who does not evidence visible depression is suffering from a depressive condition. Such depression is often said to be masked or somaticized-that is, expressed through bodily complaints or behavior.

The concept of disease is an abstract one. The physician observes certain symptoms that appear to fit a particular pattern. He or she identifies this pattern with a disease label, which often serves as a theory and an explanation of the basic condition troubling the patient. The diagnostic process will be explored further in the next chapter; I note here, however, that, while some psychiatrists think the observable symptoms and signs suggest a particular underlying disease, others regard them only as part of a reaction pattern.

The term *reaction pattern* suggests that although certain symptoms go together, they need not imply any particular disorder. Those who view the behavior of psychiatric patients as reaction patterns rather than as the result of disease conditions point out that the same condition may manifest itself in many different ways, while different conditions may lead to behavior patterns that appear to be similar. Although this view is usually attributed to Freud, it has many roots. Vilfredo Pareto, an Italian sociologist who wrote in the latter part of the nineteenth century, differentiated the deep, persistent, and important aspects of the personality, which he called *residues,* from the more superficial and varying aspects of the personality, which he referred to as *derivations.* He maintained that the same residues might lead to widely varying derivations. For example, a love of pornography or a desire to legislate against pornography may be derivations of the same basic residue. Similarly, Sigmund Freud, in introducing the concept of reaction formation, posited that a basic human need might find expression through its vigorous denial and repudiation. Much of U.S. psychiatry and clinical psychology in past years had been based on the assumption that reaction patterns are not fully meaningful until their psychodynamics have been explored and their basic roots understood. In contrast, European psychiatry placed much greater emphasis on the identification of underlying disease through observation of the patient's symptoms. In recent years, U.S. psychiatry has become more biologically oriented and more sympathetic to the disease formulation.

Disease, Personality Disturbance, or Problem in Living

In recent years there has been increasing evidence and a growing consensus that the major mental disorders such as schizophrenia, bipolar–affective disorder, and major depression are significantly influenced by inheritance and other biological factors and that it is appropriate to think of them as disease conditions no different than other medical disorders. But excluding the most severe disorders, there still remains a broad spectrum of opinion about whether most disorders should be seen more as diseases or as disturbances in the functioning of the personality, or even as problems of living. These views frequently overlap, but mental health professionals may put more emphasis on a particular perspective. In a trivial sense, all professionals know that the mind is part of the body and that psychological events have biological counterparts. Those who strongly endorse a biological disease perspective, increasingly those among recent cohorts of psychiatrists, are likely to believe that genetic and other biological factors play a prominent part in causing these conditions. Those who view mental illnesses as disturbances of the personality conceive of such problems as repertoires of behavior and patterns of feeling that have their origins in childhood and adolescent social development and persist through time, despite their inappropriateness, disruption of functioning, and personal discomfort. Although most mental health professionals accept the importance of biological influences and vulnerabilities, they may emphasize in their practices and explanations of "mental illness" influences other than biology or deep-rooted psychological disorder. Instead, they may focus on problems in living that develop because of distorted cognitive orientations, confusions in communication, distortions in social roles, investments in inappropriate and harmful personal relationships, unrealistic expectations, and social and personal stresses. In the 1960s and 1970s many social scientists and some psychiatrists maintained that persons were labeled as mentally ill because they failed to conform to certain social standards, either because of their own unique understandings and viewpoints or their failure to develop certain social skills that others defined as essential. Although these ideas are part of a comprehensive view, few professionals today endorse these ideas as a central perspective.

Social Adjustment

In addition to emphasizing bizarre behavior and personal suffering, psychiatrists and other mental health professionals frequently view illness in terms of the failure of persons to adjust adequately to their social surroundings or to fit into a recognized social group. They frequently assume that such adjustment failures result from certain biological or psychological deficiencies in the person. The basic assumption that failure to conform implies disorder leads some mental health professionals to regard all deviants as sick, and they attempt to explain such behavior by seeking its psychological or biological roots. In applying a psychiatric viewpoint to deviance in general, we often fail to appreciate the extent to which nonconforming behavior is a consequence of learning processes whereby persons within particular subgroups and social settings normally develop attitudes, values, and behavior patterns that are illegal or disapproved of within the larger society. No doubt, some deviants suffer from particular biological propensities and profound psychological disorders, but just as it is irresponsible to argue that all deviant behavior is acquired through normal learning processes, so it is irresponsible and shortsighted to conceive of all behavior we disapprove of as sick.

These conflicting views lead to defining a wide variety of conditions as mental illnesses. Some mental health workers treat only patients with specifically defined psychiatric problems; others believe in also treating those who are unhappily married, or fail to live up to their potential in school, or are bored and dissatisfied with life, or are criminals, delinquents, or prostitutes. Such multiple definitions of the responsibility of mental health professionals and the range of the problems they deal with make it difficult to describe their work clearly.

Patterns of Mental Health Utilization

Services for persons with mental health problems are provided by a wide range of facilities and professionals. When we think of the specialty mental health sector, we typically think of psychiatrists, psychologists, social workers, community mental health centers, psychiatric outpatient departments and clinics, psychiatric hospitals, and drug and alcohol treatment facilities. On an inpatient basis, care for psychiatric patients is provided, typically, in general voluntary hospitals, private psychiatric hospitals, and in county, state, and Veterans Administration hospitals. In the general hospital sector, psychiatric care may be provided in specialized psychiatric units or in scatter beds among other types of units. Despite this large specialized mental health sector, which we will examine in detail later, most persons with mental health problems either receive no professional care or obtain treatment from physicians with little specialized mental health training. The doctor of first contact is most typically the primary care physician (a family practitioner, general internist, or pediatrician), and such doctors see many patients who suffer from high levels of psychological distress.

The best data currently available on mental health utilization of services comes from the Epidemiological Catchment Area (ECA) study of populations in five areas of the United States, and, more recently, from the National Comorbidity Survey, which provides a representative sample of the adult population of the United States. Both studies are of major importance, and we will consider them in greater detail later. The data from the former study indicate that mental health visits to general physicians constitute from 41 to 63 percent of all mental health visits, depending on the geographic area studied. In New Haven, Connecticut, for example, where the number of psychiatrists was relatively large, people were more likely to turn to the specialized mental health sector. In Baltimore, Maryland, or Saint Louis, Missouri, in contrast, people were more likely to depend on the general medical sector (Shapiro et al. 1984). Even these estimates of the use of general physicians may be low, because many patients with depression, anxiety, and serious psychosocial problems do not define their problems in mental health terms and present primarily somatic symptoms and nonspecific physical complaints when seeking care. Estimates vary greatly on the proportion of medical visits that can be so characterized, but almost everyone agrees that such visits are highly prevalent. Since these visits are not reported as mental health visits by patients, they are typically not counted even if the doctor provides counseling or prescribes psychoactive drugs. In one study involving esti-mates from the National Medical Care Utilization and Expenditure Survey (NMCUES), the investigators noted that including such nonspecific complaints as "nerves" would increase estimates of mental health utilization by as much as 50 percent (Taube, Kessler, and Feuerberg 1984).

In the National Comorbidity Survey, 7 percent of the noninstitutionalized population ages fifteen to fifty-four reported using a professional service for an emotional problem (Kessler et al. 1994). Among persons who had a mental disorder in the prior twelve months consistent with the criteria used in this study, 21 percent used some form of professional service such as that provided by a psychiatrist, general physician, nurse, or social worker. Approximately half of these persons (11.5 percent) received these services from a psychi-atrist, psychologist, or substance use facility. Help seeking from the mental health spe-cialty sector was almost twice as high among persons who were assessed as meeting the study criteria for three or more disorders, suggesting that the most seriously ill are most likely to receive care from the mental health specialty sector.

Using the previously mentioned data from the ECA study, and standardizing it to the 1980 U.S. Census, Regier and his colleagues (1993) provided a depiction of the patterns of service use among persons with mental illness and addictive disorders. Although the proportions of persons seeking help from the general medical sector and the mental health specialty sector are similar, those in the specialty sector have on the average many more visits per client. If one also includes reported help seeking from self-help groups, family, and friends, these informal types of help account for approximately 40 percent of all con-tacts. The remainder of all contacts are to the general medical sector (11 percent), specialty mental health and addiction services (38 percent) and other human services (12 percent).

In 1977 my colleagues and I collected data on the need for and use of mental health care from a cross-section of persons living in north central Wisconsin. We asked the fol-lowing question: "Sometimes when people have a personal problem, such as with their feelings or marriage, they go someplace for help. In the past year, have you gone to any of the following for a personal problem?" Because the population area we studied had a wide range of services available, the responses to this question gave us some sense of the scope of the help-seeking network. It is essential to realize in examining the responses to this question that many people do not necessarily recognize depression, anxiety, or other symp-toms as personal problems. The responses, therefore, tell us only what people who define themselves as having personal problems do.

First, we found that the lay network was the most prevalent source of help for personal problems. Thirty-three percent of respondents reported seeking help from a friend, and 28 percent reported seeking help from a relative. Professional sources of help reported in order of importance were clergy (6 percent), lawyers (4 percent), nonpsychiatric physi-cians (4 percent), social workers (4 percent), psychiatrists (2 percent), public health nurses (2 percent), social agencies (2 percent), psychologists (2 percent), chiropractors (1 per-cent), and mental health centers (1 percent). The possible source of helpers for personal problems was diverse.

My colleagues and I also carried out an epidemiological study of help seeking for per-sonal problems among a representative sample of 1,502 students at the University of Wisconsin–Madison (Greenley and Mechanic 1976; Mechanic and Greenley 1976). Most students discussed personal problems with friends, relatives, and dorm counselors. Among those using more formal sources of help, 83 percent reported seeking one type of assistance in the three months before the interview, 15 percent reported using two services, and 1 percent, three or more services. The most common source of help was faculty members, followed in importance by general physicians, clergy, psychiatrists, and counseling services. Students with more serious problems used a wide range of helpers, including psychiatrists, psychologists, a women's counseling service, a telephone suicide prevention center, drug information centers, a community law office, and many others. The factors that influence the use of varying types of helpers will be examined later.

The Mental Health Professions

The four main professions that deliver mental health specialty services are psychiatry, clinical psychology, psychiatric social work, and nursing. A psychiatrist is a medical doctor who has usually completed four years of a psychiatric residency that provided intense involvement in clinical psychiatric problems. A clinical psychologist is not a medical doctor, but has had several years of graduate work in psychology and a clinical internship. Often a clinical psychologist holds a Ph.D. degree. The graduate program in clinical psychology is a blend of theory, practice, and research training. There is also a professional psychology degree (Psy. D.) for psychologists who have less interest in research. Although psychiatrists are more likely to have had intensive practical experience in handling different types of clinical psychiatric problems during their residency training, the clinical psychologist is likely to be better versed in psychological theory and research, to have a clearer understanding of the scientific bases of assessment and treatment, and to have a more critical awareness of research. Psychiatric social workers usually hold a two-year postgraduate degree. Graduate programs in social work have traditionally emphasized psychodynamic factors, social casework, and group organization. In recent years such training has become more diversified, giving attention to coping theory and crisis intervention, family therapy and behavior modification, the development of community care programs, and social administration.

Each of the major mental health professions reflects a somewhat different orientation and background, and each has its distinctive strengths and weaknesses. Theoretically, psychiatrists, clinical psychologists, psychiatric social workers, and nurses are able to work together as a harmonious team in which their distinctive skills complement one another, but their relationships are often characterized by competition and resentment. Psychiatrists are usually on top of the heap, gaining dominance through their M.D. status, their monopoly over the prescription of psychoactive drugs, and their greater ability to be reimbursed for services under a variety of insurance programs. Clinical psychologists, having research and other technical skills often lacking among psychiatrists, have substantially gained independence from psychiatric dominance, and in most localities licensed psychologists now have direct access to reimbursement for psychological services without having to work through a psychiatrist or clinic. In recent years some clinical and professional psychologists have been advocating for the legal authority to prescribe a limited range of psychiatric drugs, and these efforts are being strongly resisted by psychiatry. With the growth of managed care it is not inconceivable that psychologists with such interests will find allies and will ultimately succeed in these efforts, but in the short run it seems unlikely. Psychiatric social workers, the weakest politically of the mental health quartet, most often work on a salaried basis in clinics and social agencies, although many aspire to be individual therapists. Attracting independent reimbursement is a major difficulty, although some states require that services for mental illness provided by certified social workers be reimbursable. Since social work services are less expensive than those provided by psychiatrists and psychologists, it is likely that managed care will strengthen the position of social work over time, although not necessarily for independent reimbursement. Managed care organizations find it quite useful to substitute therapy by social workers for other professionals and more opportunities in these organizations should be available for social work in the future. But the emphasis will be on short-term and directive therapies rather than the types of psychodynamic therapies often taught in graduate schools of social work.

Nursing plays a major role in mental health services, but there is large variability in nursing personnel from the nurses' aide and licensed practical nurse to registered nurses, psychiatric nurses, psychiatric nurse specialists, and nurses with Ph.D's and postgraduate training. In 1992 there were almost 80,000 fulltime equivalent registered nursing positions in mental health organizations in the United States (Center for Mental Health Services 1996), but most occupants have no specialized training in psychiatric nursing, although many have a great deal of experience with persons with mental illness. Nurses working in mental health settings are typically drawn from the large population of registered nurses. These nurses have different types of training, varying from two-year associate community college degrees to the increasingly more common four-year bachelor of arts (B.A.) degrees. The nursing profession seeks to phase out less intensive programs and to make the BA qualification a requirement for becoming a professional (registered) nurse. In 1988 there were only 10,567 nurses who had master's degrees in psychiatric nursing, and less than 4,000 were certified in either adult or child psychiatric nursing (Merwin et al. 1996). Interest in graduate training in psychiatric nursing has been diminishing over several years, with such nurses declining from 16 percent of all nurses receiving graduate training in 1979–1980 to 10.3 percent in 1989–1990. Nurses have had a highly adaptable set of skills, and many nurses readily make the transition to caring for persons with mental illness without great difficulty. But despite nursing's numerical importance and centrality in the care of persons with serious mental illness, nursing has not successfully trained leaders who play a major role in mental health policy.

There are many other mental health personnel as well, although their numbers are much smaller than the four major mental health professions and they will not be found in every service program. Among them are case managers, recreational therapists, counselors, specially trained clergy, job coaches and occupational therapists, rehabilitation therapists, and mental health aides. The definitions of these roles, however, are *ad hoc* and may vary a great deal from one place to another. For example, some functions, such as case management can apply to master's-level and even Ph.D. professionals who perform a complex set of therapeutic, linkage, and administrative responsibilities, or to others with less than a college education and no specialized training. Thus, knowing only the title tells you relatively little about the skills and capacities of the occupant.

Social workers practice the same types of psychotherapies as psychologists and psychiatrists (Henry, Sims, and Spray 1971), and there is reason to believe that the personality and interactive styles are more important than the theoretical inclinations of therapists or the special slant of their training. However, most social workers are employed in organized mental health settings such as mental hospitals, specialized psychiatric units in general hospitals, and mental health centers and clinics, where they often function under the authority of medical personnel and are disadvantaged as well by the lower prestige and power of social work as compared with its competitors. Social workers have also been predominantly women, and disproportionately members of minority groups, and discrimination on the basis of gender and other cultural orientations has held social work back. But this, too, is changing. In many agencies and mental health centers, where financial pressures have reduced resources, administrative authority has commonly shifted over to social work.

Similarly, nursing has never wielded influence commensurate with its numbers and its central role in inpatient care. Nursing traditionally has been subservient to doctors in all specialties, but nursing has fought vigorously in the last decade to define sources of independent authority. They have achieved this by requiring increased credentials, by political lobbying at the state and federal levels, by developing new independent roles as nurse practitioners and nurse specialists, and by creating an independent academic structure within universities to produce nurse Ph.D.'s. They also lobbied successfully to have an independent nursing institute at the National Institutes of Health that supports nursing research and helps elevate the standing of nursing as a research profession.

Curiously, while psychiatric nursing was extremely influential in an earlier period, and the origins of many nursing national leaders, nursing has done less well in mental health more recently. One possible reason is that most nurses in mental health remain in institutional settings where medical dominance remains strong. Also, nursing in mental health must compete in practice and in politics with psychology and social work, as well as with medicine. Managed care, however, has the potential of strengthening nurse roles in mental health relative to psychiatry and psychology because nurse services cost less and nurse roles are highly adaptable, ranging from psychotherapy and medication management to unit organization, group therapy, and utilization review.

Despite the differences among mental health professionals, there is considerable similarity in the background, value orientations, and attitudes among those engaging in psychotherapeutic work. One study found that psychotherapeutically oriented psychiatrists are more similar to clinical psychologists and social workers than to their medical colleagues (Henry, Sims, and Spray 1971). Although there are many political and economic divisions among the mental health professions, the common values shared by many types of mental health professionals provide opportunities for effective cooperation and team efforts.

Psychiatrists continue to have the most influence over the mental health sector despite their small numbers because of the prestige of their medical background and the advantage they have in being recognized by all payers as reimbursable providers. They also have the largest influence on care provided in medical settings.

Mental Health Personnel and Work Patterns

It is difficult to know the number of active psychiatrists. Any doctors, whether they have specialized training in psychiatry or not, can declare themselves as specialists in psychiatry. One way of arriving at a reasonable estimate is to take all members of the American

Psychiatric Association and add to them nonmembers who declare themselves as psychiatric specialists in the files of the American Medical Association, the best available listing of physicians. This was done in a survey in 1988–1989 by the American Psychiatric Association and resulted in an estimate of 44,255 psychiatrists, of whom approximately 33,000 to 38,000 were neither retired nor in training (Dorwart et al. 1992; Koran 1995). In contrast with the past, most psychiatrists in clinical work function in many different settings and only about 10 percent work exclusively in private, office-based practice (Olfson et al. 1994).

Most psychiatric work, however, takes place on an outpatient basis in solo or group office-based practice (Chartock and Shin 1996). About a fifth of psychiatrists are primarily based in private psychiatric hospitals and in general hospitals, and a tenth work for public agencies (Olfson et al. 1994). Where a psychiatrist works substantially affects the mix of patients seen and the types of therapies used. Hospital-based psychiatrists see more seriously ill patients, including patients with schizophrenia, major depression, bipolar–affective disorders, and substance addictions. Office-based psychiatrists primarily see patients with mood disorders such as major depression and dysthymia, anxiety disorders, and personality disorders (Schappert 1993). The most common treatment is psychotherapy (in about nine of ten visits), and about half of all visits are concerned in some way with medications (Schappert 1993; Olfson et al. 1994). In only about 5 percent of cases is medication prescribed without psychotherapy, most commonly in problems involving children such as mental retardation, developmental disorders, and other childhood disorders.

It is clear from recent data that psychiatric practice has in the last decade shifted more toward inpatient services with other mental health professionals taking on more of the psychotherapeutic function. Between 1970 and 1992, the number of private psychiatric hospital beds increased from approximately 4,295 to almost 44,000 and specialized psychiatric beds in general hospitals from 22,394 to more than 52,000 (Center for Mental Health Services 1996). Between 1990 and 1992 the number of beds in both settings began to decline (Center for Mental Health Services 1996), suggesting what may be a long-term trend as managed care more aggressively reduces hospital admissions and length of inpatient stays. However, many patients formerly treated in public mental hospitals are now being treated in general hospitals, creating new demand for the use of general hospital beds.

In recent years psychology and social work have assumed a much larger role in providing mental health services. While psychology has increasingly competed with psychiatry for office-based clients, social work has gained ground in mental health centers and other agency practice. It has not become a major competitor in private practice because it is often not covered by third-party insurance. In an analysis of mental health visits using data from the 1980 National Medical Care Utilization and Expenditure Survey, psychologists had reached parity with psychiatrists in mental health visits (Taube, Kessler, and Feuerberg 1984). Psychiatrists continue to be greatly involved in outpatient care but are less commonly employed in mental health centers than previously, and social workers and psychologists provide the major leadership and most of the services in these institutions.

It is difficult to count accurately the number of psychologists providing mental health services. A 1992 survey of members of the American Psychological Association's 73,268 members found that 28,890 either claimed provision of services as a primary activity or paid a special assessment by the APA on psychologists in clinical practice (Kohut 1995). The vast majority of these individuals had doctoral degrees and about half were in independent practice. Some of these psychologists may be health clinicians outside the mental health area working in hospitals, medical schools, and clinics, but most probably work in the mental health field. All states license the practice of psychology and most, in addition to the doctoral degree, require two years of supervised clinical training and passing a state-administered examination (Dial et al. 1992). These psychologists largely function as independent professionals, but there are many more individuals with bachelor's and master's degrees in psychology who work in more supervised roles in mental health service agencies. In 1992, more than 25,000 full-time-equivalent psychologists at the bachelor's level or higher were employed by mental health organizations (Center for Mental Health Services 1996). Since psychological practice is typically licensed and the use of the term restricted, individuals providing psychotherapeutic services will often be designated as mental health workers, counselors, case managers, or therapists of various kinds.

Estimates of the numbers of social workers working in mental health are even more difficult. The master's in social work (M.S.W.) is the professional clinical degree, but, in addition, many more students receive the B.A. in social work with limited clinical experience. The Ph.D. in social work is a research degree, and while most who receive this degree also have an M.S.W., some do not. So, as with psychology, the number arrived at depends very much on what is counted. A survey of the membership of the National Association of Social Workers, which had 134,240 members in 1991, most with M.S.W. degrees, found that about 85,000 were employed full time in some aspect of mental health services (Gibelman and Schervish 1995). Most worked in mental health clinics and child services, followed by medical clinics, family services, and other areas such as schools and substance abuse services. Twelve percent were in private practice by themselves and another 5 percent were in private group practice. Most states license or certify social workers, and there are in addition post-graduate qualifications that can be attained, the most important being admission to the Academy of Certified Social Workers. These qualifications may be required to be eligible for reimbursement for providing social work services under some insurance programs.

Another way of estimating the number of mental health personnel is to examine full-time-equivalent staff in mental health organizations. Such data exclude private practitioners and, thus, significantly underestimate the involvement of psychiatrists and psychologists who are heavily involved in office-based settings. Such information, however, helps us understand better the roles of nursing, social work, and other occupations in the mental health arena. In 1992 there were almost 600,000 scheduled full-time-equivalent positions in mental health organizations. Of the major mental health professions, nurse positions were most prevalent (78,677), followed by social workers (43,628), psychologists (25,091), and psychiatrists (22,858). Fewer than half of the psychologists had a Ph.D. degree (11,757) but most social workers have at least a M.S.W. degree (43,628). The most typical mental health worker had less than a B.A. degree (128,034). The mix of professions differed, depending on the type of setting (Center for Mental Health Services, 1996). Public mental hospitals depended most on nurses and other mental health workers and had relatively fewer psychiatrists, psychologists, or social workers. Psychiatrists predominate in general hospital psychiatric units relative to other settings. Social workers and psychologists are found most commonly in multiservice mental health organizations like community mental health centers, and general physicians predominate in public mental hospitals, probably as a result of the difficulty these institutions have in recruiting psychiatrists. However, numerically there are about twice as many psychiatrists as general physicians in public mental hospitals.

Data on the work of office-based psychiatrists, some of which I have already reported, come from the National Ambulatory Medical Care Survey, based on information recorded by office-based practitioners on standardized encounter forms. This is a survey of visits and not a survey of patients. In 1993, there were more than 20 million visits to office-based psychiatrists, constituting 2.9 percent of all visits to office-based doctors (Woodwell and Schappert 1995). Only about 16 percent were new patients, and two-thirds of these patients were self-referred. Detailed data on psychiatric visits from the 1993 survey have not been reported. Further information comes from the two-year period 1989–1990, where an estimated 37.6 million visits were made to office-based psychiatrists (Schappert 1993). Almost two-thirds of visits to psychiatrists were self-paid, which was twice the proportion compared to visits to other specialists. The most frequent reasons for visits were depression (28.2 percent), and anxiety or nervousness (15.9 percent). Most other specific reasons occurred with much lower frequency. The greatest percentage of visits were made by women (59 percent), individuals between the ages of twenty-five and sixty-four (80 percent), and whites (92 percent). Men, nonwhites, children, and the elderly were underrepresented relative to their proportions in the general population. The average duration of a psychiatric visit was 42.7 minutes, compared with 15.5 minutes with other office-based doctors.

There is a long-standing pattern of differential geographic access to mental health services and particularly to psychiatrists. Mental health services, other than public mental hospitals, have long been concentrated in highly populated urban areas, and most office-based psychiatrists have traditionally practiced in large cities like New York, Boston, and Los Angeles that had population subgroups receptive to psychotherapy. Federal policy for many years has sought to make mental health services more accessible to the entire population, and there has been reasonable progress in this objective. Almost all counties in the United States, with the exception of rural and less urbanized nonmetropolitan counties, have available at least an ambulatory mental health facility (Goldsmith et al. 1994). Half of the U.S. population now living in major metropolitan areas are likely to have access to several mental health facilities and most of the U.S. population has an overnight facility if needed. Only about 1 percent of the population, living in the most isolated areas of the country, have no reasonable access to any facility. Psychiatrists, in contrast, are distributed geographically in a much more uneven way. The ratio of psychiatrists per 100,000 population in 1988 varied from 15.9 and 12.6 in New England and the Middle Atlantic states to 3.5 and 4.8 in the southeast and southwest central states. Of those surveyed in 1988, more than one-fourth of all active psychiatrists were practicing in New York and California, while less than 1 percent were located in six rural states (Dorwart et al. 1992). An even more pronounced pattern is found among office-based practitioners. The National Ambulatory Care Survey found that in 1989-90 the visit rate to psychiatrists in the northeast per 100 persons was more than double the visit rate in the west (Schappert 1993). These numbers hide the much larger variations across smaller geographic areas.

Trends in Mental Health Care

Between 1955 and 1983, the number of episodes treated in organized mental health facilities increased from 1.7 million to 7 million. Prior to 1955 the severely ill were treated predominantly in mental hospitals, while those with less incapacitating conditions and adequate economic resources received care from private office-based psychiatrists or in private clinics. The number of resident patients in state and county mental hospitals in the United States climbed during the early 1950s to a total of almost 560,000 in 1955. With the introduction of new psychoactive drugs, changes in social ideology and administrative viewpoints, and growing concerns about the costs of maintaining large numbers of long-stay patients in public hospitals, a downward trend began (U.S. President's Commission on Mental Health, 1978, Vol. II, p. 94). The number of resident patients in public mental hospitals declined to less than 200,000 in 1975 despite a substantial increase in admissions (Clausen 1979, p. 101). In 1955 there were only 178,000 admissions to public mental hospitals; by 1975 admissions exceeded 435,000. Contrary to the earlier pattern, patients now stay in such hospitals for only a brief period of time before they return to the community. Many chronic patients, however, follow a "revolving-door" pattern with a large number of admissions.

The history of mental health service delivery reflects the inequalities of American medicine generally but in an exaggerated form. Traditionally, persons with means were served by private practitioners, while those who were poor were either ignored, incarcerated, or maintained in large custodial hospitals. Although there were instances in early American history of mental institutions practicing a high level of "moral treatment" (Bockoven 1972), changing social conditions in the nineteenth and twentieth centuries, including decreased community tolerance for the mentally ill and the accumulation of chronic patients in hospitals, led to the era of the large custodial mental hospital (Grob 1973). Although the development of such hospitals was stimulated by reform movements intended to separate the mentally ill from criminals and to provide a more sympathetic environment, a variety of conditions resulted in large, crowded, understaffed, and underfinanced custodial institutions.

After the progress made from 1960 to 1980, many of the traditional inequalities in mental health care are again increasing. The most severely mentally ill are commonly uninsured, frequently do not receive the welfare benefits for which they are technically eligible, and constitute a significant proportion of the homeless in most of our nation's large cities. The current situation to which much of this book is directed reflects a shameful instance of social and medical neglect of a needy and dependent population.

American psychiatry as we know it today, unlike much of European psychiatry, did not take root in the hospital context, and most public mental hospitals in the post-World War II period had few psychiatric, medical, or mental health professional staff (Deutsch 1949; Belknap 1956). The most prevalent group of employees were untrained orderlies whose major function was to maintain order, not to provide treatment. Although many were undoubtedly kind and dedicated, the need to control large numbers of disturbed patients with minimal staff created a situation in which a rigid form of authority and bureaucratic response was functional. Goffman (1961), in his essays on *Asylums,* vividly described such total institutions, the way they were managed, and their impact on patients.

In 1947 there were only 4,700 psychiatrists in the United States, and only 23,000 mental health professionals in the core areas of psychiatry, clinical psychology, psychiatric social work, and psychiatric nursing, in contrast to the large number available today. A large influence on this increase in personnel was the training and manpower programs of the National Institute of Mental Health. The majority of the new psychiatrists trained in the 1950s and early 1960s had a psychodynamic orientation and were mainly attracted to fee-for-service private practice with middle-class patients. In *Social Class and Mental Illness,* two eminent writers, one a sociologist and the other a psychiatrist, studied the prevalence of mental illness among New Haven residents in 1950 and the treatment they received. It was clear that while the lowest social classes carried the largest burden of mental illness, they received the least care (Hollingshead and Redlich 1958). Most care provided by psychiatrists was for higher-status patients with less severe disorders.

In the 1950s and 1960s psychoanalytically oriented psychiatrists dominated the major psychiatric teaching centers, and America's romance with Freud and psychoanalysis had a pervasive (probably perverse) effect not only on psychiatry but also on social work, psychiatric nursing, and clinical psychology. This not only encouraged long-term, and often unlimited, office-based therapy, but also created an inhospitable environment for developing a rigorous scientific approach to the problems of mental illness. Such power bases erode slowly, and such intellectual trends take a long time to reverse. Many older psychiatrists adhere to older ways, but the psychiatric professions have changed substantially and younger psychiatrists are adopting very different practice patterns. Psychiatric training has changed dramatically, with a strong emphasis on the neurosciences, medicine, and psychopharmacology. Few chairs at major training centers are any longer psychoanalytically oriented, and these perspectives no longer define the core practice of psychiatry. Although about a fifth of psychiatrists were members of the American Psychoanalytic Association or the American Academy of Psychoanalysis, in 1989 only 2.7 percent of psychiatrists' outpatients were receiving psychoanalysis (Dorwart et al. 1992).

Although psychiatry in most European countries developed within the field of medicine during the 1950s and 1960s and was part of an integrated medical care system, psychiatry in the United States during this period operated alongside the medical care system but was not really a part of it. In the National Health Service in England, most psychiatric specialists were part of the health care system, were employed primarily in hospitals, and worked more closely with general practitioners and other medical specialists than psychiatrists in the United States. They also contributed to developing a better balance among varying types of services and greater reform of mental hospitals than was evident in the United States during the same time.

The psychodynamic orientation of American psychiatrists during the post–World War II period made it difficult to integrate psychiatry as a consulting specialty into the general medical system. The cardinal principle of the dominant psychoanalytic perspective was that behavior was dominated by unconscious processes that could contribute to inappropriate social functioning and psychological distress. These processes could be discovered and treated only through the use of the psychoanalytic method in which the therapist and patient repeatedly and intensively explored the patient's psyche. Thus, the form of treatment advocated was expensive in terms of the therapist's time and the small number of patients he or she could treat. In short, psychoanalytic therapy required private practice and rich patients.

Psychoanalytic therapy is more "religion" than "science," and its nurturance required enough people intellectually attracted to it and willing to pay for it. The large cosmopolitan urban areas provided such a clientele, and it was in such cities as Washington, D.C., New York, Chicago, Los Angeles, and Philadelphia that such therapists concentrated. Because the therapy was viewed as requiring verbal and other middle-class abilities, the requirements for therapy justified its focus on an "elite clientele." Until the development of psychiatric outpatient services in hospitals and mental health centers, the poor and those with the most serious and incapacitating conditions had no significant source of help other than mental hospitalization or the services of primary care physicians. Although general physicians who were poorly trained in psychiatry could have benefited significantly from an effective consulting psychiatric specialty, the average doctor had difficulty understanding or sympathizing with the strange theoretical conceptions of mental illness held by the psychodynamically oriented practitioners. Psychiatrists were typically viewed as esoteric, impractical, and not particularly helpful.

Psychiatric training in recent years has been more eclectic, with growing concern for scientific rigor, more precise classification, and the investigation of biological hypotheses. After a long period of dormancy in scientific work, departments of psychiatry are engaging in more clinical, epidemiological, biological, and social research. Advances in the neurosciences and in genetics, and the technological tools made possible by the new biology and advances in brain imaging, have redirected psychiatry to its medical origins and to intense investigation of biological hypotheses. Clinical psychology has become more behaviorally and cognitively oriented, developing therapeutic approaches based on learning theory, cognitive theory, and developments in psycho-physiology and social psychology. Social work is less concerned with the psychodynamics of the patient and more concerned with coping, social networks, and social supports. Mental health workers of all types are more commonly found in organizational settings, such as mental hospitals, general voluntary hospitals, mental health centers, and community facilities, such as day hospitals, halfway houses, and sheltered workshops.

The decades of the 1960s and 1970s were years of expansion and chaos in psychiatric services. New treatment contexts were established, such as community mental health centers, specialized psychiatric units in general hospitals, and many different types of programs in preventive psychiatry and community care. By the late 1970s, professional leaders in mental health were beginning to sort out the more important and lasting changes from the excesses of the early, highly ideological community care movement. Efforts were being made to refocus on the needs of persons with serious mental illness and less on those who were unhappy, demoralized, or had more ordinary problems in living. The 1980s were years of consolidation and restructuring as biological psychiatry became more dominant and as it became clear that mental health care financing would be subjected to greater constraint than was typical during the decades of growth. Mental health services became more directive and pragmatic, with growing interest in issues of finance, organization, and delivery and how they might be investigated systematically. The 1990s have seen the emergence of managed care, which has the potential of reshaping many aspects of mental health practice. The 1990s have also been years in which the voice of consumers, families, and other advocates have been more widely heard, and where the case for equal treatment of psychiatric disorders with other medical problems has gained greater credibility and public support. The issues of managed care and health insurance reform will be big challenges for the next century.

Changing Inpatient Care

From about 1966 until the late 1970s, psychiatric care not only expanded on an outpatient basis, but greatly improved in inpatient service. The typical mental hospital is smaller, better staffed, and more treatment-oriented than in the past. The numbers of such hospitals have not changed dramatically; however, these institutions are substantially different than they used to be. Between 1970 and 1982, the average ratio of patients to employees was reduced from 1.7 to .7 and average expenditures for patients increased from $4,359 to $31,000 a year (or $12,000, after adjusting for inflation). By 1982, the typical state mental hospital had 529 inpatients and 807 employees. The number of public mental hospitals has remained relatively stable (273 in the 1990s) but the number of patients continues to decline (less than 80,000 today) (Bachrach 1996). Public mental hospital care is very expensive, with average costs per year per patient exceeding $100,000 in New York State.

Mental hospitals now deal with the sickest, most disabled, and most difficult patients. Although these hospitals now treat many fewer people, and a small fraction of all mentally ill persons, they continue to consume from one-half to two-thirds of state mental health budgets. In 1955 state and county mental hospitals accounted for 63 percent of all inpatient psychiatric episodes; by 1975 they accounted for only 22 percent (Kiesler and Simpkins 1993). Their share of all treated episodes continues to decline relative to private psychiatric hospitals and particularly general hospitals, which have become a major provider of psychiatric acute inpatient care. Many admissions now are to specialized psychiatric and chemical dependency units, but significant proportions of psychiatric admissions continue to take place on general medical and surgical units, where we refer to these patients as being in "scatter" beds because of the nonspecialized character of the inpatient units. In 1993 more than 1.8 million patients were discharged from short-stay hospitals with a primary psychiatric diagnosis. They had an average length of stay of 10.3 days (Graves 1995), a two-day drop since 1984 (Dennison 1985). This pattern occurs across the entire spectrum of medical care: managed care strategies reinforce the downward pressure on length of stay.

In the period between 1970 and 1992, beds in private psychiatric hospitals have multiplied by more than ten times, and residential treatment beds for emotionally disturbed children have doubled (Center for Mental Health Services 1996). Many elderly persons with mental illness are in nursing homes, although such institutions are used less frequently than a decade ago for persons under age sixty-five with mental illness. There has also been significant growth in adult residential care, foster care, and other types of supervised housing settings for persons with severe and persistent mental illness. In sum, we have seen a dramatic reorganization of inpatient psychiatric care, a major change in the distribution of patients among sites of care, and a transformation of the pattern of hospitalization for acute psychiatric illness.

As a consequence of reductions in the populations of public mental hospitals and the transfer of many hopeless chronic patients to nursing homes, the public mental hospital was in many instances transformed from a custodial institution to an active treatment unit. The ratios of professional to patient and staff to patient improved enormously, and active treatment and rehabilitation programs were developed to a point where in many instances there is little resemblance between the hospital as it had once been and what it has become. Although many hospitals and programs still depend substantially on psychiatric aides with limited education and training, these staff members are more carefully selected and supervised than in the past. Government programs such as Medicare and Medicaid provide entitlement to psychiatric services, and psychiatric insurance coverage has improved. Perhaps most important, new drugs and treatment techniques have been developed that provide significant assistance to many psychiatric patients, helping them to return to their usual roles and responsibilities. The mentally ill are less stigmatized than in the past, and there seems to be more public understanding of the problems of mental illness.

To note advances is not to neglect the profound problems that lie ahead, not only for the mentally ill and their families, but also for public policy. Large numbers of chronic psychiatric patients have been retained in or returned to the community without the development of appropriate services necessary to assist them to maintain a reasonable level of functioning and life satisfaction. Community sheltered care has grown considerably, and is highly variable in quality. Psychiatric insurance coverage has been broadened in many cases to cover services provided by psychologists and social workers but it is still structured to favor a medicalized approach to mental health care. Insurance coverage for mental illness relative to other disorders is still very restricted, despite growing interest and advocacy for parity in coverage for physical and mental disorders. Our knowledge of psychiatric disorders and their effective treatment is still relatively primitive, and the research infrastructure of basic, clinical, and health services research in mental health still trails developments in other disease areas.

Although the civil liberties movement in mental health brought significant gains in protecting patients' constitutional rights, it also brought new dilemmas in getting people appropriate care when they do not appreciate the need for it. The improvement of diagnostic criteria and the development of treatment standards have contributed to making concepts of disorder and treatments less vague and confusing, but much sloppy thinking and practice persist. Funding for service programs, research, and future professional development has been reasonably maintained in recent years, but with reduced government funding and the implementation of managed care prospects for the future are uncertain. With projected reductions in Medicaid and other government safety net programs, the future for patients with the most severe and disabling illnesses seems particularly under threat. Changing employment patterns, redevelopment of cities, gentrification, and reduction in housing supports pose serious problems for rehabilitation and community integration. Many mentally ill have joined the ranks of the homeless, and they are doubly vulnerable because of their mental illnesses and other social disadvantages. Substance abuse has become more common among young mentally ill persons, making treatment and rehabilitation even more challenging. Compounding these problems is the fragmentation of financing and organization of services in most localities. Public mental health systems remain in desperate need of reform and consolidation. Public systems are moving aggressively to managed care as a vehicle to address some of these challenges, but it is not clear whether reducing costs or improving quality is the highest priority.

The policy agenda, thus, is large and difficult. How should mental health care be financed, and how could funds now available be used more effectively? What incentives could be provided to manage care better and to achieve more rational organization? How can we direct more mental health services to the most disabled and needy clients? How can we best resolve the conflicts between civil liberties and the need for treatment? Exploration of these and many other public policy issues are the task of the chapters that follow. But, first, we must be clear about what we mean by the concepts of mental health and mental illness.

Chapter *2*

What Are Mental Health and Mental Illness?

If we are to discuss mental health policy, we must be aware of the scope and limits of our topic. If our goal is to develop policies to deal with the prevention and treatment of mental illness and the facilitation of mental health, then we must clearly outline the dimensions of each of these concepts. Are mental health programs to be limited to persons who come under the care of mental health workers, or are they to extend to those who see no need for psychiatric services and who have not been defined as problems by their communities? Are such programs to be restricted to persons suffering from clear psychiatric syndromes, or should they include those with ordinary problems, such as nervousness, unhappiness, and social and family conflict? Are deviations such as delinquency and criminal behavior part of the mental health problem, or are they more fruitfully dealt with outside the sphere of psychiatry? Are such situations as poverty, discrimination, and unemployment central aspects of the mental health problem, or do they relate more significantly to other fields? Is failure in performance resulting from a low level of education a mental health problem, or is it primarily a problem of education? Each of these questions and many others must be answered before it is possible to consider alternative mental health policies.

Psychiatrists, mental health workers, and the public in general disagree about the appropriate criteria for ascertaining the presence of mental illness. Much of this disagreement stems from a lack of consensus as to how broad or narrow the conception of mental illness should be: some psychiatrists restrict the definition of mental illness to a limited set of disorders, while others include a great variety of problem situations within the psychiatric sphere.

Psychiatric Diagnosis Guidelines

As with medicine in general, psychiatrists have developed descriptive diagnostic labels that they use to categorize and deal with patients. Although most psychiatrists use these designations, they do not agree on their nature, significance, or utility. Increasing numbers of psychiatrists maintain that the labels denote different disease conditions; others maintain that they apply to reaction patterns having manifest similarities but do not describe specific disease conditions. The opinions of most psychiatrists probably fall somewhere between these two; they accept some of the diagnostic categories as disease categories, and they view others as convenient ways of grouping reaction patterns. Frances and his colleagues (1995), who developed a guidebook to assist clinicians in the use of the most recent diagnostic and statistical manual (DSM), state the issue fairly:

> *The DSM "mental disorders" are best understood as descriptive syndromes likely to assist in our increased understanding of the underlying disease, but only in selected cases do they as currently defined actually represent such diseases. The descriptive syndromal system embodied in DSM-III and its successors has been and continues to be enormously useful in facilitating clinical management and research. However, it is to be hoped fervently that the descriptive system of diagnosis will gradually yield to categorization that is based on a more fundamental understanding of the pathogenesis of mental disorders (p. 17).*

The American Psychiatric Association has traditionally divided psychiatric conditions into three major groups: (1) those conditions caused by or associated with impairment of brain tissue (for example, disorders caused by infection, intoxication, trauma, and metabolic disturbances); (2) mental deficiency; and (3) disorders without clearly defined clinical cause, those not caused by structural change in the brain, and those attributed to psychogenic causes. Our discussion will focus on this third category. The American Psychiatric Association further divided this category into five subcategories:

- psychotic disorders
- psychophysiologic, autonomic, and visceral disorders
- psychoneurotic disorders
- personality disorders
- transient situational personality disorders

These subcategories descriptively depict the gross reaction patterns recognizable among patients.

The *Third Edition of the American Psychiatric Association's Diagnostic and Statistical Manual* (DSM-III) broke away from traditional usage of diagnostic terms and attempted to develop a more logical set of diagnostic criteria (Spitzer and Endicott 1978). Major categories in the DSM-III include organic mental disorders such as senile and presenile dementias, substance abuse disorders such as alcoholism, schizophrenic disorders, paranoid disorders, affective disorders such as depression or manic–depressive states, anxiety disorders including phobias and generalized anxiety, and personality disorders. The traditional distinction between organic disorders and functional disorders (those without a demonstrable organic basis or structural abnormality) was discarded because the distinction was viewed as simplistic, and the concept of neurosis was eliminated because it was too vague. These new definitions, however, did not provide adequate differentiation between *disease states* and *social behavior,* nor is it clear that such distinctions are always possible, as this chapter will make clear.

DSM-III, introduced in 1980, was widely adopted as the official diagnostic system by almost all mental health facilities and by other organizations such as insurance companies and the courts. Efforts to fine-tune DSM-III, and correct errors and inconsistencies, began in 1983 and resulted in publication of DSM-IIIR (revised) in 1987. Work began on DSM-IV in 1988, not because a new version was needed, but because the World Health Organization was preparing a tenth revision of the International Classification of Disease (ICD), diagnostic codes used widely throughout the world. The American Psychiatric Association believed it was important to coordinate the two coding systems and to achieve as much convergence as possible. In substance, however, DSM-IV (American Psychiatric Association 1994) remains quite close in content and definitions to DSM-III and DSM-IIIR, and while it is more carefully documented, it contains no substantial innovations. Publication of the DSM manual and its various guidebooks and aids is big business (DSM-III sold more than a million copies), and some believe that this is no small incentive for revision. In any case, DSM-IV is the official accepted diagnostic manual for mental health services and research in the United States, and it has a powerful influence on practice and reimbursement.

DSM-IV organizes psychiatric diagnoses under seventeen categories. For our purposes, the most important are substance-related disorders, schizophrenia and other psychotic disorders, mood disorders, anxiety disorders, adjustment disorders, and personality disorders. Also included, however, are sleep disorders, eating disorders, somatoform disorders, and so on. DSM sets up a multiaxial system with five major levels. Axis I is simply a diagnosis (with the exceptions of personality disorders and mental retardation, which are arbitrarily listed on axis II). This encourages the clinician to consider further after making a diagnosis whether the patient also has personality and retardation problems. Axis III lists general medical conditions, which may be implicated in or independent of the psychiatric disorder. Axis IV takes account of psychosocial and environmental problems, and axis V provides for a global assessment of functioning. Although all five axes are important in a well-rounded assessment of patients, in practical terms, axis I, the psychiatric diagnosis, gets most of the attention.

As an example, consider how a clinician would make a DSM-IV diagnosis of a major depressive episode. First, the patient must have had five or more of a list of nine symptoms, present for a two-week period, and representing a change from previous functioning. One of the symptoms must be either depressed mood most of the day, nearly every day, or else a marked diminished interest or pleasure in all, or almost all, activities most of the day, nearly every day. Among the other symptoms are recurrent thoughts of death or suicidal ideation, fatigue or loss of energy, diminished ability to think or concentrate, indecisiveness, insomnia, or hypersomnia, feelings of worthlessness or excessive or inappropriate guilt, and so on. To be counted, each of these symptoms should occur almost every day. Moreover, the symptoms should not be due to bereavement or the direct physiological effect of a medical condition or a substance, and they should cause clinically significant distress or impairment in social, occupational, or other important areas of functioning. The symptoms should not meet the criteria for a mixed episode, which would be classified differently.

DSM has had a major influence on psychiatric thinking and diagnosis, but the system is largely based on pragmatic description rather than any underlying theoretical basis. It constitutes a committee effort to achieve uniformity among psychiatrists with radically varying theoretical orientations, ranging from the biological to the psychodynamic. The controversy is often more political than scientific in its character, and political compromises are necessary to achieve consensus. One of the most bitter disputes involved the classification of neurotic disorders, and in all likelihood these disputes will continue through subsequent revisions of the DSM. As Bayer and Spitzer (1985) note in their discussion of the controversy over neurosis and psychodynamics, "the entire process of achieving a settlement seemed more appropriate to the encounter of political rivals than to the orderly pursuit of scientific knowledge" (p. 195).

Despite the limitations of the DSM, the process of codification and the efforts to be as specific as possible about diagnostic criteria have encouraged greater care in diagnosis and more uniformity in the use of psychiatric designations. Most psychiatrists give DSM serious regard, and greater precision in the use of psychiatric labels has facilitated clearer communication among professionals. The DSM has also been extremely important for research, because research criteria based on these definitions facilitate defining samples of patients more precisely and help communicate better to which groups of patients the findings apply. On the negative side, the codification process takes on a life of its own, such that insurance companies, courts, and other social agencies attribute to DSM definitions more validity than they truly have.

Varieties of Mental Illness

Mental health professionals deal with a large variety of psychiatric conditions, but this is not the context to review them. For those unfamiliar with these conditions, it is useful to peruse the DSM (American Psychiatric Association 1994). For purposes of discussing mental health policy, I focus on mood disorders and schizophrenia. I give less descriptive attention to anxiety disorders, alcohol and drug problems, and personality disorders, but they are clearly important and are often comorbid with psychotic and mood disorders. Many important disorders are not even mentioned. Throughout the discussion I will also refer to individuals who have severe and persistent disorders. Although there is no agreed-upon definition, this concept generally has three components:

- the presence of a serious psychiatric disorder such as schizophrenia, bipolar disorder (frequently referred to as manic–depressive disorder), or major depression
- persistence of the disorder over time or frequent reoccurrences
- a high level of disability affecting the ability to perform occupational and social roles and to carry out ordinary activities of daily living

Mood disorders are highly prevalent, and the depression and/or elation can be extraordinarily painful, disabling, and disruptive to everyone around the person. Depression, the more obvious of the two types of mood disturbance, can vary from a painful but not disabling sense of sadness to a sense of despair that is truly devastating (see Styron 1992).

Much of the public and many physicians have not fully recognized how destructive depression can be in people's lives. Many studies consistently demonstrate that depression is an extraordinarily disabling condition. The Medical Outcomes Study, for example, an investigation of 11,242 outpatients in varying medical settings found that patients with depressive disorders or even depressive symptoms that did not meet clinical criteria for a disorder had comparable or greater disability than patients with eight other major chronic medical conditions, including diabetes, arthritis, ulcers, and problems of the spine. Generally, those with depression had worse physical, social, and role functioning, worse perceived health, and greater bodily pain. These patients also spend more days in bed than patients with such conditions as diabetes and arthritis. Only current heart disorders had disabling effects comparable to depression (Wells et al. 1989b).

Distinctions are made between major depression and bipolar disorder (manic–depressive disorder), in which manic episodes are evident. Bipolar disorder is less prevalent than major depression and has a different epidemiology, suggesting that it is a separate condition or set of conditions. Persons with major depression and bipolar disorder each appear to have genetic vulnerability, although this seems especially the case in bipolar disorder. Patients with a bipolar disturbance respond to the drug lithium, while most depressed patients do not, also suggesting that bipolar disorders are separate conditions.

Paranoid reactions are typically characterized by persecutory or grandiose delusions or delusional jealousy. The suspiciousness characteristic of the paranoid is commonly seen in the general population, and its more extreme forms frequently accompany schizophrenia. When extreme symptoms occur without hallucinations and cannot be attributed to schizophrenia, they are separately diagnosed, but the differentiation of these diagnoses is unclear. Although extreme paranoid disorders are not extremely prevalent, the resentment and anger associated with these states are believed to be associated with potential violence and thus require careful management. Such patients who become violent are also often schizophrenic or substance abusers, and thus the relationship between paranoia and dangerousness remains unclear.

People who have schizophrenic reactions often face long-term disability and a continuing need for care. Although they comprise a relatively small component of all mental illness, their care consumes vast public resources. Thus, schizophrenia represents the prototype of the challenge that public policy must intelligently address. Although psychiatrists generally agree that schizophrenic reactions encompass different conditions with surface similarities, there is little evidence that subtypes can be reliably differentiated, and, under ordinary conditions of practice, even the gross diagnosis is less than fully adequate in its reliability. Because schizophrenia is one of the most important psychiatric conditions—and the one perhaps most studied and written about—I will illustrate some of the general problems of psychiatric conceptualization using schizophrenia as an example.

Schizophrenia: An Example in Psychiatric Conceptualization

As Frances and his colleagues (1995) note in the guidebook to DSM-IV:

> *Schizophrenia is a clinical syndrome of unknown etiology and pathophysiology.*
> *No symptoms are pathognomonic to schizophrenia, and there are no clinically*

*useful laboratory or imaging markers. The characteristic features of schizophre-
nia are heterogeneous, and the boundaries with other disorders can be difficult to
delineate. All of this makes for quite a diagnostic challenge, as well as creating
problems for research (p. 166).*

Psychiatrists usually diagnose schizophrenia on the basis of bizarre behavior characterized by inappropriate verbalizations and distortions of interpersonal perception as evidenced by the presence of delusions and hallucinations. Persons with schizophrenia often
withdraw from interpersonal contacts and engage in a rich and unusual fantasy life. In its
more extreme manifestations, schizophrenia is associated with disregard for conventional
expectations and with habit deterioration. One definition describes schizophrenia as a set
of reactions involving disturbances in reality relationships and concept formation, accompanied by a variety of intellectual, affective, and behavioral disturbances varying in kind
and degree. McGhie and Chapman (1961) note that early schizophrenia often involves disturbances in the processes of attention and perception (including changes in sensory quality and in the perception of speech and movement), changes in motility and bodily awareness, and changes in thinking and affective processes. Patients classified as schizophrenic
often give the impression that they are retreating from reality and are suffering from unpredictable disturbances in their streams of thought. Depending on the stage of the condition
and the level of personal deterioration, schizophrenia may be easy or difficult to identify.

*The diagnosis of schizophrenia is either very easy or very difficult. The typical
cases, and there are very many such, can be recognized by the layman and the
beginner; but some cases offer such difficulties that the most qualified experts in
the field cannot come to any agreement. Such difficulties hardly can be surprising; there is no clear, fundamental definition of schizophrenia. In general, the
diagnosis of schizophrenia is made too frequently; we are inclined to believe that
the less skilled the psychiatrist, the more often the diagnosis of schizophrenia. As
the diagnosis still has a connotation of malignancy and grave implications for
patients and their families, it encourages drastic therapies and should be made
with great circumspection. It is based entirely upon psychological and rather subjective criteria. All too often the diagnosis is made without specification of stage
and severity (Redlich and Freedman 1966, pp. 507–508).*

In recent years considerable effort has been made to improve the diagnostic classification of schizophrenia and to achieve greater reliability in diagnostic assessment from one
context to another. DSM-III and IV have contributed to clearer diagnostic specification,
and interest in biological models results in more attention to careful diagnosis. DSM-IV
notes five characteristic symptoms of schizophrenia: delusions; hallucinations; disorganized speech; gross disorganized or catatonic behavior; and negative symptoms such as
affective flattening. A number of approaches have been developed for more systematic
diagnosis. John Wing, for example, has developed a technique of interviewing patients—
called the *present state examination*—that has been used in a variety of diagnostic studies
(Wing 1978). The procedure involves a set of rules based on clinical experience that allows
allocation of patients to diagnostic categories. This system has been computerized (known

as CATEGO) (Wing, Cooper, and Sartorius 1974) and has been established to have high reliability for the classification of schizophrenia in different cultures (John Wing et al. 1967; World Health Organization 1973). Its usefulness to predict prognosis, however, is unclear (Kendell, Brockington, and Leff 1979).

Symptoms used in the diagnosis are divided into various classes. In the case of an acute problem, the central symptoms that account for two-thirds of all clinical diagnoses of schizophrenia include thought insertion, thought broadcast, thought withdrawal, auditory hallucinations of a specific type, and delusions of control. Thought insertion is the experience that thoughts other than one's own are being inserted into the mind. The patient believes that alien thoughts are inserted into his or her mind through radar, telepathy, or some other means. Careful questioning is required to establish that the patient truly understands and that he or she is not exaggerating a commonly occurring experience. In fact, the symptom is rare. Other groups of symptoms may also be used to establish a diagnosis of schizophrenia, such as other types of delusions or hallucinations or persistent talking to oneself. Still other symptoms are more ambiguous, and it becomes difficult to make a clear differential diagnosis between schizophrenia and other clinical conditions. In the case of more marginal symptoms, agreement among psychiatrists decreases.

The chronic schizophrenic is often highly disabled socially. Two main types of symptoms tend to be present: (1) "a syndrome of 'negative' traits, such as emotional apathy, slowness of thought and movement, underactivity, lack of drive, poverty of speech, and social withdrawal"; and (2) "incoherence of speech, unpredictability of associations, longstanding delusions and hallucinations, and accompanying manifestations in behavior" (Wing 1978, p. 110). The consequences of these types of symptoms and their effects on work, interpersonal relations, and family life make the chronic schizophrenic a major challenge for any program seeking to achieve reasonable community adjustment (Estroff 1981). It is difficult to rehabilitate the schizophrenic patient, and limiting the chronicity of the condition is itself a formidable challenge. Recent studies, however, demonstrate that the prognosis of schizophrenia is less discouraging than clinicians have typically believed and that well-conceived and appropriately managed programs of care can significantly limit the disabilities associated with schizophrenia and improve patients' level of function and quality of life. These points are of great importance and require brief summary here.

Clinicians have expressed pessimism about the inevitable deterioration associated with schizophrenia and the intractability of the disease to intervention. In contrast, longterm studies show extraordinary variability in adaptation and function over time, suggesting that these patients have much greater potential than many clinicians believe. Each of five long-term studies reported since 1972 shows varied outcomes with significant numbers of long-term remissions (Harding, Zubin, and Strauss 1987). For example, in a remarkable clinical study carried out over twenty-seven years, Manfred Bleuler (1978) studied the course of disorder among 208 patients in Zurich in various cohorts over two decades. He described the continuing adaptations among these patients who fluctuated between varying outcomes. One-half to three-quarters of the schizophrenic patients achieved long-term recoveries, and only 10 to 20 percent became severe chronic schizophrenics. The estimate of recovery is conservative, since it only includes patients reaching an end-state, and, as Bleuler notes, prognosis of all schizophrenia combined is better. Moreover, in some patients, even after forty years of psychosis, marked changes still occur.

Long-term studies carried out by Ciompi (1980) in Lausanne and by Huber, Gross, and Scheuttler (1979) in Bonn confirm Bleuler's conclusion on the variable and often favorable course of schizophrenia.

In the American context, follow-up after an average of thirty-two years of a group of 269 chronic patients released from Vermont State Hospital revealed that one-half to two-thirds had significantly improved or recovered, confirming European results (Harding et al. 1987a,b). The patients studied had, on average, been totally disabled for ten years and had been continuously hospitalized for six years. Most were functioning adequately in the community in later life, although ten years after release many of these patients had uncertain adjustments and were socially isolated. Using records, the investigators rediagnosed patients, selecting those 118 patients who met DSM-III criteria for schizophrenia at hospital admission in the mid-1950s (Harding et al. 1987b). At follow-up most were living in the community and needed little or no help in meeting basic needs. Two-fifths of patients of working age were employed in the prior year, a majority had few significant symptoms, and about three-quarters were assessed as leading "moderate to very full lives." The picture that emerges is one highly divergent with clinical assumptions, and suggests that the image of inevitable deterioration that dominates the psychiatric literature may have been a self-fulfilling prophecy. Similar findings have been reported by Clausen, Pfeffer, and Huffine (1982), and while Tsuang, Woolson, and Fleming (1979) found in a thirty- to forty-year follow-up that schizophrenics had a less favorable course than patients with affective disorders, a significant number of schizophrenics had "good" outcomes.

It is not too difficult to reconcile the lack of congruency between these studies and the level of pessimism found among many clinicians. Clinicians are often unaware of the epidemiological picture because they see their patients primarily in a short-term, cross-sectional perspective (Harding, Zubin, and Strauss 1987). Moreover, many patients who function well may no longer seek care or require intensive treatment, giving more salience to those patients who do not get well and repeatedly return for inpatient care. The difficult and intractable cases come to dominate the clinician's time and perceptions. A longitudinal perspective, in contrast, would not only provide a more hopeful picture, but also provides the perspective necessary for understanding the types of care essential for this needy population. A number of studies, which we will review later, show persuasively that effectively organized community alternatives to hospital care can achieve superior results whether measured by clinical outcomes, psychosocial participation, levels of function, or patient and family satisfaction.

The causes of schizophrenia remain unknown, and there is still much disagreement about its classification. Theories of its origins have ranged from biologically oriented models (Kety 1986) to those that posit the roots of schizophrenia in social interaction and family life (Mischler and Waxler 1965). Debate continues as to whether it is more valuable to view schizophrenia as a variety of diseases with common manifestations or as reaction patterns. In recent years, the dominant view has moved closer to biological and biomedical models, but almost everyone accepts the idea that both biology and environment play some role. As John Strauss (1979) notes: "No single variable, biological or psychosocial, appears to be necessary or sufficient to make someone schizophrenic" (p. 291).

With the growing dominance of the biomedical orientation, there is much more attention devoted to specifying precise diagnostic criteria, as was noted in our discussion of the

DSM, and more interest in diagnostic reliability. In contrast, those who view schizophrenia as a convenient term for a particular reaction pattern that has no underlying disorder use the label more loosely and are less concerned with the reliability of the concept because the diagnosis is not seen as the primary factor in decisions concerning the care and treatment of the patient. But even these new efforts at diagnostic clarity, such as DSM-IV, are empirically derived and have no clear theoretical basis. There are now many operational definitions using different criteria and combinational rules and giving varying importance to longitudinal considerations. McGuffin, Farmer, and Gottesman (1987) note that "disappointingly, a straightforward 'Chinese menu' set of criteria such as DSM-III appears to be more serviceable. . . . However, we consider that the work of constructing appropriate criteria is not yet done and that there must still be a continuing process of revision and reassessment" (p. 154).

As research proceeds, most scientists have developed a complex multifaceted view of schizophrenia, but the following statements reflect the wide range of approaches and theoretical conceptions that have guided efforts in this field over the years.

> *Virtually all the participants in the Conference subscribed in some form to a diathesis-stressor framework (DSF) for explaining the appearance of schizophrenia. With the exception of Kringlen, the contributors . . . emphasize a large and rather specific genetic 'something' interacting with non-specific, perhaps universal environmental factors. (Gottesman 1978, p. 60)*

> *Environmental factors play a considerable role in schizophrenia development. The results give no support to any simple dominant or recessive transmission. If one accepts a polygenic transmission, one has to admit that based on these data the polygenic predisposition is of a rather modest degree. More than 70 percent of children of two schizophrenic parents do not develop schizophrenia despite a double risk genetically and environmentally. (Kringlen 1978, p. 23)*

> *It is now clear that several chemically different types of drugs attenuate the manifest schizophrenic symptoms in many patients, and that a blockade of dopamine synapses is their common pharmacologic action. One would hesitate to conclude that the dopamine system therefore plays a primary role in the etiology of schizophrenia. Since the dopamine system interacts with many other transmitter systems, including serotonin, GABA, norepinephrine and certain polypeptides, any of these or others still undiscovered could be the site of the biochemical alteration, the existence of which is implied by the genetic evidence. (Kety 1978, pp. 156–157)*

> *A great many observers have attempted to explain the manifestations of schizophrenia as being the result of disturbed interactions between the parents and the child who later develops a schizophrenic illness. These investigators have focused on the psychological disturbances of the ego functions that result from deviations in normal development, maturation, and ego integration. (Rubinstein and Simons 1981, p. 613)*

Social withdrawal, for example, is a characteristic of most forms of chronic schiz-
ophrenia, irrespective of social setting, and a biological component (seen at its
most extreme in catatonic stupor) must be accepted. (Wing 1963, p. 635)

Confusion may arise if one does not keep in mind the nature of the concept of schiz-
ophrenia. It is not, and should not be treated as, a disease entity of a biochemical or
genetic nature, but merely a reaction type which has been selected more or less arbi-
trarily because of its operational usefulness. (Ødegaard 1965, p. 296)

In psychoanalytic terms, the schizophrenics represent those who have failed to
evolve the ego interactive processes or strengths necessary to resolve flexibly con-
flicts between their (id) drives and over-demanding superego attitudes and the
aspirations of the ego ideal. They are thus defective in the capacity to adapt to the
social demands confronting them and to their own drives. They thereby lack a
harmonious self-concept and ego ideal with clear goals and motivations. Much of
their adaptation is made, instead, through partially satisfying regressive or fix-
ated infantile behavior. (Kolb 1977, p. 375)

Varying Conceptions of Mental Illness

These descriptions indicate the diverse conceptions of the character and cause of schizophrenia; similar controversy surrounds many other mental disorders including the mood
disorders, personality disorders, and substance abuse. It is not surprising that in the
absence of causal understanding many different conceptions prevail and compete. Uncertainty also allows ideological beliefs to play a major role, since how mental illness is
viewed has implications for social reform efforts and for concepts of personal change and
autonomy.

The ideological debate reached its perhaps most divisive form during the decades of
the 1960s and 1970s, a period characterized by optimism about the potential of social
reform and strong advocacy for civil rights and civil liberties. Those who believed strongly
in human betterment through environmental manipulation resisted biological and genetic
explanations because they feared that if mental illness was seen as biologically caused
there would be less sympathy for social efforts to improve people's lives. In contrast, if
mental illness was a product of social environments, there would be an additional strong
incentive for social programming. There is, of course, no clear or simple relationship
between conceptions of etiology and society's willingness to attack social problems, but,
in general, those who endorse strong biological positions tend to be more skeptical about
the potentials of social reform and more conservative in their political views.

A second ideological dimension concerns liberty interests in contrast to therapeutic
ones. Following a long history of philosophical debate, there are those who strongly
believe in maintaining and protecting the rights of individuals to live as they wish without
interference from the state for whatever reason. In their view, people must retain the right
to personal autonomy even if in the view of others they behave in ways highly damaging
to themselves. In contrast, those with a therapeutic ethic believe that intervention should

override individual liberties if the person is mentally ill and in need of treatment. Those endorsing liberty interests argue that interventions should be minimized and are only justifiable in instances of imminent danger to others. The laws shift from time to time with changing public opinion, but the issue itself is irresolvable because it reflects deeply felt opposing positions about the nature of people and their relationships with society.

In the 1960s the liberty interests were championed by public interest lawyers who came out of the civil rights movement, many social scientists, and some psychiatrists. As a spokesperson for the extreme libertarian position, Thomas Szasz (1960, 1974), a professor of psychiatry and a psychoanalyst, vigorously maintained that mental illness was a myth and that the standards by which patients are defined as sick are psychosocial, ethical, and legal but not medical. Although Szasz's use of the myth metaphor did little to stimulate reasonable and rational debate, he presented a point of view that requires serious scrutiny.

Szasz argued, and continues to argue today, that the concept of mental illness results from conditions such as syphilis of the brain, in which it is demonstrable that peculiarities in behavior and thought are linked with a physiological condition. He argued that, in contrast, most symptoms designated as mental illness are not the result of brain lesions or biological dysfunctions but rather are deviations in behavior or thinking. Thus, Szasz contends that the metaphor of illness is used to characterize problems having no underlying biological basis and that judgments of mental illness are based primarily on ethical or psychosocial criteria. He concedes that specific disorders in thinking and behavior result from brain dysfunctions, but he argues that it is better to say that some people labeled as mentally ill suffer from a disease of the brain than to assert that all of those called mentally ill are sick in a medical sense. In Szasz's opinion, the use of the concept of mental illness to characterize both disorders of the brain and deviations in behavior, thinking, and affect due to other causes results in confusion, abuses of psychiatry, and the use of medical terminology to deprive patients of their civil liberties through involuntary hospitalization and other forms of coercion.

The issues in the debate between those advocating a disease model of schizophrenia and those maintaining that it is primarily a deviant response pattern have been posed sharply by a demonstration in which eight "normal" pseudopatients complaining of a bogus symptom presented themselves at twelve hospitals.

> *After calling the hospital for an appointment, the pseudopatient arrived at the admissions office complaining that he had been hearing voices. Asked what the voices said, he replied that they were often unclear, but as far as he could tell they said "empty," "hollow," and "thud." The voices were unfamiliar and were of the same sex as the pseudopatient. The choice of these symptoms was occasioned by their apparent similarity to existential symptoms. . . . Beyond alleging the symptoms and falsifying name, vocation, and employment, no further alterations of person, history, or circumstances were made. The significant events of the pseudopatient's life history were presented as they actually occurred. . . . Immediately upon admission to the psychiatric ward, the pseudopatient ceased simulating any symptoms of abnormality. (Rosenhan 1973, p. 251)*

All of the patients were admitted to the psychiatric hospitals. In every case but one, the pseudopatients were discharged with the diagnosis of schizophrenia "in remission." The remaining diagnosis was simply schizophrenia. Length of hospitalization averaged nineteen days with a range of seven to fifty-two days. The pseudopatients were given 2,100 pills, including antipsychotic agents such as Stelazine, Compazine, and Thorazine. Rosenhan describes the powerlessness and depersonalization characteristic of psychiatric hospitalization and the extent to which the assumption that these patients were ill influenced interpretations of what they said and did. Rosenhan concludes that "we have known for a long time that diagnoses are often not useful or reliable, but we have nevertheless continued to use them. We now know that we cannot distinguish insanity from sanity" (Rosenhan 1973, p. 257).

There have been many critiques of Rosenhan's demonstration, but the most careful review has been provided by Robert Spitzer (1976), a research psychiatrist. Spitzer argues that all Rosenhan has actually demonstrated is that patients reporting unusual symptoms frequently associated with a serious psychiatric ailment are suspected of having that ailment and can be admitted to a hospital. From the perspective of differential diagnosis, the absence of symptoms other than auditory hallucinations excludes most alternative diagnoses. One alternative would be that the patient is trying to deceive the physician by malingering—a situation that sometimes occurs—but it is a relatively unlikely alternative because few patients feign schizophrenia, and there are likely to be few benefits to such deception. Quoting Kety, Spitzer makes the point that if a patient drank a quart of blood and came to a hospital emergency room vomiting blood, the hospital staff would assume that the patient had internal bleeding. Kety then asks whether such a demonstration would argue convincingly that medicine does not know how to diagnose peptic ulcers. Furthermore, Spitzer maintains that the discharge diagnosis of all but one of the pseudopatients as having schizophrenia in remission is highly atypical, suggesting that these pseudopatients were puzzling to the psychiatrists who evaluated them.

There is nothing in the Rosenhan demonstration that addresses in any definitive way the usefulness or validity of psychiatric diagnosis. What Rosenhan has shown is that hospital staff can be fooled by a patient who reports a serious symptom that cannot be independently validated, a situation characteristic of many areas of medical practice. In much of medical practice, problems are identified by the fact that patients experience pain and discomfort and come seeking help; the patient's history and reports of symptoms are important aspects of the assessment. Rosenhan, however, like many others before him, does raise important issues concerning typical psychiatric practice. His study suggests the bias of physicians toward active treatment in situations of uncertainty, when the treatment may potentially do more harm than the symptoms disturbing the patient. He showed how readily psychiatric hospitalization was achieved, particularly if the patient was receptive to hospital admission. Such practices have implications not only for the patient and his or her self-concept but also for the medical care system, because hospitalization is an expensive endeavor. Of course, in the managed care environment it is far less likely that hospitalization would occur in such circumstances. Rosenhan, like Szasz, raised more issues about the manner in which psychiatrists perform than about the usefulness of a medical disease model for psychiatry.

The position stated by Szasz and others that the concept of mental illness is largely a social judgment of deviant and disturbing behavior is contested strongly by most psychiatrists. They contend that mental illness does not simply connote nonconformity but also disturbance of psychological functioning as evidenced by delusions, hallucinations, disorganized thinking, and disturbed emotional states, such as extreme anxiety or depression. (For a classic statement of this view, see Lewis 1953.) Although there are no valid laboratory tests or diagnostic procedures to assist judgments of psychological dysfunction, they believe that these psychopathological criteria are as relevant as the criteria used in the diagnosis of physical illness. The problem that leads to such great controversy is that psychiatric assessments of pathology depend almost exclusively on the clinician's judgment, while in physical medicine more objective investigatory procedures are frequently available in making such assessments.

One of the typical problems in such debates is that the adversaries are not really addressing the same point. Szasz bases his argument on the observations that psychiatrists frequently define mental illness solely on the basis of social and psychosocial criteria, that psychiatrists often become involved in questions of ethics and in conflicts of interest rather than being concerned with illness per se, and that the psychiatric role is used to deal with social problems and to achieve social goals that are only remotely related to clinical assessments of pathology; he is correct in all these observations. However, he never really adequately addresses the possibility of assessing mental illness on the basis of disturbances in psychological processes, and it is to this question that his critics usually respond.

The difficulty with the notion that mental disease is a myth is a logical one. The diagnostic disease approach is a tool used for identifying, studying, and treating persons with particular types of problems. By refining the definition of a particular problem, we can then study it, try to ascertain causes, and observe what happens to the problem over time and the way it responds to different types of influences. Most typically, patients come to doctors in distress; they are suffering and want some relief. Differential diagnosis is a technique the doctor uses to identify the specific nature of the problem and what medical knowledge may have to offer. In any given instance, one can ask how useful it is to approach certain types of problems with a disease model as compared with some other intervention. To ask whether the disease model is true makes no more sense than asking whether a shovel is true. Both the disease model and shovels are tools—they are useful for dealing with some problems and not with others. Both can be inappropriately used in situations in which they cause more damage than good, as when a shovel is used to try to jack up a car with a flat tire or the disease model is used to try to help a student who has difficulty understanding this book.

Calling a condition a disease is a social judgment based on cultural concepts of what is disturbing. We typically view conditions as diseases if they shorten life, disrupt functioning, or cause pain and distress. But whether we feel pain or not depends not only on our physical being but also on cultural conditioning and social expectations. What may be painful and limiting in one social context may be viewed differently in another. Behavior occurs in a social context, and our goals and definitions of self are culturally shaped. Science and medicine are part of the larger culture and help define the meanings we attribute to various events. Every outcome has causes; the challenge is to identify these determinants correctly. The disease model is one approach to studying causes of the human response patterns that we regard as significant and needing some form of remedy.

Studying a problem requires us to identify it and differentiate it from other problems. By doing so, we can better locate its determinants, the way it evolves over time, and the way it can be successfully modified. In the study of disease, efforts are made to identify clusters of symptoms on the assumption that they stem from some underlying dysfunction. By accurately describing and studying these symptoms, we are better able to advance our knowledge of them and identify causes and treatments. Over the years we have learned a great deal about many diseases—patterns of typical and atypical symptom occurrence, symptom development over time, causes, and effective treatments. In other instances we have incomplete knowledge or very little knowledge. At any given point in time, the physician must work with disease models, some of which are well developed and highly useful, others that are incomplete and of more dubious value.

Confirmed disease theories provide all the necessary information concerning the cause of the condition, what is likely to occur if it is untreated, and what regimen is available to retard it. A correct diagnostic assessment thus leads to correct action. It should be obvious why diagnostic reliability is so important; if the patient has pernicious anemia and the physician diagnoses the condition as tuberculosis, he will be proceeding on incorrect inferences concerning the cause of the problem and the appropriate actions that will remedy it. (For a more complete discussion of this issue, see Mechanic 1978, pp. 95–105.)

Although the debate as to whether a particular problem is a disease or not most commonly occurs in the psychiatric area, there is no difference in the application of disease models in medicine or psychiatry. The debate rages in psychiatry because the disease theories used by psychiatrists have a lower degree of scientific confirmation than many such theories in general medicine, although both areas have many unconfirmed theories. We are talking about a matter of degree. When a physician assigns the label of pernicious anemia to a patient's problem, the doctor's understanding of the problem and its treatment derive directly from the diagnosis. In contrast, if, as Ødegaard (1965) maintains, assignment of the label of schizophrenia to a patient's condition does not affect the choice of therapy or chance of recovery, the advantage of using a disease model can be questioned because it might detract attention from more effective approaches. Psychiatric disease models, however, are not as poor or unspecific as the critics suggest. Differentiation of bipolar and other types of depression usually results in different specific treatments, and depression is typically treated differently from schizophrenia. In everyday ambulatory medical care, it is estimated that one-quarter to one-half of all patients do not fit existing models of disease (White 1970), and primary care physicians are increasingly adopting a problem-assessment approach in managing such patients in contrast to imposing disease labels on them.

The defining characteristics of disease models are constantly changing. What we can or cannot do depends on the state of our knowledge and understanding at the moment. The fact that a confirmed disease theory does not exist for a particular cluster of symptoms, signs, or problems tells us little about the future state of our understanding. Knowledge about mental disorders and human behavior is increasing. Although psychiatrists with a psychodynamic perspective tend to apply a similar approach to most conditions that they regard as treatable, there is a growing tendency to use specific treatments for particular disorders. Obviously, the overlap in treatment techniques for differing conditions reflects the ambiguous and uncertain state of the field, but the overall level of ignorance is not so large as some would imply.

In deciding whether a disease orientation is useful, it is necessary to balance the gains achieved from using such a perspective against its various disadvantages. The adoption of a disease perspective involves certain risks. Characterizing a particular problem as a mental disease may lead to greater stigmatization than alternative definitions. The implications that the condition is within the individual rather than in the social situation and that it is not subject to his or her control or that of others may, under some circumstances, lead to attitudes that are serious deterrents to rehabilitation. The most serious result of using disease models when they yield little information is the possible encouragement such a model may provide for failing to explore alternatives for rehabilitation outside the disease perspective. Gerald Grob (1966), an intellectual historian who has studied the history of mental hospital care, notes the following problems.

> *The continued insistence by psychiatrists that their profession was truly scientific, however, exerted a profound, though negative influence over the character of the mental hospital. As we have seen, the assumption that mental disease was somatic in nature invariably led to therapeutic nihilism. Moreover, somaticism often precluded alternative approaches, particularly along psychological and other nonsomatic lines. Lacking any visible means of therapy, psychiatrists tended to engage in a vast holding operation by confining mentally ill patients until that distant day when specific cures for specific disease entities would become available. (Grob 1966, pp. 356–357)*

Developmental Models

The major competing view to the disease perspective is one that conceptualizes problems in terms of their psychodynamics. Instead of concerning themselves with establishing a disease diagnosis, psychodynamic psychiatrists and other mental health professionals attempt to reconstruct a developmental picture of the patient's personality; they believe that such an exploration will provide an understanding of the way the disturbed state of the patient has developed and the functions that the disturbed behavior has in the patient's adaptation to the environment. Kolb (1977), in instructing the psychiatrist on the examination of the patient, made the following observation.

> *The purpose of the psychiatric examination is to discover the origin and evolution of such personality disorders as may be interfering with the happiness, satisfactions, efficiency, or social adjustment of the patient. One seeks, therefore, to secure a biographical-historical perspective of the personality, a clear psychological picture of the living person as a specific human being with his individual problems. It will be found that there is a logical continuity in any personality manifestations, whether the manifestations be those that are called normal or those that are called abnormal. The fundamental dynamic laws of behavior and of personality development are the same for both. (Kolb 1977, p. 197)*

A basic assumption of the psychodynamic therapist is that disturbed behavior is part of the same continuum as normal behavior and is explained by the same theories that govern our understanding of normal personality development and social functioning. If disturbed behavior is a form of adaptation of the personality in response to particular situations and social stresses, then it is logical to study such behavior from the same perspectives and orientations as those from which we study any other kinds of behavior.

Psychodynamic therapists do not make serious attempts to ascertain whether or not the patient is mentally ill, for this is not a meaningful perspective within their frame of reference. They assume the existence of mental illness or personality disturbance by the fact that the patient is suffering and has come for help or by the fact that the patient's social behavior is sufficiently inappropriate to lead others to bring him or her to the attention of care providers. Using a developmental approach, the therapist attempts to ascertain what aspects of the person's past experience have led to the development of patterns of functioning that have created the current difficulty. Strong inferences in this approach are that the source of the difficulty is within the patient's personality development and that the problem can be alleviated or remedied by changing some aspect of functioning.

Because the psychodynamic perspective does not differentiate mental illness from ordinary problems of mental discomfort or social adjustment, professionals of this persuasion tend to accept for treatment people with a wide variety of problems, such as marital dissatisfaction, poor adjustment to school, neurosis, and feelings of lack of fulfillment. Although such professionals may be attuned to some extent to the social aspects of some of these problems, they basically proceed as if these problems stem from the personality of the patient rather than the social situation, deprivation and injustice, or other environmental contingencies.

In recent years psychotherapeutic perspectives have diversified, and there are many competing concepts of appropriate therapy. Varying therapies focus on early development, communication, family role conflict, behavior modification, and other areas. Explanations for psychological distress vary from conflicts in early family development to faulty learning and increasingly emphasize such factors as self-confidence and assertiveness, social stress, social support systems, conflicting expectations, and emotional repression. Therapies range from individual encounters with professionals to interactions in families, groups, and larger social networks. Competing with more formal therapies are encounter groups, self-help organizations, and recreational sensitivity group experiences (Back 1972). The term *therapy* has come to encompass the most diverse ideas, varying from a range of reasonable theoretical approaches as in interpersonal theory and behavior modification to the inane and "insane." In this arena it seems as if anything goes, and whatever else can be said about it, it is evidently a "flourishing industry."

Discounting the abuses and obvious charlatanism characteristic of the "therapy movement," it is evident that it reflects a change in focus from early development to situational problems and discomforts. There is increasing emphasis on the idea that personal distress flows from a discordance of individual personality and individual needs and the nature of the person's social environment. It is commonly noted that persons with similar personality strengths and weaknesses may make better or poorer adjustments depending on social circumstances. Persons with strong aggressive needs, for example, may or may not have problems depending on whether they are in positions of authority or in subordinate jobs. In addition to the question of fit between person and environment, much attention is given to the way people relate, express intimacy, and become entangled in confused role structures. The growing emphasis on behavioral therapies, in part a result of demonstrated effectiveness of behavior modification in a variety of situations, has focused more attention on the idea that many maladaptive responses are learned and can be extinguished under appropriate conditions.

Among the many different therapeutic approaches to psychological disorder, a few have been consistently useful and have gained wide acceptance. The application of learning principles through behavior therapy is widely accepted, and these learning approaches are used in a great variety of therapies seeking to modify behavior and dysfunctional thinking processes. Cognitive therapy and interpersonal therapy are widely used in the treatment of depression, and their efficacy has been studied by the NIMH in a large-scale collaborative study. In this study, these two therapies were compared in a randomized controlled trial with patients receiving a tricyclic antidepressant drug (imipramine) and placebos. Cognitive therapy, developed by Aaron Beck (1976), seeks to change the meanings individuals attach to their life situations, which he believes lead to different types of emotions. Interpersonal therapy focuses more on interpersonal relations and on conflicts in roles and relationships (Klerman et al. 1984). In the short term all three approaches performed better than placebo. Imipramine brought improvement more quickly than the psychotherapies, but after three months the drug and therapy groups were comparable. Interpersonal therapy appears to outperform cognitive therapy, particularly for the more severely depressed patients. Studies most generally show that combining drug and psychotherapy approaches outperforms any single approach (Conte et al. 1986). The extent to which short-term therapy of any kind produces lasting results remains an issue to be carefully explored.

While some patients with mild and moderate disorder may benefit from short-term therapy and retain such benefits well into the future, this acute treatment model may not be appropriate for other patients. Many schizophrenic patients, for example, require long-term and continuing care and quickly relapse when they discontinue their medication. An acute care model serves these patients badly, and proper care should be seen as more like the appropriate care of a diabetic patient who requires insulin and continuing monitoring than like the care of a person with an acute infectious disorder who returns to a normal situation after the infection is successfully treated. The issue of appropriate treatment perspectives is a crucial one for public policy, since the application of the wrong model not only contributes to great personal suffering but also to poor public understanding and disillusionment with the mental health system of care.

Changing Conceptions of Mental Illness

Conceptions of both the causes of psychological disorder and modes of dealing with it are shaped by their cultural context and reflect not only the state of scientific knowledge and belief but also larger social forces. In the 1950s, the dominant view of such disorders, influenced by psychoanalytic thinking and the larger cultural milieu, was that they were intrinsic to the personality and its development. Although the impact of social conditions was not discounted, it was felt that a well-integrated and "healthy" personality could cope with all but the most extreme circumstances and that persons who do get into difficulty usually have significant weaknesses of personality. Thus, dissatisfaction and distress among women was seen as a personal problem and not a consequence of blocked opportunities and unequal roles. Illegitimacy among blacks was viewed as a problem of personality in contrast to being a consequence of cultural norms, poverty, discrimination, and a welfare system that penalized members of intact families.

The decade of the 1960s brought rapid social changes, increased opportunities, and much social disruption. There was a growing rejection of the idea that biology and personality limit social potential and an emphasis on explanations that viewed social problems and personal disorganization as consequences of a social structure with inequalities, blocked opportunities, and exploitation. The focus was on social environment and social reform, based on the assumption that personality was completely malleable if only we could diminish inequalities and injustice. Psychiatry discovered the concepts of social class, community, and political structures. Psychiatrists were encouraged to play doctor for communities as well as for individual patients. The strict environmental bias of the 1960s, like the earlier personality bias of the 1950s, failed to explain why in the same circumstances most persons manage to adapt while others have great difficulty. If dissatisfaction, illegitimacy, and failure were simply a consequence of social structure, why, indeed, did so many deprived persons cope so well?

The decade of the 1970s was a period of theoretical consolidation, characterized by a growing appreciation of biological limits, developmental influences, and structural pressures. The excessive psychobiological determinism of the 1950s and exaggerated social determinism of the 1960s have yielded to a more balanced, complex, and sophisticated picture of social behavior. There has been a resurgence of biological interest within psychiatry, a growing appreciation of genetic studies, and much greater concern with the interaction of individual predispositions with environmental pressures and the way such pressures are modified by varying types of social supports or exacerbated by vulnerabilities.

Much of the interest in psychiatry has shifted toward biology and the neurosciences, hoping to capitalize on the advances in biotechnology and imaging techniques. Such new technologies as positron emission tomography (PET) and nuclear magnetic resonance (NMR) allow us to image the brain in a way difficult to imagine just a short time ago. Advances in molecular biology make it possible to develop molecular probes to identify markers for genes that increase susceptibility to specific mental illnesses. Such developments are exciting and deserve encouragement and support, but with some cautions.

The current excitement in biology is no justification to neglect research and understanding in the behavioral and social sciences. Most mental illness is a product of biological factors interacting with varying vulnerability factors, and these conditions are shaped by the social environment as well as by biology. Improved understanding of the social environment and behavior may contribute as much to prevention and intervention as advances on the genetic and molecular levels. It would be wise not to neglect the lessons of history concerning excessive enthusiasm for biological solutions. In undermining support for social factors and good social care, under the assumption that illness was biological, great harm resulted for patients and their families.

The evidence now available suggests that biology, development, and the shape of the environment all contribute importantly to serious mental illness. In many instances, the application of a disease model remains uncertain and its ultimate value unclear. In other instances, the disease model has done much to encourage careful thinking, to stimulate research, and to improve care. However we proceed, we must also make sure that the assumption that mental disorders are diseases does not undermine the use of other approaches in helping afflicted persons. Whatever the dominant view of mental disorder, such conditions tend to involve unique problems in their recognition and care. We now turn to a discussion of some of these problems.

Social Conceptions of Mental Illness

We usually recognize and define psychiatric problems through the appearance of particular patterns of deviant behavior or deviant feeling states. Sometimes individuals come to view themselves as having psychiatric problems on the basis of their conceptions of normal functioning and their own knowledge and experience. On other occasions people become aware of their problems as psychiatric ones only after others in their milieu point them out as such. Kadushin (1958) cites an example of the way such a definition may be formed.

> I think I have had an emotional disturbance for some time, and I finally decided to do something about it. . . . Before my marriage I had a lot of conflict between my mother and myself. . . . My mother visited us . . . about two weeks ago, and she is always complaining that I never confided in her, and why I wasn't happy at home with my husband . . . and I sort of put the blame on her. She would patch things up after each conflict, and a couple of days after her visit I got an eight-page letter which told me off. She said she noted my unnatural feelings toward my son. That I give more affection to the cat. . . . Several years ago she said that she would take me to a psychiatrist, without my knowing it. . . . Because, she said, that I didn't love my husband. Now, I didn't see it that way. But now I think I need it. I get upset very easily. . . . I'm very emotional. (Kadushin 1958, p. 395)

On other occasions, individuals or those closest to them resist a definition of mental illness; they are eventually defined as being mentally ill when a crisis develops because of their bizarre and difficult behavior or when they come into difficulty with community social agencies. The following example illustrates the process.

> Mr. B's wife had become violently distrustful of him, especially in the past eighteen months, but the first indication had come nearly five years ago. He recalled: "It was when Sue [the daughter] was about three months old. My wife was jealous if I played with the baby. She resented it." From this time, Mr. B thought of his wife as having "a nasty streak in her that made her act jealous." She was frequently accusatory and he was frequently angry with her, especially when she falsely accused him of running around with other women. Still, she was a good mother to the children and when she flew off the handle, he would go out for a walk to avoid further conflict. He first thought that the problem might be serious when she said that someone had "done something" to the alarm clock to change

its shape. She began to restrict the children's play. When a neighbor came to see how Mrs. B was, she ordered her former friend out of the house, waving a butcher knife. Lorraine B. moved out of her husband's bed, but frequently kept him awake much of the night while she prowled the house to "protect her papers and books." These events led eventually to medical intervention. (Adapted from Clausen 1961, pp. 128–129)

The recognition of mental illness generally takes place in community contexts; therefore, we should understand the way the public forms its conceptions of mental illness.

From the point of view of lay definitions, the two most pervasive and influential perspectives on deviation are those based on the health-illness and the goodness-badness dimensions. Each of these perspectives represents one aspect of our conflicting philosophical conceptions concerning deviant behavior. While we predicate our legal system and much of our social life on the assumptions that individuals are able to control their actions and must be held accountable for their responses (or, in other words, their actions are consciously motivated and willful), the sciences and scientific perspectives have encouraged a contrasting view based on the assumption that deviant behavior is the product of a particular developmental history and cannot seriously be viewed as being within the control of the individual. Because both views are important in social life, we tend to pave a middle path between them, often accepting the assumption of accountability for behavior but at the same time arbitrarily recognizing certain exceptions to this assumption.

The view taken of the deviant largely depends on the frame of reference of the observer and the extent to which the deviant appears to be willing or able to control his or her responses (Mechanic 1962a). The evaluator usually judges an act within the context of what is believed to be the actor's motivation. If the actor's behavior appears reasonable and if it appears to enhance self-interest in some way, then the evaluator is likely to define the deviant response in terms of the goodness–badness dimension. If the behavior appears to be peculiar and at odds with the actor's self-interest or with expectations of the way a reasonable person is motivated, the evaluator is more likely to characterize such behavior in terms of the sickness dimension. Most people, for example, find it difficult to understand why a rich person would steal small items from the five-and-ten-cent store; they are likely to view such a person as being sick rather than as being bad because it is not clear how such acts serve self-interest. More people would label the same act committed by a working-class person as being bad. The difference in definition lies not only in the act but also in the motivation imputed to the actor.

Most physical illnesses fall within the usual conception of sickness rather than badness. We rarely hold people responsible or accountable for their physical ills, and, although persons may not always take the necessary precautions to avoid illness, we assume that illness happens to people, that it is not in their interest, and that it is, therefore, not motivated. For the community, difficulties in defining an act as sick or bad arise most frequently in the area of psychiatric disorders. Many psychiatrists take the positions that many delinquents and criminals are sick rather than bad. But, although emotional difficulties can certainly be observed among such violators, we have difficulty establishing that the disturbing behavior is a result of the emotional makeup of the person rather than of some aspect of social character. As the behavior and motivations of the individual become more bizarre and difficult to understand, we more readily apply the definition of sickness, but psychiatric conceptions of behavior include large residual categories, such as the disordered personality and character disorders, that clearly overlap with public and community conceptions of badness.

The tendency for many mental patients to be viewed as being responsible for their condition, in contrast to the usual absence of such motives being attributed to the physically ill, explains in part the stigma associated with psychiatric disturbances. This stigma is also attributable to the fact that mental illness is frequently socially disruptive; it may threaten and frighten others, and it may involve a large element of social unpredictability. Although some physical conditions can lead to similar social problems, most persons who are physically ill do not threaten the community in the same way that many psychiatric patients do. Most people have at one time or another suffered from physical morbidity, and they recognize that becoming ill is a common occurrence, but they less commonly recognize themselves as having suffered from psychiatric conditions, and they do not necessarily accept the idea that people like themselves become mentally ill.

The lack of correspondence in the public's attitudes toward physical and mental illness also stems from the common tendency to equate all mental illness with psychoses. A large proportion of the population conceives of the mental patient as being crazy, but the depressed, or highly anxious, or withdrawn person is not thought of as suffering from a mental illness. Even many people who have been patients in mental hospitals, including those who have been admitted several times, fail to conceive of themselves as being mentally ill; they frequently characterize their difficulties in physical terms (Linn 1968). In addition, unlike physical illness, mental illness is usually thought of by the public as characterizing the whole person rather than just one aspect of functioning. The implication is that because mental illness marks the entire person, he or she cannot be trusted to understand the situation or to make decisions concerning his or her welfare. This assumption is often untrue, and it is not difficult to understand why patients wish to resist being viewed in this way.

Although it is convenient to refer to *persons with mental illness* or *psychiatric conditions* as we do in this book, such general terms have little real meaning because of the heterogeneity of these categories. We would not, for example, sensibly talk about *people with physical conditions,* since almost everyone in the population will have several acute physical conditions each year (like the common cold) and many have one or more chronic diseases. Meaningful discussion requires specificity, since it is one thing to have acne and quite another to have AIDS. However, it has been much more conventional to talk about mental illness in a global fashion, even though the conditions involved vary in character, severity, the extent of disability they cause, and in many other ways. Because people are less likely to make these distinctions, the concept of mental illness associates *any* emotional difficulty with the stereotypes of severe psychoses and encourages an image of people who are unpredictable and incapable of caring for themselves. In reality, some psychiatric conditions are like the flu or a gastrointestinal disorder; they are relatively short-lived and do not greatly disrupt one's life. Others are more like serious heart disease and cancer, causing great discomfort and disability, and sometimes threatening life.

Views of Mental Illness in Relation to Social Policy

It is appropriate to inquire how varying mental health conceptions affect the formulation of public policy. It is reasonable to maintain that if people need help, it is in the public's interest to provide it, whether or not it falls within the confines of mental illness, but limitations always exist on the resources available. Decisions concerning the way such resources are to be allocated among those who need help depend, therefore, on our conceptions of the problems that constitute greater and lesser need.

Since optimal mental health is a utopian ideal, therapeutic programs always encounter neverending layers of problems. Because the provision of services is one of the conditions affecting the demand for services, if the field is defined too broadly, infinite amounts of money, personnel, and time could theoretically be absorbed in providing mental health care. Resources, however, are never unlimited; we must weigh investments in mental health care against investments in education, transportation, recreation, housing, and the like; we must base such decisions on some concept of priorities and some notion of the criteria by which these priorities are to be established.

Priorities always depend on values; two paramount values are ordinarily applied in thinking about mental health needs. The first is a humanitarian value—the concept of *need;* it is based on the idea that services should be made available to those who need them despite the cost, the difficulty in obtaining them, or the pressure on resources. The second concept—the notion of *gain*—is based on the idea that services should be made available when the result achieved is equal to the investment or greater than alternative investments. The widespread use of cost–benefit and cost-effectiveness analysis has focused increasing attention on the concept of gain. This concept, however, clearly comes into conflict with humanitarian needs and values at some point, and, therefore, public policy usually involves some marriage, however uncomfortable, between the notions of need and of gain.

From the perspective of cost-effectiveness (gain), several very different issues require resolution before an intelligent public policy can be formulated. The provision of services to the mentally ill and decisions regarding allocation of available resources should, in part, depend on the efficacy of alternative services, but such decisions are difficult to make. Vast investment in unproven and ineffective services may result in little gain beyond the humanitarian gesture of offering help to a person in need. Indeed, just as in the case of the use of drugs, X-rays, or other diagnostic and treatment procedures, some psychiatric services may harm the patient by adversely affecting concepts of self, the reactions of others, or social opportunities. One long-term study of predelinquent boys randomly assigned to treatment and control groups in Massachusetts found that the treated boys had more repeated arrests, more job dissatisfaction, and earlier deaths than those in the control group (McCord 1976). In another study involving the California Youth Authority, delinquent boys were treated through a confrontation technique in a "therapeutic community." Those receiving the treatment did considerably worse than matched delinquent controls (Robins 1979a,b). We cannot assume that treatment is benign and that people do not suffer from many of the approaches that are now prevalent. It would be foolish to invest large amounts of public money to subsidize therapies that have no demonstrated efficacy. We obviously need sufficient data to make informed assessments for the most reasonable directions for publicly subsidized programs.

Efficiency is also gained if the therapy provided not only manages the illness when it occurs but also retards possibilities of recurrence or more extensive illness later on. With all other factors constant (which they never are), we would expect curing the condition of a child or a young adult to result in continuing gains throughout the person's life. The same cure in the case of an older person would not produce an equal yield. Social values and humanitarian concerns often take precedence over the concept of gain, and services are provided in many situations on the basis of need, irrespective of cost-effectiveness. Extensive use of the concept of gain obviously conflicts with a sense of compassion.

It has been argued that major emphasis should be placed on preventive psychiatric services and early treatment on the assumption that such programs locate morbidity conditions early, retard continuing morbidity and disability, often prevent disability entirely, and stimulate positive mental health (Felix 1967). We still cannot be confident, however, that we have the appropriate knowledge and skills to do these things effectively. Some preventive programs involve risks of iatrogenic illness—morbidity that results from the services rendered rather than from the condition itself. Because many neurotic symptoms and fears are widely distributed and transitory in nature, treating them as though they were aspects of emotional illness may encourage a feeling of helplessness in the patient. Such treatment may structure the symptom and the condition as part of one's self-identify and discourage persons from realistically coping with and overcoming their problems.

There are some promising opportunities for preventive interventions although we should be modest and realistic about such preventive capabilities. There is growing evidence in many areas that enhancing protective factors such as social supports, improved coping and life skills and reducing known risk factors such as child abuse and poor parenting can reduce the occurrence of some mental disorders. However, there is no significant evidence that we can prevent such major disorders as schizophrenia, bipolar disorder, or even major depression, although there are some promising possibilities in the later case. There are strategic points for preventive intervention. Children of mentally ill parents, for example, are particularly vulnerable. Programs that improve parenting and provide support to such children may reduce the risk. Controlled studies of interventions to help deal with major stressful events such as loss of employment have shown both improved function and reduced depressive symptoms (Price et al. 1992). A major evaluation by the Institute of Medicine provides a rich review of the preventive literature and many promising possibilities for preventing or reducing the severity of many important types of psychiatric morbidity, including depressive symptoms and use of substances (Mrazek and Haggerty 1994).

The conception of mental illness underlying public policy is important because different views suggest varying approaches to classifying psychiatric conditions and to caring for the patient. If we assume that psychological difficulties and problems are pervasive throughout the society and have always been so and that those who suffer from psychiatric disease are fundamentally different from the mass of people who have common psychological problems, we are in a very different position than if we believe that mental illness is a continuum on which all these problems fall, depending on their degree of seriousness. The kinds of interventions attempted depend on the assumptions made about the nature of mental illness itself. We must carefully consider the full implications of each of the relevant alternatives if we wish to understand the nature of the commitments we are making.

Limited resources and the need for priorities necessitate some limits to the concept of psychiatric need. If mental illnesses are fundamentally different from ordinary problems in living and are defined not by social standards but by medical diagnoses of disease, public health policy should give highest priority to those patients who are clearly sick in a traditional psychiatric sense. Here we might assume on the basis of considerable evidence that many ordinary problems are transitory, while psychiatric disease states are more persistent. Thus, public policy must give greatest emphasis to limiting and alleviating the more serious conditions.

In contrast, if the psychoses and other serious conditions are part of the same continuum as other problems, we can treat all such conditions in fundamentally the same way—chronic disability is simply a manifestation of untreated and neglected illness. Indeed, early intervention may prevent chronic and severe mental illness. If one accepts these assumptions—and they are assumptions rather than proven facts—it is reasonable to devote considerable resources to preventive work and to treating mild and moderate psychological disabilities.

One can understand the significance of these diverse approaches by looking at a difference of opinion that developed at a government-sponsored mental health conference. Alexander Leighton (1967) took the position that mental disorders should be seen as part of a continuum.

> *Typologies of this sort are able to handle the complex continuity that appears to exist between patterns of health and patterns of illness. One can picture this, diagrammatically, as comprising two extremes in a field: one side, health behaviours, is a dense population of white dots, and the other, psychiatric behaviours (symptoms) is a dense population of black dots. As one looks across the field from light to dark, the whites grow less and less and the blacks become thicker and thicker. (Leighton 1967, p. 339)*

Paul Lemkau took strong exception to Leighton's formulation.

> *We cannot properly look at our problem in this way, at least not all of our problems in this way; when we do so, we make the assumption almost automatically that the same kind of program will apply all the way across the board, all the way across these various shades of gray. All we need to do is intensify or de-intensify a panacea-like program. I think this is false. I think it covers up the complexity of the task we have to do in therapeutic and preventive psychiatry. You don't cure phenylketonuric oligophrenia with psychotherapy, you prevent it by adjusting diet.*
>
> *Now, I don't think that that fits in this scale of grayness. One can go on and on with these kinds of things and point out that the preventive and therapeutic programs are very large in number if we are going to fit the particular cases that, in reality, exist. I think Dr. Leighton does us a disservice when he tries to tell us that the matter is just gradations of the same thing. It isn't, and I don't think the abandonment of proper classification of illnesses is the answer to this kind of problem. (Kramer et al. 1967, p. 363)*

By drawing these positions sharply, we can exaggerate the extent to which two separate camps exist. Most mental health professionals are probably not clear about their views of mental illness or the assumptions that underlie them. They usually hold both opinions simultaneously, although the opinions themselves may be contradictory in a formal sense. Other complications bring the two views together. Moderate problems (even if they are not regarded as psychiatric illnesses) may become severe problems that incapacitate the individual in carrying out social roles. These serious problems are worthy of help regardless of whether they are part of the same order of phenomena as schizophrenia or other recognized psychiatric conditions.

The development of a coherent and intelligent public policy depends partially on the perspectives taken but mostly on the resolution of specific empirical questions. Which untreated conditions and problems become chronic, and which ones are transitory? Obviously, no rational person would suggest that a large bulk of our medical resources be given to the treatment of the common cold because the condition is self-limited in any case. Similarly, we must be able to identify psychiatric conditions analogous to the common cold. We must be able to specify the effects of varying types of intervention. Which social services and policies limit disability and handicap, and which ones exacerbate such problems? Do preventive psychiatric services increase the number of iatrogenic disturbances or encourage psychological hypochondriasis? How successful are preventive psychiatric services in insulating persons from future serious morbidity and disability? Although the answers to many of these questions are unknown, we must continue to ask them in a way amenable to empirical investigation. Finally, although public policy must continue to develop despite the uncertainty of knowledge, the importance of such information should lead those government agencies financing care to insist that serious attempts be made to evaluate program effectiveness.

The Patient and the Society: An Insoluble Dilemma

Because there are varying ways of looking at mental illness, the views of different evaluators may come into conflict. Most typically, psychiatric difficulties are defined in terms of the distress a person is experiencing or in terms of the performance of social roles. Although psychological comfort may contribute to adequate social functioning, the factors influencing these two aspects of adaptation may vary. Individuals and communities have long-range as well as short-range goals, and they must frequently incur immediate psychological costs to achieve more important but more distant goals. In addition, successful adaptation as the long-range goal requires learning to cope successfully with adversity and acquiring a sense of efficacy, control, and self-esteem. There are both theoretical (Seligman 1975) and empirical reasons (Elder 1974) to believe that exposure to adversities that persons can overcome contributes to the development of adult well-being.

No society in history has been completely devoted to eliminating personal discomfort and pain. We usually work to alleviate forms of distress that have no social function. Our most valued social institutions, however, do much to produce psychological stress, and we need to go no further than the educational system to illustrate this point. University education frequently undermines students' most cherished beliefs; students are not infrequently failed in courses and dismissed from universities. The educational system is always setting goals that some students cannot meet, resulting in a sense of failure and a loss of self-esteem. Implicit in the value structure of universities, however, is the idea that the incentives for performance or the need for acquisition of information and skills requires inducing some stress and personal pain into the student's life. Most societies operate on the premise that stress provides incentives and facilitates the development of important instrumental goals. Therefore, although it is often possible to relieve personal distress by reducing obligations and responsibilities, we frequently choose not to do so.

A major dilemma in psychiatry involves the emphasis to be placed on performance in contrast to that placed on the control of personal distress. Psychiatrists employed by particular institutions, such as the military, seek to minimize the number of psychiatric casualties from the perspective of social performance, but, no doubt, the performance is achieved at some cost to the psychological comfort of the people involved. When a time dimension is built into perspectives on mental health problems, such problems become even more complicated. The value of one alternative in relation to others obviously depends on the long-range goals of individuals and groups and on the extent to which societal pressures are necessary to achieve such goals. If we minimize psychological distress at one stage in a person's life, at some cost to performance and the extent to which new skills are developed, we may find at some later point that this lack of skills is an important cause of the current distress. Conversely, if we neglect the issue of personal distress and place value only on the development of performance skills, we may "stress" a person to the extent that he or she is continuously uncomfortable and may refuse to function at all. We must achieve some balance between mastery of the environment and individual comfort, not only for humanitarian reasons but also to facilitate continuing performance and mastery.

Social Problem or Mental Illness?

We have already discussed the consequences of viewing disturbances in psychological functioning from the perspective of personality development as contrasted with a biological or social perspective. Although mental illness is clearly a social problem, it is not obvious which social problems fall within the domain of mental illness. Many women are distressed and lack self-confidence, but to define such problems mainly from the psychiatric perspective neglects the social and environmental problems that lead to such distress. Although women are more likely to suffer from depression than men (Weissman and Klerman, 1977; Weissman et al. 1996), simply defining this as a clinical problem is a disservice to both women and society. Similarly, delinquency thrives in impoverished areas and among certain minority groups. To define delinquents as children in need of psychiatric care, although many may have such needs, may divert us from considering the social forces and conditions that lead to behavior defined by the larger society as unlawful. The concepts of mental health and mental disorder are frequently used in an imprecise and ambiguous way and come to encompass a wide range of social problems. These psychiatric definitions implicitly suggest that these problems reside more in individuals than in the organization and patterning of the community itself. Another implication is that the proper means of changing these conditions is through changing the personalities and inclinations of individuals rather than through changing the structure of the society itself. Some mental health professionals believe that persons who illegally use drugs must be emotionally disturbed; it is equally plausible to consider whether certain laws pertaining to the use of specific drugs are truly consistent with scientific knowledge and, indeed, whether the inclination of many people to experiment with drugs is a reasonably normal response.

I do not mean to suggest that psychiatrists are unaware of the societal difficulties faced by women or the social influences affecting delinquent behavior or the use of drugs among college students. As long as the craft of psychiatry is practiced, however, the problem of mental illness will inevitably be approached from the viewpoint of changing the patient rather than changing the society. This contradiction has led some psychiatrists to reject traditional psychiatric roles and to direct themselves instead toward changing society itself. Some of these efforts are characterized as preventive psychiatry. Many psychiatrists, however, have overreacted to their professional dilemma. In conceptually moving from the individual to the society, they have argued that mental illness in general is a product of social forces and social structure and that the psychiatrist must be concerned with the community. This position widely expands the horizons of psychiatric work and the scope of psychiatric activity and places the psychiatrist in the political arena.

Another alternative to the psychiatric dilemma exists, however. By noting that the problems of various groups in society are rooted as much in the influences of the society as in the conditions of individuals, we might appropriately conclude that such problems realistically are not the province of psychiatry at all, unless the person is also mentally ill in the more narrow sense. These problems are frequently associated with general conditions in the society rather than with specific conditions characterizing the person's inability to make an adequate adjustment without profound suffering. The mental health professional, in order to perform a specific function in society, cannot hope to be all things to all people. He or she must be trained to take on tasks that make a specific contribution. My view is that psychiatrists should have a limited function—to provide help to individuals who are disabled because they suffer from the specific kinds of problems that psychiatrists are uniquely trained to handle. There are many more such patients than psychiatrists can easily provide care for, and while psychiatrists have increased the scope of the problems they deal with in society, they have neglected the patients suffering from more traditional psychiatric syndromes.

Psychiatric problems, of course, may contribute to larger social problems, and social problems may cause profound psychological distress. The issues that require clarification are whether it is reasonable or fruitful to treat most social problems as problems of mental health and whether the same professionals who are trained as experts in treating schizophrenia, depressive disorders, and other more typical psychiatric conditions are those who can most appropriately deal with problems resulting from environmental impoverishment, cultural deprivation, social change, economic and social discrimination, and other societal conditions. Because the availability of mental health professionals is limited, their involvement in social problems leads to the neglect of the victims of hard-core mental illness.

In raising such issues, I do not wish to imply that the society should not devote large resources to alleviating social problems and the many forms of inequality that exist. We must, however, entertain the hypothesis that in allowing the psychiatric perspective to muddy the social waters, we may be diverting attention from more important questions involving both social problems and mental illness. Many of the major social problems we face require a large effort to develop an adequate system of social, economic, and educational services and opportunities available to all. The major problem of mental illness is to treat and, if possible, to prevent the psychological suffering and social handicaps evident among those so afflicted. Whether such problems are better attacked as separate questions or together is an important social-policy issue.

In suggesting that psychiatry, as a profession, might give greatest emphasis to the development of its specialized and traditional skills, I do not mean to indicate that the contexts for treating the mentally ill need to be separated from contexts in which other medical and social difficulties are handled. The same patients may frequently have a variety of difficulties and problems—some requiring psychiatric assistance, some requiring help from other professionals. It is desirable to coordinate and integrate the care such persons receive, both to facilitate their understanding of their needs and to allow professionals to provide the best overall program for their care and rehabilitation.

It is difficult to find agreement on policy questions pertaining to mental illness because different persons have varying conceptions of these disorders, and such conceptions determine in which direction it is most appropriate to move. We should therefore inquire more fully into the way patients come into contact with the mental health system, the varying conceptions of the causes of mental illness, and the measures that might prevent their development. The next two chapters deal with these issues.

Chapter 3

Psychological Disorder and the Flow of Patients into Treatment

The Study of Psychiatric Epidemiology

The study of mental illness requires the identification of specific disorders and the way persons who are treated for these disorders differ from those who are not. Cases of psychiatric illness are most easily identified in treatment institutions, but in studying such cases it is difficult to separate the factors related to the occurrence of these conditions from those that affect the processes of seeking and receiving help. Although the study of treated cases of severe mental illness may approximate all such cases, many who are afflicted, even with schizophrenia, do not make contact with conventional psychiatric facilities.

We have learned a great deal from the study of treated cases and have depended on such studies because of the difficulties of carrying out community investigation. It has become evident that in many areas of concern treated cases only poorly approximate the sick population in general, and persons with similar conditions may not receive treatment at all or may be treated by general practitioners, social workers, or religious counselors. We must either increase our scope of identifying cases in other than psychiatric facilities or initiate community epidemiological surveys in which case-finding assessments are made within community populations.

Psychiatric epidemiology faces two major problems. The first is to differentiate as carefully as possible new cases from cases that have continued over some long period of time. The epidemiologist distinguishes *incidence* (the number of new cases that occur during a particular interval) from *prevalence* (all cases existing during a particular period of time). The prevalence rate includes all new cases that develop in the interval as well as those that began at some earlier time but continued. While prevalence gives some indication of the total magnitude of the problem and the need for services, incidence is a more useful statistic for the study of causation. The second problem is having clear criteria for identifying cases of a particular disorder and differentiating it as precisely as possible from other disorders. Rigorous case identification is also an essential prerequisite for study of causation.

In order to understand the causes of a disorder, it is helpful to differentiate factors that contribute to its initial occurrence from those that affect its course—whether it persists, disappears, or fluctuates. For example, the treatment of a streptococcal infection with antibiotics will eliminate the infection, but the lack of such treatment, allowing the illness to persist, is not a cause of the infection. Although the incidence rate will tell us the number of new infections that occur during a specified period, the prevalence rate combines these with older infections that have persisted. The study of prevalence will not allow us to separate clearly the factors *causing* a condition from those that affect its *course.*

Similarly, as we noted in our discussion of disease models, it is essential to be as precise as possible about the entity being studied. Disorders are extraordinarily varied and complicated and have different causes, natural histories, and biological and social consequences. If the condition being studied is poorly defined and combines different disorders, the knowledge generated will also be confused. Precise definition makes it more likely that we will learn something new in psychiatric epidemiology. Although this field is in part handicapped by the inadequacies of our current systems of classification, we should not make matters worse by being careless about case definition.

Epidemiologists of mental disorder often face difficult practical problems. Schizophrenia, for example, is a relatively infrequent condition in populations. If it is to be studied in community samples, large samples would have to be examined to identify a sufficient number of new cases for causal studies. Obtaining such samples is both expensive and strategically difficult. In contrast, treated samples have the difficulties associated with selective help seeking we have already noted, especially when they come from only one or a limited number of treatment institutions. One compromise is to select samples of treated cases from community case registers gathered from a wide range of institutions or from existing administrative data files. Registers or data files, which maintain records of patients contacting many different facilities, allow for a broader sample of cases in the study of any particular disorder (Wing and Hailey 1972). However, they cannot provide information on persons who do not seek care or those who contact practitioners not covered by such registers, such as primary care physicians. Also, when data are reported from a variety of facilities and institutions, reliability of diagnosis and other information becomes problematic. Registers are very expensive to maintain and involve serious legal and ethical issues, and it is usually difficult to maintain long-term cooperation from reporting institutions. Although some registers have been useful for sampling and other research purposes, they have not achieved the high expectations associated with their development. Administrative data files are more easily available but typically are incomplete, cover only services reimbursed by a particular program, and are restricted in their use because of the need to protect confidentiality.

Identifying Psychological Problems in Community Populations

As the extent of social selection in seeking treatment became evident to researchers, they sought to study the prevalence of psychiatric disorder in community populations. In some classic studies, psychiatrists personally interviewed the populations of entire communities for the purpose of identifying all persons with psychiatric illnesses (Essen-Möeller 1956, Hagnell 1966). Although such studies provided valuable information, they were dependent on the psychiatric conceptions of the interviewers and had uncertain reliability and validity. It was also exceedingly expensive for psychiatrists to interview personally large numbers of people in community populations; consequently, such epidemiological studies were very limited.

During World War II the practical needs of the military required screening instruments to identify prospective soldiers likely to suffer psychiatric breakdowns. Researchers developed an instrument—the Army Neuro-Psychiatric Screening Adjunct—that could differentiate to some extent between psychiatric and normal populations. Following the war, when epidemiologists turned to the problem of studying psychological disorder in community populations they used this instrument as a basis for developing measures of impairment. The Midtown Manhattan Study (Srole et al. 1962) stimulated the development of a variety of interview measures for screening persons in community populations. These techniques all tend to include items measuring depression, anxiety, and psychophysiological discomforts but not psychotic symptoms or antisocial behavior. They focus more on *neurotic* distress than disturbed thinking. One of the most commonly used measures of this kind in the postwar period—the Langner twenty-two-item scale (Langner 1962)—differentiated between normal and treated psychiatric populations and was correlated with such variables as sex, social class, and stressful life events (Langner and Michael 1963, Dohrenwend and Dohrenwend 1969). Examples of the twenty-two items in the scale are:

I feel weak all over much of the time.

I have had periods of days, weeks, or months when I couldn't take care of things because I couldn't "get going."

Have you ever been bothered by your heart beating hard?

Are you ever bothered by nervousness?

You sometimes can't help wondering if anything is worthwhile any more.

Do you ever have trouble in getting to sleep or staying asleep?

Many of the items were scored by the frequency of symptom reports and not by simply reporting the symptom.

The value of such global measures of psychiatric impairment and their appropriate use have generated much critical debate. At the methodological level, it has been suggested that these scales suffer from various response biases, such as yea saying/nay saying among certain respondents, distorting effects because of different perceptions of the social undesirability of items, and confusion of symptoms of physical and psychological illness (Manis et al. 1963; Crandell and Dohrenwend 1967; Phillips and Clancey 1970; Seiler 1973; Tousignant et al. 1974). It was noted that such biases resulted in persons with physical illness reporting more symptoms than their psychological state warranted because of confusion in the items, and that persons of varying ethnic groups saw the symptoms as more or less stigmatizing, thus affecting the way they would respond. At the substantive level, concern was raised by the finding that psychiatric outpatients score higher on such items than more severely disabled inpatients (Dohrenwend 1973), and that competent youth—such as college students—may score extremely high (Mechanic and Greenley 1976). Also, correlations among psychiatric patients who were retested a year later were higher than were correlations between test and retest results in community samples (Dohrenwend 1973, pp. 485–486), suggesting that among patients the scales measure some stable problem while among a community sample they may reflect transient stress to a larger extent.

Despite the criticisms, further study suggests that these scales measure disabling distress and, although not comparable to psychiatric diagnoses, persons with these symptoms suffer and use many types of medical and psychological assistance (Greenley and Mechanic 1976; Wheaton 1978; Dohrenwend et al. 1979). The question is, what do these scales actually measure? Dohrenwend and his colleagues, who have studied these scales in some detail, observe that they particularly seem to tap anxiety, sadness, psychophysiological symptoms, lack of enervation, and a perception of poor health, and that this tends to constitute a single dimension of response. In my own work on the Langner scale, I found results comparable to those reported by Dohrenwend (Mechanic 1979b).

Dohrenwend and his associates (1979) explored various explanations of high scores on such scales: that they measure neurosis; that they reflect a particular mode of expression in which the individual reports dissatisfactions mainly within him- or herself; that the scales measure something akin to fever in physical illness; or that they measure a *quasi neurosis* reflecting psychological discomfort and maladjustment. Dohrenwend favors as an explanation Jerome Frank's concept of *demoralization*—a situation in which a person cannot meet expectations, but also cannot get out of (Frank 1974). Demoralization is believed to be associated with constitutional defects, environmental stress, learned incapacities, existential despair, psychiatric symptoms, and physical illness. In my own work on the development of such distress syndromes (Mechanic 1979b), I have developed the hypothesis that they partially reflect a learned pattern of illness behavior involving a focus on internal feeling states, careful monitoring of bodily sensations, and a high level of self-awareness and introspection. This pattern of illness behavior is associated with and contributes to disabling psychological pain. This response pattern is learned in part, I believe, and is reinforced through childhood illness, parental behavior toward the child (particularly negative behavior), socially acquired attitudes, and social stress. A great deal still needs to be learned about what these scales measure and their implications for social policy. The meaning of a high distress pattern still requires further research, but we have some useful information about the implications of distress for perceptions of illness and the utilization of care.

In recent years there has been significant improvement in screening instruments for psychiatric disorder, for measuring general well-being, and for ascertaining levels of depression, anxiety and social impairment. Some are more commonly used than others, but considerable disagreement remains as to the extent they have overcome the types of problems already discussed and how individuals with high scores on these measures compare with patients treated in psychiatric settings. In other words, there is concern about the validity of these measures as true representations of disorder. Typically, researchers establish a level of reported symptomatology that is presumed to reflect a high probability that an individual is likely to have a problem worthy of attention.

There are too many of these research screening scales to allow review here, but some examples are helpful in illustrating developments in this field. For example, two of the most frequently used scales in the literature are the Center for Epidemiological Studies Depression Scale (CESD) (Radloff 1977) and the General Health Questionnaire (GHQ) (Goldberg 1972). The CESD consists of twenty items reporting on the frequency of relatively common symptoms of depressed mood, such as feeling sad, lonely, depressed, completely helpless, or fearful; having crying spells; wondering if anything is worthwhile anymore; not being able to get going, and so on. It has high reliability and is quite successful in screening for persons who may have a serious depressive problem. However, the measure is very nonspecific and yields large numbers of persons who score high but would not be regarded by clinicians as clinically depressed. The GHQ is a sixty-item screening scale that covers several types of distress states such as depression, anxiety, social impairment, and hypochrondiasis. It was developed as a first-stage screening instrument for psychiatric illness, with patients who score high being examined more closely by a clinician, but the GHQ and some of its subscales are commonly used in surveys without follow-up. The instrument is not intended to have diagnostic specificity, but there are subscales that relate to specific diagnostic types such as depression. For example, items intending to tap depression include feeling unhappy and depressed, being unable to concentrate, thinking of yourself as worthless, and thinking life is entirely hopeless and not worth living. The GHQ has good test–retest reliability and is reasonably good at identifying psychiatric disorders, but, like many other such measures, it is not diagnostically specific and yields a significant number of false positive cases. This is not a barrier if used as a first-stage screening instrument, but it is a problem when the GHQ or any of these instruments are used as exclusive measures.

Estimates of Prevalence of Disorder in Community Populations

It is difficult to estimate prevalence of psychiatric illness using global measures of psychological distress. Although many community studies have been carried out, estimates of mental illness vary a great deal, depending on the broad or restrictive nature of the concepts of disorder (from 1 percent to more than 50 percent of the population). Dohrenwend and Dohrenwend (1969), considering only more thorough studies involving direct interviews with subjects, note a tremendous increase in rates for functional psychiatric disorders in studies published after 1950 as compared with those before 1950. The only plausible interpretation of these findings is that there has been a broadening of definitions of psychiatric disorder, and what one finds depends on the assumptions of the researcher as to what constitutes disorder. The Dohrenwends (1969, 1974a,b) have worked these studies over laboriously, but it is impossible to make the results of studies based on such varying definitions of disorder compatible, especially in respect to less disabling nonpsychotic disorders. Although estimates for schizophrenia might vary from 0.5 to 3.0 percent of the population, and there is agreement that manic–depressive psychosis is relatively uncommon (less than 0.5 percent), reported rates of neurosis, depressive disorders, and personality problems vary substantially from one study to another. The estimates available to the President's Commission on Mental Health (1978, Vol. II, p. 16) of neurosis (including nonpsychotic depressive disorders) were 8 to 13 percent. Estimates have now been improved through the Epidemiological Catchment Area Program (ECA) and the National Comorbidity Survey (NCS).

The Epidemiological Catchment Area Program and the National Comorbidity Survey

As the foregoing suggests, the availability of measures that could be administered at a community level stimulated epidemiological work, but there was much uncertainty as to the meaning and clinical significance of the distress measures used. The development of DSM-III and the more refined specification of diagnostic criteria contributed to a revitalization of epidemiological measurement and led to the establishment of the Epidemiological Catchment Area Program (ECA) involving a collaborative epidemiological study of about 20,000 individuals in five sites: New Haven, Baltimore, Saint Louis, Los Angeles, and Durham, North Carolina (Eaton and Kessler 1985). All sites used the Diagnostic Interview Schedule (DIS), developed by Lee Robins at Washington University, Saint Louis, which allowed diagnoses to be made by diagnostic algorithms according to DSM-III criteria and was adaptable to other diagnostic systems as well (Robins et al. 1984, 1985). The purpose of the ECA project was to obtain prevalence rates of specific mental disorders and to examine their relationship to demographic factors, family history, life events, and neurobiological variables. The ultimate purpose was to gain a better understanding of etiology, clinical course, and treatment response in relation to specific disorders (Regier et al. 1984, National Institute of Mental Health 1985, Robins et al. 1991).

The National Comorbidity Survey (NCS) was a congressionally mandated study that extends the ECA by administering a structured diagnostic interview to a representative sample of the noninstitutionalized civilian population of the United States between the ages of fifteen and fifty-four (Kessler et al. 1994). Unlike the ECA, which was restricted to five population areas, the NCS allows representative diagnostic estimates for the United States. The diagnostic interview used was a modified version of the Composite International Diagnostic Interview (CIDI), which was an adaptation of the DIS used in the ECA study. Like the DIS, the interview is administered by trained interviewers who are not clinicians. The format allows diagnostic estimates consistent with DSM-IIIR criteria. The interview also allows some comparisons consistent with the criteria of DSM-IV and the ICD-10 diagnostic criteria for research. The survey was highly sophisticated and achieved a response rate of 82.6 percent. A supplemental survey followed up nonrespondents aggressively to understand selective biases in who responded; these nonrespondents tended to have higher rates of disorder. Rates of disorder were, thus, statistically adjusted to take account of selective response.

The ECA project has been the source of many extensive analyses. The description of results here primarily relate to the first three sites studied (New Haven, eastern Baltimore, and Saint Louis), but some findings from all five sites (including Durham, North Carolina, and Los Angeles) are also noted. Six-month, twelve-month, and lifetime prevalence are reported, but the shorter-period measures are emphasized here because these data are less likely to be distorted by memory, respondent reconstructions of past events, and other biases associated with the methods used. Validity of the results has always been a critical and debated issue (Anthony et al. 1985; Robins 1985). The cases identified by these interviews are not necessarily the same as those that would be identified by clinicians interviewing the same patients. Since clinician judgment is not necessarily reliable or valid, one can question why clinician assessment should be the "gold standard," but most people would favor the views of a well-trained clinician over these standardized questions that can be misunderstood by respondents.

Considering the five sites, the five most common disorders over the previous twelve months were phobia (8.8 percent); alcohol use/dependence (6.3 percent); generalized anxiety (3.8 percent); major depressive episode (3.7 percent); and drug abuse/dependence (2.5 percent). Other reasonably frequent and disabling conditions included antisocial personality (1.2 percent); panic (0.9 percent); schizophrenia or schizophreniform conditions (1.0 percent); and manic episodes (0.6 percent). Based on the five sites, ECA investigators estimated that 32 percent of Americans had one of the disorders studied at some point in their lifetime and that 20 percent had an active disorder (Robins and Regier 1991). An active disorder was defined as one where the diagnostic criteria were met at some point in the person's life and at least one symptom or one episode had been present in the prior year.

Phobias and major depression were the most common diagnoses for women and alcohol abuse and/or dependence was the most common diagnosis for men. Rates of disorder were lower in the group older than age forty-five, with the exception of cognitive impairment, which is substantially higher in the elderly group. Rates for different disorders varied a good bit among sites (Myers et al. 1984; Robins and Regier 1991). Tables 3.1 and 3.2 show the most frequent DIS/DSM-III disorders by age and sex in three sites, and provide estimates of the number of Americans likely to be affected by each disorder based on size of the American population in 1980.

The National Comorbidity Survey reports on most of the same diagnostic categories as the ECA for a national representative sample, although the age groups covered are somewhat different (fifteen to fifty-four versus eighteen to sixty-five). The NCS found that almost half of the respondents surveyed had a lifetime disorder and almost 30 percent had a disorder during the previous twelve months. As in the ECA, the most common disorders over the previous twelve months were phobias (16.7 percent); substance abuse/dependence (11.3 percent); and major depressive episodes (10.3 percent). As expected, women were more likely to have affective and anxiety disorders and men to have substance abuse/dependence and personality disorders. Disorders were most prevalent in the twenty-five to thirty-four age group and prevalence of most disorders was less among persons with higher socioeconomic status.

Most of the findings of the NCS confirm other studies, but valuable new information is provided on patterns of comorbidity. More than half of all the lifetime disorders identified in the study occurred among about one-seventh of the sample who had three or more comorbid disorders. Almost three-fifths of disorders in the prior twelve months occur in this subsample. This smaller subgroup of respondents accounts for most people who had a severe disorder, who have high levels of impairment, and who especially require mental health services. From a public policy standpoint, persons with comorbidities constitute the most critical population and the greatest challenges.

While the NCS confirms and extends many other estimates, it makes clear that simply counting the number of people with disorders is not particularly helpful in understanding policy needs. Reporting these large numbers from the ECA and NCS projects helps alert the public to the magnitude of mental health need and conveys that mental disorders are very common, but it combines very serious and persistent disorders with many others that are transitory or not disabling. Thus, the large numbers reported are somewhat misleading. Moreover, there is good reason to believe that the procedures used for approximating DSM categories are overinclusive, resulting in a significant number of

TABLE 3.1   Four Most Frequent DIS/DSM-III Psychiatric Disorders[1] by Rank, Sex, and Age, Based on Six-Month Prevalence Rates

	Age Group				
Rank	18–24	25–44	45–64	65+	Total
Male					
1	Alcohol abuse/ dependence	Alcohol abuse/ dependence	Alcohol abuse/ dependence	Severe cognitive impairment	Alcohol abuse/ dependence
2	Drug abuse/ dependence	Phobia	Phobia	Phobia	Phobia
3	Phobia	Drug abuse/ dependence	Dysthymia	Alcohol abuse/ dependence	Drug abuse/ dependence
4	Antisocial personality	Antisocial personality	Major depressive episode without grief	Dysthymia	Dysthymia
Female					
1	Phobia	Phobia	Phobia	Phobia	Phobia
2	Drug abuse/ dependence	Major depressive episode without grief	Dysthymia	Severe cognitive impairment	Major depressive episode without grief
3	Major depressive episode without grief	Dysthymia	Major depressive episode without grief	Dysthymia	Dysthymia
4	Alcohol abuse/ dependence	Obsessive compulsive disorder	Obsessive compulsive disorder	Major depressive episode without grief	Obsessive compulsive disorder

Source: National Institute of Mental Health, *Mental Health, United States 1985.* DHHS Publ. (ADM) 85-1378, 1985, p. 5.
[1]Dysthymia included. The basis for ranking was the six-month prevalence rates for New Haven, Baltimore, and St. Louis combined. DIS indicates Diagnostic Interview Schedule.

false positive judgments (Wakefield 1997). There are many methodological issues in such studies, and significant questions about the clinical validity of these estimates, but even if we assume wide confidence levels, these studies convincingly substantiate many other community studies documenting high levels of psychological disorder in general populations and associated limitations of function (Dohrenwend et al. 1980). Even the 14 percent of the population with three or more disorders is a very large number, including some 35 million people.

From still another point of view, these figures are not really surprising. Most people have many acute illnesses, and even chronic medical conditions are very common. Surveys repeatedly show that many of these conditions go untreated. Contact with the medical care system is influenced by severity of symptoms and disability, illness behavior orientations, and factors characterizing the financing and organization of services (Mechanic 1978), an issue to which we now turn.

TABLE 3.2   **Six-month Prevalence of DIS/DSM-III Disorders for Estimated Number and Percent of U.S. Civilian Population, Based on 1980 U.S. Census and Three ECA Sites[1]**

Disorder	Estimated U.S. Population Aged 18 or Older	
	Number (in millions)	Percent
Any DIS disorder	29.4	18.7
Any DIS disorder except phobia	22.6	14.4
Any DIS disorder except substance abuse	22.1	14.0
Substance abuse disorders	10.0	6.4
Alcohol abuse/dependence	7.9	5.0
Alcohol abuse	7.2	4.6
Alcohol dependence	4.6	2.9
Drug abuse/dependence	3.1	2.0
Drug abuse	2.1	1.3
Drug dependence	1.7	1.1
Schizophrenic/schizophreniform	1.5	1.0
Schizophrenia	1.4	0.9
Schizophreniform	0.1	0.1
Affective disorders	9.4	6.0
Manic episode	1.0	0.7
Major depressive episode	4.9	3.1
Dysthymia	5.1	3.2
Anxiety/somatoform disorders	13.1	8.3
Phobia	11.1	7.0
Panic	1.2	0.8
Obsessive compulsive	2.4	1.5
Somatization	0.1	0.1
Antisocial personality	1.4	0.9
Cognitive impairment (severe)	1.6	1.0

Source: National Institute of Mental Health, *Mental Health, United States 1985.* DHHS Publ. (ADM) 85-1378, 1985, p. 4.

[1]The three ECA sites were not chosen to be a representative sample of the United States, so the study results cannot be used to estimate precisely the number of Americans afflicted. However, by projecting the data and standardizing the rates to the 1980 Census on the basis of age, sex, and race, an approach is provided for those who wish to make projections to the total population.

Psychological Disorder and Utilization of Care

The distress syndromes and DSM disorders measured by the instruments described involve components suggesting poor self-assessments of physical health as well as poor mental health. Studies show that people react to their health in a global or holistic way, and psychological difficulties or psychosocial problems influence the extent to which they view their health as poor even if differences in physical health status are controlled (Tessler and

Mechanic 1978). Distressed people are not only more likely to visit psychiatrists, counselors, and social agencies of various kinds (Greenley and Mechanic 1976; Greenley, Mechanic, and Cleary 1987), but they are also more likely to visit nonpsychiatric physicians (Tessler, Mechanic, and Dimond 1976). Such patients may or may not have an identifiable psychiatric diagnosis, but they constitute a major component of demand for medical and psychiatric services.

The relationship between having a DSM disorder and the need for care remains uncertain. Data from the ECA study indicate that while most of those with a DIS/DSM-III disorder had no care for this problem during the prior six months; about one-third of those who sought care for an emotional problem had no DIS/DSM-III disorder. Of course, the fact that a person does not have a specific diagnosable disorder does not exclude the possibility of great pain and disability. The NCS substantiates the findings that most persons who have mental disorders do not receive treatment for these conditions. Less than two-fifths of persons with a lifetime disorder had ever received professional treatment for it, and only one-fifth of those with a recent disorder have received such care. More than 40 percent of those with three or more lifetime disorders never received professional help, and almost two-thirds of those with three or more lifetime disorders who had a disorder during the previous year received no professional help during the past year (Kessler et al. 1994). When receiving professional help in the past year, only about half of those with disorders received such help from the mental health specialty sector. Those with three or more disorders were more likely to receive help from mental health providers than persons with fewer disorders. Many factors other than diagnosis affect the help-seeking process and selection into care.

For example, Brown, Craig, and Harris (1985), in a study of depressed women in Islington, a section of London, England, rigorously studied a population sample of women with levels of depression comparable in severity to depressed patients typically treated by psychiatrists. Those who were actually referred to psychiatrists did not differ in number of core symptoms of depression compared with those who only received care from general practitioners. However, psychiatric referral occurred when the depression was expressed in certain disruptive ways such as threats or plans of suicide, exhibition of socially disruptive behavior such as violent outbursts, and abuse of drugs. This suggests that referral depends not only on the severity of the illness, but also on the social consequences of its expression as in high risk behavior. General practitioners may be more likely to refer such patients because they believe them to be more disturbed or feel unable to cope with the behaviors involved. Larger quantitative studies also confirm that referral to psychiatry and admission to a psychiatric hospital are influenced more by risk such as suicide threats and social disruption than by severity of symptoms (Mechanic et al. 1991).

Such studies help explain why diagnosis is inadequate by itself to explain either need for care or referral processes. Consider, for example, the DSM-IV definition of a major depressive disorder. Criteria for such a diagnosis include five symptoms that are present during the same two-week period and represent a change from previous functioning (American Psychiatric Association 1994, p. 327). At least one of the symptoms must be either depressed mood or loss of interest or pleasure, but the other four can be any from a list of seven other possible types of symptoms. Thus, from the diagnostic point of view, the other symptoms are comparable in importance. They vary, however, from such symptoms as insomnia nearly every day, significant weight loss or gain when not dieting, and fatigue or loss of energy every day to a suicide attempt or specific plan for committing suicide or psychomotor agitation or retardation nearly every day observable to others. Clearly, the social risks associated with some of these symptoms are much greater than with others, and doctors and families respond to risk as well as to diagnosis. Contingencies associated with symptoms of depression such as risk and social disruption contribute to definitions of *need* and to referral processes. The ECA and NCS projects reflect DSM diagnostic criteria and incorporate both their strengths and limitations.

Approximately two-thirds of individuals in each of three ECA sites who were assessed as having a recent DSM-III disorder, as measured by the Diagnostic Interview Schedule, made an ambulatory visit for health services of some kind during the previous six months (not necessarily for a psychological disorder) (Shapiro et al. 1984). Depending on site, this was only about 8 to 10 percent more than in the population as a whole. In contrast, the average number of medical visits was considerably higher among those with a psychiatric diagnosis, as were inpatient admissions. Inpatient admissions for mental health reasons, however, explain most of the excess, and in one site (Saint Louis), excluding mental health admissions resulted in a lower proportion of respondents with DSM-III diagnoses having hospital admissions than among those with no diagnosis. A majority of visits and admissions occur in the general medical sector, in contrast to psychiatric settings, with considerable variation among study sites.

Most important is that a majority of patients in almost all disorder categories received no care for a mental health problem during the six-month period under consideration. Such care seeking is particularly low among persons with cognitive disorders and substance abuse and/or dependence. More detailed data have been reported on help-seeking patterns for Baltimore (Shapiro et al. 1985) and New Haven (Leaf et al. 1985). In Baltimore, 62 percent of persons judged to have a DSM-III disorder in the prior six months did not receive any mental health services during that period from either physicians in general or the specialized mental health sector. Those diagnosed as schizophrenic were most likely to receive some care (55 percent), while the group least treated were those with severe cognitive impairment (25 percent). Receipt of care for a mental health problem was particularly low among the elderly and nonwhites.

In the New Haven sample, efforts were made to assess use of mental health services provided by a wider range of health professionals and clinics. Sixteen percent of the sample met criteria for a DSM-III disorder during the six months prior to interview, but most received no mental health services. In the sample overall, 6.7 percent had a mental health service in the six-month period: 2.6 percent only from general physicians; 3.2 percent from the specialized psychiatric sector; and 0.9 percent from both (Leaf et al. 1985). Utilization was highest for schizophrenia, panic, antisocial behavior, and somatization, and lowest for alcohol or drug abuse or dependence.

Leaf and his colleagues used regression analysis to examine a variety of factors associated with having a mental health visit during the previous six months and number of such visits, controlling for DSM-III disorder. Among the factors limiting the likelihood of such visits were being male, being under age twenty-four or over age sixty-five, nonwhite and lower educational status, and not being married. Persons who lacked a regular source of care, who had less receptive attitudes to mental health professions, and who faced barriers to access also were less likely to receive such care. If patients entered the specialized mental health system, they had many more mental health visits than those treated solely by generalists (a mean of 15.6 for those exclusively treated by the specialty sector as compared with 2.1 for those treated by generalists).

The more recent NCS, as we have seen, confirmed that the majority of persons with psychiatric disorders receive no treatment, and few receive treatment from mental health professionals. Indeed, treatment rates were lower in the NCS than in the ECA study. The Rand Health Insurance Experiment also provides extensive information on services utilization for insured persons, but controls for magnitude of illness are based on symptom scales and not on specific psychiatric diagnoses. In any case, both the original Rand study and subsequent further analyses of these data indicate considerable selection into mental health specialty care controlling for symptoms. Women and younger members of the sample and those with more education were more likely to have a mental health specialty visit. Income, however, was not a statistically significant determinant when other factors were taken into account (Mechanic et al. 1991).

It is difficult to correctly estimate help seeking for emotional problems from the general medical sector. Survey questions related to such ambulatory visits will typically not identify patients who emphasize somatic aspects of psychiatric disorder in their presentations and patients who believe it is inappropriate to present emotional symptoms as a basis for a medical visit. Cross-cultural studies indicate that patients present symptoms they believe to be consistent with the help-seeking context (Cheung and Lau 1982). Patients visiting general physicians are likely to focus on the physical concomitants of distress and may be unwilling to discuss emotional problems or to do so only when physicians give indications of interest in such symptoms (Ginsberg and Brown 1982).

The relationship between the presence of a DSM-III disorder and need requires careful examination. The fact that as many as 45 to 63 percent of schizophrenics, 55 to 75 percent of depressed patients, and the vast majority of phobic patients are out of contact with any mental health services for as much as six months prior to being assessed as having these disorders suggests major unfilled needs, even if we make allowances for substantial overestimation of cases. It is reasonable to expect that many of these patients could benefit from professional care. In some instances of substance abuse, antisocial personality, and severe cognitive impairment among the elderly it remains unclear what benefits would derive from increased mental health intervention. Often, there is little that mental health professionals can do, and some patients have learned through experience with the mental health system that they get limited help. We need better data to define clearly which of these patients should be induced into care through public policy initiatives and what types of services they should receive. Even in the case of cognitive impairment among the elderly it is important to assess to what degree such impairment may be a function of depression and whether patients could be assisted in learning skills that help maintain functioning despite memory loss.

Assessing the issue of need and appropriate care requires information on the long-term course of treated and untreated DSM-III disorders as measured both clinically and by survey, particularly among subpopulations who choose not to seek care from the medical care system or who do so but in the more narrow context of physical complaints. It is essential to distinguish patients who present their complaints somatically because they perceive such presentations as appropriate to the context, but are receptive to explicit mental health interventions, from those who are not. In the case of the former, there is some evidence suggesting that attention to mental health issues reduces the use of nonpsychiatric medical services (Jones and Vischi 1979, Smith, Monson, and Ray 1986). Patients with psychiatric morbidity and distress use more outpatient and inpatient care than others in the population (Mechanic, Cleary, and Greenley 1982). It remains uncertain whether savings in total expenditures are achieved when use of both general medical care and mental health services are taken into account (Borus et al. 1985). Among those resistant to mental health treatment, physicians have little alternative but to treat patients with a more narrow medical definition and provide whatever support and encouragement feasible.

Despite the inadequacy of definitions of need, the data identify a variety of barriers to care. These include: (1) the unwillingness of many patients to define themselves as having a mental or emotional disorder, or to seek care for such a problem from a mental health professional; (2) perceived stigma associated with mental health services and the lack of support from significant others in using such services; (3) barriers to access to appropriate care including the lack of a regular source of medical care, inadequate insurance coverage for mental health services, and high levels of copayment in using such services; and (4) lack of knowledge or sophistication among physicians in recognizing mental health problems and making appropriate referrals, or attitudes among physicians that inhibit appropriate care and referral. Primary care studies suggest that how physicians manage patients with mental health needs depends substantially on their attitudes, interests, workload, and on financing mechanisms (Shepherd et al. 1966; Mechanic 1974, 1976; Goldberg and Huxley 1980). Referral to specialized mental health settings, in turn, depends on the doctor's confidence and interest in managing the patient, attitudes toward mental health professionals, the patient's wishes and inclinations, and the overall structure of reimbursement as it affects both the doctor and patient.

Social Factors Associated with Psychiatric Conditions in the Community

We now have a large number of community studies using broad measures of psychological distress and impairment, as well as the more specific diagnoses derived from such instruments as the DIS. Generalized distress and impairment are greater among persons of low socioeconomic status, among women, among the divorced and separated, and among blacks (Dohrenwend and Dohrenwend 1969, 1974; Pearlin and Johnson 1977; Kessler 1982; Kessler and Neighbors 1986). As one examines specific diagnoses, however, the associations with social and demographic factors vary. This should be no surprise since mental illnesses are varied, have many different causes, and, therefore, should have different correlates. The only acceptable generalization is that the burden of illness and disability is much greater among the poor than the affluent. More detailed statements require examination of the epidemiology of each condition. Some examples illustrate the issues.

The single most consistent finding in the epidemiological literature is the relationship between socioeconomic status and the prevalence of schizophrenia (Dohrenwend and Dohrenwend 1969). The onset of schizophrenia is usually in young adulthood, but it does not markedly vary by sex, region, or cultural area. There is some indication, however, that schizophrenia may be more prevalent in urban than in rural areas, but these differences are not large (Dohrenwend 1975, p. 370). For the past fifty years, there has been much speculation concerning the link between social class and schizophrenia.

Despite many studies on class and schizophrenia, there are few studies with sufficient numbers of new cases of schizophrenia. The limited and flawed incidence data—such as in the Hollingshead and Redlich (1958) study—suggest that an incidence difference in relation to social status may exist, but the large number of lower-class schizophrenics is particularly apparent in prevalence data. These and similar findings have generated a long debate between advocates of a social causation as compared with a social selection interpretation. Those favoring a social causation view argue that there is something about the environment of lower-class living that increases vulnerability to schizophrenia. Melvin Kohn (1973, 1977) maintains that a genetic vulnerability, social stress, and an inflexible and rigid value system that hampers coping interact to produce an excess of schizophrenics in the lower class. The more common view, and one I believe to be better supported by the existing evidence (Mechanic 1972a), is that the lower-class status of schizophrenics is largely a result of the debilitating effects of the condition itself. Persons with the condition are hampered in their work and either suffer downward mobility or fail to rise with increased opportunity, as their peers do (Turner and Wagenfeld 1967). Although there is persuasive evidence that stress contributes to the occurrence of schizophrenic episodes (Brown and Birley 1968), differences in stress cannot explain the link between schizophrenia and social class.

Bruce Dohrenwend has spent several decades exploring the extent to which social causation or social selection is more important in schizophrenia and other types of disorder. He developed an unusual strategy to test this idea. He reasoned that while mental impairments would interfere with social mobility, ethnic discrimination would operate similarly, keeping people from advancing in their socioeconomic status. Persons from ethnic minorities, thus, who were not psychiatrically impaired would have difficulty in mobility, while nondisadvantaged groups could move up the social ladder more easily. If schizophrenia was socially caused by the stresses associated with lower socioeconomic status, ethnic minority groups would be particularly disadvantaged and would be expected to have a higher level of disorder than nonminorities. But if social selection was the predominant influence, healthy ethnic minorities would have more difficulty moving upward because of discrimination and blocked opportunities and more of such persons who remained in the lower social strata would be psychologically healthy than those unlikely to experience discrimination.

Finding an appropriate research setting has been a particular challenge for testing this hypothesis. Using Israel's population register, Dohrenwend and his colleagues (1992) identified a birth cohort of 4,914 young Israelis who were born to European and North African families. "Oriental Jews" from North Africa are relatively disadvantaged and experience considerable prejudice and discrimination. The sample was then screened by psychiatrists in a standardized way, and those with conditions were given specific diagnoses. These data then allowed examination of comparative illness rates by diagnosis. Rates of schizophrenia were higher for those of European than North African background in low socioeconomic groupings, suggesting support for the social selection hypothesis. In contrast, social causation seemed to be much more influential in the case of depression in women and substance abuse and antisocial personality in men.

In recent years, depressive illness has been receiving more attention, and measurement of cases for epidemiological study has improved. There is strong and consistent evidence that depressive illness occurs more commonly in women than in men (Weissman and Klerman 1977). It has been hypothesized that women express distress inwardly while men are more likely to act out through alcoholism, drug addiction, violence, and other antisocial activities. These differences are not clearly understood, but the fact is that there are more depressed women than men in both the population at large and among treated populations.

Community sample studies provide more representative cases for epidemiological investigation. The most ambitious study of depression carried out in a community setting was done by Brown and Harris (1978). They compared a population of women in the Camberwell district of London with depressed women receiving outpatient care. This study allowed comparison between women within the community sample who became depressed and those who did not, as well as between depressed women in the sample who were untreated and those receiving outpatient care. Brown and Harris found that stressful life events, such as losses of relationships, status, or love, occurred more commonly to the women who became depressed than to those who did not. Women who had no intimate relationship, who had three or more young children in the home, who did not have an outside job, and who lost their mothers early in life were more vulnerable to depression. These circumstances existed more frequently among lower-class women, explaining the higher rate of depressive conditions in this social stratum. The same conditions were found in the psychiatric outpatient sample. Within the model presented by Brown and Harris, stressful life events are provoking agents. The way women deal with these agents depends on their vulnerability, on the presence or absence of social support available to them through intimacy, and on the extent to which there is reinforcement outside the home, such as a job. Depression results from a lack of resources to deal with life provocations, leaving the person feeling helpless.

The various predictors such as an outside job or the number of children at home are simply proxies and may vary, depending on the population being studied and the social context. The meaning of these predictors in particular social contexts is most important, and these are still being explored. For example, we found that having children in the household was especially stressful for working women, but particularly among those with low family incomes (Cleary and Mechanic 1983). These data suggest that among working women the relationship between having children at home and depression depends on the time and work demands from this dual role and the help available, which more affluent mothers can afford.

Loss of mother in childhood as a vulnerability factor is more difficult to explain in its relation to depression, but Harris, Brown, and Bifulco (1987) have begun to explicate how this major life event affects subsequent life transitions. Their tentative explanation is based on the fact that early loss of mother is associated with lack of adequate care, which in turn is associated with premarital pregnancy, less effective coping, and early and often unsuitable marriages. Although these patterns are linked with lower social class, the process is seen as having importance beyond the effects of social class itself. This perspective of the development of the life course assumes that experience at any point is dependent on earlier influences and choices that affect the range of options at subsequent points. Choices about schooling, job, marriage, childbearing, and their timing establish the conditions for future transitions (Brown 1986).

Brown and his colleagues have substantially elaborated and refined their conceptions of the origins of depression, based on extensive research using an elaborate and influential instrument they developed, the Life Events and Difficulty Schedule (LEDS) (Brown and Harris 1989). They have successfully woven their theoretical thinking about depression and other conditions into a life course perspective examining the contingencies that may push life onto one or another trajectory. Using the LEDS to pursue their research on depression among women, Brown and his colleagues found that feelings of humiliation and entrapment following a severely threatening event, as well as measures of loss or danger, account for most of the occurrence of depression in both clinical and community samples (Brown et al. 1995). Humiliation, as defined by the researchers, conveys events in which a person is devalued in relation to self or others. Entrapment refers to events lasting at least six months that involve ongoing marked difficulty, with indications of persistence or deterioration.

The work of Brown, Harris, and their collaborators reflects the shift in focus of psychiatric epidemiology from description to investigation of stressful events, vulnerability factors, social supports, and coping. Although it is widely accepted that adverse life events are associated with all types of pathology, the crucial issue involves why persons react so differently to such disturbing events. It is not remarkable that people succumb to major stressful events, but rather that so many remain resilient despite enormous difficulties and exposure to adverse environments. Social epidemiologists have turned to identifying people's capacities and resources, their social networks and sources of social support, and the developmental experiences that facilitate their resistance to provoking agents. Interest is increasingly focused on the reasons why many children of two psychotic parents adapt adequately while others have major difficulties. Major measurement problems remain to be solved because coping capacities and social support are relatively new concerns, but they raise exciting questions. Elder (1974) studied a cohort of children born in 1920–1921 who were part of the Oakland Growth Study and who grew up during the Great Depression. Data were available concerning adult adaptation as reflected in anxiety and tension, psychosomatic illness, behavior disorders, serious somatic illness, and psychotic reactions. Children from the working class faced greater adversities during the Depression and had more problems of adaptation later. More interesting, however, was the fact that middle-class children who faced deprivation during the Great Depression were more symptom-free in adult life than those who were sheltered from deprivation. Twenty-six percent of the nondeprived middle class had behavior disorder problems, as compared with 7 percent of the deprived group. Heavy drinking in adulthood was much more common in the nondeprived middle class than in the deprived middle class (43 percent versus 24 percent).

These findings, as well as similar findings from other studies, suggest some provocative hypotheses. Are persons who are insulated from difficulties that allow for the development of competence and mastery handicapped as a result of a life experience that is too protective? What are the positive social functions of stress, particularly when it is not overwhelming and when persons learn to deal with it effectively? How much stress is necessary in early life to prepare persons for later adversity? The results of such studies as

Elder's are consistent with the experimental work in the area of helplessness (Seligman 1975) that suggests that individuals' beliefs in their ability to affect what happens to them is important for well-being. Dealing effectively with adversity reinforces a sense of competence and confidence.

The Epidemiology of Antisocial Behavior and Behavior Disorders

There is impressive evidence from epidemiological longitudinal studies that antisocial behavior during childhood often results in many adult difficulties (Robins 1966, 1979a,b). Resistance to authority during childhood, as reflected by delinquency, drinking, and sexual behavior, seems to be correlated with the development of serious problems in adulthood, such as employment difficulties, problems with the law, alcoholism, drug abuse, and early death. Children in this group are often identifiable early in their school experience by low IQ, poor reading and poor school performance in general, and truancy. The causal factors relating to such behavioral development are complex and poorly understood. What emerges from many studies is the sad trajectory that so many of these children follow, the compounding of problems as they grow older, and the disastrous outcomes for both them and society. In marked contrast, children with neurotic symptoms often tend to have transitory problems and are much more likely to develop satisfactory adjustments in adult life.

As Robins (1979b) notes in her extensive reviews of the developmental literature, there is a great deal of consistent data suggesting that achievement patterns, social skills, and aggressiveness develop well before adolescence and set the stage for future life adaptations. This does not imply that children with conduct problems, school difficulties, and poorly developed skills cannot successfully overcome these problems in adult life, but the risk of adult difficulties for such children is considerable. A major challenge for mental health workers—and for policy makers—is to identify interventions that effectively block the realization of such poor prognoses and improve the life chances of these children (Mrazek and Haggarty 1994).

Although violent and aggressive behavior in childhood does not necessarily ensure such patterns in adulthood, such behavior is unlikely to develop in adulthood if it was absent in childhood. The effects of social deprivation, low social status, and certain cultural environments can be overcome. Children living in well-functioning homes under such conditions do well in adult life. Poor social and economic conditions, however, are more conducive to family pathology, child abuse, alienation, and lack of encouragement for achievement, which increases the probability that children growing up under such conditions will have difficulties. Many of the negative factors, such as social deprivation, broken homes, illegitimacy, parental deviance, child abuse, and little parental supervision or interest in the child are correlated, making it difficult to isolate the central causal factors contributing to behavior maladjustment.

There has been a massive amount of work in the past decade on stress, coping strategies, and social support processes, and this discussion has only provided a brief sample of the scope and richness of such inquiry. Work is increasingly focusing on the intervening processes between stress and outcomes to elucidate causal pathways. Many important questions remain, such as the extent to which individuals select themselves into certain stressful situations, the developmental benefits of adversity and exercising mastery, negative as well as positive effects of some types of social networks and social supports, and structural and cultural constraints on coping flexibility. Thoits (1995) presents an excellent review of many of these issues. In Chapter 4, we turn to a more detailed examination of conceptions of the causes of mental illness and the implications of such conceptions for social policy.

$$C \ h \ a \ p \ t \ e \ r \quad \textbf{\textit{4}}$$

Conceptions of the Causes of and Means of Controlling Mental Illness

Psychiatry today has no dominant perspective. Its concerns span the range of genetic factors, brain and behavior relationships, psychopharmacology, psychodynamics, social learning, communication patterns, stress and coping, and larger structural forces. This chapter briefly reviews these major perspectives, particularly as they pertain to larger social policy issues.

The Impact of Environment on Mental Illness

Mental health professionals agree that environmental influences have an important impact on the development and course of mental illness as well as on the process of help seeking. They differ on such questions as whether or not environmental factors have the major impact on the causes or course of mental illness, and how environmental forces influence and interact with biological and personality influences. At one extreme are those investigators who believe that a biological or a physiological defect is a *necessary condition* for a serious mental illness and that such conditions as schizophrenia, bipolar disorder, and even major depression occur only when persons with such inherited defects are faced with adverse circumstances that bring out their latent biological vulnerabilities. At the other extreme are those who see psychiatric morbidity as simply the result of compounded stresses and adverse environmental events.

In discussing the impact of the environment on psychiatric conditions, it is necessary to separate the effects of environment on the causes of specific psychiatric conditions, its effects on the development of secondary disabilities (the course of the disorders) (Lemert

1951; Wing 1962), and patterns of illness behavior and responses to care (Mechanic 1978). Most mental health professionals are aware that persons with the same primary condition—such as depression or schizophrenia—may fare better or worse depending on the social and environmental circumstances they face and the kind of treatment and support they receive. Although in some instances social forces may affect both the occurrence of the condition and the subsequent disability, in other instances the environment is most important in determining the extent of handicap. It is important to be as precise as possible as to the way environmental factors may affect a condition.

Because it is impossible, given the state of our knowledge, to come to any definitive view on such issues, all I can do here is to present some of the contrasting positions concerning the etiology of mental disorders and develop some of the implications of each. I shall discuss the following perspectives: heredity, psychosocial development, learning, social stress, and societal reaction. Although I shall attempt to polarize these views to illustrate their distinctive aspects, it is important to recognize that most investigators adopt an eclectic view that synthesizes elements of each of these perspectives.

The Question of Inheritance and Environment

The evidence is strong that genetics play an important role in major mental illness such as schizophrenia and manic–depressive illness, and there is further evidence supporting its relevance in severe alcoholism, sociopathy, and suicide (Kety 1986). But genetic factors in these conditions do not follow conventional patterns, and there is no clear understanding of the mode of genetic transmission. Schizophrenia has been studied more intensively than other conditions, and various studies show a higher concordance of schizophrenia among identical as compared to fraternal twins. Although these studies are not above criticism, they provide as much basis for a heredity theory as any other (Rosenthal 1970; Gottesman and Shields 1982; Cloninger et al. 1985).

Evidence for a genetic etiology of schizophrenia also comes from studies comparing the offspring of schizophrenic parents with those of parents who were not mentally ill. Heston (1966), for example, compared the adjustment of forty-seven adults born to schizophrenic mothers with a matched control group of adults born to mothers who were not mentally ill. Those in both the subject and the control group were separated from their natural mothers during the first few days of life and were reared during their early years in foster homes. The investigator found that the occurrence of schizophrenia and other pathologies was higher among the offspring of schizophrenic mothers than among the matched controls. Because the subjects of the study were removed from their schizophrenic mothers shortly after birth, we cannot conclude that the higher rate of pathology was a result of interaction with a schizophrenic mother.

This theory, however, does depend mostly upon studies of twins, and further consideration of the implications of such studies is necessary. Perhaps most influential among early studies were the investigations carried out by Franz Kallman (1953). He found that although schizophrenic concordance varied from 10 to 18 percent among fraternal twins, it was 78 to 92 percent among identical twins. If we assume Kallman's findings to be correct, even though there were considerable inconsistencies among the findings of other studies of twins, they still leave room for positing factors other than genetic ones. If genetic factors were the only ones operating, the identical heredity of monozygotic twins would produce a perfect concordance rate.

Interest has persisted in the investigation of the heredity hypothesis, and studies have been relatively consistent in demonstrating a higher concordance for schizophrenia in identical as compared with fraternal twins or siblings. Studies of adopted children of schizophrenic mothers and adopted monozygotic twins reared separately also provide confirmation of a hereditary link (Rosenthal 1970). However, in more recent years, the levels of concordance in schizophrenia found among identical twins have been lower than in prior investigations—more in the range of 15 to 20 percent. These lower levels of concordance reflect tighter methodologies and minimization of investigator bias as well as sampling differences and the use of schizophrenic patients who are less severely affected by the illness. If schizophrenia is a group of conditions influenced by a variety of genes and if such genes vary in their penetrance, selecting less severe cases might lessen the probability of finding concordance.

What should be noted, however, is that even in those studies finding high concordance—as in Kallman's studies—concordance rates are much lower than the 100 percent one would expect on the basis of a pure heredity hypothesis. Kallman's position was that "a true schizophrenic psychosis is not developed under usual human life conditions unless a particular predisposition has been inherited by a person from both parents" (p. 98), but that the disease resulted from the intricate interactions of genetic and environmental factors. He maintained that schizophrenia could be prevented or cured. Because environmental and psychosocial elements could predispose a person to, precipitate, or perpetuate psychoses, understanding of and control over such elements could retard the disease process. Even in instances where both parents are schizophrenic, less than half of their offspring develop this illness during their lifetime (Gottesman and Shields 1982). The functional psychoses do not follow simple Mendelian patterns of inheritance (Cloninger et al. 1985).

Theorists have analyzed the situation extensively, but they have not clearly defined the precise environmental factors contributing to a schizophrenic breakdown. Various evidence, however, shows that a psychotic breakdown is frequently preceded by a stressful event of some magnitude. Brown and Birley (1968) studied fifty patients suffering from an acute onset or relapse of schizophrenia and a group of 377 normal controls. These groups differed in the proportion experiencing at least one major change in their lives in the three-week period preceding investigation. Although 60 percent of the patient group had such an experience, only 19 percent of the control group were so affected. Possibly, environmental stress leads to the initiation of treatment rather than the illness itself, and persons similarly ill who do not suffer severe environmental stress are less likely to define themselves as requiring treatment. Because the condition studied, however, was a severe one, this interpretation probably does not explain the result obtained. This study is impressive in that the investigators separated the social changes into categories according to the extent to which the patient may have had control over them. The fact that the relationship held for events over which the patient had no control as well as for those he or she could affect supports the idea that this finding could not be explained by the argument that schizophrenic patients tend to get themselves into social difficulties because of their illness. The study suggests, in contrast, that significant changes in the patient's life adversely affected his or her psychological and social functioning. Other studies also suggest a relationship between the cumulation of stresses in a person's life and the occurrence of psychiatric morbidity, but the causal links in such relationships are not clearly understood.

Various theories have been formulated to explain the link between the occurrence of changes in a person's life and schizophrenic breakdown. Studies have found that schizophrenic patients living in family situations of high emotional involvement (mainly negative involvement) are more likely to have a recurrence of their symptoms (Brown et al. 1962; Vaughn and Leff 1976; Leff and Vaughn 1985). One conception of the process is that those genetically predisposed to schizophrenia are particularly vulnerable to the intense brain stimulation that might occur during stressful life events or intense emotional involvement. The schizophrenic might be seen as a potentially vulnerable person whose illness is triggered by a highly stimulating life situation. Consistent with this is that social distance from relatives and maintenance phenothiazine medication seem to protect against relapse. Study of patients' psychophysiological responses in the home confirm the fact of biological arousal in the presence of relatives with whom the patient has high emotional involvement (Tarrier et al. 1979). An alternative explanation for the vulnerability of schizophrenics to major changes and intense emotions involves the assumption that such events or situations are threatening to persons who lack the ability to handle problems. Because of biological incapacities or inadequate social training, schizophrenics may lack the coping skills that assist in facing and dealing with challenging situations, and the combination of biological vulnerability and personal inadequacy increases the probability of breakdown. There are many other formulations of the process of schizophrenic breakdown, but the fact is that we just do not really understand this condition. At best we have some leads and many hypotheses that have not achieved confirmation; we are still a long way from understanding the causes of this illness.

Despite the limitations of our knowledge, direction over environmental forces acting on the patient or on the patient's capacity to tolerate or cope with particular changes may allow us to contain and to control illness and disability. The difficulty, however, is in specifying the particular environmental supports that are most conducive to an optimal outcome. In the past, hospitals were much more willing to release schizophrenic patients who returned to family surroundings than they were to release those who had to make other living arrangements, but research findings suggested that particular family environments may not provide the best context for an optimal outcome (Carstairs 1959; Freeman and Simmons 1963). Subsequently, treatment orientations changed and many programs sought to establish living arrangements for patients independent of their families. The reality is, however, that a large number of persons with mental illness live with their parents and other relatives and their management must be addressed in a family context. Whatever the final determination of such matters, mental health workers believe that schizophrenics and other mentally ill persons in the community require the kind of supportive care that helps them deal more effectively with inevitable crises.

Studies of the affective disorders are more recent, but considerable progress has been made in a relatively short time span. It is clear that these disorders aggregate in families, and both twin and adoption studies support a genetic basis for both bipolar (manic depressive) and unipolar affective disorder. The extent of these effects are difficult to estimate because they vary a great deal among studies and no specific process of transmission has been established (Reich et al. 1985). Bipolar disorder appears to be different from unipolar affective illness and has a distinct epidemiology, but the siblings and offspring of those with bipolar disorder have an elevated lifetime risk of both bipolar and unipolar disorder. The risk of disorder is higher in families with bipolar illness, suggesting a stronger genetic effect than is characteristic of unipolar disorders, which appear to be more closely linked to the social environment.

Over time, developments in psychiatric genetics have become more sophisticated at both the molecular and epidemiological levels. Although biologists are using new tools to identify genes that increase susceptibility to particular mental disorders, workers in epidemiological genetics are exploring increasingly complex hypotheses about how such susceptibilities may interact with various types of familial and other environmental factors. The questions being asked and the research designs to study them are increasingly complex and sophisticated. We know that even very early in life children have temperamental characteristics that elicit different environmental reactions that can be either damaging or protective (Werner and Smith 1992). We also know that people are not passive actors, but through their temperaments and inclinations—such as impulsivity, warmth, and aggressiveness—they create different environments around them. Researchers are increasingly exploring the extent to which family environments are responsive to the unique characteristics of each individual and the degree to which family environments are shared, the extent to which environmental effects are contemporaneous or long-acting, and the extent to which genetic and environmental risk factors vary over time (Kendler 1995). They are also seeking to understand whether genes can make individuals more sensitive to the damaging effects of particular environments and how such genes might function. There is increasing evidence that particular environmental factors are rarely general but may act on people differently depending on their susceptibilities (Kendler 1995). Work in genetics is moving toward greater collaboration with the social sciences in an effort to better understand how these complex interactions occur.

In sum, work in genetics and the neurosciences has demonstrated a very considerable role for biological substrates of mental illness. In addition to genetic factors, just briefly reviewed, is the growing understanding of biological mechanisms in the brain. It is now established that chemical neurotransmitters operate at most brain synapses, and they are now described as multidimensional nodes that are "genetically endowed but variously modified by a host of environmental influences" (Kety 1986, p. 23). Moreover, particular types of drugs act specifically on various symptoms of major mental disorders. As we better understand the activity of the chemical transmitters, we are likely to develop more effective and less adverse drugs.

A Note on Psychiatric Drugs

For several decades psychiatry was dependent on a fairly fixed range of drug types and was limited in its understanding of how they acted on the brain to modify particular psychiatric conditions. In the last decade, new classes of drugs have been developed and new neuroscience technologies have advanced our understanding of how they affect brain receptors. Such methodologies as positron emission tomography (PET) and single-photon emission computed tomography (SPECT) allow examination in a safe fashion of brain action as it occurs. Through the use of radioligands specific for particular neuroreceptors and the study of brain glucose metabolism, we can now image changes in the brain in response to various pharmacological agents (Pickar and Hsiao 1995). Psychopharmacology and its effects on the brain have thus become an expanding and exciting field.

Since the introduction of the phenothiazines in the 1950s, antipsychotic drugs have played a major role in reducing the most disturbing psychotic symptoms and in helping manage schizophrenia and other psychotic disorders. Although a number of new antipsychotics have been developed over the decades, no one particular drug has been better than others in antipsychotic effects. Each works better for some patients than others. All of the earlier drugs have risks of uncomfortable and often serious side effects, particularly extrapyramidal symptoms and especially tardive dyskinesia, and none of these drugs are free of dangers. Bothersome side effects have been a major barrier to maintaining many schizophrenic patients on neuroleptic drugs, and continuity of medication adherence is a major challenge in psychiatric practice. The action of antipsychotic drugs is poorly understood, but it is widely believed that psychotic symptoms result from excesses of dopamine or oversensitivity of dopamine receptors in the brain. The antipsychotics are believed to interfere with the binding of dopamine to its receptor sites.

Several new antipsychotic drugs have recently entered the market or are under development. One of the most commonly used new drugs prescribed for patients with schizophrenia is risperidone (Risperdal®), which seems to block the action of serotonin and dopamine. It is often the first drug prescribed for persons newly diagnosed with schizophrenia or other psychotic disorders. The advantage of risperidone is that it seems to improve some negative symptoms such as apathy and withdrawal, as well as the positive symptoms such as delusions and hallucinations. The action of this drug is not fully understood, but it appears to have less side effects than conventional neuroleptic drugs and seems less likely to cause extrapyramidal side effects like tremors and muscle rigidity. Because it is a relatively new drug, it will take some time to assess occurrence of tardive dyskinesia. Several other new drugs have been introduced or are being developed which also are designed to affect the dopamine and serotonin transmitters in the brain.

The introduction of clozapine (Clozaril®) in the United States in the early 1990s was greeted with excitement, since it almost never causes extrapyramidal motor side effects and seems to have efficacy in some 30 to 40 percent of patients who have failed to improve with other antipsychotic drugs (Pickar and Hsiao 1995). This was the first indication since the introduction of neuroleptics that one drug seemed to be superior to others available. Clozapine, however, has a 0.5 percent to 2 percent risk of agranulocytosis, a potentially fatal blood-related condition, and its use, thus, requires frequent monitoring of the white blood count (Pickar and Hsiao 1995; Yudofsky et al. 1991). Thus, the drug is only recommended for use if standard antipsychotic treatment has failed, and when it is used the patient's blood requires weekly monitoring. Clozapine treatment is estimated to cost $5,000 to $10,000 per patient per year; coverage of such treatments puts enormous stresses on state mental health budgets that pay for most long-term psychotic patients. Thus, the cost-effectiveness of the drug becomes central to public policy considerations.

A study in Connecticut of the use of clozapine found that discharge rates did not differ between those treated with clozapine versus traditional care but those on clozapine were less likely to be readmitted to inpatient care (Essock et al. 1996). There is growing indication that despite its cost, clozapine is a cost-effective therapeutic agent; however, definitive studies are yet to be completed. Any new drugs that allow disabled people to return to levels of functioning that support community reentry will be (and should be) strongly supported from a humanitarian perspective, even if uncertainties remain about their cost-effectiveness. The policy challenge is to ensure that those patients who can benefit receive this treatment. As this is written, a new drug, olanzapine, has entered the market. Sold under the brand name Zyprexa®, this drug has a similar chemical composition to clozapine and appears to have comparable effects without the same risk of agranulocytosis. However, it may increase the risk of extrapyramidal side effects. It is too early to evaluate the long-term potential of this drug, however.

Patients with major depression have options of a number of major types of drugs: heterocyclic (also called tricyclics); monamine oxidase inhibitors (MAOIs); serotonin specific drugs; and newer antidepressants that have mixed or compound synaptic effects. None of these drugs have superior effects, and people respond differently. The drugs do differ greatly in their side effects and the ease with which they can be used as suicide agents. Researchers tend to believe that depression occurs in the absence of sufficient norepinephine, epinephrine and/or serotonin at the brain's neurotransmitters. These drugs are believed to act partly by blocking the uptake of these chemicals by modifying the mechanisms by which the brain clears them, but modes of action are complex and diverse and not fully understood (Thase and Kupfer 1996). These varying drugs act on different biological compounds and through different mechanisms. A common problem in the use of heterocyclic antidepressants like amitriptyline (Elavil®), imipramine (Tofranil®), or doxepin (Sinequan®) is annoying side effects such as blurry vision, dry mouth, urinary retention, and constipation. These drugs have many other less frequent side effects and also pose a risk of an unintentional overdose or suicide. MAOIs like phenelzine (Nardil®) and tranylcypromine (Parnate®) interact with foods with toxic results due to life-threatening increases in blood pressure. Taking these drugs requires very careful dietary restrictions. Many patients have resisted taking heterocyclics and MAOIs because of annoying and dangerous adverse reactions.

Prozac®, a serotonin-specific inhibitor, began to dominate the U.S. market in antidepressants in the late 1980s and has been an enormous success because of less severe side effects and its comparative safety. Great claims have been made for the potential of Prozac® to modify human personality, but Prozac® seems no more effective than most other antidepressants and significant personality modifications, if they occur, are relatively rare. Because the drug can be taken safely and can be taken without discomfort, it probably is prescribed more readily than the earlier antidepressants. World use of antidepressants grew at a 42 percent compound annual rate between 1986 and 1991 largely as a result of the use of Prozac® and other new serotonin reuptake inhibitors such as sertraline (Zoloft®), paraxetine (Paxil®) and fluvoxamine (Luvox®) (DiMasi and Lasagna 1995; Berger and Fukunishi 1996). Other new antidepressants (venlafaxine, nefazodone) are also being introduced and evaluated that are different in structure and neurochemical effects (Thase and Kupfer 1996).

The availability of comparatively safe antidepressants, and the inflated expectations of their positive effects on mood, have led some clinicians to prescribe these drugs more readily for persons with moderate and transitory depressions rather than restricting their use to the more serious cases of major depression. There is division of opinion as to whether this is appropriate and whether drug treatment is replacing problem-oriented psychotherapies that help individuals cope better with their life circumstances. Further, there is concern that many individuals come to depend on drugs as a crutch rather than persevere to resolve life problems and develop greater mastery. Many conflicting trends underlay this debate. Part of the debate concerns values and the extent to which stoicism is valued. Some believe that Americans are becoming too soft, too dependent on pharmacological supports. Others argue that Americans are far too stoical, and that too many people suffer quietly when they could be substantially helped. There is, perhaps, some basis for both arguments, but the epidemiological evidence supports the latter much more strongly. Drugs, of course, are a big business, and the drug industry has a great stake in promoting wider use. Also, as we increasingly move into a managed care environment, utilization reviewers may be more willing to pay for drug interventions than for extended forms of psychotherapy. These are all open issues difficult to resolve, but there is little question that improved drugs have contributed importantly to reductions of distress and disability.

The Psychosocial-Development Perspective

Much research in the mental health field has been based on the premise that early psychosocial environment and family interaction are influential in the development of personality and of mental disorders in later life. In the United States the importance of psychoanalytic and neopsychoanalytic theories of psychological and social development had a pervasive influence on the hypotheses developed and the research undertaken.

Intrinsic to the psychosocial approach is concern with how children are socialized, how parents react to their behavior and train them, and, most importantly, the emotional tone of family interaction and of the relationships among the child, siblings, and peers. Among the variables frequently studied are the use of punishment by the parents, the degree of parental warmth, the dependency patterns in the family, the means of handling aggression, the forms of parental social control, and the family role structure (Maccoby 1961).

In the study of schizophrenia, several early research groups attempted to specify aspects of family functioning and relationships that predispose members to a schizophrenic reaction pattern. Bateson and his colleagues (1956) emphasized the idea of the *double bind,* a situation in which a person is subjected to incongruent or conflicting messages; the appropriate response is unclear, and the danger of being rebuked exists regardless of which message the person responds to. Other investigators with a psychosocial perspective saw schizophrenia as confusion in identity resulting from distorted family role structures. Lidz (1963) described two kinds of schizogenic families—one built around a sick, dominating parent, usually the mother, and the other characterized by chronic hostility and mutual withdrawal of family members. Other approaches gave primary emphasis to family interaction and communication, the organization of family role patterns and identities, and the peculiar use of sanctions (Mischler and Waxler 1965). Many of these earlier studies viewed families as causal agents in mental disorder and such work was deeply resented by family members who felt blamed and stigmatized by prevalent theoretical conceptions.

Other early investigators pointed to early peer relationships and adolescent problems to explain schizophrenic conditions. Harry Stack Sullivan (1953) emphasized the importance of preadolescence—the period when, he believed, the capacity to love matured. Sullivan theorized that this capacity is first developed through association with a chum of one's own sex. Such a relationship allows preadolescents to see themselves through others' eyes and provides them with consensual validation of their personal worth. During the adolescent period, the maturation of competence was particularly important; if individuals successfully negotiated this period, they developed self-respect adequate to almost any situation. Such theories have encouraged various investigators to explore peer contacts and social isolation during adolescence in attempts to account for schizophrenic illness, but findings in this area have not confirmed these views (Kohn and Clausen 1955).

The importance of psychosocial development and the role of the family in psychiatric disorder have been accepted and extensively studied, but it has been difficult to identify consistent psychosocial predictors of schizophrenia, depression, behavior disorders, or generalized psychological distress (Frank 1965; Marks 1973; Robins 1979b). The earlier literature was characterized by dogmatism, conjecture, and wild and irresponsible statements. Careful evaluation of the literature and systematic studies fail to show the importance of such frequently cited influences as child-rearing practices, family communication and role constellations, and maternal and other parental qualities. It has become increasingly clear how little we really know about the development of these disorders, how inadequate our research models have been, and how important it is to differentiate varying types of disorders in pursuing predictive studies.

Some firm findings, however, are emerging from careful longitudinal studies, as noted in the previous chapter. Aggressiveness, achievement patterns, and social skills development in children are generally established before adolescence, and childhood problems in these areas frequently persist into adulthood (Robins 1979b). Antisocial behavior in childhood increases vulnerability to a variety of mental disorders, alcoholism, and other problems in adult life. In contrast, children with neurotic problems often do quite well in adulthood, suffering much less illness, disability, and maladjustment than the antisocial child (Robins 1966; Rutter 1972). Children having difficulties with authority figures often end up having problems with alcohol, sex, and the law. Seriously disturbed children, such as those with childhood psychoses, have serious and disabling adult disorders. Fortunately, such disorders are relatively infrequent. (For outstanding reviews of the longitudinal studies, see Robins 1979a,b, 1983; Mrazek and Haggarty 1994.)

Although theorists are very interested in the psychosocial aspects of schizophrenia and other mental illnesses, they have little conclusive evidence on which to base preventive work. The usual variances in child-rearing patterns appear to play a relatively small part in producing the profound difficulties that we are concerned with here, and indeed, the relevance of different child-rearing practices in personality development in general has not been established (Sewell 1952). Any relatively warm, accepting family climate that nurtures a sense of self-esteem in the child and provides training experiences somewhat consistent with social realities will probably produce a "normal" child. Despite the earlier theoretical assumptions that perpetuated the myth of the fragile child, children are exceedingly flexible and adaptive and relatively strong and invulnerable to modifications in their environments. Indeed, adversity in childhood that is manageable may lead to the development of mastery and strength (Elder 1974). The contexts that appear to breed pathology are those that are emotionally bizarre or highly deprived and those in which the child experiences profound rejection, hostility, and other forms of physical and emotional abuse and is exposed to inadequate, ineffective, and incongruous models of behavior.

Family factors most frequently predicting adult functioning "include family size, broken homes, illegitimacy, adoption or foster placement, socioeconomic status, supervision by parents, attitudes of parents toward the child, parental expectations for the child's achievement, behavior problems in the parents and siblings, and psychiatric disorder in the parents" (Robins 1979b). These factors all tend to be intercorrelated and reflect many other aspects of family life and position in the society in addition to genetic transmission, and its is difficult to identify causal mechanisms.

It is not fully clear why such extensive effort to identify precursors has yielded so little understanding of the major mental disorders. The problem may be that there are just too many contingencies in the life course, and outcomes may depend on complex pathways that are in no sense inevitable. As George Brown (1986) notes, "the study of various life stages in a series of separate studies is of limited use. For many problems it is necessary to follow an individual from childhood through adult life to determine how various experiences interrelate" (p. 191).

The longitudinal study by Quinton and Rutter (1984a,b) of girls in local authority care (the British equivalent of a foster institution) and an appropriate comparison group found that those who received institutional care were more likely to have pregnancies early in adult life, to enter unstable cohabiting relationships, to have serious problems in relating to and caring for their children, and to have psychiatric disorders. They were less likely to plan their relationships with men and more likely to cohabit with a person who had significant personal problems and who provided little support. When such women had a supportive spouse, many of the parenting difficulties were alleviated. Retrospective study of these women who were in institutional care as children suggested that they more commonly had adverse childhoods than comparison mothers, comparable to those now being experienced by their own children. These experiences included teenage difficulties, leaving home early because of rejection or conflict, and early pregnancy. Thus, many of the noxious patterns of child care and ineffective coping seemed to replicate themselves across generations.

The research literature suggests complex causal mechanisms, and much attention has shifted to the study of stressful life events, coping, sense of control, and social supports. It seems clear, however, that while it is difficult to isolate any single factor particularly promotive of mental illness, social and family environments characterized by abuse and neglect are major contributors, and these conditions are more prevalent in impoverished environments. Sexual abuse is an increasing focus of investigation and many studies find it to be an important risk factor. In one NCS study Kessler found that rape and sexual abuse entirely accounted for the 100 percent excess of posttraumatic stress disorder in women as compared with men, and other studies suggest that such abuse may play an important role in depressive disorders. Healthy parents who create a warm and constructive environment for their children, make them feel valued, and encourage their acquisition of skills can do much to protect against psychological disorder, although biological vulnerabilities can be manifest in the best and most loving environments. In recognizing the importance of a high quality of parental caring, we must not make the mistake of blaming parents whose children develop disorder.

Many conditions contribute to poor parenting, including premature parental roles and a lack of child-care skills. Parents who are themselves mentally ill or who face difficult life stresses with which they cannot cope have more difficulty attending to the needs of their children (Feldmen et al. 1987). These problems are exacerbated by poverty, poor housing conditions, inadequate schooling, and discrimination. Poverty increases risk, but most poor children develop reasonably and acquire the necessary psychological and coping skills. The relative role of biological predisposition and environment depends of course on the specific disorder being considered. Such issues as altering living patterns, improving housing conditions, eliminating social discrimination, and providing good schools are very much intertwined with political and social processes, and society will probably not alter its priorities and decisions merely because mental health workers feel that current conditions may lead to poor mental health. These and similar battles, if they are to be fought at all, must be fought in the political realm—a realm in which mental health workers have demonstrated no special ability.

The usual approach taken by workers with a psychosocial perspective is to alter individual family conditions and understandings that they believe are not conducive to the mental health of its members. They contend that encouraging people to seek supportive help and counseling when difficulties and crises first occur alleviates problems and avoids future complications conducive to morbidity. Family problems and patterns of interaction, however, are frequently hard to solve or alter. Mental health workers are not at all sure just what aspects of family functioning are central to the morbidity condition. Also, the therapeutic relationship, even if properly directed and effectively organized, constitutes such a small part of family interaction that it may not be able to overcome the more common experiences family members have with one another and with their community. Finally, we cannot always separate those aspects of family interaction that were conducive to family pathology in the first place from those that constitute adaptive responses to the presence of pathology. The frequent occurrence of a dominant mother and a weak, withdrawing father in families with a great variety of social and psychiatric problems suggests that family structures may be a reaction to sickness in one of the members rather than an important risk factor.

The literature evaluating psychosocial interventions to either prevent or alleviate mental disorders or behavior pathologies suggests a need for cautious optimism. There have been very few studies demonstrating important long-term outcomes resulting from treatment (Robins 1973), and, as previously noted, even seemingly helpful approaches have sometimes been linked to adverse outcomes. Even the best motives and personal dedication can be harmful if therapists do not know what they are doing. Behavior modification approaches seem more promising at least in specific instances, such as the treatment of childhood fears and phobias, but many of these symptoms have a high rate of spontaneous remission in any case (Marks 1969).

In a study involving the use of child guidance facilities at a well-known mental hospital, Shepherd, Oppenheim, and Mitchell (1966) matched treated children with other children having similar problems who were not receiving treatment. Varying parental needs and patterns of illness behavior accounted for the fact that some children were treated but others with identical problems were not. When the researchers reevaluated the treated and untreated groups of children two years later, they found little difference in rates of improvement. Even within the treated group, the amount of improvement was unrelated to the amount of treatment provided. Approximately two-thirds of both groups of children—treated and untreated—had improved in the two-year period. How are we to interpret these findings?

The investigators concluded that many of the treated symptoms were no more than temporary exaggerations of reaction patterns occurring normally in human development. They believe that clinicians who have concentrated on morbidity have an incomplete appreciation of the normal range of reaction patterns and give exaggerated significance to symptoms and problems that are not really pathological and do not ordinarily require treatment (Robins 1966, pp. 300–303). Those more skeptical about such studies point out an important differentiating factor between the treated and untreated groups. The fact that some children were brought into treatment suggests that their parents were either unable or unwilling to cope with their problems, and the findings suggest that such parents also had fewer resources for dealing with the difficulties of their children. Because these children did no worse than those whose parents had more effective coping resources, therapy may have been helpful and effective. The data on hand do not really allow us to evaluate the opposing arguments conclusively. However, even if we accept the argument of the proponents of child therapeutic services, the outcomes achieved by such services are at best very modest. We must be willing to consider the possibility of using equivalent resources in a manner encouraging a larger and more effective return.

Providing children's mental health services is particularly challenging because of the multiple social systems often involved (family, school, social services, criminal justice) and the complexity of services delivery. In recent years great emphasis has been given to the need to develop a comprehensive community services system for children with mental illness in which care is carefully case managed and in which a wide range of services can be mobilized. The basic notion is to make a wide range of resources available to the case manager, which can be *wrapped around* the child and family in the most appropriate environment and which support and promote improved access, service provision, and function. This concept is widely endorsed and promoted as an ideal way of providing child mental health services, but there has been little large-scale or rigorous evaluation.

From 1989 to 1995, the U.S. Army funded an $80 million demonstration study at Fort Bragg, North Carolina, to study the effects of providing a total continuum of services with comprehensive intake and management of complex cases by case managers and interdisciplinary treatment teams. The study, a randomized, controlled trial between traditional CHAMPUS insurance (basically traditional indemnity coverage) and the experimental treatment approach sought to evaluate costs as well as outcomes, since it has been widely assumed that gaps in the traditional services system led to inefficiencies and waste. The experimental program provided inpatient and residential treatment, therapy at home, treatment services after school, day treatment, therapeutic homes, specialized group homes, twenty-four-hour crisis management, "wraparound services," and intensive outpatient care (Bickman 1996). By flexibly drawing on this broad array of alternatives, it was assumed that treatment would be more individualized and more continuous with timely transitions among types of care, that services would be provided at the most appropriate and least restrictive levels, and that less children would drop out from treatment. The researchers found, however, that while the experimental demonstration provided a high-quality system of care, it was more expensive and had clinical outcomes no better than the traditional system (Bickman 1996). Thus, once again, what seemed intuitively sensible and attractive could not be demonstrated in this very thorough and ambitious effort.

Any study as large, complex, and important as this one elicits much critical evaluation, as it should. Proponents of case-managed comprehensive care approaches are not likely to be converted by any single study, and they offer many explanations for why this particular study failed to find some of the expected positive effects. Friedman and Burns (1996), two children's services researchers, for example, note that the demonstration was applied to all children with mental health problems and was not restricted to the more disturbed population of children that are usually thought of as the main target for such comprehensive programs. They note some difficulties in the implementation of the demonstration and focus on findings that imply greater success, such as greater parental satisfaction and some small positive clinical findings among the many measures used. The results of this study will continue to be debated and will contribute to the sophistication of future studies. Nevertheless, a clear conclusion from the Fort Bragg study is that the claims of those who advocate a comprehensive case-managed approach remain undemonstrated.

The Learning Perspective: Behavior Therapy

Over the years psychologists have achieved substantial understanding of the learning process. Although some early attempts were made to translate these findings into a therapeutic approach, such attempts have now become a major investment and an enterprise of some importance in therapeutic research.

One of the first systematic attempts to link learning theory and psychoanalytic practice was presented in *Personality and Psychotherapy* written by John Dollard and Neal E. Miller in 1950. They brought together the formulations of Hullian learning theory and various psychoanalytic concepts and tried to specify the conditions under which habits are formed and changed. They reformulated various psychoanalytic concepts such as the unconscious, conflict, and repression into stimulus-response terms using the concepts of drive, cue, response, and reward. They pointed out that repression is the learned avoidance of certain thoughts. Because some thoughts arouse fear (a secondary drive stimulus), ignoring them leads to drive reduction and to reinforcement; in this way the response becomes a learned part of a person's repertoire.

Although various efforts to analyze psychotherapeutic processes within a learning frame of reference continued, *Psychotherapy by Reciprocal Inhibition* by Joseph Wolpe (1958) gave considerable impetus to the use of learning theory in psychotherapy. Wolpe maintained that psychotherapeutic effects were produced mainly by complete or partial suppression of anxiety responses by the simultaneous evocation of other responses physiologically antagonistic to anxiety. He also maintained that neurotic behavior is a persistent but learned and unadaptive anxiety response acquired in anxiety-generating situations. Such anxiety responses are unadaptive because they are manifest in situations that contain no objective threat. Given these assumptions, Wolpe and others have developed therapeutic approaches, such as desensitization, relaxation, and operant conditioning, techniques now commonly practiced in psychotherapy.

The learning approaches to psychotherapy, or what is more commonly called *behavior therapy,* are based on the idea that it is possible to develop reinforcement schedules that weaken unadaptive responses and reinforce more adaptive behavior. This approach is specifically directed toward changing particular aspects of the person rather than toward such ambitious but unrealistic results as psychic reintegration.

Critics of behavior therapy have charged that such procedures may change symptoms but are not directed toward basic causes, an argument that has weakened over time. They also have maintained that except for specific conditions that are dominated by a single symptom, such as phobias and sexual impotence, mental conditions are characterized by complicated syndromes for which it is difficult to discern and develop specific reinforcement schedules or other remedial procedures. They argue that one must understand the relevant, important cues and stimuli in the patient's illness before proceeding but, more frequently than not, learning these requires a long period of therapeutic work.

The contention that behavior therapy just reduced particular symptoms or substituted one for another has proved to be an invalid criticism. Implicit in it is the assumption that a more basic cure is possible, but little evidence supports such a claim. Changing destructive, specific patterns of behavior, such as self-mutilation or fear of leaving one's house, is anything but trivial. The second argument, concerning the difficulty of locating specific cues and the patterns of behavior and thinking to which they are associated, points to a more serious problem. But over time, the techniques of behavior change have been incorporated into a wide variety of therapeutic approaches. If we are to evaluate behavior therapy, we must consider the way it compares in each specific instance with the other forms of therapy available.

A major problem with many psychotherapeutic approaches is that they are diffuse and vary little from one patient to another regardless of the problem, the patient's situation, or the needs for practical action. The psychodynamic therapist, for example, approaches many different types of patients in the same way, taking a global approach in contrast to clearly specifying the patient's problem and defining a series of specific goals toward which both therapist and patient can work. A major contribution of the behavioral approach is its emphasis on specifying precisely what is to be accomplished in terms of observable behavior by designating intermediate objectives and working toward modifying more complex patterns of response (Bandura 1969).

Behavior therapy is no panacea, but there is much evidence that it is a constructive and relatively effective approach to modifying behaviors that are painful to people and that cause them difficulty in relationships with others. Although this approach has limited value as a cure for persons with serious mental disorder, as in the case of the schizophrenic patient, it facilitates modification of certain behaviors that help the rehabilitation and community adjustment of the patient. Such behavior modification may not only be valuable on its own terms but may also contribute to the patient's sense of psychological comfort, psychological control, and self-confidence.

Behavior therapy consists of a series of techniques including systematic desensitization, flooding, modeling, and stress inoculation (Sutherland 1977). In systematic desensitization, the patient is introduced to the disturbing stimulus in increasing intensity so as to develop tolerance of it. As the patient masters fear in response to one of the graded exposures, rewards may be given, such as encouragement and compliments. In flooding, the patient is asked to imagine the most frightening examples of feared objects until the fear diminishes. Although this technique may make the fear worse if the patient cannot tolerate the imagined scenes, the method is often combined with the use of tranquilizing drugs that reduce anxiety. In modeling, the patient is encouraged and rewarded in repeating the behavior of the therapist in dealing with some troubling situation. Rewards and punishments are increasingly used on hospital wards in an explicit way to induce constructive behavior. Token economies have been used in mental hospitals to encourage patients to take responsibility and to cooperate in ward endeavors. In stress inoculation, patients learn slow breathing and muscular relaxation (which inhibit anxiety) while being exposed to electric shock. They also learn to reassure themselves and engage in thinking conducive to coping. These learned techniques are then used in real-life situations that are threatening to the person.

An extension of behavior therapy involves self-control, in which the person learns to induce self-selected behaviors without external reinforcement or contingency schedules controlled by outsiders (Halleck 1978). Techniques that are taught include control over the stimuli to which people expose themselves, self-observation, self (positive and negative)-reinforcement, self-instruction, and developing alternative response sequences. One application of this technique is to teach patients to recognize when they are having symptom exacerbations, to teach them to reduce exposure to events upsetting to them, and to shape their expressions in a less stigmatizing way so that they are less frightening to others. These techniques have been used with psychotic patients by inducing self-monitoring and self-evaluation, which presumably leads to self-control through changes such as reducing or increasing particular types of activities. It has even been suggested that it may "be possible to teach schizophrenic patients a behavioral approach for talking themselves out of their symptoms" (Breier and Strauss 1983, p. 1141). Although these techniques are no panacea, they can be a useful adjunct to the care process.

Behavior therapy, in short, is a practical response to many types of behavior problems. It is not only used by therapists and counselors, but is increasingly taught to patients, clients, and their families to assist them in modifying their own behaviors. The underlying conception, perhaps most forcefully and extremely stated by Skinner (1971), is that maladaptive behavior and symptoms are largely learned, and by appropriately modifying reinforcement schedules implicit in the social structures of communities, families, schools, and hospitals, we can shape the future behavior of man.

The Social-Stress Perspective

The study of stress has been one of the most active areas of social research in psychiatry. As we have already noted, stressful life events have been associated with the occurrence of schizophrenic episodes and are believed to play a major role in depression. Although concern with stress goes back a long way in psychiatric discussions, there has been an enormous growth of research in the last decade or two on the relationship of stressful life events to a wide range of physical and psychiatric conditions (Dohrenwend, B. S., and Dohrenwend, B. P. 1974, 1981; Brown and Harris 1989; Goldberger and Breznitz 1982; Thoits 1995). The research itself is increasingly specific and sophisticated, and methodological refinements are evident.

In its simplest form, stress conceptions suggest that all people have a breaking point and that mental illness and psychiatric disability are the products of the cumulation of misfortune that overwhelm their constitutional makeup, their personal resources, and their coping abilities. Stated in this way, the perspective is not very useful for it cannot successfully predict who will break down, but in retrospect it can explain everything. There is considerable evidence that many persons can withstand pronounced stress without psychiatric difficulty and that psychoses do not increase substantially during major catastrophes, such as war, disasters, and other calamities (Murphy 1961; Reid 1961; Fried 1964). Pronounced exposure to extreme stress and deprivation, such as occurred in concentration camps, resulted in a high prevalence of long-term psychiatric disability, however, and there is considerable evidence that increased stress is associated with nervousness, anxiety, and other physiological symptoms (Dohrenwend and Dohrenwend 1969).

Workers in the stress area are differentiating among types of events, types of personal vulnerabilities and assets and types of disorder. In the case of events, one issue is whether all life changes—favorable as well as adverse ones—produce disruptions in feelings and functioning. Are there different types of adverse events—for example, events involving loss of a loved one or an important relationship—that have a greater influence than other types of adverse events—loss of money or a job—on such conditions as depression? Although the occurrence of some conditions such as depression seems to follow primarily adverse events and particularly loss, other conditions such as schizophrenia may be precipitated by an intense positive experience. This suggests that we need clearer specification of the way different types of life changes affect certain conditions. Stress theory, as stated in a global and general sense, encompasses different and even competing conceptions.

Life change events may be hypothesized to play a role in the formation of a disease process, to trigger a disease process to which a person is constitutionally vulnerable, to stimulate help seeking, or to shape the mode of expression of distress. Brown and Harris (1978), in their research on depression, maintain that life events play a significant causal role in the occurrence of depression; however, they argue it is not any type of event that is important, even if very unpleasant, but rather only certain severe events involving long-term threat.

> *The distinctive feature of the great majority of the provoking events is the experience of loss or disappointment, if this is defined broadly to include threat of or actual separation from a key figure, an unpleasant revelation about someone close, a life-threatening illness to a close relative, a major material loss or general disappointment or threat of them, and miscellaneous crises such as being made redundant after a long period of steady employment. In more general terms the loss or disappointment could concern a person or object, a role, or an idea. (Brown and Harris 1978, pp. 274–275)*

Such events are by their very nature adverse, and positive life events do not cause depression.

A contrasting view of the way life events may affect disorder is suggested by the previously reviewed research studies of schizophrenia (Brown et al. 1962; Brown and Birley 1968; Vaughn and Leff 1976). These studies suggest that events in general—not only adverse ones—contribute to schizophrenic breakdown. The hypothesis here is that schizophrenics, because of biological constitution or genetic makeup, are particularly vulnerable to high levels of arousal, and events that excite the patient trigger symptoms. Unlike the depression analysis, events within this conception are more a trigger than a basic aspect of the illness.

Still a third conception is that events may not affect the illness itself, but may induce greater concern with symptoms and result more readily in the acquisition of help. Studies indicate that a stressful event and the distress associated with it increase the probability that assistance will be sought. A final conception is that certain events may influence the way the illness is expressed. Being fired from one's job will not cause paranoid schizophrenia, but this event might provide substance for the patient's paranoid ideation. In sum, although it is very difficult to do in practice, it is important in discussing stress and mental disorder to specify clearly the types of stresses involved, the particular disorders referred to, and the specific influences relating the stress events and the varying aspects of the illness process.

As research on stressful life events progressed, it has become clear that such events by themselves predict outcome measures to only a modest degree. Stress is common in people's lives, but some manage it much better than others. Attention has thus shifted to intervening variables that either increase vulnerability or contribute to resilience. Such factors include personality, coping strategies, and social support. Personality factors include such concepts as type A (Friedman and Rosenman 1974), sense of control (Rodin 1986), and hardiness (Korbasa 1979). Coping includes problem-solving approaches, modes of information acquisition, anticipation and planning (Leventhal 1970); focus is often on whether persons emphasize problem-oriented or emotion-oriented approaches. Social support has been approached in many ways including both subjective and objective measures of social networks available and the help given and received.

Each of the relevant component areas of the stress-coping paradigm (the measurement of stress, the description of social networks, and depiction of the coping process) is characterized by vigorous debates about assumptions, conceptualization, and methodology, but these debates have significantly sharpened thinking. In the measurement of stress, divergent views abound on the emphasis to be given respectively to positive and negative life events, subjective and objective measures, and major life events as compared with daily irritations. There also has been controversy as to the methodology of measuring events (whether by respondent report or independent evaluations), the significance of precisely timing the event, and the need to distinguish carefully between events totally outside the individual's control, as compared with those to which the person could have contributed, such as divorce, loss of job, or economic difficulties (Brown and Harris 1978; Dohrenwend and Dohrenwend 1981; Lazarus and Folkman 1984). The value of focusing on independent events is clear, but relatively few stressors are completely independent of a person's past history or behavior.

The concept of social support has been subjected to similar types of debates. While the evidence linking measures of social support to health outcomes has been substantial, neither the measurement of the concept nor the results have been fully consistent. The concept may refer to the extent and structure of social networks, the availability of intimate others, social contacts, voluntary community participation, and similar phenomena. Theories underlying alternative approaches to measurement have not always been clear, and the specific causal mechanisms intervening between support and outcomes are not well developed, although specification of alternative statistical models has advanced (Wheaton 1985). Studies of support have been relatively one-sided, with little attention having been paid to the constraints, responsibilities, and stresses often associated with kinship ties and other close interpersonal relations (Thoits 1995).

Decisions about measurement often involve assumptions that close the opportunities to examine particular theoretical ideas. Life event scales that failed to differentiate clearly between positive and negative life changes made it impossible in many studies to test the assumption that life changes, independent of positive or negative features, contributed to morbidity. Existing evidence suggests that loss events relate to depressive illness, but that a wider range of events may be relevant to triggering schizophrenic episodes. Measurement approaches must allow testing of the underlying assumptions that motivate investigation in the first place. Similarly, the counting or scoring of life change events, in examining direct relationships between life change and health outcomes, ignores much developmental research, which suggests that growth and competence are attained through mastering challenging life events. Within this context, stress describes a relationship between a situation and an individual's resources to deal with it and not a specific event (Mechanic 1962b; Lazarus and Folkman 1984). The most typical measurement models are not always well constructed to capture the richness of our ideas.

The examination of people's sense of personal control and the exercise of "mastery" is a large and promising research area; this has immediate practical implications because it is possible to intervene in many social contexts to enhance people's control over their immediate environments (Rodin 1986). It is also consistent with developments in clinical psychology and cognitive therapy that relate to helplessness and depression. In some contexts studied, such as nursing homes, small changes in personal control have an impressive effect on psychological response, health, and even mortality (Rodin and Langner 1977), but questions about this remain unanswered. It is not apparent to what degree these effects operate within the normal range of human control, compared with situations of deprivation. Nor is it evident how enhanced control interacts with personality, attribution styles, cultural values, age, and other variables. The area remains an important one for continuing research and development.

Our understanding of the interaction of life events with other factors in affecting psychiatric morbidity, though still primitive, is used as an important rationale for preventive and community mental health efforts. Building on the idea that outcome depends on the ability of individuals to withstand adverse life events through coping skills and social supports, efforts are made to provide increased assistance during transition crises, such as divorce, and to assist people in actively coping with the problems associated with their life situation. While some self-help groups make assistance available to anyone going through the experience, such as Parents Without Partners (Weiss 1975), other groups, such as Alcoholics Anonymous, are provided for individuals suffering from a specific disorder. There are few examples of effective programs in preventing the occurrence of mental illness, but successful programs based on a model of teaching coping techniques and providing social support have been developed that have minimized secondary disabilities associated with mental illness and prevented the hospitalization of the patient.

The Labeling Perspective

In the 1960s and 1970s, labeling theory played a major role in the ideological debate that helped shape the deinstitutionalization movement. Conceptions of labeling and its effects varied greatly from those who presented labeling theory as a causal model to explain mental illness to others who viewed labeling primarily as a process contributing to chronicity and disabilities that extended beyond those that were direct results of mental disorder. Labeling theory was derived from a theoretical approach in the study of deviant behavior and societal reactions that focused less on the origins of deviant response and more on those social forces that help structure, organize, and perpetuate such reactions. Advocates of this perspective argue that deviant response is reinforced and perpetuated by social reactions to it, by the manner in which it is labeled, and by the resultant exclusion and discrimination against the deviant. The basic assumptions underlying this approach are that each society produces its own deviants by its definitions and rules and that such processes of definition help maintain the boundaries of the society (Lemert 1951; Erickson 1966).

The model most usually presented is a sequential one in which, over time, a pattern of deviant response is labeled in a fashion that increases the probability that further similar responses will occur (Becker 1963). As the definition of the deviant response persists and as normal roles become more difficult for the deviant to assume because of limited opportunities and growing exclusion, deviant acts become organized as part of one's social identity and as an ongoing deviant role. Thus the labeling process itself helps convert transitory, common deivant behavior into a more stable pattern of persistent deviant response.

In the case of mental illness, Scheff (1984) argued that such disorders are residual forms of deviant behavior for which we have no other appropriate labels and that such behaviors arise from fundamentally diverse sources. He maintained that the occurrence of such symptoms or deviant responses is frequent and is usually neither labeled nor defined. Because such behavior occurs within normal and conventional response repertoires, it is usually temporary and nonpersistent. However, when such behavior is explicitly identified and labeled, the forces produced help organize the behavior into a social role. Scheff hypothesized that, although deviants do not explicitly learn the role of the mentally ill, they are able to assume it because they have learned stereotyped imagery of what mental illness is from early childhood; movies, television, radio, newspapers, and magazines inadvertently but continuously support and supplement this imagery. Scheff believes that deviants labeled as mentally ill may receive a variety of advantages by assuming the role and enacting it, although their assumption of the role need not be a conscious process. He argued that when such persons attempt to return to normal, conventional roles, their opportunities are restricted, and they may be punished as a result of the stigma associated with their past difficulties. They often have problems in obtaining adequate employment and have difficulties in relations with others because they have been classified as mentally ill. As Scheff sees it, the transition from mental symptoms as an incidental aspect of social performance to mental illness as a social role occurs when the individual is under considerable personal and social stress. In such circumstances, the persons may themselves accept the societal definition of their status and develop deviant concepts of their identities.

Although the societal-reaction approach is provocative and obviously identifies processes that occur to some extent in the definition and care of mental patients, the relative importance of such processes were very much exaggerated. No one would deny that social labels can have powerful effects on individuals, but little evidence supports the idea that such labeling processes are sufficiently powerful to be major influences in producing chronic mental illness. The labeling process is not sufficient in itself to produce mental illness, but existing theories of the societal reaction are extremely vague in defining clearly the conditions under which labeling will or will not produce deviant behavior. Some patients get well rather quickly and stay well, while others, such as schizophrenics, commonly develop chronic disabilities. The theory of labeling does not explain why such differences occur.

Robins (1975) has presented a useful critique of labeling theory, specifically examining the theory in relationship to existing knowledge about alcoholism. She notes numerous inconsistencies between what labeling theory suggests and the facts. First, she observes that predictors of deviance are similar for both labeled and unlabeled alcoholics if the severity of the problem is taken into account. Second, while all common forms of deviant behavior decrease with age, cumulation of labeling associated with deviance must obviously increase over the life span. Thus, from this perspective, deviance should increase with age. Third, labeling theory would suggest that persons labeled in a certain way—say as a prostitute or thief—would increasingly display such behavior. In contrast, however, specific types of deviance in younger life are associated with later deviance, but often the content of the deviant behavior changes. Young girls caught stealing are more likely in later life to attempt suicide or to be sexually promiscuous or alcoholic than they are to be adult thieves. Fourth, several studies show that parents' deviance is associated with the probability that their children will be schizophrenics or alcoholics even when the children are separated from their parents and do not know the parents' identification, as in the case of infant adoptees. Moreover, Robins argues, the process of labeling itself is quite different from theoretical conceptions. The alcoholic, for example, is usually labeled only after many years of excessive drinking, and it is typically the family and not public authorities who become concerned about the problem. Although labels of *alcoholism* are withheld from many heavy drinkers for many years, the behavior is often self-sustaining and may lead to physical dependence. The most successful group approach to containing excessive drinking—membership in Alcoholics Anonymous—requires persons to label themselves as alcoholics in order for behavior change to proceed.

There is considerable stigma associated with mental illness, and many people associate the term with psychotic behavior in contrast to the variety of emotional problems that occur in populations. For those who have contact with the mentally ill, concepts of illness, perceptions of danger, and degree of stigma are associated with the nature of the experience one has (Clausen 1981; Link and Cullen 1986). Individuals test their general impressions against actual experience and often revise their expectations in a favorable direction. While labeling and its consequences may be important, the form and content of such labeling is highly interdependent with the behavior of the mentally ill. Some mental patients behave in a stereotypical fashion, but most do not and their families and the community differentiate among different patterns of behavior. As Robins's critique suggests, labeling theory is vague in its formulations, in its specification of the ways labeling affects illness, and in the specific types of disorders that may be affected more than others.

Although labeling theory has not been very useful in clarifying etiologic questions, it is a powerful perspective for examining how the definitions of a problem and its management affect its course or social outcome. It suggests that the manner in which the community defines and deals with sick and vulnerable people may either encourage disability, sick role behavior, and dependency or else prevent it. The expectations we communicate to the mentally ill are important indeed, and the range of potential functioning of the mentally ill is fairly large, depending on social definitions and social arrangements in the community. The political aspects of this problem can be considered under the designation of *collective mobilization.*

Collective Mobilization

Mental illness or any other type of deviant behavior may be viewed as a central or tangential aspect of a person's social identity. It can be considered an incidental aspect of persons' social roles and community participation or as the major fact of their social existence. Severe chronic mental illness, by its very nature, affects the person's family life, work, and social networks, but the way the community views problems and the identity of those who have them may allow for varying degrees of normal social participation and, therefore, different levels of social disability.

In recent years there has been growing recognition that many of the disabilities experienced by persons with mental illness and with other impairments are as much the product of social expectations, social stigma, and exclusion from opportunities as they are a direct function of mental or physical impairments. Organizations representing these groups are becoming politically active and more militant, demanding that their constituencies not be excluded from educational opportunities, jobs, and access to social participation simply because they are impaired or different. These efforts are increasingly supported by legislation that affirms the rights of the disabled to equal opportunity and provides a context in which they can participate more fully in community activities. Such collective mobilization efforts to change social definitions and to alter opportunities for the impaired have important effects on the degree of social disability and dependence they suffer. Modification of community expectations and social arrangements has enormous potential for preventing the elaboration of disability and suffering. It constitutes an essential preventive strategy for those concerned with the welfare of people with disabilities.

In sum, many of the social problems associated with chronic mental illness, as well as other types of disabilities, stem from physical and social arrangements in the community as well as from individual behavior. As patient groups and their representatives have come to recognize this, they have initiated political campaigns to modify arrangements that exacerbate their problems. Such social movements successfully modify social definitions and social policies that limit people with disabilities from leading more normal lives.

In this chapter and the previous ones, I have tried to illustrate some of the difficulties in clearly defining the realm of mental illness, the varying conceptions of this phenomenon, competing etiological viewpoints, and some implications for possible intervention. We now turn to a review of mental health policies and the way they have evolved to the present before we examine directions for future policies.

Chapter 5

The Development of Mental Health Policy in the United States

In the decades following World War II, a strong coalition emerged emphasizing environmental factors as prominent contributors to mental illness and championing the importance of substituting new patterns of community care for the traditional reliance on public mental hospitals for the seriously mentally ill. In the period from approximately 1955 to 1975, this coalition vastly influenced public policy toward the mentally ill and shaped the federal role in mental health policy (Grob 1987).

Those associated with this movement often assumed that mental illness was a simple continuum from mild to severe dysfunction in contrast to a heterogeneous collection of unrelated disorders, that early intervention could prevent serious mental disorder, that population dynamics and the populations at risk were unchanging, and that use of mental health resources for outpatient psychiatric care was always more cost-effective than hospital care. These were all testable assumptions, but they were mostly accepted on faith. In the 1960s the rhetoric of community care developed a momentum of its own, importantly shaping agendas and debates on mental health policy and broadly influencing the thinking of intellectual elites, public policy makers, and the general public (Grob 1987). In the process, many dedicated professionals and reformers lost touch with the heterogeneity of mental health problems and the tough realities of designing and implementing effective programs appropriate for the most seriously mentally ill.

Understanding the history of mental health policy, particularly in recent decades, provides a necessary perspective for understanding the forces that shaped the evolution of the mental health sector and possible points of leverage for constructive policy reform. Between 1955 and 1983, the number of mental health episodes treated in mental health specialty settings increased from 1.7 million to 7 million episodes; the community hospital became an important site for acute inpatient psychiatric care; and there was a vast growth in the number of mental health professionals of all kinds. Despite these changes, there is persistent evidence of significant neglect of the most seriously ill long-term patients, and many have become pessimistic about our capacity to care appropriately for these patients in the community. This negativity has been shaped in part by the excesses of ideology in the earlier decades, naive advocacy about labeling and normalization processes, and more recently by the persistence of homelessness among many persons with mental illness and the erosion of welfare programs. These conceptions and situations have provided a target for critics of deinstitutionalization, who focus on exaggerated claims and obvious failures of community care and proclaim the intent of deinstitutionalization as naive and counter-productive. Neither exaggerated claims nor criticisms serve the needs of the mentally ill well or contribute to a well-informed public. By identifying some of the dominant mis-conceptions and defining issues more carefully, we can develop targeted and efficacious strategies that offer potential for bringing improved care to this most needy population.

In planning for the future, we can often obtain insights from the past; therefore, we should attain some perspective on events that have already occurred and on the social, cultural, and ideological forces that have influenced them. Mental illness is not a new prob-lem; the mentally ill have always existed in society. Methods of caring for the mentally ill have not followed a consistent developmental pattern; rather, they have been characterized by stops and starts, by advances and setbacks. Indeed, many of our conceptions of mental illness and many current proposals were not only advocated but also practiced a century ago. Milieu treatment, a concept widely popular today, existed in the nineteenth century in both Europe and the United States under the rubric of moral treatment (Bockoven 1972). Moral treatment was based on the assumption that psychiatric illness could be alleviated if patients were treated in a considerate and friendly fashion, if they had the opportunity to discuss their troubles, if their interests were stimulated, and if they were kept actively involved in life. Close relationships between staff and patients often prevailed, and patients were treated in a personal and sympathetic way. In the passage that follows, a doctor in New York State writing in 1911 describes his conception of moral treatment.

> *(It) consists in removing patients from their residence to some proper asylum; and for this purpose a calm retreat in the country is to be preferred: for it is found that continuance at home aggravates the disease, as the improper association of ideas cannot be destroyed. . . . Have humane attendants, who shall act as servants to them; never threaten but execute; offer no indignities to them, as they have a high sense of honour. . . . Let their fears and resentments be soothed without unnec-essary opposition; adopt a system of regularity; make them rise, take exercise and food at stated times. The diet ought to be light, and easy of digestion, but never too low. When convalescing, allow limited liberty; introduce entertaining books and conversation. (Quoted in Deutsch 1949, pp. 91–92.)*

The idea of moral treatment is attributed to the French physician Philippe Pinel, who broke the pattern of harsh custodialism associated with mental institutions and substituted a program based on kindness and sympathy. It was not difficult to demonstrate that men-tal patients respond to sympathy and care, and Pinel had a profound influence on psychiatrists not only in Europe but also in North America. Pinel's program was based on his belief that psychological factors were important causes of emotional disturbances, as were social factors and an inadequate education. Treatment of the insane, he believed, was only a form of education, and intelligent understanding associated with a minimum of mechanical restraint would bring good results.

Although moral treatment was established at institutions throughout the world, the sense of social responsibility toward the unfortunate, which is more developed today, was not very strong, and most patients received no better care than they had previously. Mental patients were undifferentiated from the destitute poor. When moral treatment was practiced, it was mainly available to relatively affluent persons. Dorothea Dix, who became concerned about the inhumane care received by most of the mentally ill, was able to rally influential persons to support her initiation of a far-reaching reform movement. This nineteenth century movement was directed toward improving the care of those mentally ill paupers who were severely punished for their condition or who received no care at all. It is ironic that this reform movement, inspired by lofty motives, led in the United States and elsewhere to the development of large custodial institutions that have set the tone for the care of the mentally ill until recently. Although some smaller institutions practicing moral treatment existed at the time, for the most part the impoverished mentally ill were excluded from them. Dorothea Dix's movement was directed toward providing a minimum amount of help, and this was a significant advance in the care of the mentally ill at the time. Events later proved that once a particular system of care had developed, it was difficult to alter it.

Even the institutions that practiced moral treatment were not immune to social changes. Social conditions accompanying the industrial revolution resulted in an increased tendency to hospitalize those who could not adapt to new circumstances (Grob 1966). Although industrialization was changing the nature of work, family life, and community tolerance for bizarre behavior or incapacity, the unfortunate were exposed to great difficulties in the new industrial environment. As family structure changed, making it more difficult to contain old and disabled members within the family unit, and as the number of old people increased because of changing mortality patterns, the mental hospital often became a refuge for the old. The changing patterns of disease, particularly the increasing numbers of patients with paresis, and the dementia associated with it, resulted in more chronic and hopeless populations of patients (Grob 1983).

In New York State, 18 percent of all first admissions to mental hospitals in 1920 were diagnosed as being senile or suffering from cerebral arteriosclerosis. By 1940 they accounted for 31 percent of all admissions (Grob 1977). What was true of New York State described other states as well. In the absence of other social institutions, the mental hospital became a refuge for persons who could not cope with society on their own or for those who had no kin who could or would take responsibility for their care. Goldhamer and Marshall (1953), in studying patterns of mental hospitalization in Massachusetts over a 100-year period, could find no evidence that mental illness was increasing, but over this period admissions to mental hospitals for the aged group significantly increased. Brenner (1973), examining trends in mental hospitalization in relation to changes in the economy over a period of 127 years, found that admissions increased following periods of economic misfortune. During these periods it is the poor and dependent who fare worse, and this helps explain the large inflow to mental hospitals of poor aged and foreign immigrants who had the least capacities to care for themselves and the weakest social supports available in the community. It remains unclear whether adverse economic circumstances contributed to the prevalence of mental illness or undermined tolerance and supports for the mentally ill in the community. Whatever the case, economic and social instability produced large numbers of persons in need of care, and the mental hospital in the absence of other alternatives assumed this function.

With the limited facilities and resources available, mental hospitals were confronted with many more patients than they could effectively handle. The burden of their numbers made it more difficult to maintain an active program, such as moral treatment (Rothman 1971). Hospitals, limited in staff and money, dealt with these new conditions by regimentation of patients and the development of bureaucratic procedures through which large numbers of patients could be handled by limited staff (Goffman 1961). There were, of course, variations from one area to another and among different kinds of hospitals; any general depiction must leave room for the variability that existed (Grob 1973). Studies of individual hospitals provide a clearer view of some of the social forces and ideological influences that affected the structure of mental hospitals. We now turn to a review of the early history of one such hospital.

The Early History of Worcester State Hospital

In a sophisticated history, Gerald Grob (1966) traces the various social forces that affected the growth and the organization of Worcester State Hospital, established in 1830 as the first state hospital for the mentally ill in Massachusetts. The interest in establishing a mental hospital in Massachusetts was encouraged by the inadequacy of informal methods of caring for the indigent and insane and was activated by vigorous, enlightened reformers who were motivated by a strong sense of religious and social responsibility. The new hospital, in its earliest period (1833–1846), practiced moral treatment and offered its patients an optimistic and humanitarian climate. Early records of the hospital suggest considerable success at rehabilitation, not because of the efficacy of any particular psychiatric treatment, but probably as a result of the hopeful and encouraging climate, which supported the patient and inspired a feeling of being helped. Moral treatment, however, did not persist, and for most of the nineteenth century, the hospital was guided by a pessimistic psychiatric ideology that mirrored its custodial nature.

As Grob shows so well, the organization of psychiatric care was responsive to social, economic, and ideological influences in the society at large. Industrial and technological changes in Massachusetts, coupled with increasing urbanization, brought decreasing tolerance for bizarre and disruptive behavior and less ability to contain deviant behavior within the existing social structure. With the growing number of patients—the mass of them held in low esteem by the community as well as by mental hospital personnel—many of whom were chronically ill, it was impossible to maintain the administrative and environmental attitudes necessary for moral treatment. Moreover, with a growing number of patients and limited resources, it was necessary to develop more efficient custodial attitudes and procedures. The contempt in which the hospital held its clients and the low social value accorded them by the society at large neither stimulated hospital administrators to demand greater resources to care for their patients nor encouraged the community to provide further and more intensive support.

Other forces as well led to the deterioration of the hospital. As Grob argues, new psychiatric ideologies and professionalization among psychiatrists did much to retard the care of the mentally ill. These ideologies were in part the product of psychiatrists' own attitudes and beliefs, molded by their social backgrounds and influenced by their need to maintain and increase their status. Grob believes that psychiatric insistence that the profession was scientific exerted a negative effect on mental hospitals. The emphasis on somatic factors within the traditional medical model had little to offer in the treatment of patients, and it undermined alternative approaches that could have produced improvement in patients by communicating a sense of confidence and hope (also see Bockoven 1957, 1972). Furthermore, he argues that the development of a professional psychiatric subculture erected barriers between psychiatrists and other interested groups and was used to justify the exclusion of laymen who had provided much of the impetus for the improvement of mental health care. Finally, the trend toward professionalism isolated psychiatrists from the more humanitarian and compassionate ideologies existing in the society and replaced these with a barren, alleged objectivity that offered little help or hope. Professionalization of psychiatrists thus hampered the administration of psychiatric care.

Grob's history of Worcester State Hospital provides an important cautionary tale for professionals and policy makers. The disappointment with "Great Society" programs has resulted in an ideology of futility, a loss of interest among psychiatrists in social and community programs, and a return to biological and medical approaches. The concept of disease and traditional medical care certainly plays an essential role in the care of the most severely mentally ill, but the social, organizational, and humanistic contexts of care are also crucial. Molecular biology and the neurosciences offer great promise for the future but relatively little to current patients who desperately need a broad array of care and rehabilitation services. However sophisticated our biological approaches, social and behavioral factors will continue to play an important part in the occurrence and course of mental illness and in good psychiatric care. In turning back toward biology and medical concepts, it would be tragic if psychiatry once again contributes to weakening the forces of reform and the humanistic basis of care that inspire a sense of hope so important to millions.

More Recent Developments in Mental Health Policy

American psychiatry and mental health policy, as we know them today, are for the most part post–World War II developments. At the beginning of World War II, there were only 3,000 psychiatrists in the United States, and shortages among other treatment and research personnel in the mental health field were even more acute. Progress is reflected in the fact that there are now approximately 44,000 psychiatrists in the United States. Even more impressive increases have occurred in psychology, psychiatric nursing, psychiatric social work, and other mental health fields.

Except for their traditional role in mental hospitals, psychiatrists became most extensively involved in public policy issues during World War II, initially through their participation in selective service screening. Between January 1942 and June 1945, an estimated 1,875,000 men among the 15 million men examined were rejected for service because of alleged psychiatric disabilities. Of the men inducted, a large proportion of those later separated from the armed forces on a disability charge were discharged specifically for neuropsychiatric reasons (Felix 1967, pp. 28–29). These facts created great concern and stimulated interest in improving basic preventive and treatment services and research in the psychiatric area.

In noting the influence of such involvement, we should also point out that psychiatric participation in selective service was less successful than one might have anticipated, given the claims of its advocates. Partly because of the shortage of adequately trained professionals, partly because of the meager development of psychiatric criteria for screening, and partly because of the way selective service was administered under the pressure of manpower requirements, such screening was for the most part a failure (Ginzberg et al. 1959). Deutsch (1949) describes the situation in this way:

> *It had been recommended that one psychiatrist be assigned to draft examining boards for every fifty registrants, and that a minimum of fifteen minutes be devoted to every psychiatric examination. When the many millions began to pour through selective service centers, however, these proposals became scraps of paper on the wind. Instead of fifteen minutes, an average of barely two minutes was devoted to the psychiatric examination of Army recruits. It was not unusual for a single psychiatrist to examine 200 men daily. The course of psychiatric screening throughout the war was highly irregular. In some states and in some centers, men with long mental hospital records were rushed into the armed forces; in many centers, no effort was made to ascertain institutional histories for psychotic episodes; at others, men with histories of very mild emotional disorders were summarily rejected. The pendulum directives swung from one extreme to another during the war; at one period, practically everybody not obviously psychotic was accepted for service; at another, nobody with the slightest trace of neurosis passed the examining board. (Deutsch 1949, p. 463)*

It would be totally inappropriate to evaluate the possibilities for psychiatric screening on the basis of the selective service experience. As Deutsch points out, the conditions under which these psychiatric examinations took place were totally unrealistic, and the examinations were frequently performed by general physicians with little or no training in psychiatry. However, one important observation can be gained from this experience, and it has relevance to the present. Selective service officials had a low opinion of psychiatry. When war appeared imminent, they did not give high priority to psychiatric selection. Most of the encouragement for psychiatric screening came from groups within the psychiatric profession, so psychiatrists were in no sense innocent maidens in this affair. Many of the psychiatric recommendations were absurd in light of existing knowledge and the psychiatric manpower situation. The recommendations for psychiatric screening did not show an adequate appreciation of the administrative needs of selective service and the relative priorities given to its goals—the major one was manpower procurement. Later in the war, mechanisms were devised that facilitated psychiatric screening, but the responsibility for the failure of screening must reside largely within the psychiatric profession, which encouraged the entire venture and made unrealistic claims as to what could be achieved.

In current mental health literature, programs that are promoted are commonly unrealistic in terms of manpower, the existing state of psychiatric knowledge, and organizational and community resources. All too often programs are advocated and encouraged without sufficient attention being given to their feasibility or to their consequences for social and political goals outside the realm of mental health. As psychiatry and public policy become increasingly linked, it is necessary that mental health advocates be more responsible in their recommendations and give attention not only to "ideal" psychiatric programs but also to practical ones.

Post–World War II Developments in Mental Health Policy

World War II not only alerted the country to mental health needs but also provided psychiatry with opportunities to develop programs for psychiatrically disabled soldiers. Although the war brought no breakthroughs in psychiatric knowledge, it did provide individual psychiatrists with broad administrative experience and gave considerable stimulus to attempts to devise new treatment techniques that were feasible in dealing with relatively large groups of patients. If selective service did little to enhance the reputation of psychiatry, the practical response of psychiatrists in the military to very difficult psychiatric problems was impressive. They showed openness to new approaches and group techniques were extensively used for the first time. Army psychiatrists also experimented with the use of sedation and hypnosis. The psychiatric problems that commonly occurred alerted psychiatrists, more than ever before, to the social aspects of psychiatric care and to the effects of environment on the occurrence of mental illness. By the time the war ended, psychiatrists had gained many friends and a somewhat more receptive response among their medical colleagues.

The publicity given to psychiatric casualties and the awareness of the large manpower loss as a result of the alleged high prevalence of psychiatric defects in the screened population provided a strong impetus for development of public policy in relation to mental health. The government and informed laymen became aware of the necessity to learn more about the causes of mental illness and the means of preventing it, to assist the individual states in developing their own mental health programs, and to build a satisfactory manpower pool in the mental health area. In 1946 Congress passed the Mental Health Act, creating the National Institute of Mental Health (NIMH). The avowed intent was to have "the traditional public health approach applied to the mental health field." This program did and continues to do much to achieve the goals set for it.

Postwar Psychiatry

The emphasis on private psychiatric care encouraged by psychoanalytic theory and practice in the 1950s and 1960s did little to facilitate the care of chronic patients in American mental hospitals, despite the overall improvement in the psychiatric manpower situation (Myers and Bean 1968). The situation improved somewhat in the 1970s, even though mental health care continued to be focused on individual psychotherapy. Psychodynamic ideology, which emphasized analysis of unconscious motivation, discouraged interest among many therapists in the more direct and "superficial" techniques of providing support, reassurance, and direction. Unfortunately, most of the professional schools for training mental health professionals attract students and faculty primarily interested in individual psychotherapy and private practice. Even social work and nursing, which have long traditions in practicing with the most needy and disabled, turned toward individual psychodynamics and attract students with aspirations to be private therapists. Few universities train professional students in optimal ways to work with the most severely mentally ill, and this area has received little priority in most of our training programs. Professional psychology, which has grown rapidly in recent years, has demonstrated the least interest in the most severely impaired patients.

Although there were significant advances in the United States in manpower development and mental health research following World War II, very little of this gain was transferred to mental hospitals, and direct federal aid to the states for mental health services actually decreased during the Korean War. Although innovations were being developed—most significantly, new psychoactive drugs—most states had neither the facilities and financial resources nor the personnel to implement new ideas in the mental health field. The Hoover Commission, looking into the entire issue of government reorganization, reported, "Although we believe that the federal government should gradually reduce its grants as the states take up the load for any given health activity, we conclude that the recent reduction in federal support has been too abrupt" (Hoover Commission 1955, p. 72). The commission noted that aid to the states had been significantly reduced while research support had been developing. Individual states were becoming acutely aware of their personnel and financial limitations at the same time that a tentative optimistic spirit was emerging in the mental health field because of reports of improved release rates with intensive personal care and drug therapies.

Concepts of community care were also developing during this period, stimulated by the interests of state governments reflected in the work of the Governors' Conference beginning in 1949 and the influential conferences on mental health sponsored by the Milbank Memorial Fund (Grob 1987). In 1954, New York State enacted its Community Mental Health Services Act, enabling the development of local mental health boards which could subsidize a range of services including outpatient care with state support for up to half its costs below a ceiling. By 1956, 85 percent of the population were represented by boards participating in the program.

Stimulated by these events and the interests of both the American Psychiatric Association and the American Medical Association for a Joint Commission on Mental Health and Illness, the Congress passed such legislation in 1955 (Grob 1987). When the Mental Health Study Act of 1955 was being considered, government officials no longer believed that large custodial institutions could effectively deal with mental illness. The emphasis on discussion of mental health care in the community was motivated as much by a desire to reduce hospital populations and concomitant costs as by a belief that such measures would have significant therapeutic value. In its deliberations, the Congress gave highest priority to considerations of manpower. The feeling was that already existing therapeutic knowledge could not be applied because of shortages of personnel and facilities. Government officials felt that possible remedial efforts could be increased significantly through the development of psychoactive drugs. In general, however, the experience with new drugs had not progressed to the point where they dominated the thinking of the Congress, and it is likely that the Mental Health Study Act would have been supported in their absence.

The Mental Health Study Act authorized an appropriation to the Joint Commission on Mental Illness and Health to study and make recommendations concerning various aspects of mental health policy. In 1961 the commission published its well-known report, *Action for Mental Health,* which argued strongly for an increased program of services and more funds for basic, long-term mental health research. It recommended that expenditures in the mental health field be doubled in five years and tripled in ten years. It argued for new and better recruitment and training programs for mental health workers. It suggested the expansion of treatment programs for acutely ill patients in all facilities, including community mental health clinics, general hospitals, and mental hospitals. It argued for the establishment of mental health clinics, suggesting one for every 50,000 persons in the population. It attacked the large state mental hospitals and suggested that these be converted to smaller, regional, intensive treatment centers with no more than 1,000 beds. It recommended new programs for the care of chronic patients as well as for after-care and other rehabilitation services. These were wide-ranging and ambitious demands, but they fell on receptive ears in Washington. Many of these recommendations led to action because of abundant funds and moral support from the federal government. The most far-reaching of such legislation was the new program for financing community mental health centers.

The new direction of mental health policies in the United States, however, did not flow directly from the report of the Joint Commission. *Action for Mental Health* was largely an ideological document, and, like poetry, it was sufficiently ambiguous to allow various interest groups to read what they wished into it. It is not surprising that a vigorous political battle at the federal level resulted between those psychiatrists with a public health viewpoint, who wished to develop completely new precedents for mental patient care, and those psychiatrists more within the traditional medical model, who felt that considerable federal assistance should be invested in improving the quality of mental hospitals and their capacities to provide adequate treatment to patients. Those who favored a more radical break with the past system of providing mental health services through state and federal hospitals were more influential with President John Kennedy, and the final decision was to give greatest impetus to community health centers, not clinics, which were to be independent of the old mental hospital system, although affiliated with it. This was a tremendously important decision and one that endorsed the viewpoint that mental illness is not inherently different from the larger range of psychological difficulties common in the community.

The implementation of the Joint Commission recommendations required more than the suggestions themselves. First, the American economy was in an excellent position, and abundant funds were available for meeting domestic needs. Second, the president himself was committed to the program in mental health and mental retardation, and, in contrast to some other proposed medical care programs, the mental health program did not involve any obvious group or value cleavages. Third, psychiatric drugs had changed the climate of mental health care as well as administrative attitudes, and the value of supporting mental health services seemed to be more obvious to laymen. Finally, the harmful consequences of the custodial-hospital environment had been poignantly demonstrated, and society had become increasingly aware of the unequal access to good psychiatric treatment for the rich and the poor.

The ideas of the Joint Commission were hardly new. In 1914 the Massachusetts State Board of Insanity recommended that "each hospital reach out in the community and be responsible for the mental health of the district covered by each" and advocated outpatient departments dealing with after-care, family care, and mental hygiene. These departments would take on such functions as working with discharged patients, boarding patients in foster families, and educating the public to prevent insanity (Grob 1966, p. 350). What made the report of the Joint Commission so important was not the uniqueness of its recommendations, but the receptive climate into which they were introduced. It is possible that any reasonable set of recommendations would have been acceptable given the timing, circumstances, and mood of the people in government.

In the 1960s expenditures increased for mental health professional training, mental health services, and construction and staffing of new community mental health centers. During this period of optimism, large numbers of mental patients were released from hospitals into the community without adequate preparation, a network of appropriate services, or consideration of the social costs. Such deinstitutionalization was consistent with economic pressures on state government. Costs of caring for discharged patients could be transferred from state mental health budgets to federally subsidized programs, such as welfare and Medicaid (Scull 1977). These trends were supported by a naive optimism and ideology that the community was good and the hospital was bad. During the 1960s mental health professionals made claims of expertise that had little basis in reality. Associated with the new public health framework was a simplistic view of prevention of mental disorder, a broad increase in the boundaries of mental health concepts, and a naive political stance concerning the functions of community psychiatry in public decision making. Although the envisioned increased numbers of mental health centers, community programs, and new mental health personnel never fully materialized, the range of providers, services offered, and clients increased substantially.

The new Community Mental Health Centers (CMHCs) were to be the key to the new public health approach. Initially they were to have five essential services: inpatient care, emergency care, partial hospitalization, outpatient care, and education and consultation. In addition, they were mandated to develop a continuum of care through linkages among the required services. Other services, such as pre-admission and post-discharge services for hospitalized patients, and specialized diagnostic services, were suggested but not required. As time went on the CMHCs were at the center of the debates about the nature of mental illness, and the mandated services had expanded to twelve including specialized services for children and the elderly, alcohol and drug abuse services, and follow-up care and transitional services for the chronically ill. The range of services grew, but a clear sense of priorities never emerged. By 1977, 650 CMHCs served almost two million people and were accessible to 43 percent of the population (Foley and Sharfstein 1983), but the system was in peril because of the turbulent social and mental health politics of the day. Facing many competing expectations and demands, they had difficulty following a clear strategy.

The Vietman War, its aftermath, and the disillusion with the programs of the "Great Society" resulted in the curtailment of funds for mental health programs. The Nixon years were a hostile time for mental health issues. Not only was the administration unsympathetic to mental health concerns, but existing programs for mental health centers, research, research training, and professional manpower development were phased down, phased out, or allowed to erode with inflation. There were serious criticisms of some of these programs. It was evident that many, if not most, of the mental health centers were concentrating their efforts on ordinary problems of living rather than dealing with hard-core chronic mental patients (Chu and Trotter 1974). Massive deinstitutionalization revealed the poor planning for release of patients into the community and the inadequacy of continuing supervision and treatment. In some areas there was a backlash of community criticism of mental health policies.

It was clear by the late 1970s that the climate in which new initiatives had flourished had changed radically. It was time to consolidate programs and assess what had been accomplished. Despite the excesses, exaggerated claims, and naive expectations in the 1960s, much progress was evident. Outpatient care and the use of psychiatric services increased dramatically. A great shift away from public mental hospitals took place, with more acute psychiatric illness being treated in general hospitals and outpatient clinics. Behavioral techniques for treating many types of problems were commonly adopted, and treatment of disorders became more focused and diversified, breaking away from the chains of a psychoanalytic dogmatism. A vigorous civil liberties movement developed on behalf of mental patients, and patients' rights in civil commitment procedures and in other areas of care were substantially clarified and strengthened. Many patients in need were recognized and treated more quickly in the community, preventing some of the secondary disabilities associated with earlier treatment modes. Understanding of new psychoactive drugs and their adverse effects increased, allowing more sophisticated pharmacological therapy. Private and nonprofit insurance companies providing medical coverage substantially increased the scope of inpatient psychiatric benefits, and many expanded outpatient coverage as well. When all was said and done, these were no small achievements.

In the late 1960s and early 1970s, the executive branch and Congress became increasingly concerned about such problems as alcoholism and drug abuse. As funds were more limited, traditional mental health monies were tapped to launch new national efforts in these areas. Within the mental health sphere, new political constituencies developed to deal with alcohol and drug abuse problems, but what eventually emerged was an umbrella agency known by the acronym ADAMHA (the Alcohol, Drug Abuse, and Mental Health Administration), incorporating the National Institute of Mental Health (NIMH), the National Institute on Alcohol Abuse and Alcoholism (NIAAA), and the National Institute on Drug Abuse (NIDA). These agencies initially had responsibility for a variety of service programs, demonstrations, research efforts, and research and professional training programs, and they were also involved in planning and public education. ADAMHA programs were under considerable attack during the Nixon years, and the administration and the Congress were locked in battle during this period as Nixon tried to reduce and dismantle many of the programs associated with Presidents Kennedy and Johnson. By 1977, the federal government had only funded 650 of the proposed 1,500 community mental health centers at a cost of $1.5 billion, but the administration had already lost interest in continuing the program. It also was increasingly evident that these centers were not serving the most severely ill patients.

By 1976, when Carter became president, the mental health federal programs were showing the effects of the hostility evident in the Nixon years. Also, the core concerns had changed since the social programs of the 1960s. The problems of deinstitutionalization were clearly evident and the need to develop community services for the most chronically disabled patients highly salient. Developing accessible and comprehensive community care is expensive, and the hopes that the nation, in the near future, would develop a universal system of national health insurance that protected the mentally ill were already fading in the face of medical cost inflation. There was, thus, much concern with the appropriate role of the federal government and with ways of garnering funds from various federal, state, and local programs to provide stable funding for essential community networks of care. Realizing that much depended on reimbursement possibilities, careful examination was directed to possible funding streams.

With improved epidemiological data and a renewed concern with primary medical care, there was recognition that many patients in need of mental health care are not found in psychiatric settings but in the context of general medical care. Attention now focused on improving general physicians' recognition and management of psychiatric disorder, the availability of psychiatric consultation to general physicians, and referral practices. Several experiments or demonstrations involving a closer integration between general medical and psychiatric services suggested that such management reduced medical utilization (Follette and Cummings 1967, Cummings and Follette 1968, Patrick et al. 1978).

In February 1977, President Carter established a Presidential Commission on Mental Health to review the mental health needs of the nation and to make recommendations. This effort, like most such commissions, was highly politicized but offered a unique opportunity because Mrs. Carter had a special interest in mental health and served as honorary chairperson of the commission. The commission made its report in 1978, addressing such issues as the organization of community services, community supports, financing, personnel, legal rights, research, prevention, and public understanding. The report argued for greater investment in mental health services, noting that although the mental health problem was one of the largest in terms of numbers of people involved and their suffering, it received only 12 percent of general health expenditures. It noted the acute need to develop community-based services, to make them financially, geographically, and socially accessible, and to make them flexible so as to serve the needs of varying social and racial groups. It argued strongly for further support for research and training, for attention to chronic mental illness, and for meeting the special needs of children, adolescents, and the elderly.

The 1978 commission, unlike its predecessor, reported in a more difficult and complex climate. Inflation was a prime concern, and health care costs increased faster than prices in the economy as a whole. Government expenditures in health were already high and largely uncontrollable, in part as a result of the structure of the Medicare and Medicaid programs. Policy makers appeared reluctant to make large new investments in health care initiatives, and during times of financial stringency the "haves" are reluctant to yield any ground to new areas.

Unlike the earlier initiatives of the 1960s, the commission functioned in an atmosphere of much greater fiscal constraints and with many more well-developed constituencies anxious to protect their interests. As a consequence, the report was quite general, advocated a broad array of conflicting ideas, endorsed most mental health interests, and failed to face the tough question of financial priorities. Thus, it provided no clear direction among competing constituencies and may have contributed to the nasty infighting that followed in its wake about how to design appropriate legislation. As the coordinator of the President's Commission's Task Panel on the Nature and Scope of the Problems, I was clear on the difficulty of the political task of balancing competing interests, but I would have preferred a more direct course of focusing on the needs of the most severely ill. While these received much attention, other vague concepts such as prevention received equal play. In endorsing everything, the report offered no clear course of action, but it brought together a great deal of information that could serve as a vehicle for advocacy.

The process of drafting the Mental Health Systems Act was long and tortuous, reflecting the conflicting interests involved, the competition with other Carter initiatives, and the growing fiscal constraints. After numerous efforts, a bill was presented to the Congress, which was then substantially modified in an effort to satisfy some of the strongly opposing groups that had a stake and to reach an acceptable consensus. The process reflected the difficult competing ideologies that persist in the mental health sector: those that favor comprehensive approaches versus those that focus on categorical groups; the desire of community mental health centers to retain their autonomy versus the concern of the states to hold them accountable; the concern to ensure treatment to disturbed persons in community settings versus the rights of patients to refuse care; and the goal to have the dollars follow the patient versus the concerns of hospital employees' unions (AFSCME) to protect their members, and so on (Foley and Sharfstein 1983). The act was signed into law by President Carter in October, 1980.

While the legislation was being developed, the Department of Health and Human Services, at the recommendation of the President's Commission, was hard at work developing an integrated federal strategy to ensure an appropriate response to dealing with the multifaceted problems of the chronically mentally ill. This was a far-ranging effort that examined the epidemiology of severe mental illness, the range of psychiatric, medical, rehabilitative, housing, and social services available and needed, issues of personnel and recruitment, and financing reforms. The report recognized the critical importance of Medicaid, Social Security Disability Insurance, and many other federal programs, and presented an incremental approach to modifying them in a constructive way (U.S. Department of Health and Human Services 1980). The report was actually completed before the passage of the Systems Act but serves as an important analytic rationale for designing an effective national system.

The story ends sadly when the Reagan administration, which took office one month after the passage of the act, chose not to implement it and instead began dismantling the building blocks of a national system through its "new federalism" initiative. The bulk of the federal mental health services monies, as well as funds from many other health and social programs, were returned to the states in block grants but with cuts in funding levels. Other federal programs on which the mentally ill depend lost ground or were cut back, including Medicaid, housing subsidies, and social services. Large numbers of chronically mentally ill persons were dropped from disability insurance by the Social Security Administration during the disability reviews in 1980 and 1981, but with the intervention of many advocates and the federal courts, many were reinstated. The more difficult access to housing and income benefits during this period is believed to have contributed to the enlarged population of homeless mentally ill found in every major U.S. city.

The Reagan program that sought to reduce direct federal operation of health programs involved both a very different philosophical orientation than the Systems Act and less willingness to support expenditures for social programs. The reduction in funding made it extraordinarily difficult to maintain services, but the ideology about giving states more authority to direct mental health services within their jurisdictions had some clear merits. The federal initiatives of the 1960s typically bypassed state authority on the theory that states that had a stake in traditional mental health care were impediments to reform. Federal officials interacted directly with local service delivery system with little involvement of state officials or concern for state priorities. Much of the hostility in negotiations of the Systems Act was a reaction to the earlier insensitivity of the federal government to state interests. And, in retrospect, it seems that the approach of the federal government contributed to the low priority that community mental health centers gave to chronic patients.

Following 1980 the federal role in providing direct leadership in mental health services diminished, and much mental health policy debate shifted to the state and local arenas. The National Institute of Mental Health had less impact on policy formulation and implementation, and its responsibilities now were primarily in the research and demonstration areas. It appeared that mental health had once again receded into the background as states struggled with budget difficulties and seemed unwilling or unable to take up the slack. In fact, much progress during the 1980s occurred quietly through the continuation and expansion of a variety of important federal programs on which persons with serious mental illness depended (Koyanagi and Goldman 1991).

Despite the opposition of the Reagan administration, Congress continued NIMH's Community Support Program (CSP). The CSP, modeled on the innovative Program of Assertive Community Treatment developed in Dane County, Wisconsin, helped states develop broad systems of care for persons with serious mental illness that extended well beyond traditional services and included attention to housing, psychosocial rehabilitation, and other important needs. Substantial extensions and improvements to such major programs as Social Security Disability Income (SSDI), Supplemental Security Income (SSI), Medicaid, and Medicare made these programs more useful for assisting persons with severe mental illness. For example, changes in the Medicaid program made possible payment for case management that could be targeted to persons with mental illness, allowed reimbursement of mental health clinics, and improved standards for the mentally ill in nursing homes. The Medicare program more recently broadened coverage for mental illness and defined a new medical management service for medication visits that reduced the usual copayment for mental health services from 50 to 20 percent. The annual outpatient treatment limit was eliminated and reimbursement to clinical psychologists and social workers was now allowed. Between 1987 and 1992 there was a 73 percent increase in the user rate and a 27 percent increase in the average number of services per user. Inflation adjusted per capita spending more than doubled (Rosenbach and Ammering 1997).

Despite these improvements, problems persisted and grew. Contributing factors included:

- growing numbers of young persons with serious mental illness whose problems were complicated by substance abuse
- increasing amounts of homelessness among the mentally ill
- cutbacks in funding levels in many federal and state programs
- difficulties faced by the states in shifting funds from institutional care to community programs that allowed dollars to follow patients as they moved from hospital to the community

With continuing deinstitutionalization, most patients were in the community, but most funding was still invested in state hospitals and inpatient care. Although states increasingly understood the needs for community systems of care, they had great difficulty in funding them appropriately.

In the 1980s, the National Alliance for the Mentally Ill (NAMI) emerged as a major advocate for clients and families of the mentally ill. It now represents about 160,000 families. NAMI, representing a large number of state and local alliances, has established a significant presence in Washington and many state capitals. The organization has been a vigorous advocate for the needs of persons with serious mental illness and their families, for basic mental health research, particularly in the neurosciences, and for parity in mental health insurance coverage with coverage for other medical disorders. NAMI has also been a major supporter of mental health services research and the national plan for its growth and development. NAMI's vigorous efforts in the 1980s and 1990s helped keep many important mental health issues on the national agenda.

In the 1990s policy makers revisited the issue of the proper location of the NIMH within the governmental structure, and mental health responsibilities were again reorganized. In its early years, the NIMH was part of the National Institutes of Health (NIH), and was able to thrive under the strong public support for research (Grob 1994). Under the activist leadership of Robert Felix, NIMH became an independent agency within the Public Health Service. Felix wished to bring a public health approach to mental health and viewed an independent agency as consistent with his objective. During the Nixon years, however, NIMH was brought into an umbrella agency (ADAMHA) that included other agencies dealing with alcohol and drugs.

As federal support for mental health diminished in the 1980s and as research funding became more competitive, many scientists believed that their interests would be better protected by the prestige of the NIH than by ADAMHA. They also argued that developments in the brain sciences, and the closer relationship between psychiatry and medicine, made bringing mental health research together with other biomedical research a logical step. Advocates for the services and demonstration components of NIMH argued that separating mental health research from services demonstrations and technical assistance would damage the integrity of these efforts, as well as their political clout. The researchers supported by NAMI, a strong advocate for brain research, won and the NIMH research program was returned to the NIH in 1992, along with the alcohol and drug research programs, each constituting a new institute within the NIH. Other mental health programs including the demonstration authorities, planning and monitoring of state plans, technical assistance, information collection and clinical training were organized into a new Center for Mental Health Services within a new umbrella agency, the Substance Abuse and Mental Health Services Administration (SAMHSA). In some sense, both advocates and opponents of these changes have been proved right. Federal deficit reduction efforts have forced cutbacks in many government programs, but mental health research has been sheltered by the prestige and public support of biomedical research. The services component, in contrast, initially experienced budget cuts that diminished its capacities.

Mental health services must seek ways to use existing resources more efficiently and creatively, but increasingly this is more a state-by-state effort than a national initiative. The most important trend is the rapid movement of states into mental health managed care as a way of constraining the growth of Medicaid and other state mental health programs. The passage of new welfare legislation in 1996, and its differential impact on various states, promises much new activity at the state level and many uncertainties. The failure of the Congress in 1996 to return the Medicaid program to the states in the form of block grants allows the continuation of many important protections for persons with mental illness, but the devolution of authority from federal to state government ensures greater variation in state performance in coming years.

During the 1970s the mental health system came close to significant reform, but much of the momentum was lost with the changing politics of the 1980s, the growth of the federal deficit, and cutbacks in mental health initiatives. In 1992 the Clinton administration proposed health care reform, which, among other things, would have made mental health a more equal partner in health care coverage. Mental health concerns gained visibility and open support from many major political figures during the accompanying debate, but the Clinton proposals failed to capture the political and public support necessary to change public policy. Nevertheless, parity in mental health care coverage has become a more acceptable political position, as reflected by some of the changes passed by Congress in 1996 that require greater equivalence in some aspects of mental health insurance. There is little doubt that parity is an issue we will hear a lot more about. It is inevitable that many of the mental health issues of the past two decades will reemerge on federal and state agendas, although perhaps in different formats and contexts.

The Organization of State Mental Hospitals

Most state mental hospitals were built in the later part of the nineteenth and early part of the twentieth centuries. Many were either developed or enlarged in response to the crusade of Dorothea Dix; their construction constituted the first attempt in many areas of the country to provide attention to persons of limited resources who were mentally ill. As we learn more about the history of mental hospitals, we discover the extent of heterogeneity and the difficulty of generalization. But as the population aged and patterns of disease changed in an increasingly urbanized society, most hospitals were faced with growing numbers of chronic patients with irreversible problems who overwhelmed staff resources and gave these institutions a custodial and often harsh atmosphere. As chronic patients came to comprise an increasing proportion of the mental hospital caseload, psychiatrists shifted their work to other settings, and there was a considerable feeling of hopelessness about constructive treatment in the mental hospital. These and other influences resulted in giving mental hospitals low priority in public perceptions and financial support. This situation persisted well into the twentieth century despite several attempts to humanize the mental hospital.

The first major humanizing influence on mental hospitals in this century was the Mental Hygiene Movement. Begun in 1908 by Clifford Beers, a former mental patient who exposed the dehumanizing aspects of mental patient care, this movement encouraged a new, humanistic ideology that stimulated some improvement in hospital conditions and public concern for the mentally ill. It did little, however, to retard the pattern of providing for the mentally ill in large and impersonal public institutions. Despite the efforts and concern of many reformers, mental hospitals maintained a custodial attitude reinforced by meager allowances for the care of psychiatric patients, limited professional staff, and dependence on untrained and unskilled manpower.

One of the most important innovations in mental patient care has been the use of psychoactive drugs, first introduced in the middle 1950s. Although these drugs do not cure patients, they do much to reduce their most disturbing symptoms; they facilitate the control of mental patients and the ability of hospital personnel to work with them. The use of drugs gave staff greater confidence in its own efficacy and helped dispel the feelings of hopelessness and apathy that had captured the mental hospital. Administrative changes were instituted, such as eliminating constraints, minimizing security arrangements, and encouraging early release. Patients under drug treatment were more tractable and cooperative, and receptivity to mental patients returning to the community increased. Finally, the feeling of hope and efficacy felt by the hospital staff was communicated to patients and the community generally and gave both renewed confidence in the ability of patients to cope with difficulties outside the hospital.

Evidence supports the contention that changes in patient retention and release patterns following the introduction of psychoactive drugs were as much the result of administrative changes in mental hospitals as they were the consequence of the drugs themselves. Some studies in English hospitals that introduced new administrative policies prior to the introduction of psychoactive drugs show that new patterns of release were observable prior to drug introduction, and they suggest that the tremendous change that took place is largely a result of alterations in administrative policies (Brown et al. 1966; Bockoven 1972; Scull 1977). Whatever the specific utility of the psychoactive drugs, the development of this new technology supported a climate of opinion and confidence, making it possible to change important policies relating to patient handling and release. Whether directly or indirectly, drugs helped bring about a revolution in psychiatric care.

Despite the widespread introduction of neuroleptic drugs in the mid-1950s, many problems remained, including issues of suitable housing, subsistence, and the need to change community attitudes. It is widely assumed that deinstitutionalization began with a vengeance in 1955, the point at which inpatients in public mental hospitals reached their peak. In fact, the timing of deinstitutionalization varied greatly by state, and for the nation as a whole the pace was relatively slow, only 1.5 percent a year between 1955 and 1965 (Gronfein 1985).

Large-scale deinstitutionalization did not come until the mid-1960s, in combination with a number of changes that addressed issues of community attitudes and subsistence. Attitude change involved three strong ideological thrusts. The 1960s were a period of civil rights activity and advocacy. The young lawyers and activists for the civil liberties of the mentally ill came out of the civil rights movement and were involved with public interest law. Civil commitment was characterized by substantial abuses and was a visible target for their efforts (Ennis 1972; Miller 1976). In these initiatives they were influenced by the social science literature on the adverse effects of custodial mental hospitals and abuses of psychiatry (Goffman 1961; Szasz 1963; Wing and Brown 1970). This work provided both the ideology and much of the substance to justify an attack on involuntary hospitalization. A third aspect was that psychodynamic conceptions of mental illness were increasingly accepted by mental health professionals, the mass media, and the public. Mental illness was commonly portrayed as a single continuum from mild to severe, caused substantially by sociocultural and psychosocial factors (Caplan 1964; Leighton 1967). Within this dominant ideology of environmental causation, it followed that bringing more benign influence to bear on the mentally ill would ameliorate their level of disturbance. That major mental disorders might be fundamentally different from common distress syndromes, or that poor community environments could have the same negative effects as poor hospital environments, were not considered seriously. The result was a strong anti-hospital ideology.

To successfully remove disabled people from hospitals required places for relocation, and it was not until the rapid expansion of welfare programs in the 1960s and 1970s that the means became widely available. Medicare stimulated a dramatic growth of nursing home beds, and Medicaid financed the cost of nursing home residence. This not only gave the states an opportunity to transfer elderly mentally ill and demented patients receiving custodial care in hospitals to an alternative institution, but also allowed transfer of significant state costs to the federal budget. The expansion of Social Security Disability Income (SSDI) in those years and the introduction of Supplemental Security Income (SSI) for those without the required work history for disability eligibility provided much of the financial support necessary to return impaired patients to a variety of community settings including families, board and care facilities, and single occupancy housing. Between 1966 and 1980 the yearly rate of deinstitutionalization averaged 6 percent. It could not have been achieved without the expansion of welfare programs.

Statistics on patients resident in mental hospitals reflect the vast changes that took place. As 1955 ended, 558,922 patients were residents in mental hospitals, but the following years show a considerable decrease in this figure. Although the number of admissions to mental hospitals rose substantially between 1955 and 1971, by the latter year, only 308,983 patients were residents in mental hospitals (U.S. President's Commission 1978, Vol. II, p. 94). Admissions dropped somewhat following 1971, and the number of resident patients continued to fall, reaching 215,573 in 1974. By the mid-1980s, inpatients in public mental hospitals fell to almost 115,000, and general hospitals had become a major site of acute psychiatric care. In 1983, there were almost three times as many admissions to general hospitals as to state mental hospitals (National Institute of Mental Health 1987).

As a consequence of reductions in the populations of public mental hospitals and the transfer of many hopeless chronic patients to nursing homes, the public mental hospital was in many instances transformed from a custodial institution to an active treatment unit. It is, of course, difficult to describe conditions in the United States because each state maintains its own mental health system and there is great diversity in the availability of facilities, funding patterns, and relative emphasis put on different aspects of care. But overall, the professional-to-patient and staff-to-patient ratios improved enormously, and active treatment and rehabilitation programs were developed to a point where, in many instances, hospitals little resembled what they had once been.

Despite these favorable changes, mental hospitals continue to be plagued by many of the problems and conditions that preceded these administrative and therapeutic advances. Some hospitals are still large and managing such institutions often demands organizational routines that are dehumanizing and that interfere with an individualized approach to the patient. Many patients still have limited individual contact with professional staff, and it remains difficult to recruit well-trained psychiatrists to such institutions. Because the less severely ill are filtered off to community programs, and those more affluent and those with insurance use community hospitals, patient populations in these hospitals tend to be more chronic and more difficult to rehabilitate. Hospitals are increasingly concerned with legal issues, requiring more time for record keeping and documentation as compared with patient care.

The statistics on the reduction of mental hospital populations, however, are somewhat misleading. Many mental patients formerly in mental hospitals were transferred to nursing homes that offered no active treatment and often a poorer environment than the mental hospital (Stotsky 1970; Vladeck 1980; Linn 1985). Others live in group homes, sheltered care situations, and isolated rooming houses that vary a great deal in the quality of environment, supervision, and social contact with others (Allen 1974; Segal and Aviram 1978; Lamb 1979). Still other patients are treated in general hospitals that may provide unimaginative programs based on a traditional medical model, and some are simply "dumped" in inadequate community housing in transitional housing areas with little support or assistance and are left to be victimized by criminal elements. Although deinstitutionalization has brought improved lives for many patients, residence in the community is no panacea, and it is necessary to look behind the label to assess the quality of life patients actually live in these varying contexts.

Programs of Community Care

Many of the added activities that have been supported by public investment in the mental health field have been in the area of community care. The community care ideology developed from the growing realization that the mental hospital as it existed often did much to isolate patients from the community, to undermine their motivation to return, to retard skills, and, in general, to induce a level of disability above and beyond that resulting from the patient's condition. As noted earlier, the report of the Joint Commission attacked the large mental hospitals and advocated their abolition. The commission supported smaller mental hospitals providing intensive care, treatment units in general hospitals, and mental health clinics. These facilities were to be close to the patients' homes and were to keep them in touch with their families and the community. The new emphasis was on outpatient care and short periods of hospitalization when necessary. Additional alternatives were urged that fell somewhere between the total separation characterized by the mental hospital isolated from the community and outpatient care, such as day hospitals, night hospitals, halfway houses, and hostels. An understanding of the importance of maintaining patients' skills and sense of activity led to added emphasis on vocational services, sheltered workshops, and continuing employment while the patient was in the hospital. Finally, great emphasis has been given to the idea that patients should be kept in their home surroundings and that the necessary services should be provided to them and their families so that they can cope with the problems that arise.

Ideologies develop more rapidly than patterns of care, and although it was not terribly difficult to change hospital policies concerning admission and retention, there are additional obstacles in providing a system of community services that can support and buttress new hospital policies so as to ensure adequate benefits for patients. While the ideology is coherent, the services provided to patients in the community are sporadic and fragmentary, and frequently the burden that had been the hospital's has been shifted to the family. Yet in most parts of the country, no system of services aids the family in meeting crises or in dealing with the patient and the problems of care effectively. Indeed, many new initiatives are now being directed toward these ends.

The Composition of the Seriously Mentally Ill Population

Deinstitutionalization has been a rallying cry for those advocating community care and a target of their critics. Because the term is used imprecisely and is not clearly tied to particular patient populations or relocation sites (Bachrach 1976), it has little empirical utility. Deinstitutionalization is viewed as a source of many current problems and has a certain currency in the ideological debate, but the debate is more a source of heat than light.

Even prior to 1955, most inpatients in public mental hospitals returned to the community. In any given year, the net releases and deaths—the typical way of tracking inpatient occupancy—almost equaled the rate of new admissions. In 1950, for example, there were 152,000 admissions, 100,000 releases, and 41,000 deaths. The longer a patient remained in the hospital, the less the likelihood of release, but a significant proportion of new admissions returned to the community within a few months. Beginning in 1956, net releases and deaths exceeded new admissions but only by 7,952 individuals. It wasn't until 1970 that net releases (excluding deaths) actually exceeded the number of new admissions during the year (U.S. President's Commission on Mental Health 1978). Moreover, in any given year, the vast majority of patients leaving were those who were admitted relatively recently.

These simple data indicate that the deinstitutionalized population is a heterogeneous collection of varying patient cohorts (for a discussion of cohorts, see Ryder 1965). Many would have been returned to the community in the absence of policy change, and common references to the deinstitutionalized seem to refer to clients who have never been part of the long-term mental hospital population at all.

Public mental hospital populations were reduced by deaths, return of a residual group of long-term care patients to nursing homes or other community settings, substantial reduction of the average length of stay among newly admitted patients (median twenty-three days in 1980), and more stringent admission criteria. Of public hospital patients resident in 1955, a large proportion either have since died or have been relocated to nursing homes. Goldman, Feder, and Scanlon (1986) estimate that some 668,000 nursing home patients in 1977 had diagnoses of mental illness or dementia. This population includes transfer from mental hospitals, but most probably came to nursing homes directly from the community. Kiesler and Sibulkin (1987) estimate that as many as half of the elderly discharged from mental hospitals in the post-1964 years came to nursing homes. Nursing homes played a significant role for relocation of the elderly mentally ill but a small role for younger patients. By 1977, only about 5,500 patients under age forty-five and primarily with mental illness were residing in nursing homes (Goldman, Feder, and Scanlon 1986).

The public discussion appears often to refer to the original hospitalized cohorts, but in fact the populations that alarm the community are later cohorts and mostly younger schizophrenics and substance abusers, most of whom have never been long-stay inpatients and some of whom have never had a psychiatric admission at all. As the organization of mental health services has changed, acute psychoses are treated typically with short inpatient admissions in community general hospitals and in reconstituted public mental hospitals. Most such patients have had entirely different histories with the mental health services system than earlier cohorts. Only some proportion of these patients would have been long-term residents of mental hospitals in an earlier era.

The amount of serious mental illness in the population, with schizophrenia as the prototype, depends on both the rate of incidence and the size of the population at risk. Much of the increasingly evident problem of serious mental illness in the community in the 1980s was not due to deinstitutionalization or even to changes in the way psychiatric hospitalization was used, but was more due to shifts in the demography of the population with large subgroups at ages with highest risk of incidence. Morton Kramer (1977) predicted these problems two decades ago simply by projecting demographic trends. The misattribution of the source of changes to deinstitutionalization, vaguely defined, encourages serious errors in policy making. Unless the society was prepared to maintain a massive public hospital system or alternative institutions for new occurrences of mental illness, the problem would have been evident in communities regardless of what we did.

Long-term care in aging provides an analogy. The demand for services is substantially a product of the growth of the elderly population, the increased prevalence of the oldest-old subgroup with high risks of functional disability, and the delay of mortality. Despite having enormously increased nursing home beds at large national expense, providing for 1.7 million residents (Harrington et al., 1977), the numbers of disabled elderly in the community far outnumber those in nursing homes.

A population of major concern to the mental health system, and to the community, are young schizophrenics and other seriously disturbed youths, who are aware of their civil liberties and hostile or indifferent to psychiatric ideologies. They are frequently uncooperative with the types of treatment made available to them, and their mental illnesses are commonly complicated by abuse of drugs and alcohol. They mix with other street people, constitute a significant minority of the homeless population, and at various points in their life trajectories are hospitalized, jailed, or live on the streets (Lamb and Grant 1982; Lamb 1984). The problems are compounded by the fact that the age groups at highest risk have increasing numbers of minority and disadvantaged youth that connect the stigma of mental illness with the social difficulties associated with color and disadvantage. This population poses difficult problems of appropriate treatment and requires approaches for establishing contact and trust that are very different from the conventional office-based mental health services. Blaming deinstitutionalization for these problems is wrongheaded, since most of these patients are not appropriate clients for long-term institutional care. The barriers to designing acceptable care are not constructively addressed by simple distinctions between hospitals versus community services. In contrast, they will depend on carefully developed strategies of community care.

The resistance of many young persons with schizophrenia to traditional psychiatric treatment is not too difficult to appreciate. In addition to the general cultural values and ideologies they have assimilated, they are also typically better educated than earlier cohorts and have hopes and aspirations, however unrealistic they may be, that have been reinforced by television and other mass media and by the broader culture. Many of these youth are undergoing the typical developmental problems of late adolescence and early adulthood in addition to their impairments. It is not easy for them to accept that they have perhaps a lifelong impairment, that they require long-term medication, and that they must yield many of their hopes and expectations for the future. The denial and resistance characteristic of this situation requires mental health workers to engage in much building of trust and to approach these clients in a supportive and patient way.

Homelessness and Mental Illness

There have always been homeless people in large urban areas in this country, but not since the years immediately following the Great Depression has homelessness been so visible (Bassuk 1984a,b). Estimates about the number of homeless have been a form of political rhetoric and have varied widely, depending in part on the political agendas of those announcing the numbers. In 1984 the U.S. Department of Housing and Urban Development (HUD) (1984) estimated the homeless population as 350,000, and most careful studies and analyses suggest that this figure was in the right ballpark (U.S. Government Accounting Office 1985; Freeman and Hall 1986; Rossi et al. 1987; Jencks 1994). Various estimates suggest that the nation's shelter population increased fivefold between 1980 and 1990 (Jencks 1994). The shelter population constitutes a diverse group, however, including both short-term homeless individuals during transitional periods in their lives and long-term residents. Persons with serious mental illness and those with substance abuse problems are more prevalent in the long-term group.

The term *homelessness* conveys an image to most people, but defining and counting the homeless involves complex and changing processes. People who do not have or share a home or apartment may live in many places, including shelters, welfare hotels, in subways and bus stations, on the street, or doubled up with relatives, friends, and acquaintances. But the public and public agencies are more worried about the visible homeless on the streets than those who are doubled up in what may be very unsatisfactory living arrangements. Numbers of homeless are fluid, in part, because should options for decent housing become available, individuals will leave housing arrangements they believe unsatisfactory and will enter shelters or even go on the streets to gain eligibility. Thus, how we respond to homelessness can contribute to the magnitude of the types of visible homelessness that alarm the public. Despite the many different interpretations of homelessness, researchers require a specific definition. One useful definition comes from the McKinney Homeless Assistance Act, enacted by the U.S. Congress, that defined homelessness as having spent "more than seven consecutive nights in a shelter, or in a car, abandoned building, public park, nonresidential building, or other nondwelling" (Bassuk et al. 1996). Various studies indicate that persons who are homeless have many needs that are both medical and social in nature (Bassuk 1984a,b; U.S. General Accounting Office 1985).

Homelessness stems from many different types of problems and encompasses different subpopulations. Thus, it is no surprise that there are disagreements about its causes and its permanence. After a careful examination of the homelessness issue, Jencks (1994) concludes that the main contributors to homelessness in the early 1980s among single adults were increases in long-term joblessness, changes that made it difficult to commit the mentally ill to hospitals involuntarily, release from hospitals of mental patients who had no place to go, the growth in the use of crack, and political restrictions on establishing flophouses. Important factors among families included single motherhood, the loss of purchasing power among mothers, and possibly increased use of crack. Jencks believes that the continuation of high rates of homelessness into the 1990s after some of these factors abated reflected the fact that homelessness policies encouraged more of the invisible homeless such as those living with friends to enter the ranks of more visible homelessness.

In a very careful study of the homeless in Chicago, more than one in three homeless people reported themselves in ill health, a rate twice as high as that found in general population surveys (Rossi and Wright 1987). More than one in four reported having a health problem that prevented their employment. Mental illness and psychiatric symptoms were major sources of disability. Almost one in four Chicago homeless reported having been in a mental hospital for stays of more than forty-eight hours. Nearly half of the Chicago homeless exhibited levels of depression that suggested a need for clinical attention. Contacts with the criminal justice system, suggesting perhaps another kind of disability, were frequent. The cumulative incidence of these disabilities was very large, with 82 percent of the homeless reporting ill health, having been in a mental hospital or detoxification unit, having received clinically high scores on psychiatric symptom scales, or having been sentenced by a court (Rossi et al. 1987).

Studies suggest that for many people homelessness is a temporary situation reflecting changing economic circumstances and housing markets. Although the housed poor have many of the same problems as the homeless population, the homeless poor often have personal and social problems that make them particularly vulnerable during economic downturns such as mental illness, substance abuse, disrupted households, the stigma of arrest and imprisonment, weak family and personal networks, and poor coping skills. A study in Massachusetts, for example, compared AFDC mothers who were never homeless with a sample of AFDC mothers who were in shelters (Bassuk et al. 1996). Those in shelters had less income, less education, a history of more residential instability, and smaller support networks. Both groups had more persons with mental disorders than the general population but did not differ from one another in overall prevalence. However the mothers in shelters had more serious problems, as reflected in higher rates of treatment and prior hospitalization for a mental disorder or substance abuse.

The demographic profile of the homeless changes with time and circumstances, but certain trends are clear. The homeless are disproportionately nonwhite young males with limited education. About two-fifths have substance abuse problems and a third serious psychiatric problems and/or a history of mental illness. A significant minority of young women with children have never been married or have disrupted marriages. In short, this is a poor, vulnerable population (Wright 1989; Bassuk 1984 a,b; Rossi et al. 1987).

Precise estimates of psychiatric problems among the homeless will vary depending on the definitional criteria used, the samples studied and how they were selected, and the particular time of the study, but all studies report high rates of psychiatric symptoms and contact with the specialty mental health system compared to the population as a whole. Incidents of acknowledged prior hospitalization vary from 11 to 33 percent among the homeless, compared to 3 to 7 percent among general adult community samples (Institute of Medicine 1988). A study of the skid-row homeless in Los Angeles using measures comparable to those used in the NIMH ECA study discussed earlier, which derived diagnostic judgments based on survey responses, found that 60 percent of the homeless met criteria for a mental illness or substance abuse disorder—about three times the rate in the general population. Peter Rossi, summarizing twenty-five studies of the homeless, estimated that 27 percent had a history of at least some mental hospital experience; a combination of seventeen studies suggested an average rate of chronic mental illness of 34 percent (Rossi 1989). These figures exceed those characteristic of other poor populations who are also vulnerable to psychiatric problems. Studies also suggest that persons with serious mental illness are more likely than others to remain chronically homeless (Susser et al. 1989.)

By the middle 1980s mental health authorities and programs began to more fully appreciate the critical nature of housing problems and to make housing development and placement a significant component of mental health services. Although mental health services were delivered more aggressively, and often on the street, it has been clear that placing patients in suitable housing with appropriate supervision is an essential part of a good mental health service and a prerequisite for further rehabilitation efforts. Both the federal government and state mental health authorities contributed to increasing the range of housing options that could be fitted to the clinical needs of the client population but the supply of appropriate and affordable housing has yet to catch up with the needs of these programs. Particularly difficult is finding housing arrangements for uncooperative or disruptive individuals who have problems with substance abuse and who get into conflicts with landlords, residence counselors, and other tenants. Some of these clients require supervision but rebel against it and have unstable housing histories.

Addressing the issue of housing and homelessness is now an important component of any serious program for persons with serious and persistent mental illness. It has received a great deal of attention in research and social policy and many new programs have been developed to house clients adequately and prevent loss of residence. The population particularly at risk for homelessness are those with a serious mental illness who also have a comorbid substance use disorder or who use drugs.

Susser and his colleagues (1997) developed an innovative homelessness prevention program structured to strengthen clients' links to services, family, and friends, and to provide emotional and practical support during the transition from shelters to community housing. They randomized 96 seriously mentally ill homeless men who were entering community housing to the "critical time" intervention and to usual services. Over an 18 month follow-up period, the intervention clients on average were homeless for 30 nights as compared with 91 nights for the usual care group. The power of the intervention remained stable over the 18 months studied suggesting that such a critical time intervention could provide protection against future homelessness.

This section of the discussion has been descriptive. Although I have reviewed some of the historical elements in the evolution of mental health policy, I have not examined in any detail the issues and dilemmas that government and mental health agencies face. Much of the rest of this book is directed at these kinds of policy issues. But before taking up such issues in detail, it is important to examine more closely the community processes that lead to definitions of mental illness and to consider some theoretical approaches to community care.

$$Chapter\ \ 6$$

The Recognition of Mental Disorders

The extent to which mental illness is seen to exist depends on the perspectives taken and the criteria used to identify its presence. It is not too difficult to play a numbers game that either maximizes or minimizes the amount of alleged mental illness by changing the criteria used. If mental illness is viewed as the presence of a clearly established disabling condition, then the estimate of its occurrence is conservative. However, if mental illness is defined as the presence of psychosomatic conditions, anxiety, or any of a wide variety of problems in living, then we can characterize a large proportion of the population as having some form of mental illness.

An early study of midtown Manhattan (Srole et al. 1962) estimated that approximately one-quarter of the more than 1,600 respondents between twenty and fifty-nine years of age were impaired. It evaluated only 18.5 percent of the total respondent group as being healthy. Other studies have made similar observations (see Leighton et al. 1963). In a study of the prevalence of mental disorders in Kalamazoo County, Michigan (Manis et al. 1964), in which various data comparable to those collected in midtown Manhattan were obtained, the investigators demonstrated that the rates of mental illness in midtown Manhattan were not greatly different from those in the community they studied but were inflated by the different criteria used.

> *Our interpretation is that the differences in reported rates of untreated illness arise primarily from lack of agreement, stated or implicit, in the criteria used to establish the cutting-point between the sick and the well. The criterion used in the Kalamazoo community study appears to identify only the extremely ill and to underestimate total prevalence. The Baltimore procedures seem to focus on a more broadly conceived spectrum of mental illness, though they, too, admit some underestimation. The rates reported for Midtown Manhattan are apparently the consequence of a very inclusive conception of mental illness. (Manis et al. 1964, p. 89)*

Plunkett and Gordon (1960), reviewing prevalence studies undertaken prior to 1960, note that percentages of the population found to be mentally ill ranged from less than 2 percent to as much as 33 percent (pp. 62–68). With the inadequacies of the measures used in various surveys and field studies, it seems reasonable to use such indices primarily for assessing relative differences among population groups rather than to treat the absolute levels of disorder reported as meaningful assessments (Davis 1965).

Bruce and Barbara Dohrenwend (1969) clearly illustrated the unreliability of various absolute estimates of psychiatric illness. In reviewing twenty-five studies of untreated cases of psychological disorder, they found that prevalence rates varied from less than 1 percent to over 60 percent of the population. Comparing epidemiological studies carried out in 1950 or earlier with those done after 1950, they found widely varying rates of pathology. The median rate in the studies after 1950 was more than seven times the one reported for the earlier studies. Because it is inconceivable that population rates have changed so radically, it is clear that these estimates reflect something other than traditionally defined psychiatric syndromes.

By considering limited categories of mental illness, one can increase the possibility of making some reasonable estimate of morbidity. Investigators in different countries, using relatively narrow concepts of schizophrenia, agree that the prevalence of active cases varies from approximately one-quarter to 1 percent of the population (J. K. Wing 1967; L. Wing et al. 1967; National Institute of Mental Health 1985). As the concept expands, of course, the prevalence rate increases. From the point of view of public policy, questions concerning the prevalence of mental illness must be linked to decisions concerning the appropriate range of facilities that should be provided. Once we have some conception of which conditions it is reasonable to treat, we can estimate the extent of the problem we have to deal with.

Planning for psychiatric services is not vastly different from planning for general medical services. If we wish to improve the facilities available for dealing with a variety of diseases for which medical care is important, and we require estimates of community needs, we do not survey the population to determine the prevalence of common self-limited complaints. Similarly, in deciding the magnitude of psychiatric need in the population, we must not confuse the psychiatric conditions causing profound distress and disability with the prevalence of mild difficulties and mild psychophysiological complaints. I do not wish to imply that help should not be available to those who have mild difficulties, but, just as we do not confuse the common cold with heart disease, so we should not confuse psychoses and major depression with occasional sadness and other common complaints. The DSM has now eliminated neurosis as a psychiatric category because of its imprecision, but the concept is still widely used among mental health professionals and the lay public. Estimates of the proportion of the population who were neurotic ranged from less than 5 percent to almost everyone. Some mental health professionals with a psychodynamic perspective argued that we are all to some degree neurotic and could all benefit from a better understanding of our intrapsychic needs and repressed desires. While such a point of view may have some value as a philosophical statement, the absence of clear criteria for discriminating among those more or less needy makes such statements useless in the development of social policy.

As already noted, a significant proportion of the U.S. population have a mental illness as defined by the DSM. But such estimates are not very helpful unless we can differentiate the extent to which persons with various conditions suffer distress, are incapacitated, and can successfully be treated. It is irresponsible to confuse mild and self-limited conditions with those that cause severe discomfort and prevent persons from performing social roles and preferred activities. Although it is essential to provide help to people in despair, in the allocation of treatment resources it is also important to consider which conditions benefit most from treatment and the relative cost-effectiveness of different ways of treating particular conditions. If in some instances less-expensive drugs work as effectively as more-expensive, long-term psychotherapies, it is difficult to justify the more expensive, but no more effective treatment. Public policy requires some flexibility. Some patients cannot tolerate drugs but still require treatment and others may do best with combinations of drugs and psychotherapy. But when the public is subsidizing the cost of services, people cannot simply demand whatever they want.

Except in the case of the clearest psychiatric conditions demanding public intervention, it is very difficult to estimate the need for facilities because the need for care is ordinarily not defined by professional criteria, but rather by members of the community who decide whether to seek psychiatric care for themselves or others and under what conditions. Because definition and intervention occur within the community, we should understand the social and personal processes through which persons come to see themselves or others as suffering from a psychiatric condition and the way they come to the attention of psychiatric facilities.

Mental Illness, Illness Behavior, and Entry into Psychiatric Care

Every society recognizes behavior outside certain limits as deviant, and madness exists in every culture.

> *Explicit labels for insanity exist in these cultures. The labels refer to beliefs, feelings, and actions that are thought to emanate from the mind or inner state of an individual and to be essentially beyond his control. . . . Almost everywhere a pattern composed of hallucinations, delusions, disorientations, and behavioral aberrations appears to identify the idea of "losing one's mind," even though the content of these manifestations is colored by cultural beliefs. (Murphy 1976, p. 1027)*

The conditions under which individuals, their significant others, and a community are sensitive to particular symptoms or behavior depend on their knowledge and beliefs and the impact of the deviance in a particular context. Whether their concept is broad or narrow, whether they intervene readily or only reluctantly, and whether they are blaming or supportive vary by time and place. As Clausen and Huffine (1975) note, however, the social definition of mental illness depends not so much on one or another symptom as on the accumulation of many inexplicable actions. These can be judged only by social context, and even clinicians in making judgments of mental processes within a narrow conception of psychiatric illness must take the context into account in evaluating the abnormality of thought and behavior.

Depending on the culture and social group, illness may be readily recognized and defined by the persons themselves or only after it becomes a social issue and others in the community demand some action. A wide range of variables affects the recognition of disorder and initiation of care (Mechanic 1978, 1982), and these are briefly described in the following list. Interestingly, these same variables apply to the definition of physical and psychological disorder:

1. The visibility, recognizability, or perceptual salience of deviant signs and symptoms
2. The extent to which the person perceives the symptoms as serious (that is, the person's estimate of the present and future probabilities of danger)
3. The extent to which symptoms disrupt family, work, and other social activities
4. The frequency of the appearance of deviant signs or symptoms, or their persistence, or their frequency of recurrence
5. The tolerance threshold of those who are exposed to and evaluate the deviant signs and symptoms
6. The information available to, the knowledge of, and the cultural assumptions and understandings of the evaluator
7. The degree to which autistic psychological processes (perceptual processes that distort reality) are present
8. The presence of needs that conflict with the recognition of illness or the assumption of the sick role
9. The possibility that competing interpretations can be assigned to the symptoms once they are recognized
10. The availability of treatment resources, their physical proximity, and the psychological and monetary costs of taking action (including not only physical distance and costs of time, money, and effort, but also stigmatization, resulting social distance, and feelings of humiliation resulting from a particular illness definition)

It may appear curious that I should attempt to group together factors affecting the recognition and the definition of both psychiatric and nonpsychiatric disorders because we know that mental patients are often brought into care through different pathways from those followed by people who suffer from general medical conditions. A large proportion of psychotics among the lower class are first recognized as mentally ill when their bizarre behavior becomes visible to community authorities; such persons are frequently brought to a psychiatric facility by police. Alcoholics and drug addicts brought into treatment often come through official routes, such as the courts, the police, or community social agencies. Despite these different pathways to care, the social processes leading to the recognition and the identification of general medical conditions and those leading to the recognition of psychiatric problems are similar. All illness is defined because the person directly concerned or others become aware that some deviation from a normal state has taken place. The community may have more tolerance for a person with a broken leg or for one who is shy and withdrawn than for the alcoholic who disturbs others or the schizophrenic who verbalizes thoughts no one can understand. The differences, however, in defining a person with a broken leg and in defining a disruptive alcoholic stem not from different social processes but rather from the manner in which these problems become manifest and from their effect on social life, social activities, and social values. If you are aware that a member of your living group has active tuberculosis and refuses to seek treatment—thus exposing you to the disease—you might choose to use official agencies to ensure that the ill person is removed from contact with you and does not threaten the public safety. What makes ordinary medical conditions different from some psychiatric ones, from the public's standpoint, are the various ways in which psychiatric disorders differ in terms of the ten dimensions already noted.

We have no way of predicting the specific response to any condition. The definitions of normality by which deviation is judged vary among medical practitioners as well as among lay persons, especially in the area of psychiatric disorders. More frequently than not, individuals come to view themselves as ill on the basis of their own standards of functioning as well as on their previous knowledge and experience, and when marked deviations are apparent they tend to seek medical confirmation. On other occasions individuals do not recognize themselves as sick but come to accept this definition when some other person defines them as ill (for example, persons who are informed that they have hypertension or tuberculosis, although they may not actually recognize that they are ill). In some instances of mental illness, persons defined by others as sick vigorously resist this diagnosis. The definition that one is mentally ill involves a considerable change in one's self-identity, and the effects of treatment are often perceived as uncertain or harmful. Even the difference between psychiatric and nonpsychiatric conditions can be exaggerated, however, and the overlap is considerable.

The manner in which deviant feelings or behavior becomes evident may have varying disruptive effects on social life and may be associated with more or less stigma. Although some mentally ill persons withdraw from social interaction and cause no disruption in the community, others engage in visible, bizarre behavior that is threatening and frightening to others. The person whose symptoms are not disruptive is not so readily defined because the public's conceptions of health and mental illness tend to be sharply polarized. Because the behavior of mentally ill persons is viewed as markedly different from that of normal individuals, the public frequently stigmatizes persons so defined. Psychiatric conditions, as opposed to nonpsychiatric ones, tend to be more disruptive and associated with greater stigma, but we should again note that this difference is a quantitative rather than a qualitative one. We do not need to consider the social processes underlying the definitions of psychiatric and nonpsychiatric conditions separately, as long as we give attention to such factors as social disruption, stigma, and resistance to accepting a definition of illness.

The ten categories pertain equally to situations in which individuals define themselves as ill and in which others regard them as *sick*. Let us consider the way these categories apply to a person suffering from a self-defined depressive condition and to an alcoholic defined as a problem by the community. The recognition of a depressive illness may follow a period during which a person experiences feelings of sadness and emptiness more profound than usual, difficulty getting going, loss of interest in life, and sluggishness. Depression, however, is a fairly common symptom, and the person must recognize that this depression is more serious than previous episodes. This recognition, in turn, depends on the extent to which the symptoms disrupt activities, the persistence of the depression and associated symptoms, and tolerance for psychological pain. A self-definition of illness may depend on whether the depressed state is sufficiently profound so the person cannot get out of bed, get to work, or take on usual responsibilities and activities, and on whether the symptoms are persistent or fluctuating. It may be possible to assign competing definitions to the symptoms. If there has been some adversity, such as the death or injury of a loved one or a personal defeat in work or family life, the person may define his or her feeling state and condition as a temporary response to a frustrating and unhappy situation. But should these symptoms occur independently of adversity, the problem is likely to be viewed as coming from within the individual.

These categories can be applied equally well to definitions of alcoholics, schizophrenics, or other persons often designated by the community as mentally ill. The community is more likely to define individuals as alcoholics when their drinking is visible rather than private and when their drinking pattern extends beyond that ordinarily thought of as conventional. The definition of and response of others to such excessive drinking depend on the extent to which the drinking disrupts work, family, and other community activities and the frequency with which the person becomes drunk. If drinking leads to work absenteeism, conflict within the family, and embarrassing family situations, people are more likely to be defined as problems than if they drink themselves to sleep at night and do not disrupt family life or fail to meet social obligations. Persons in the community may have more or less tolerance for drinking and drunkenness. They may not take note of a happy drunk but may react punitively to a drunk involved in fights or driving a motor vehicle. They may react differently to drunk men and women. It is not my intent to go into each of these matters in any detail. The point is that from a conceptual view, we do not need to develop separate categories for the factors underlying the social definition of illness made by the persons themselves and for those underlying the definitions made by others (for a more complete discussion, see Mechanic 1978).

There has been considerable work directed at examining the selective processes by which individuals with various types of symptoms find their way to different types of care (Goldberg and Huxley 1980; Mechanic 1982). David Goldberg and Peter Huxley (1980) have defined four filters between a community population and an inpatient unit that can be examined in elucidating the psychiatric help-seeking process. First, there are studies at the community level, such as the ECA studies reviewed earlier, that attempt to ascertain who in the population have varying conditions and what types of help they seek. The first filter defines who in a population arrives at helpers of first contact. Most studies focus on physician use, but any type of informal or formal care seeking could be the object of inquiry. A second filter concerns whether the source of care (typically a physician) recognizes the patient's psychiatric distress, symptoms, or conditions. A third filter concerns referral to a secondary source of care, such as a mental health specialist. Depending on the illness behavior of the patient, the second filter is commonly bypassed and patients come directly to a mental health specialist, particularly in the United States. The fourth filter is admission to a psychiatric bed. This perspective can be extended to examine exchanges between acute and chronic beds, hospital beds and nursing home beds, partial-care and total-care beds, and the like, but there are limited returns in elaborating the number of filters. The number of filters to be studied, and the level of detail, depends on the policy issues of greatest importance. The more basic idea to remember is that many individual, social, cultural, and economic factors affect the exchanges among levels of care and how individuals come to pass through various selective filters.

For example, a considerable literature supports the observation that mental health status, insurance, sociodemographic variations, attitudes, social networks, other social and cultural variables, and characteristics of the health care delivery system all affect the likelihood of a mental health contact. In New Haven, the relative odds of a mental health contact of any kind within the previous six months were substantially greater among those who had a regular source of medical care (3.06 to 1), who were receptive to professionals (2.42 to 1), who were young adults (2.11 to 1), who used clinics (1.76 to 1), and who were white (1.95 to 1), unmarried (1.64 to 1), female (1.49 to 1), and had some college education (1.42 to 1) (Leaf et al. 1985). In Baltimore, unmet need for mental health care was found to be most substantial among the elderly, among nonwhites, and among those with eight or less years of education (Shapiro et al. 1985). A number of behavioral models have been developed to account for the wide variety of social, cultural, and attitudinal factors that affect the use of mental health services (Mechanic 1975; Greenley, Mechanic, and Cleary 1987). Some of these factors affect help seeking in general, while others help explain alternative choices among mental health providers (Greenley and Mechanic 1976; Greenley, Mechanic, and Cleary 1987).

Various investigators have studied the conditions under which a particular set of symptoms is viewed from a psychiatric frame of reference or from another perspective. Charles Kadushin (1958), in interviews with 110 persons using a psychiatric clinic, attempted to ascertain how they decided to undertake psychotherapy. He found that such a decision is a five-step process:

1. Persons must decide that they have a problem and that it is an emotional one.
2. They must decide whether to discuss the problem with relatives and friends.
3. They must decide at some point whether they are adequately dealing with the problem and whether to seek professional help.
4. If they choose to seek professional help, they must choose an appropriate profession from which to seek help.
5. They must select a particular practitioner.

In his clinic sample Kadushin found four characteristic ways of recognizing a problem: being told by others; experiencing painful physical symptoms; being unhappily married; and feeling unhappy in general. In a further analysis of social distance between client and professional, Kadushin (1962) found that stable interaction is most likely when there is little social distance between role partners, so that professionals who are socially close to clients are likely to be consulted. He further points out that the patient's lack of familiarity with the psychotherapist's role can also be a problem. Kadushin thinks that some of these problems are alleviated through the presence of a subculture of friends and supporters of psychotherapy, and he argues that knowing others who have had psychiatric treatment, being told by one's friends to go to a psychiatrist, having one's problems noticed by others, and reading works on psychoanalysis are characteristics of those belonging to this subculture (1962, p. 530, 1966). Kadushin's analysis pertains only to some kinds of psychiatric patients; the process of defining oneself as mentally ill may vary substantially from one type of psychiatric condition to another.

If the subculture Kadushin describes exists and makes persons more receptive to particular treatment contexts, then the use of some psychiatric services may depend not so much on the seriousness of the person's condition as on whether he or she is a member of the informal subculture. A study by Scheff (1966) of users and nonusers of a student psychiatric clinic sheds some light on this issue. Scheff compared a sample of student applications for psychiatric help with a random sample of the population that had free access to this psychiatric clinic. The items on the questionnaires administered to both groups were almost identical; they had been developed from studying the problems of previous students who had applied for psychiatric help. Scheff found that the number of problems students reported was strongly related to application for psychiatric care: 59 percent of the clinic applicants had ten or more problems, while only 35 percent of the nonusers had a similar number. The most striking aspect of this result, however, is the extensive overlap between clinic applicants and the random sample in respect to the problem inventory. An equally impressive result is that religion and religious participation were more effective predictors of clinic applications than was the number of problems students had. Overall, Scheff found that the clinic sample had an overrepresentation of persons with similar social backgrounds and similar social activities.

Linn (1967), in another study of the same psychiatric clinic, provides evidence in support of the general idea developed by Kadushin. In comparing clinic applicants with a random sample to whom clinic services were available, Linn argued that there would be an overrepresentation of applications from the group of students who were less integrated into traditional social institutions, who were more likely to identify with other students who were cosmopolitan, who were more likely to report that they had friends with socioemotional problems, and who discussed such problems with others. Linn found considerable evidence in support of these ideas. He found an overrepresentation of clinic applications among those who reported that their friends were interested in psychology, were concerned about meaning in life, and were sensitive and introspective. He found an underrepresentation of those who reported that they liked football games, were religious, and had friends who were usually well dressed (see also Bart, 1968).

Although these studies were provocative, they fail to resolve several important issues. First, they fail to indicate to what extent the characteristics associated with psychiatric use reflect their correlation with symptoms as compared with patterns of seeking help. If certain patterns of behavior are associated with more symptoms, it may be the symptoms and not the behavior that results in going to a psychiatrist. Second, persons with the same problems may go to varying types of helping facilities or cope in other ways. It is not clear from these studies whether the patterns associated with going to a psychiatrist are linked with a general tendency to seek help or, more specifically, associated with going to a particular source of help.

To study this problem, my colleague James Greenley and I examined who among a random sample of more than 1,500 university students who sought psychiatric and counseling care (Greenley and Mechanic 1976; Mechanic and Greenley 1976). Although the magnitude of psychological symptoms was the most important influence in seeking help, cultural characteristics, attitudes, knowledge, and group identifications among students with comparable symptoms had an important effect on the propensity to seek care for psychological problems. We found, however, that most predictors were specific to a particular source of care. Jewish students were more likely to go to the outpatient psychiatry clinic; Catholic students were more likely to seek help from religious counselors on campus. When we took account of most types of formal help seeking, only very few characteristics differentiated those who sought help from those who did not. Women, for example, were more likely than men to seek help from general physicians, psychiatrists, and the counseling center. Students who sought help were more inclined toward introspection, were acquainted with more users of services, and had a higher reported general propensity to seek help for psychological problems. These findings support the idea that the occurrence of symptoms encourages persons to search out the meaning of their experiences and feelings. Certain orientations, such as introspection and psychological awareness, push the person toward defining the problem in a psychological context. Once the student decides to seek care, sociocultural influences, social networks, and personal values as well as knowledge of available facilities orient the student to a particular type of assistance. These results have been replicated in a large community population (Greenley, Mechanic, and Cleary, 1987).

In recent years, researchers have been giving more attention to attribution processes—the way people interpret their experiences and the causes of events. Psychological distress may be interpreted in many ways—as a psychological, social, or moral problem, for example. The schemas available in the person's social context may have major effects on the way feelings and experiences are construed (Mechanic 1972b). The women's movement is an interesting example of the emergence of widely accepted social explanations of women's distress. In earlier decades, housewives feeling a sense of malaise and unfulfillment as wives and mothers had difficulty explaining their feelings in terms other than their own inadequacies or failures. The women's movement, however, now gives support for explaining such distress less in personal terms and more as a result of inequalities, blocked opportunities, and exploitative role arrangements. The source of distress is defined outside oneself and offers different opportunities for coping.

Community Definitions of Mental Illness

Many psychiatric conditions are defined not by the persons themselves but by others in the community who note bizarre behavior or failure to meet expected standards. Such labeling of a particular person as mentally ill depends on the various contingencies discussed earlier. In addition to the influences of different personal and social factors, the character of the symptoms themselves exerts a considerable effect on whether a person is defined as mentally ill. Although there are vast differences in willingness to tolerate bizarre and difficult behavior, few relatives are willing to house a patient who is suicidal, homicidal, incontinent, hallucinatory, delusional, or disoriented (Angrist et al. 1961). If the patients are sufficiently bizarre and disruptive, the probability is extremely high that they will come into care. Social definitions of illness are relevant because many serious illnesses do not develop in a particularly striking way. The ambiguity surrounding the occurrence and the severity of illness makes sociological variables important.

Although the public's conception of mental illness has been changing, there is still considerable reluctance to define a relative or friend as mentally ill and a strong tendency to normalize and to deny symptoms that become apparent. Many people still visualize mental illnesses as extreme states of disorganized behavior and as a sharp break from usual or familiar patterns. Lesser psychiatric difficulties are often viewed as physical conditions or as indications of normal variabilities in personality. When persons' symptoms are accompanied by physical indications, they are often urged to seek medical help; but should their difficult behavior be inconsistent with a physical interpretation, then it is often attributed to stubbornness or moral defects rather than to illness.

Clausen and Yarrow (1955) and their colleagues, in a unique study of mental health definitions, described five trends characterizing the process through which wives of psychiatric patients attempted to cope with their husbands' mental illness and increasingly difficult behavior: (1) the wife's first recognition of a problem depends on the accumulation of behavior that is not readily understandable or acceptable to her; (2) this recognition forces her to examine the situation and to adjust her expectations for herself and for her husband to account for his deviant response; (3) the wife's interpretation of the problem shifts back and forth from seeing the situation as normal on one occasion to seeing it as abnormal on another; (4) she tends to make continuous adaptations to the behavior of her spouse, waiting for additional cues that either confirm her definition or lead to a new one—that is, she mobilizes strong defenses against her husband's deviant behavior; and (5) finally, she reaches the point at which she can no longer sustain a definition of normality and cope with her husband's behavior. Yarrow et al. (1955) observe the following tendencies.

> *The most obvious form of defense in the wife's response is the tendency to* nor-malize *the husband's neurotic and psychotic symptoms. His behavior is explained, justified, or made acceptable by seeing it also in herself or by assuring herself that the particular behavior occurs again and again among persons who are not ill . . . when behavior cannot be normalized, it can be made to seem less severe or less important in a total picture than an outsider might see it. . . . By finding some grounds for the behavior or something explainable about it, the wife achieves at least momentary* attenuation *of the seriousness of it. By* balancing *acceptable with unacceptable behavior or "strange" with "normal" behavior, some wives can conclude that the husband is not seriously disturbed. . . . Defense sometimes amounts to a thoroughgoing* denial. *This takes the form of denying that the behavior perceived can be interpreted in an emotional or psychiatric framework. (Yarrow et al. 1955, pp. 22–23)*

The strong tendency of relatives and the community to normalize difficult patterns of behavior until they can no longer be tolerated has relevance for public policy because it encourages long delays in seeking treatment. Awareness of such common tendencies has encouraged public health psychiatrists to support efforts toward public education. Many argue that it is first necessary to educate the public to recognize the appearance of mental illness in its earliest manifestations and to view seeking aid for these problems as appropriate. Efforts have been made in recent years to provide community facilities that are especially prepared to deal with these problems. The evidence is that such public education and the increase in access to acceptable psychiatric and other counseling facilities and practitioners have resulted in many persons with mild and moderate problems receiving care. A research group from the University of Michigan's Institute for Social Research studied public views of mental illness in 1957 (Gurin et al. 1960) and completed a similar study of over 2,000 respondents in 1976, using many of the same questions (Institute for Social Research 1979, Kulka, Veroff, and Douvan 1979, 1981). They found that over the twenty-year period, use of professional help for psychological problems increased from 14 to 26 percent, although the levels of well-being in the population were approximately the same.

A number of questions asked on the University of Michigan surveys were repeated in 1996 on the General Social Survey with a representative sample of the U.S. population. (Swindle et al. 1997). In the period from 1957 to 1996 there was substantially increased help seeking for mental health problems in the population and some major changes in the types of help sought. Most dramatic has been the growing dependence on informal sources of help, from 4 percent of the population in 1957 to 26 percent in 1996. Use of mental health specialists also increased from 1 percent to 22 percent during this period. Within the formal system of care, people now depend less on general medical care and psychiatric treatment and more on treatment provided by social workers and counselors. In 1996, almost 15 percent reported having seen social workers or counselors for a "nervous breakdown" or mental health problem as compared with only 3.5 percent reporting seeing psychiatrists.

Despite these gains, however, the fact is that seriously disturbed patients who require care do not come into treatment. Weissman and Myers (1978) in their New Haven study found that only one-quarter of the respondents studied with any diagnosis, including major depression, sought professional help for the problem in the previous year. Brown and Harris (1978) noted comparable findings concerning depression in the Camberwell area of London. These findings were replicated again in the ECA Study (Leaf et al. 1985; Shapiro et al. 1985). The relatively low proportion of persons with DSM diagnoses who sought help was confirmed again in the National Comorbidity Study (Kessler et al. 1994).

Families cope with mental illness in various ways. Sampson et al. (1964) found that husbands withdrew from their symptomatic schizophrenic wives, thus insulating themselves from their wives' disturbed and bizarre behavior. Contrary to popular belief, depressed women in families are not passive, but often are irritable and combative (Weissman and Paykel 1974). One way in which family members deal with such behavior is to withdraw emotionally and ignore the distressed person. Often there is a vicious cycle, with the withdrawal and rejection resulting in even more depressed and disturbed behavior. Symptoms that are not physically threatening or not so bizarre that they result in social difficulties may be tolerated for years before action is taken. Treatment may be sought when the family's ability to cope breaks down because of some change in the family's internal or outside relationships. One finding of a study of children brought to a clinic, compared with children having similar symptoms but not brought into treatment, was the inability of the mother to cope and her own anxiety and depression (Shepherd, Oppenheim, and Mitchell 1966).

This failure to recognize mental illness and at times the blatant denial of it are not such simple or clear-cut issues as they may seem. Large costs may be involved in recognizing oneself, one's spouse, or one's child as mentally ill. The definitional act itself often involves major changes in the structure of interaction in the family; indeed, the recognition that a member of the family is mentally ill requires a major reorganization of the family itself. Once the definition is made and action is taken, the act is in many ways irreversible. The meanings that members of the family assign to one another have been changed, the stigma of mental illness is difficult to completely reverse, and perhaps what is most important of all, psychiatric assistance may not make any significant difference in restoring "normality" to the situation.

From a policy perspective, there is at least one other consideration. Many of these crises may be transient ones, and the usual patterns of family living may be restored without psychiatric intervention. The studies and observations on normalization are extremely biased ones. They concentrate on situations in which the *normalization process has failed and has led to further problems.* Although we have no adequate data to make an absolute judgment, these situations may constitute a small percentage of the total population of cases in which bizarre behavior occurs and normalization takes place.

In many cases early and effective treatment of disorder may reduce suffering, minimize disability and family disruption, and even prevent suicide. Excellent treatments now exist for controlling some of the worst symptoms of schizophrenia, bipolar depression, other major depressive disorders, and phobias. In many other areas, however, treatment and its value are more dubious, and there is limited benefit in encouraging persons into treatment considering the monetary and psychological costs. Although encouragement and support of persons undergoing life crises are necessary, the act of defining people's behavior as indicative of a psychiatric condition may undermine their limited self-confidence and efforts at continuing to cope in work and family life, and it may encourage a stance of dependency that leads to further disability and the acceptance of illness. The major challenge faced by new programs is to provide sustenance and help to those who are going through difficult crises without defining and structuring their problems so as to increase the probability of disability.

To some extent, the experience of the military illustrates the consequences of various alternatives. Evaluations of the use of psychotherapy in dealing with neuropsychiatric casualties indicate that the manner of providing care has a bearing on the effectiveness of the soldier. Glass (1953) reports that when psychiatric casualties were evacuated to mental health facilities during the North African and Sicilian campaigns in World War II, few soldiers were salvaged for combat duty. The psychiatrist, prior to the development of new military mental health policies, usually assumed that the patient was ill and "sought to uncover basic emotional conflicts or attempted to relate current behavior and symptoms with past personality patterns" (p. 288). This administrative policy seemingly provided patients with rational reasons for their combat failures. Both the patient and the therapist were often readily convinced that the limit of combat endurance had been reached. In contrast, when psychiatrists treated soldiers in the combat zone with such interpersonal devices as suggestion and influence, a much higher percentage of men returned to combat. Glass (1958) argued that neuropsychiatric illness was often the result of an attempt to adapt to or withdraw from dangerous combat circumstances.

> *It should be recognized that both symptoms and behavioral abnormalities represent a meaningful effort at adaptation under stress. Inability to cope with threatening or dangerous situations evokes substitute behavior of an evasive or regressive pattern in an effort to reach some satisfactory compromise solution for both*

internal needs and external demands. Even in the bizarre types of combat psychiatric breakdown, such as mutism or uncontrolled panic flight, one can discern primitive attempts to withdraw or escape from a terrorizing environment. Less severe abnormalities, such as hysterical paralysis, self-inflicted wounds, and AWOL from battle, more readily portray their purposeful nature. In the more mild forms of combat fatigue, characterized by tremulousness, tearfulness and verbal surrender, a childish dependent adaptation is quite evident. The form or type of psychological noneffective behavior displayed in combat is not determined so much by individual personality characteristics as it is dictated either by the practical circumstances of the battle situation or by group (including medical) acceptance of such symptoms or behavior. (Glass 1958, pp. 194–195)

We can make a rough assessment of the scope and importance of social definitions in determining morbidity by evaluating the effects of changing psychiatric policies in the military. Despite the shifts in military psychiatric policy from before World War II to after the Korean War, there was an impressive consistency in the rates of admission to hospitals for armed forces personnel. This consistency suggests that changes in policy had little effect on the occurrence of psychoses requiring hospital care. The invulnerability of rates of psychosis to changing public policies is also supported by the facts that such rates are approximately the same in wartime and in peacetime and that they did not differ appreciably in the two wars under consideration. Additional evidence shows that extreme combat conditions or exposure to bombing attacks does not have any apparent effect on the rate of occurrence of psychotic conditions (Glass 1958; Group for the Advancement of Psychiatry 1960, pp. 290–291; also see the discussion of the influence of stress in Chapter 4).

In contrast, the rates of admission for psychoneurotic conditions fluctuated widely. Among army active-duty personnel, they were considerably higher in wartime than in peacetime and considerably higher in World War II than in the Korean War. The conflicting conceptions of psychoneurosis and the lack of reliability in its diagnosis allow such rates to be easily manipulated. In all overseas theaters in World War II, approximately 23 percent of all evacuations resulted from psychiatric causes; in Japan and Korea from September 1950 to May 1951, the comparable figure was only 6 percent. Military psychiatric policies during these periods appear to have had considerable influence on the rate of defined neurotic conditions.

Good evidence suggests that the much lower proportion of evacuations for psychiatric reasons in the Korean War resulted from more than the manipulation of the definition of psychoneurosis. During the Korean War, the Army developed a preventive program to retain manpower and to cut down the level of neuropsychiatric casualties. The core of the new program was to provide brief supportive treatment in the combat zone and to avoid a hospital atmosphere or one conducive to the soldier adopting a patient role. Studies of such neuropsychiatric cases returned to duty show that their performance was comparable to that of other returnees hospitalized for disease or injury or excused for administrative reasons (Group for the Advancement of Psychiatry 1960, pp. 291–292). The Navy's experience was similar to that of the Army. In the Korean War, marines were given supportive treatment close to the front; few were evacuated, and psychiatric casuality rates were one-tenth of those in World War II (Group for the Advancement of Psychiatry 1960, p. 294).

Such programs of administrative support and therapy based on viewing the soldiers' difficulties as being within the normal range under stress do not necessarily cure psychiatric problems, but they do ensure more effective behavior. Few forms of therapy are curative. From the perspective of the military, the psychiatric policies pursued during and after the Korean War were less costly and more useful in promoting effective behavior than were those used in previous wars.

The military situation also sheds light on another matter discussed in Chapter 4 that must be kept in mind. Incidence of psychoses shows little responsiveness to changing conditions and administrative policies, and this suggests—although it cannot be proved—that such conditions are not part of the same continuum as psychoneurotic conditions, which appear to fluctuate widely under varying stress conditions. If we can apply the military experience to other contexts, then mental health policy in relation to chronic mental conditions of a psychotic nature must be formulated on the basis of different considerations from those given to psychoneurotic conditions and other problems of living. What is true of the incidence of psychoses is not necessarily true of their course, however. Understanding social and environmental factors helps considerably in maintenance and rehabilitation of psychotic patients.

The Course of Schizophrenia

Clinicians have commonly viewed schizophrenia as an intractable condition with an inevitable deteriorating course. A large number of studies now refute this conception and demonstrate the possibilities for minimizing disabilities and maintaining a higher level of function than most psychiatrists believed likely. Such traditional perceptions by clinicians reflect the limited perspective through which they see patients. Their conceptions are very much influenced by the treatment failures they see over and over again and less by the larger epidemiological picture. Both epidemiological and clinical follow-up studies demonstrate that the actual course of events is more positive. These studies show extraordinary variability in adaptation and levels of functioning, and they were reviewed earlier. Our focus here is with factors that possibly explain the variable course of the disorder.

Findings from studies converge in suggesting a complex and differentiated course of illness depending on social and environmental conditions. A good illustration is the International Pilot Study of Schizophrenia, which followed 1,202 patients in nine countries (World Health Organization 1979). At two-year follow-up, 27 percent of schizophrenics had a complete recovery after the initial episode, and 26 percent had several psychotic attacks with periods of complete or partial recovery. Five-year follow-up in a subsample of American patients was highly correlated with appraisals at two years (Strauss and Carpenter 1977). Most striking in the international study is the large variation between developed and developing countries, with proportions of patients showing complete recovery varying from 6 percent in Denmark to 58 percent in Nigeria.

There was some skepticism expressed about these findings by researchers who noted that patients studied were not representative samples of schizophrenic patients in each society, and, thus, selection biases might have occurred. Thus, in a second collaborative study (Sartorius et al. 1986), efforts were made to identify representative samples of new cases of schizophrenia in each of ten countries. This was achieved by monitoring defined populations over a two-year period to identify first contacts of psychotic patients with a wide range of helping agencies, including indigenous healers. Great care was taken to identify patients in different cultures by the same criteria, and, in fact, subsequent analysis showed that the symptom profiles of schizophrenic patients in varying samples were similar. Again, the investigators found that the two-year pattern of schizophrenic illness was more favorable in developing countries; while 56 percent of schizophrenics in such countries had a mild course over the two-year period, only 39 percent had comparable outcomes in the developed nations studied.

Waxler (1979), in a careful five-year follow-up study of schizophrenics in Sri Lanka, found that 45 percent were symptom-free as measured by the Psychiatric Status Schedule developed by Spitzer and colleagues. Fifty percent were rated by the psychiatrists as having adjusted normally; 58 percent were seen by their families as having normal social performance; and 42 percent had no impairment in the previous six months. Almost half of the patients were said to have worked continuously over the previous five years, according to their families. Even allowing for errors in measurement, this is an impressive outcome, and at variance with typical Western conceptions of the course of schizophrenia. Waxler carefully examined possible artifacts in her results and makes a persuasive case that her findings are indicative of important cultural differences, and she suggests a social labeling model as the best approach to understanding these differences.

Another alternative is that in rural contexts schizophrenics can more easily continue to play an economic role and can insulate themselves from interpersonal stresses and intense associations. In some cultural contexts, there may be strong mutual expectations within kinship structures that encourage efforts at functioning from the patient and more acceptance from the community (Kleinman and Mechanic 1979). Family members may be less critical of the patient, a factor associated with less exacerbation of symptomatology (Leff 1978). While some of the best outcome results have been noted in underdeveloped countries or in rural contexts in developed nations, good outcomes have also been reported from industrialized cities in Europe, suggesting a more complex process than can be explained by such gross comparisons alone. Predictors of long-term course have not been effectively identified, but continuing efforts in this area are necessary.

In the short term, expressed emotion seems to be an important prognostic factor. A growing body of research indicates that schizophrenic patients do less well in family environments characterized by negative emotional relationships and criticisms (Brown et al. 1962, 1972; Vaughn and Leff 1976; Leff 1978; Leff and Vaughn 1985). While these effects are attenuated to a considerable degree when patients are maintained on neuroleptic medications, differences in outcome persist even among medicated patients. Patients who have less face-to-face contact with relatives are also less likely to relapse in families with high expressed emotion (Vaughn and Leff 1976; Leff 1978).

The work on expressed emotion has now been examined in the context of India (Wig et al. 1987), a country that has been found to have a more favorable prognosis of schizophrenia in the World Health Organization studies. In large part, the findings in Western countries have been replicated, but with some intriguing differences. First, in the Indian context, hostility of significant others was the primary predictive factor. Unlike the West, criticism was often not associated with hostility, and criticism by itself was not predictive of relapse. Even more instructive was the fact that Indian relatives made fewer critical comments, fewer positive remarks, and demonstrated less overinvolvement with the patient. This was much more the case in rural areas, where the traditional kinship system was stronger than among city dwellers who were more expressive. The actual mechanisms by which expressed emotion works remain unclear, but this is a very important area for further exploration.

In an intriguing analysis, James Greenley (1986) reanalyzed the original data collected by George Brown and colleagues (Brown et al. 1972). He hypothesized that the essence of the measure of expressed emotion was a type of informal social control he labeled *high intensity interpersonal social control.* Such control, Greenley argues, involves people trying to shape others' behavior "by suggesting, nagging, threatening, arguing, criticizing, playing on feelings of obligation and guilt, and so forth" (Greenley 1986, p. 25). Greenley hypothesized that if his conception is correct, expressed emotion should be associated with family fears and anxieties when they believed the patient was not ill but recalcitrant. In contrast, he reasoned, if they felt that the behavior derived from an inherent illness they would be less likely to believe that they could shape it by informal control and, thus, would be less likely to display high levels of expressed emotion. The analysis supported these hypotheses. Greenley's analysis does not explain why psychiatric patients seem so vulnerable to this form of social control, since it is ubiquitous in family interactions in normal families as well.

The prognostic research on schizophrenia suggests that successful maintenance is a complex task involving a balance between maintaining a sufficient level of demand and activation to encourage motivation and functioning without excessive excitement or stimulation. If patients are left alone or isolate themselves, they often lapse into inactivity and withdrawal, and the negative features of the condition tend to become exaggerated (Wing 1978). Similarly, involving the patient too intensely in interpersonal relations or in highly stressful situations triggers vulnerabilities. The expressed emotion research also identifies an important role of medication in protecting the patient in situations of overinvolvement and criticism. Expressed emotion as measured consists mostly of negative affect, and, thus, it remains unclear to what extent and under what conditions intense positive affect can have comparable effects. Since intense involvement commonly involves both positive and negative affect, it is reasonable to speculate that schizophrenics are vulnerable to intense emotional relationships more generally, but this is yet to be convincingly demonstrated. Research work in this area has important implications for public policy as it affects intervention programs.

C h a p t e r 7

The Financing and Delivery of Mental Health Services

The availability and use of mental health services depend on the financing and reimbursement system. For the first half of the century, mental health services were sharply bifurcated. The poor received little mental health care, but if sufficiently disordered or disturbing, they were maintained in public institutions with minimal active treatment. The rich bought services from private practitioners on a fee-for-service basis; if they needed hospitalization, they would receive care, at least initially, in private mental hospitals. The cost of such care was prohibitive, and even affluent patients with chronic mental illness were frequently transferred to public institutions if they did not respond to treatment after some initial period. This pattern of services allocation did not really begin to shift significantly until the 1960s with the development of community mental health centers, the extension of psychiatric outpatient facilities in hospitals, and the improvement of psychiatric benefits under private and nonprofit health insurance programs (Follmann 1970). The passage of Medicare in 1965 provided some modest psychiatric benefits to the aged, although on a more prejudicial basis than other types of medical services covered by the program. Similarly, Medicaid provided significant funds to pay for mental health services for the poor. The Medicaid program, however, organized within the welfare system (Stevens and Stevens 1974) and tied to traditional federal–state welfare relationships, has been implemented from one place to another in an uneven way. As a result of these various developments in both public and private programs, there has been a vast increase in the use of services, but not in a particularly well-balanced way. Mental health services are now undergoing a process of significant transformation. Managed care now dominates, and the challenge is to achieve a more balanced pattern of services across the various aspects of care.

Mental Health Coverage and Expenditures

Despite disagreements about what mental illness is, mental health benefits have expanded under private, nonprofit, and government health insurance programs. It is estimated that in 1994 expenditures for mental health and substance abuse services exceeded $68 billion, approximately 7 percent of all national health expenditures. About $28 billion were expended through private insurance programs, $20 billion through Medicaid and other government programs, and another $20 billion through state and local programs (Frank et al. 1995).

The most recent information on health insurance coverage comes from surveys of employers by the Bureau of Labor Statistics of the Department of Labor. Most people who now have health insurance have coverage for mental health and substance abuse treatment, but such treatment is typically subjected to more restrictions than treatment for other illnesses. In the case of hospital care, most plans restrict care to thirty to sixty days per year, compared with 120 days or unrestricted periods for other illnesses. Plans have also typically set lower dollar maximums per year and per lifetime on mental health benefits, such as a $50,000 lifetime cap, but recent federal legislation restricts such discrimination. People with insurance typically face restrictions on outpatient utilization with most plans covering fewer outpatient visits than for other illnesses. Moreover, mental health outpatient insurance usually involves a 50 percent coinsurance rate compared with 20 percent for other medical conditions. Also, outpatient mental health expenses often cannot be used to meet the employee's maximum out-of-pocket expense limit, and they must continue to pay the large coinsurance rate no matter how large their expenditures. Similar restrictions apply in the case of substance abuse treatments.

Most HMOs only provide an acute care benefit for mental health and substance abuse services, imposing strict limits on the number of inpatient days per year (typically fifteen to thirty) and the number of outpatient visits to a mental health clinician (typically ten to twenty). Most HMO members are expected to copay for each mental health visit, usually about ten to twenty dollars. Some plans modify the copayments, increasing them for additional visits beyond a defined limit or when the plan does not believe that further visits are "medically necessary."

As already noted, there is large concern in the mental health community about discrimination in mental health coverage, and mental health advocates actively lobby for parity in coverage with other medical conditions. In 1996 Congress passed the Domenici–Wellstone Amendment, effective in 1998, to require parity for lifetime and annual dollar limits between mental health and other medical conditions. Although the amendment is an advance for mental health it has many restrictions and limitations.

For example, employers who wish to avoid the parity requirement can completely drop coverage for mental health services, although this is unlikely to occur often. Also, the requirement does not apply to businesses with fifty or fewer employees, and thus excludes perhaps 15 to 20 percent of the population. Moreover, insurance companies can adjust coverage for numbers of days or visits, copayment rates, or definitions of medical necessity, taking back some of the benefits provided by the parity requirement. Also, businesses are exempted from the requirement if their premiums rise as a result of the parity requirement by 1 percent or more. The net effect of this new requirement, thus, is to redistribute services and expenditures among different categories of mental health service users. The persons most likely to have exceeded the maximum allowable limits are those with severe and persistent illness, and this amendment can be viewed as a redistribution to that population. It is difficult to predict how businesses will respond, but it is likely that the overall effect will be to increase mental health services slightly as a proportion of all expenditures.

Traditionally, indemnity insurers defined as legitimate treatment whatever services the designated experts (usually psychiatrists) decided to administer. Increasingly, however, managed care companies through HMOs and utilization review seek to be more precise about what conditions should be treated and about the length and types of treatments that are medically necessary. Treatment for diagnoses not covered by the DSM are unlikely to be covered, although DSM is sufficiently broad to allow most patients to receive a diagnosis. The extent to which a rigorous test is applied for allowing treatment depends on the intensity and cost of the treatment involved. Sustained treatment usually requires a significant diagnosis such as schizophrenia or major depression, and there is little inclination to pay for much care for prevalent problems in living. Moreover, much effort is given to avoid inpatient admissions, to reduce inpatient length of stay, and to truncate long courses of treatment. Whenever possible, managed care seeks alternative treatments that are less intensive and less costly. As a result, long-term psychotherapy is being replaced by brief psychotherapy, medications are substituting for psychotherapy, and community treatments are substituting for inpatient care.

Psychologists, social workers, and other non-M.D. clinicians find themselves in uncertain circumstances with insurance changes. On the one hand, the fact that such clinicians are less expensive than psychiatrists provides employment opportunities in managed care organizations and public agencies, and many insurers now reimburse licensed psychologists and certified social workers directly for clinical services without the supervision of a medical doctor. On the other hand, insurers challenge claims about the effectiveness of psychotherapy and prefer medication treatment, which improves patients' symptoms more quickly. Although in some instances psychotherapy has effects comparable to drug treatment, it requires more intensive clinician involvement and greater costs. Psychotherapy continues as an important insured benefit, but the pressure is to keep such treatments brief, and psychotherapists are increasingly closely monitored. Also, managed care companies and insurers are now much tougher bargainers over fees, and nonmedical therapists face considerable fee pressures that limit their earnings. Even in the case of medication treatments, there is concern in professional communities that managed care practices discourage the use of the most expensive (but sometimes most effective) drugs and frown on keeping patients on necessary maintenance treatment. It seems clear that health care system changes are altering mental health practice in significant ways, limiting the autonomy and discretion of clinicians, changing the balance between clinical judgment and administrative expectations, and introducing and applying practice guidelines to the treatment of specific conditions.

The changes taking place are qualitative as well as quantitative. In the past insurers could control mental health expenditures by limiting the number of reimbursable providers, and they protected themselves through high coinsurance and deductibles, limits on numbers of days and visits, and maximum allowable expenditures. For the most part they did not get into the business of assessing what types of mental illnesses should be treated or how. Although many of these insurance rationing approaches persist, they are being significantly modified. Insurance companies and managed care reviewers are increasingly in the business of assessing *medical necessity* and *appropriate treatment,* both relatively slippery concepts given the uncertainties of knowledge of mental illness and the heterogeneity of patient populations.

The Pattern of Inpatient Services

Among the important changes brought about by insurance coverage was the expansion of specialized psychiatric units in general hospitals, as well as an enormous growth of outpatient care. Between 1970 and 1992, the number of nonfederal general hospitals with separate psychiatric services increased from 797 to 1,616 (Center for Mental Health Services 1996), and many other general hospitals without such units treated patients with psychiatric disorders in beds in general medical or surgical units (called *scatter beds*) or in small subunits of these general units. Private psychiatric hospitals also increased very rapidly during this period. In 1992 there were more than 1.7 million discharges from short-stay hospitals with a primary mental health diagnosis (Graves 1995). More than 908,000 were for patients with a diagnosis of psychosis; 258,000 for patients with a diagnosis of alcohol dependence; and the rest largely for nonpsychiatric depression, anxiety disorders, and personality disorders. Average hospital length of stay of patients with a primary psychiatric diagnosis was 10.9 days, and only 12.9 days for patients with psychoses. The predominant pattern, even for psychotic illness, is a short hospital stay to stabilize the patient's symptoms and a rapid return to the community and outpatient care. This pattern of care will be even more accentuated as managed care takes root and puts considerable emphasis on finding alternatives for very expensive inpatient care.

Many forces converged to bring about a rapid expansion of the general hospital inpatient sector. The insured public increasingly had insurance that paid for a limited number of hospital days for psychiatric illness but provided much less coverage for outpatient service, creating an incentive for inpatient care. As states closed or reduced the size of their public hospitals, they looked to the general hospital to be their first line of care in the treatment of acute psychiatric illness. States also had an incentive to shift inpatient care to general hospitals because when they did so, the federal government shared the cost of such care for patients in the Medicaid program, thus reducing the state's financial burden.

In the psychiatric inpatient private-hospital sector, individual entrepreneurs and hospital chains realized that this could be a highly profitable business and aggressively moved into markets and market niches where there were bed shortages. One major area that private psychiatric hospitals promoted was the inpatient care of children and adolescents, an area in psychiatry where treatment standards were particularly uncertain. Private psychiatric hospitals have greatly expanded, from 2.7 percent of all psychiatric inpatient beds in 1970 to 16.1 percent in 1992; the number of such hospitals increased from 150 to 475, and admissions grew from approximately 92,000 in 1969 to almost 470,000 in 1992 (Center for Mental Health Services 1996). Full-time-equivalent (FTE) staff in these hospitals increased from 21,504 in 1972 to more than 77,000 in 1992, and patient care FTEs increased more than fivefold. In the last two decades private inpatient psychiatry in general hospitals has also been a growth sector, serving primarily insured persons with less severe problems than those in public and nonprofit general hospitals and disproportionately serving children (Olfson and Mechanic 1996).

The distribution of inpatient admissions for mental disorder varies according to type of hospital. State and county mental hospitals have the largest proportion of schizophrenic admissions and a high rate of alcohol-related admissions, these two areas accounting for three-fifths of all admissions. A similar situation characterizes the Veterans' Administration's mental hospitals, although they have fewer schizophrenics and more alcohol-related problems. Public mental hospitals have more patients with previous admissions indicating greater chronicity. In contrast, community general hospitals and private psychiatric hospitals have only about one-third schizophrenic and alcoholism admissions and a much larger proportion of admissions for affective disorders: 31 percent in community hospitals and 43 percent in private psychiatric hospitals (National Institute of Mental Health 1985, p. 19). The public mental hospitals are clearly dealing with the tougher and more chronic problems. Similar patterns also are evident within the general hospital sector. Data from the 1993 Hospital Discharge Survey show that patients with schizophrenia constituted 23 percent of discharges from public hospitals but only 13 percent of discharges from private hospitals. In contrast, patients with depression made up a third of all discharges from private hospitals but only 15 percent of discharges from public hospitals. Nonprofit hospitals fell in between (Olfson and Mechanic 1996).

The introduction of prospective hospital reimbursement under Medicare in which hospitals received a fixed payment for care of patients classified in one of 468 diagnostic related groups (DRGs) tightened hospital reimbursement, but many psychiatric units were exempt because of the difficulty of using diagnosis to predict resource use (Taube, Lee and Forthofer 1984; English et al. 1986; Horgan and Jencks 1987). Thus, psychiatric patients were attractive to hospitals who could use their bed capacity to attract cost-based reimbursement. Although such reimbursement was scheduled to change, the problem of predicting psychiatric resource use has remained relatively intractable. The old reimbursement system continues in many instances because a classification system that fails to recognize important differences among patients creates incentives that distort the care process and reduces quality of care (Jencks, Horgan and Taube 1987).

Managed care is the new element in the equation that is now constraining inpatient care. Up to now, for-profit development in inpatient psychiatry concentrated on areas of inpatient coverage for insured individuals with affective disorders, substance abuse, and adjustment disorders that were profitable, and located new institutions disproportionately in regions of the country where there was less competition and where there was less reimbursement regulation. Utilization review and the growth of HMOs will affect future inpatient practices significantly.

Utilization of Services and Financing Patterns

The extension of psychiatric services through expanded insurance benefits had important implications for the distribution of care. It followed and may have reinforced an existing trend toward providing services to groups in the population who needed them less. The most comprehensive insurance coverage is frequently available to the most advantaged segments of the employed population, and even among those with comparable insurance coverage, persons with higher incomes, education, and greater sophistication use the most services (Leaf et al. 1985), despite the inverse relationship between socioeconomic status and mental health impairment (Dohrenwend and Dohrenwend 1969, 1974; Kessler 1982; Kessler et al. 1994). One early study found that insured persons with college degrees, as compared with those with a grade school or less education, were six times as likely to seek psychiatric care, and they used office psychotherapy visits almost ten times as often as those who were less educated (Avnet 1962). These gaps have closed over time as access has increased and as seeking help for psychological problems has become more acceptable to the population, but large differences remain. For example, data from the 1987 National Medical Expenditure Survey show that 6.4 percent of persons with sixteen or more years of education used an outpatient mental health service during the survey year, but only 3.7 percent of those who had eleven or less years of education did so. Whites were twice as likely to use a mental health service as blacks (Olfson and Pincus 1996). Such differences are substantially due to differences in insurance coverage and financial access, but they are also due to the kinds of social and cultural differences discussed earlier. People differ substantially in their receptivity to psychological interpretations of their distress and to mental health treatment. Use of services also depends on geographic and social accessibility of care. Differences in the availability of psychiatrists, for example, between metropolitan, rural, and central city areas have been as high as twenty- to thirtyfold (Brown 1977). Access among states varies enormously (McCloskey et al. 1996).

Mental health coverage through Medicare and Medicaid has substantially improved access to mental health care, although the latter program has much more comprehensive coverage and is a major financial component of the system of care for persons with serious and persistent mental illness. Medicaid has become the safety net for many seriously mentally ill persons, offering a broad range of services in many states, including case management and psychosocial rehabilitation. The National Advisory Mental Health Council (1993) estimated that approximately 15 percent of Medicaid expenditures go for mental health. One consequence is that the poor, who are most likely to have Medicaid coverage, are almost as likely to have a mental health visit as those with high incomes. The near-poor have the lowest rate of such visits among income groups (Olfson and Pincus 1996). This subgroup is least likely to be protected by either private or government insurance.

A traditional insurance structure that includes relatively good coverage for inpatient care but much more limited outpatient coverage provides strong incentives for hospital care that may not really be needed and encourages a medical approach to mental health problems, in contrast to community treatment alternatives and educational and rehabilitative models. It may take some time before managed care changes the incentives that have built a disproportionately large inpatient sector.

The Economics of Mental Health Care

In recent years, we have learned a great deal about the economics of mental health care, the effects of financial incentives on consumers, professionals, and institutions, and the cost-effectiveness of alternative ways of organizing services Although our knowledge of the effects of insurance and copayment on the demand for mental health services has advanced, too little attention has been given to the economics of the public mental health sector or to financing of care for the most seriously mentally ill. The Medicaid program and its complex eligibility and administrative requirements, discussed later in this chapter, is a continuing focus of attention in the larger health care arena.

Not only are cost-sharing features and service limits more characteristic of mental health than other medical services, but they also appear to inhibit outpatient services even more than in other areas (Frank and McGuire 1986). McGuire (1981), for example, in a study of psychotherapy among more than 4,000 patients, found that this service is particularly sensitive to insurance coverage and that the effects for lower-income persons were greater than for more affluent groups. McGuire's excellent study, however, focused on patients and, thus, pertains to volume of use and not to whether help would be sought.

The best source of data on the effects of cost-sharing is the Rand Health Insurance Experiment (HIE). This study, carried out between 1974 and 1982, randomized 6,970 respondents into insurance plans with varying coinsurance requirements and, in one setting, an HMO (Group Health Cooperative of Puget Sound in Seattle). In some cases there were no coinsurance requirements (labeled the "free care" group), while in other cases families had to pay 25, 50, or 95 percent of their bills up to a $1,000 per-year maximum. There were other variations (Newhouse 1974; Newhouse and the Insurance Experiment Group 1994), but for our purposes what is most important is the different obligations families had to share in their costs of care. Most insurance programs in the United States have some cost-sharing, and in recent years such requirements have increased substantially in employment-related health insurance plans. Deductibles and coinsurance also play an important role in Medicare, although the Rand group did not study the Medicare age group.

In the Rand study, physician use was demonstrated to respond substantially to insurance variations. Persons in the "free" plan (no coinsurance or deductibles) accrued expenditures of about 50 percent more for ambulatory care than those with 95 percent coinsurance (Newhouse et al. 1981). Visits in these contrasting groups varied from 5.5 to 3.5 visits per person each year. This effect was found in all subgroups studied.

The Rand HIE provides an opportunity to examine use of mental health services in the context of overall medical care. In early publications, the Rand researchers reported that cost-sharing affected use of mental health services in a way comparable to its effect on other services (Wells et al. 1982), but these results were subjected to considerable controversy. Ellis and McGuire (1984, 1986) suggested that the Rand researchers underestimated the mental health coinsurance effects due to a special design feature, the maximum dollar expenditure (MDE) level for a family. Once a family reached the MDE in a particular year, services at that point became free for the remainder of the period. The probability that families in programs with different coinsurance requirements reach the MDE at varying rates may distort estimates of the size of the effects of cost-sharing on mental health expenditures.

In an extension and reanalysis of the data, stimulated by the Ellis and McGuire (1984) observations, the Rand researchers concluded that outpatient mental health use is indeed more responsive to price than other types of medical care (Keeler et al. 1986). There was a fourfold variation between extreme coinsurance groups, and those with 50 percent coinsurance and no limits on cost-sharing spent only two-fifths as much as those with "free care." Coinsurance primarily affected the number of episodes of treatment, but once a person entered care the duration and intensity varied less. Since relatively few patients seek specialized mental health care whatever their insurance levels, the per-person cost in the study for such services was low. Other factors found to affect use in addition to mental health status and insurance included educational level and age (better educated persons and young adults used more), and there were also variations by site. Seattle and Massachusetts had more use than Dayton and South Carolina. The site effect is probably a product of the different availability of mental health providers in the sites and varying cultural dispositions toward mental health services in the geographic areas.

Psychiatric Care under Prepayment Plans

The pattern of insurance benefits evolved under fee-for-service plans has been designed to accommodate the existing psychiatric marketplace, which has been largely organized around office-based psychotherapy. Stringent controls on the definition of reimbursable providers were necessary because psychotherapists, particularly those with a psychoanalytic orientation, would carry out long courses of "treatment" at great expense with patients who had minimal impairment. The effect of paying for such services was to subsidize disproportionately the most affluent and educated groups in the population.

An alternative model is found in many health maintenance organizations (HMOs) that maintain greater control over the referral process and the assessment of the need for services. Such programs can provide outpatient benefits without the usual cost-sharing deterrents. Experience in a variety of such plans has shown that outpatient utilization can be maintained at reasonable levels if the primary physician plays a gatekeeper role (Follette and Cummings 1967; Cummings and Follette 1968; Goldberg, Krantz, and Locke 1970; Fullerton, Lohrenz, and Nycz 1976). These plans require the primary care physician's referral, which has a moderating effect on the claim for services. The number of psychiatrists and other mental health clinicians available in the plan and the queue for service set a natural ceiling on how many services can be consumed and with what intensity. When the mental health personnel are themselves employees of the plan, when they are conscious of the cost implications of utilization, and when they have no economic incentive to prolong counseling or psychotherapy, treatment tends to be less intense and to be provided for shorter periods of time. Also, it is likely that such plans select psychiatric personnel who are more attuned to pragmatic approaches to psychiatric care and to short-term and group psychotherapy.

From an organizational view, the prepaid plan offers an advantage in that it facilitates the use of nonmedical personnel in providing mental health services. Such programs may employ psychologists, nurses, and social workers and can, therefore, provide services less expensively than programs that depend primarily on psychiatrists. In contrast, most traditional insurance policies until recently have reimbursed only medical personnel and psychologists in the fee-for-service sector, creating an unnecessary dependence on the most expensive types of manpower when other mental health personnel can do as well. Capitation-type plans, that are paid a fixed amount per enrollee, may facilitate the provision of a broader range of services at reasonable cost, are potentially able to make use of the entire spectrum of suitable personnel, and forge a closer alliance between general medical care and more specialized mental health services.

Prepaid group practices or other health maintenance organizations need not organize their own mental health services. Many managed care behavioral health companies now contract to organize, manage, and provide mental health services for employers, health insurance programs, and health maintenance organizations. The mental health component of the plan can be *carved out* and treated separately from other medical services. The behavioral health company can contract simply to manage the service or agree on a capitated basis to accept the financial risk for the mental health component of care, a pattern that is increasingly common. This industry has grown very rapidly and now arranges for and manages mental health services for much of the population. In 1996, the four largest companies alone managed the care of more than 65 million people (Cutting Edge 1996). One advantage of *carve-outs* is that they allow for recruitment and management of a specialized network that is beyond the capacities of many health maintenance organizations or self-insured employers. It has also been argued that using carve-outs can moderate risk selection, which is a difficult problem for competing health care programs (Frank et al. 1996). A significant disadvantage of carve-outs is that it becomes more difficult to integrate and coordinate mental health with general health services.

This is not the context for a detailed review of the large and important literature on health maintenance organizations (Mechanic 1986b, Miller and Luft 1994, Zelman 1996). Since the way health services are organized importantly affects access, costs, service mix, and health outcomes, a brief review of studies of the performance of prepaid practice is appropriate, however.

A large literature supports the conclusion that prepaid group practice significantly reduces costs by limiting hospital admissions by as much as 40 percent and yields an overall cost savings of 20 to 30 percent (Luft 1981; Mechanic 1979a, 1986b). These differences have been found to persist when controls for population characteristics, out-of-plan use, and other factors are considered as well. Yet these studies could not exclude the possibility of significant selection effects relating to the health status of enrollees who choose prepaid practice plans for their medical care needs. In the Rand HIE, however, families were randomized into a prepaid group practice in Seattle (Group Health Cooperative of Puget Sound). This provided an opportunity to examine the impact of this type of organization independent of selection effects.

Group Health was found to have 40 percent less admissions than the free-care experimental group, although both populations faced no financial barriers to care. Overall, expenditures in Group Health were 28 percent less than in the free-care condition (Manning et al. 1984). A subsequent analysis of health status suggested that poor sick patients randomized into prepaid practice did slightly less well on outcome measures than those assigned to the fee-for-service free-care condition (Ware et al. 1986). These data are not fully convincing, but they are consistent with other studies that suggest that less educated patients have difficulties negotiating the bureaucratic barriers typical of organizational types of practice (Mechanic 1979a). Such barriers can be overcome through well-designed outreach efforts to enrollees at high risk.

Organization and financing affect mix of mental health services as well. The Rand researchers carried out analyses of the use of mental health care in the fee-for-service conditions as compared with prepaid practice. More enrollees of prepaid practice actually used mental health services than those in the "free-care" fee-for-service condition, but they were provided much less intensively. Those in prepaid practice were more likely to receive mental health services from a general medical provider, and overall mental health expenditures were only one-third of the free-care condition ($25 per year per enrollee versus $70). When prepaid enrollees saw a mental health provider, they had only one-third the number of mental health visits of the comparable fee-for-service free-care group. Group Health relied more on social workers than psychiatrists or psychologists and less on individual therapy in contrast to group or family therapies (Manning et al. 1986, Manning and Wells 1986). These results are similar to those found in nonexperimental studies.

The Rand HIE also found that when patients received mental health care from general physicians in contrast to the specialty mental health sector, the intensity and cost of services was less. More important, they found that whether patients sought care from general physicians or specialists was unrelated to mental health status at enrollment or to the level of insurance coverage. But those who visited general physicians for a mental health problem accounted for only 5 percent of total outpatient mental health expenditures because of the low intensity of mental health care provided by general physicians (Wells et al. 1987).

Since approximately half of all mental health care occurs in the general medical sector, understanding patterns and quality of such care is important. Most studies find that patients in the mental health specialty sector are more impaired on the average than those cared for by general physicians, but there is a large degree of overlap between sectors. The restricted character of the HIE sample exaggerates the extent of overlap since the population studied underrepresents the most seriously mentally ill, who would be more likely to get care from specialists. The findings, however, should alert us to the importance of carefully distinguishing between mental health visits and the content, appropriateness, and quality of care. Mental health researchers conveniently differentiate between services provided by general physicians and those provided within the specialty mental health sector. The most seriously mentally ill have complex relationships with various parts of the medical, mental health, and social services systems, and we need deeper understanding of the interacting sectors and how they affect the longitudinal care of patients.

The Rand observation of little difference in severity of problems among those seeking mental health care from the two sectors reinforces the importance of help seeking and illness behavior discussed in the previous chapter. The sociocultural attitudes and illness behavior patterns that shape patients' help seeking lead to different transactions with the health care system and different degrees of care. There is, for example, much concern about the failure of general physicians to recognize depression and manage it appropriately and the inappropriate use of psychoactive medications (Wells et al. 1996; Mechanic 1990). From a quality point of view, different types of mental health visits are not necessarily equivalent. The cost-effectiveness of one pattern of care versus another requires careful and continuing investigation if we are to make sound policy choices.

Although, in theory, the prepaid model offers the most rational and efficient way to handle mental health problems of the most common types, and the evidence supports the notion that they provide such services efficiently, we know relatively little about how well they do in terms of outcomes in serious mental illness. The feasibility of this model has been demonstrated from an economic perspective, but it would be helpful to have a better understanding of the referral decisions made by primary care physicians, of who obtains and fails to get treatment, and of the quality of mental health care provided. The prepaid organization has an intuitive logic to it, but we need more careful study of the way the system really works, the determinants of the referral process, and the outcomes of care in relation to alternative approaches.

The Structure of Insurance and Needed Mental Health Benefits

Developing an appropriate structure for providing mental health benefits is difficult because the needs of persons with mental illness are broad and diverse, requiring decisions about the relationships between acute and long-term care; between medical, behavioral, and social services; and between services provided by physicians and a range of other mental health care professionals including psychologists, social workers, and rehabilitation specialists. In this sense, the parity discussion oriented toward advocacy for an insurance system that does not discriminate against mental health services only addresses part of the problem. Simply providing the same insurance coverage available to the privately insured would not adequately meet the needs of persons with serious and persistent mental illness who require often a much broader array of social and rehabilitative services than those covered by conventional health insurance.

Coverage for mental health needs comes from a patchwork including private health insurance, Medicaid, Medicare, and other public mental health programs, the expenditures of state mental health authorities for institutions and other services, and out-of-pocket payments. Traditionally, mental health services for persons with serious conditions were a state responsibility and states and localities made large investments in their mental hospital systems. In the forty years between 1955 and 1995 resident patients in public mental hospitals declined by more than 90 percent to a population of 77,000 (Bachrach 1996). Although existing mental hospitals now serve only a small minority of seriously ill patients, and there is broad agreement that money should follow the patient, these institutions still retain much of state funding. The two-thirds of all expenditures commonly cited is an exaggeration, reflecting how budgets are reported and the different ways in which federal and state dollars flow through the mental health system, but there is little doubt that traditional state investments in institutions are highly resistant to change and that communities, institutions, and unions representing hospital workers resist reallocation from inpatient to community care. In 1992, state and county hospitals had more than $8 billion in revenues, with almost 75 percent of funds coming through state appropriations (Center for Mental Health Services 1996). Moving state funding from institutions to community care is a slow and politically difficult process.

The Medicaid program provides a significant safety net for persons with serious and persistent mental illness and can be seen realistically as a core component of the mental health services system for the disabled and many other people in poverty. Over time, however, Medicaid coverage of the poor has not kept pace with the growth in the poverty population. In 1975 Medicaid eligibility covered 71 percent of the poor in the average state (Curtis 1986), but in recent years the proportion has been around 45 percent (46 percent in 1994), and there is great variability in coverage among the states (McCloskey et al. 1996).

Moreover, the high demands of the Medicaid program on federal and state budgets has led to efforts to reduce funding, limit eligibility, cut reimbursement and eliminate federal mandates to allow each state to design its own program. The fear is that in the absence of federal requirements, poorer and more conservative states might too sharply reduce eligibility and needed benefits and thus damage the safety net designed to protect our most vulnerable citizens (Baxter and Mechanic 1997). Since Medicaid is so important in caring for persons with serious mental illness, it is important to examine the program more closely.

Medicaid is a federal–state categorical program to provide medical assistance to low-income families with dependent children and low-income aged, blind, or disabled persons. Depending on the economic position of each state, the federal government matches state expenditures under the program from 50 to 83 percent. To receive the funds, states must include certain eligible groups and services, but others are optional. However, within broad requirements, states can establish criteria for eligibility, determine and administer reimbursement, and define the amount, duration, and scope of covered services. In addition, the federal government may waive some requirements so states can modify their programs to develop innovative forms of delivery. It is increasingly common for state managed care programs to function under the federal waiver authority.

Medicaid is a large and incredibly complex program that has grown rapidly with new federal mandates introduced in the 1990s. In 1994 more than 35 million patients received Medicaid services at a cost of approximately $123 billion (Levit et al. 1996). Expenditures, however, are distributed very differently over the various eligible groups covered. Although low-income children in 1994 constituted 49 percent of the Medicaid population, they accounted for only 16 percent of program expenditures; the 16 percent of low-income disabled persons used 39 percent of all expenditures. Similarly, the 11 percent of low-income elderly used 31 percent of all payments, largely for nursing home care (Health Care Financing Administration 1996). Although the public often thinks of Medicaid in terms of the large number of mothers and children on welfare, Medicaid provides the safety net for persons with psychiatric disabilities and the government long-term care program for the elderly poor.

The mandatory services under the Medicaid program cover the basic hospital and outpatient services traditionally covered under private health insurance. The optional services, for which states can also receive 50 to 83 percent federal subsidy, allow states to develop more comprehensive services for persons with serious mental illness including clinical services, occupational therapy, prescribed drugs, psychologist services, diagnostic services, screening services, rehabilitative services, inpatient psychiatric services for persons under age twenty-one in public hospitals, case management, and transportation services, among others. Medicaid, thus, has allowed skillful state administrators to build more responsive systems of mental health care by combining federal and state dollars that would not be possible simply within the structure of private health insurance, even if it was available to all (Mechanic and Surles 1992). In most states, disabled persons who became eligible for Supplemental Security Income (SSI) also receive Medicaid, and persons with mental illness have been one of the fastest growing groups in the SSI program. In the early 1990s, persons with a primary diagnosis of mental illness were a quarter of all adults under age sixty-five receiving SSI on the basis of blindness or disability, a doubling since the 1970s

(Mashaw and Reno 1996). Among the reasons for this growth has been aggressive efforts on the part of social workers and other mental health professionals to get clients in the community into these programs providing basic subsistence and Medicaid coverage.

Despite the tremendous contributions of Medicaid, it is a flawed program in many respects. Because it funds defined service benefits with inpatient care as a basic benefit, it has perpetuated an inpatient bias. Thus, disproportionate Medicaid expenditures go into institutional psychiatric services in general hospitals, private psychiatric hospitals, and other settings. This has limited opportunities to maximize the use of Medicaid funds to develop community mental health care with appropriate support systems. The efforts on the part of many states to use federal waivers to put the mentally ill into managed care programs is one strategy to contain these inpatient care expenditures. Massachusetts was one of the first states to put all Medicaid beneficiaries in a statewide managed care plan, and a four-year evaluation found that inpatient care for patients with schizophrenia declined about a quarter and average length of stay declined by about three days (Dickey et al. 1996). The study, however, was not informative on whether adequate alternative community services were developed. A small increase in admissions within thirty days of discharge suggests a need for concern and caution. The challenge is not simply to reduce inpatient utilization but to develop a balanced system of care with alternative care of appropriate quality.

Medicaid as a program has other limitations as well. It gives a great deal of discretion to states, and while some states like Massachusetts, New York, New Jersey, New Hampshire, California, and Connecticut have capitalized on Medicaid opportunities, other states, particularly in the south and southwest, have much more limited programs. Even in cases where the federal government pays most of the cost, poor, low-tax states have been reluctant to make the necessary investment. The result is that the quality of one's benefits under the Medicaid program depends greatly on where one lives. States face a trade-off between who they make eligible for services and how much they spend per recipient. They also face a trade-off between eligibility and benefits and reimbursement rates to providers. States that seek broader coverage often attempt to gain savings through their reimbursement policies.

There also are large differences in coverage and expenditures per recipient. For example, Rhode Island has a very inclusive policy, covering 1,770 persons for every 1,000 people with incomes of less than 100 percent of the federal poverty level in 1994; the comparable rates for Nevada and Idaho were 410 and 540. Large states like New York and California had rates of 920 per 1,000 people in poverty. New Hampshire, which had a rate of only 740, spent an average of $10,654 per Medicaid user, while Tennessee, with a rate of 920, only spent $1,899 per user (Health Care Financing Administration 1996). Expenditures depend in significant part on the composition of the Medicaid population. The elderly and disabled populations cost much more than children or their mothers on welfare. In any case, the important point is that there is large variation in Medicaid depending on where one lives.

Medicaid is a large and complicated program with considerable federal oversight and regulation. Some states resent recent new congressional mandates and insist that they could use their resources better if they had more flexibility to design their programs as they like. Federal officials, in contrast, believe it important that states meet certain minimum standards and priorities in the use of federal funds. They also argue that the waiver program provides ample opportunity for states to innovate in their service delivery systems, and in recent years the federal government has approved many such waivers. While it is plausible that some states left on their own to use federal Medicaid funds could be more innovative and effective, the danger is that other states would draw back from health care commitments in the face of competing budgetary needs and ideological interest groups, increasing the range of program integrity among states. A nationally supervised program maintains a minimum decent standard for states that have a limited commitment to the disabled population, poor children, and the elderly. Civil rights offers a good analogy where, in the absence of federal standards, large disparities among states may have persisted.

Medicaid, however important, is only one source of mental health financing. In considering President Clinton's proposed health plan in the early 1990s, much attention was given to the issue of how to integrate mental health services into the mainstream health care system. The Clinton initiative failed, but the issue remains a core concern. Even if we had a uniform system of health insurance, including the approximately 40 million people who are currently uninsured, we would still be required to carefully design the benefit package. We would have to take into account the finding reported earlier that outpatient mental health care is more responsive to insurance coverage than general medical services (in economic language, that such services involve a higher level of moral hazard). One perspective favored by some Clinton advisors was to cover all "necessary" mental health services on the same basis as any other but control their availability through capitation and utilization management. Although it is still early in the managed care era, there is a great deal of evidence that such management can keep costs within a reasonable range for the general population. There is still much to debate in defining medical necessity and how such decisions should be administered. The definition of "medical necessity" is especially crucial in the care of persons with severe and persistent mental illness.

Many issues are applicable to both managed care and more traditional types of insurance. First, criteria are needed to specify the types of problems that should be eligible for services. Should such benefits be limited to major diagnosed psychiatric disorders such as major depression and schizophrenia, or should they extend as well to marital counseling, unhappiness, problems with children, and difficulties in life transitions such as divorce or death in a family? Since broad coverage substantially increases the number of potential clients, some NAMI members have advocated mainly covering *biological illnesses* but not ordinary life problems. While it is not clear how to differentiate *biological* from other disorders, NAMI advocates would define coverage by the patient's diagnosis.

Decisions also must be made as to which institutions and practitioners will be eligible for reimbursement. Should payment be restricted to medical institutions and medical doctors, a broader range of mental health professionals including social workers and case managers, or be available to any practitioner, including family counselors, recreation therapists, holistic healers, clergy, or whatever? One way of limiting the list is to only include practitioners licensed by states to provide professional mental health services, but this could vary from state to state, depending on the politics of licensing. To what extent should social workers and nurses be reimbursed as independent mental health practitioners outside of organized mental health settings?

These have been emotional issues. Over the years, the medical field has tried to exercise professional dominance (Freidson 1970; Starr 1982), and professional psychologists, nurses, and social workers have fought for status as independent practitioners. Although physicians have often posed the issue as purely a technical one, pertaining to their expertise in diagnosis and use of drugs, the battle is substantially one of gaining public and political legitimacy. Nurse practitioners are now allowed to prescribe some medications in underserved geographic areas, and clinical and professional psychology clinicians have been debating whether psychologists should be trained to medicate patients as well as provide diagnostic and psychotherapy services.

From the patient's point of view, an important issue concerns the extent of copayment. Such requirements may moderate some frivolous or less important use of services, but they might also restrain patients in need from obtaining appropriate and efficacious medical care (Lohr et al. 1986, Newhouse and the Insurance Experiment Group 1993). Such economic barriers also have a disproportionate influence on the utilization behavior of the poor as compared with those more affluent. Economists favor cost-sharing because they fear that moral hazard in the absence of cost-sharing will result in excessive and wasteful care. The mental health service most likely to involve moral hazard is psychotherapy, which individuals may seek more for educational purposes or to achieve greater personal understanding and self-actualization than because they are suffering from a mental illness. One solution is to use the same deductible and coinsurance rates used for general medical care for most mental health services but retain a 50 percent coinsurance rate for psychotherapy. Although such a high rate will constrain utilization, it might not effectively separate those who really need the service from those who do not. An alternative, used by some HMOs, is to provide a few visits at a low rate of coinsurance, or none at all, but then link the required coinsurance to a professional assessment of the need for care. The intent would be to make it easy for those who need the service to get it, while discouraging those who could cope adequately without it.

As employers, insurance plans, and government agencies turn to managed care companies to administer and manage health services for their employees and clients on a capitated rather than a fee-for-service basis, there are significant challenges to providing high-quality mental health services. People with psychiatric disorders use more medical care than others, and treatment for those with serious mental illness can be very expensive. Moreover, the pattern of expenses for those people is highly unpredictable. Thus, a health care provider has an incentive to avoid enrolling such individuals unless adequately compensated for the added risk, and one way of doing this is to offer limited or mediocre mental health services so that clients with mental illness go elsewhere. Thus, a way of either adjusting capitation rates to take risk into account, or sharing or limiting risk, is needed.

Methods to adjust capitation for people with mental illness have limited reliability, and thus health providers may avoid patients who they anticipate might be too costly and try to recruit those who they believe would be profitable. Thus far, most risk-adjustment approaches fail to explain much variance in resource use, although approaches that better gauge severity, disability, and risk of danger and disruptiveness may do better. Ultimately, improved measures will be devised, but in the shorter run adjustments based on past patterns of expenditure will be helpful. Using reinsurance to protect the provider against risk beyond some reasonable level is also useful. Another alternative is for the purchaser (employer or state program) to agree to share risk in various ways with the provider, but in a manner that provides incentives to use resources carefully. One common technique used in contracts is to establish risk corridors within which providers are put at risk and can earn profits through efficient practices but costs or gains beyond these corridors are shared or assumed by the purchaser.

An appropriate public framework requires that we determine the type of financing structure best fitted to meeting mental health needs in their broad sense, that we ensure that priorities in care go to those who are most seriously impaired and least able to help themselves, and that the structures we use promote efficient and effective use of the available resources. We are now in a period of transformation and experimentation as different approaches to manage care compete. The structures we adopt will establish how services are delivered and to whom, the types of personnel that we need to train and recruit, and the types of relationships not only between mental health and general medical care, but also with other vital services like housing and vocational assistance. In a study of 552 clients with serious mental illness, Tom Uttaro and I found that clients wanted help in a great many areas, but the areas in which they felt the greatest unmet need—in addition to recognizing and controlling their symptoms—were finding a way of keeping busy and preventing boredom and loneliness, making and getting along with friends and more intimate associates, and finding or keeping work and housing (Uttaro and Mechanic 1994). Psychiatrists emphasize determining the appropriate medication and achieving compliance, and this is clearly an essential area. Most clients, however, were receiving assistance in this area, and only 5 percent wanted more help with medications, the least of all fifteen areas in which clients were questioned.

It should be clear why simply expanding traditional insurance coverage to cover mental illness will not by itself do the job. Such insurance reinforces a narrow medical model when patients have enormous sociomedical needs that require a thoughtful integration of traditional medical and other types of services. An effective approach must have a strong focus on handling the needs of persons with severe and persistent mental illness living in the community and ensuring that the reimbursement system facilitates the development of necessary community services. A poorly designed financing approach may simply fix in place some of the weak features of traditional service systems. In the past two decades state health authorities, in collaboration with the National Institute of Mental Health and the Center for Mental Health Services, helped put in place many essential community services. As states now contract out mental health responsibility to behavioral health care companies, it remains unclear whether they will have the incentives, and money, to maintain the strengths of this public support system. These trends have to be watched carefully.

In sum, underlying many technical insurance issues that have to be resolved are a variety of important philosophical problems. First is the care of the psychiatric patient to be seen as primarily a medical issue, or is such care more appropriately viewed within psychological, social, or educational models? Second, are boundaries of mental health care properly narrow, primarily focused on traditional types of impairment, or should public policy encourage services for a wide range of social and psychological maladjustments? Third, should needs for containment of costs limit the range of disorders covered or the definition of what providers could be reimbursed, or should cost controls be achieved through other means? Although it would be foolhardy from a public policy standpoint to reimburse any psychological service, it is equally foolish to restrict services to a narrow medical approach. My view is that, although services should be broadly available, highest priority should be given to those patients who are most impaired and to those interventions that have been proven most effective. My preference would be to design an insurance program that facilitates reimbursement for care of chronic patients in community programs as well as in hospitals. Consistent with this belief, I will describe what a reasonable approach to the organization of mental health services might look like.

An Epidemiological Approach to Psychiatric Need

Examining the way patients with a range of problems flow from the community into different service contexts is useful in assessing the dimensions of need for care (Lewis, Fein, and Mechanic 1976). Simply assessing service utilization of particular types of facilities, such as psychiatric hospitalization or outpatient psychotherapy, fails to map the variety of problems people face or their different means of coping with them. Although the epidemiological picture is incomplete because of the difficulty of adequately defining mental illness in community settings, the data available are instructive.

Regier and his colleagues (1993), using data from all five ECA sites, estimated that 14.7 percent of the population sought some kind of help for a mental or addictive disorder in a one-year period using a broad definition of help seeking. Almost 6 percent sought help from the mental health/addiction speciality sectors, a similar proportion sought help from general physicians, and 3 percent sought help from other human service professionals. Almost 1 percent sought help from self-help groups, 3.5 percent from family and friends, and 4 percent from voluntary support networks. Although some received help from several sources, most people with disorders received no professional help. The more recent National Comorbidity Study, based on a representative sample of the United States and not simply on selected sites as in the ECA study, found even less professional help seeking than the ECA study, with estimates 25 percent below the ECA reported rates (Kessler et al. 1994).

Community epidemiologic studies vary a great deal in case definition, but most find a large reservoir of problems characterized by depression, anxiety, psychophysiologic discomforts, insomnia, unhappiness, and alienation (Dohrenwend et al. 1979). Although most of these problems do not constitute psychiatric disorders as conventionally defined, many of these persons suffer significantly and feel a need for assistance. At any point in time, such persons may constitute as much as one-quarter of the population, but this estimate includes both mild and more serious disturbances. Unfortunately, we have too little understanding of the natural history of these symptoms and the benefits to be gained from varying levels of support and treatment. We do know, however, that there is considerable overlap in symptoms between those treated in a variety of outpatient settings and those who receive no treatment at all.

Regardless of whether we use DSM criteria or psychological distress indicators, the evidence suggests that mental health problems are significantly undertreated. Many such problems may not require treatment, but the numbers of severely mentally ill who fall outside any system of services are a cause for concern. The issue is how to achieve the most effective triage and continuing responsibility for those most in need. Access to care and help seeking determines who enters the care system in the first place, but the first point of evaluation is commonly the doctor of first contact, the primary care physician.

The Role of Primary Medical Care

Primary medical care is an important focus because most people have access to such services, and the vast majority of the population visit a doctor at least once a year (Robert Wood Johnson Foundation 1983). Thus, effective primary care can do a great deal to support patients in distress and refer those needing more intensive and sophisticated services to appropriate professionals and facilities. Large numbers of patients coming to doctors either report or show evidence of serious psychosocial and emotional difficulties, and many physicians feel at a loss in knowing how to deal appropriately with such patients (Institute of Medicine 1979). Even the estimates from the ECA studies that 41 to 63 percent of all mental health visits occur in the primary care sector underestimate such morbidity because many patients do not define their problems in mental health terms, presenting their complaints in somatic or nonspecific ways. Physicians are, thus, often ambivalent and uncertain about appropriate treatment and referral, are commonly insecure about diagnosis and psychotropic medication, and must cope with the somatization of psychological distress and the unacceptability of mental health diagnoses to many patients.

Referral to the specialized mental health sector depends on the seriousness of the disorder, the physician's knowledge and attitudes toward mental health professionals, the availability of insurance, and the physician's perception of the willingness of the patient to accept mental health treatment. Patients' cultural background and attitudes toward the use of psychological services are significant factors affecting referral (Mechanic 1978, 1982). Studies comparing independent standardized psychiatric assessment of primary care patients to how such patients were diagnosed and managed indicate that primary care physicians commonly do not recognize psychiatric symptoms, and even less frequently make a mental health diagnosis or prescribe appropriate psychotropic medication for these patients (Wells et al. 1996). Accuracy of diagnosis appears to depend on the way the doctor interviews patients, personality, and academic ability; it is not related to self-assessment of psychological skills or experience (Goldberg and Huxley 1980).

Of those patients seen by primary care physicians, relatively few are ever referred for specialized care. Those who come or are referred to psychiatric settings tend to have more severe symptoms and social and cultural orientations that enhance their receptivity to psychiatric care (Greenley and Mechanic 1976; Greenley, Mechanic, and Cleary 1987). The majority of patients, however, receive whatever treatment they obtain from primary care physicians. Estimates vary a great deal as to the proportion of patients in general medical settings who suffer from these types of symptoms, but there is wide agreement that they constitute a considerable burden of demand on ambulatory care facilities (Andersen et al. 1977; Institute of Medicine 1979). The distress associated with these patients' problems triggers a demand for medical service (Tessler, Mechanic, and Dimond 1976), and such patients are often recipients of intensive medical and surgical care that achieves little of value. Support, reassurance, and relief of suffering through pharmacological intervention, in contrast, are of some use.

The largest amount of attention has been given to the treatment of depression in primary care, since it is common and it substantially impairs function. Treatment is often inappropriate, with heavy emphasis on minor tranquilizers and insufficient use of antidepressant medications. Even when primary care physicians use antidepressants, they typically use too small doses and do not maintain sufficient continuity of drug treatment (Wells et al. 1996). One hypothesis is that primary care physicians are reluctant to use antidepressants because of their side effects, and they often underestimate the extent to which depression is disruptive of their patients' lives. With the acceptance of new types of antidepressants discussed earlier, such as the SSRIs, which have fewer side effects and are tolerated more easily, primary care physicians may treat depression more adequately in the future. In the early 1990s, prescriptions for antidepressants increased dramatically (Wells et al. 1996) and Prozac® began to dominate the antidepressant market (Berger and Fukunishi 1996). Other SSRIs such as Zoloft® and Paxil® are also very commonly used. A recent randomized controlled trial found that motivated family physicians and internists trained to follow a standardized pharmacotherapeutic approach can achieve outcomes comparable to psychiatrists in the treatment of major depression (Schulberg et al. 1996). Uncertainty, however, characterizes treatment of less severe depressions. Medication treatment has been demonstrated to be effective in the treatment of major depression, but the evidence is far less convincing for many of the less severe depressions, common in primary care.

Attitudes toward the use of psychoactive drugs depend very much on values. Some believe that people should make efforts to cope without pharmacological assistance and that drugs should be a last resort. Others believe that drugs are prescribed too sparingly and that many people's lives could be made better by wider use of psychoactive drugs. Although it is an old debate, the attention given to Prozac® and some of the claims made for its positive personality effects, and the popularity of the book *Listening to Prozac,* rekindled the debate. Prozac® and other SSRIs are safer to use than earlier antidepressants, but patients on drugs need to be monitored carefully. Murphy (1975a,b) found that 71 to 91 percent of patients who committed suicide had been under recent care of a physician. More than two-thirds of these patients had histories of suicide threats or attempts, but these suicide gestures were known to only two-fifths of the physicians who provided care for them. There was evidence that three-quarters of the patients were depressed, but this diagnosis was rarely made by nonpsychiatrists, nor was the depression treated. More than half of those who died by overdose had an unlimited prescription of the substance ingested or had received a prescription within a week or less before their deaths.

Any effective system of primary medical care services must take account of these issues. However much physicians may wish to limit their responsibilities and the scope of their work, such patients will continue to constitute a significant component of patient demand. From a public policy perspective, it would be neither productive nor economical to attempt to shift all these patients to more specialized care. We have no evidence of the effectiveness of such care in most instances, and such a shift would take scarce resources from patients with more profound disabilities who need the available specialized services. Planning to ensure that patients with distress syndromes receive supportive assistance from the general medical sector is highly desirable, however. This can be facilitated by improving the capacity of primary care practitioners to recognize more reliably such common problems as depression, alcoholism, and anxiety, and by increasing their confidence in their ability to deal with such problems. Perhaps most importantly, primary care physicians must improve their pharmacological knowledge of psychoactive drugs and their knowledge of effective psychotherapeutic interventions.

With the growth of managed care, whether in the form of group prepaid practice or more loosely structured capitated Independent Practice Associations (IPAs) and networks, much attention is being given to better integrating behavioral health services with general medical services. A variety of models are being tested, but there is little definitive information on which work best. A great deal depends on local circumstances, the attitudes and capacities of involved health care professionals, work demands and time pressures, and the incentives or disincentives to work together. It has generally been assumed that as physicians become more organized in capitated groups it will be easier to integrate nonphysician mental health personnel into primary care to provide counseling, behavior therapy, and supportive assistance and to assist in organizing and coordinating self-help and group-help efforts.

Functionally integrated models seek to provide mental health care as part of overall health care in a seamless pattern. One approach is to have primary care physicians provide most mental health services, receiving guidance, support, and sometimes direct assistance from mental health professionals who work closely with them and help develop their capacities to provide mental health services. In a New Haven, Connecticut, HMO, for example, a consultant–psychiatrist role was developed for primary care to provide backup assistance and support for the primary care practitioner (Coleman and Patrick 1978). Primary care doctors took on more mental health issues, but with many changes taking place it was difficult to attribute this increase specifically to the intervention. This type of approach follows the inpatient function of *liaison psychiatry,* where a psychiatrist serves as a consultant to doctors who are managing patients whose problems are complicated by mental health problems. Although liaison psychiatry is an accepted subspecialty, research on its effectiveness in primary care is quite mixed (Katon and Gonzales 1994). Outcomes seem to be better when the consultant psychiatrist becomes more involved with the primary care doctor and patient and does not simply guide the primary care doctor, when treatment is more intense, and when there are structural changes in patterns of care (Saravay and Strain 1994).

Many group HMOs maintain their own mental health department for referrals from primary care physicians, an internal "carve-out" arrangement. How well this works seems to depend on the quality of the mental health services and the ties that develop between primary care doctors and mental health providers. To the extent that high general medical care costs of patients with psychiatric disorders are reduced when attention is given to their mental health needs, the HMO benefits. An integrated capitated plan also provides opportunities to reduce the intensity of mental health interventions. The Group Health Cooperative of Puget Sound, the HMO included in the RAND health insurance experiment, represents such an internal carve-out. As we already noted, access to mental health care was relatively easy but the intensity of service was low. There was no evidence that the less-intense pattern of care resulted in poorer outcomes. The poorer performance of HMOs in treating depression observed in the Medical Outcomes Study was primarily concentrated in the IPA-type of HMO and not the staff and group models, such as the Group Health Cooperative of Puget Sound or Harvard Pilgrim Health Care (Wells et al. 1996). However, a pattern of service for the patient in moderate distress may not fit the needs of patients with more serious illness.

A common approach used by some HMOs that lack the interest or capacity to provide mental health services is to *carve out* mental health from the health insurance package and contract with a behavioral health company to organize and manage the necessary services through a network they develop and maintain. These are increasingly risk contracts where the company can make profits or experience financial losses depending on how successfully they manage care. While such carve-outs have advantages in enlisting an experienced and motivated network of mental health practitioners to provide services, some of the advantages of integration are lost if both the medical care provider and the behavioral health provider do not maintain close contact and cooperation. Such cooperation may be difficult in this type of arrangement.

As HMOs have more experience with organizing services using primary care gatekeepers, they may find it convenient to use gatekeepers who have more intensive mental health training. Some postgraduate programs are beginning to be developed to train practitioners who have specialty qualifications in both family practice and psychiatry and who can better manage within a single practice patients with both medical and mental health needs. This has great advantages, because patients often resist referrals to mental health services and prefer to receive their treatment within a nonpsychiatric setting. Finally, there is continuing experimentation with expanded models of care that cover a broader range of medical and long-term care services. These models are primarily being organized for the frail elderly rather than for persons with mental illness, but similar principles apply.

In the case of persons with severe and persistent mental illness, it may ultimately be more wise to develop models of integrated care within a specialized mental health HMO, where primary responsibility for organizing and managing services is given to the mental health organization. In this model the mental health HMO receives a capitation sufficient to cover needs for housing, medical care, and social services, as well as psychiatric care, and the HMO contracts with other agencies to ensure that the broad needs of their clients are adequately met. Some organizations of this type have shown promise (Mechanic and Aiken 1989), but development costs are high and the process is difficult.

The Management of Psychological Distress

The response of the doctor to the patients' distress is affected by conceptions of etiology. To the extent that such common problems as depression and substance abuse are masked by the presentation of general physical complaints and are linked to unalterable life stresses, severe disappointments, or grave misfortunes, the physicians realistically may not see themselves in a good position to do very much beyond prescribing drugs to relieve symptoms. The patients' somatization may be adaptive as compared to intolerable alternatives, and it may be unproductive to undermine patients' defenses when they are unwilling or unable to deal with the conditions of their lives (Corney 1984). A cross-cultural example brings this issue sharply into focus.

In China, neurasthenia is a common diagnosis in psychiatric outpatient clinics and perhaps the most common *psychiatric diagnosis* in general medical settings. Such patients typically complain of somatic complaints characteristic of depression in Western countries but usually do not report comparable affective disturbance. Kleinman notes that psychiatrists in China routinely view neurasthenia as a "disorder of brain function involving asthenia of cerebral cortical activity" (Kleinman 1982, 1986). In a project at the Hunan

Medical College, Kleinman identified eighty-seven patients with this diagnosis who met DSM-III criteria for major depression and treated them with antidepressants. At follow-up, while a majority appeared to show significant improvement in psychiatric symptoms, there was much less effect in decreasing help seeking, maladaptive functioning, and social impairment. The patients remained skeptical of the value of the drug treatment.

Kleinman views neurasthenia as a bioculturally patterned illness experience, and he links it to extraordinary hardships in the lives of patients from which they could not escape given the harsh realities of the Chinese social system. The somatic discourse used by patients, and accepted by doctors, serves as a limited escape from involuntary and taxing life situations, and the illness idiom offers greater legitimacy than alternative escape routes (Kleinman 1986). The issue is whether modifying the Chinese doctor's concept of the clinical problem serves any constructive purpose. To the extent that the patient needs the illness, and neither the doctor nor the patient have the means to modify the harsh circumstances of the patient's life, the diagnosis, and its underlying meanings, may serve a useful purpose in providing a release, however limited, from restrictive and unalterable social conditions. The organic etiology attributed to the condition is culturally acceptable, while a diagnosis of depression or another emotional diagnosis is more suspect and more stigmatized. From one perspective Chinese medical practice appears out-of-date; from another, it seems to fit the cultural and social conditions exceedingly well.

In Western societies, physicians have more influence than in China, and the societies offer more opportunities for life changes. Moreover, there is a strong belief in psychological phenomena and a widely shared view that it is desirable that people be in touch with themselves, views that have increasingly affected conceptions of primary medical care and the orientation of physicians to patients with psychological distress. This trend, which some physicians intuitively if not openly resist, is as much the result of a psychological ideology as it is of an established foundation of empirical results. It is undoubtedly true that some patients experience relief of physical symptoms by acknowledging their feelings and sharing them with an empathetic person. Specific forms of psychotherapy focused on interpersonal relations or cognitive orientations appear even more helpful. But it is also true that in many instances denial is an extraordinarily effective coping device and that excessive exploration of feelings and thoughts may increase negative affect and a sense of physical discomfort (Mechanic 1979b). Psychologizing medical practice has its benefits but also its risks.

The primary care physician, better aware of psychiatric morbidity, however, can use such information constructively. The practitioner can communicate an interest and willingness to listen, a cue many depressed patients feel is lacking and inhibits expression of their distress (Mechanic 1972b; Ginsberg and Brown 1982; Roter and Hall 1992). Such information also alerts the physician to suicide and related risks and encourages greater supportiveness, vigilance, and referral when the physician is insecure. Knowledge of psychiatric syndromes and appropriate specific medication also allows more competent management. All of this can be accomplished without imposition of psychological interpretations, without undermining the patient's coping efforts, and without requiring the patient to adapt to an unacceptable definition of the problem. This is a skill highly dependent on cognitive and communication capacities, and the skillful practitioner is in a strong position to relieve the patient's symptoms, offer meaningful support, and assist in strengthening coping capacities. With trust and patience and communication of willingness to listen, even recalcitrant patients shed some of their defenses and become more amenable to influence. Much of the potential of the doctor–patient relationship, even in an age of high technology, arises from the authority of the physician and the patient's faith (Frank 1974). These assets are extraordinarily powerful and a significant force if used prudently.

Although efforts must be made to integrate more psychiatric care into the mainstream of medical care, sustained categorical efforts will be required to provide effective services to patients with chronic disorders that involve considerable handicaps. Emphasis should be given to interventions that have the highest probability of minimizing disability and reducing suffering. When care is given primarily to comfort and support, priority should be given to patients with the greatest distress and impairment. Interventions should be measured by the degree to which they enhance well-being and social functioning.

Although many people have mental disorders of one kind or another, most do not need specialty mental health services. The subpopulation most in need of specialty mental health services are those with severe and persistent disorders that cause considerable impairment and diminished quality of life. Estimates from the ECA suggest that approximately 2 to 3 percent of the population fall within this category of severe and persistent illness (National Advisory Mental Health Council 1993), involving some 5 million to 8 million people. For many such patients, the need for care will be a short interlude in their lives, as in the case of many depressions; others, such as patients with schizophrenia, may require continuing treatment throughout their lives and will consume considerable mental health resources. Still others, such as those with bipolar disorder, alcoholism, and drug addiction, will need periodic treatment, depending on the severity of the problem. In theory, many of these patients could be cared for in general medical settings, but the practicalities make it unlikely that an adequate pattern of services for highly impaired patients can be sustained in these settings.

Although some primary care physicians with an interest in psychiatry may be able to manage chronic patients between episodes of more serious problems, the demands on primary care facilities make it inevitable that these impaired and frequently difficult patients will be inadequately monitored and neglected. Given the complexity of their problems and the intractability of their conditions, they will frustrate physicians and will suffer stigmatization by both medical and nonmedical personnel. These patients require a sustained community approach in addition to whatever medical and drug treatment they receive, and it is unlikely that an unspecialized medical context can effectively organize such services.

Whatever efforts are made to extend general insurance benefits for traditional psychiatric services must not overshadow the needs of the severely impaired patients who require services organized independently of the traditional medical sector. Such services will have to be provided largely by nonmedical personnel. Services for these patients must include diagnosis and assessment, appropriate medical care, sheltered care and preparation for limited employment, aggressive monitoring and training for community living, and continuing social supports. Although a variety of viable models have been developed (Stein et al. 1975; Stein and Test 1976, 1985), we have as yet failed to develop any sustained way of financing these efforts on a continuing basis. Such programs are difficult to organize and maintain. Without financial stability they have little chance to become established.

In sum, we might generally think of patients as having three levels of need, varying from the most prevalent conditions needing only modest interventions to those less frequent but more severe conditions requiring a wide range of medical and social services. The largest group of problems, involving a lack of general well-being and a sense of psychophysiological discomfort, is most properly managed within the general medical sector as a component of comprehensive medical care. A second category of more disabling conditions such as major depression, severe anxiety disorders, and substance abuse might best be managed through a collaborative process involving the general medical sector, but with considerable assistance from mental health professionals. The most severely ill patients and those whose disorders are complicated by comorbidities should receive highest priority for specialized categorical services that involve not only medical and psychiatric services but also the entire spectrum of essential community care services.

The epidemiological approach presented here departs significantly from the past, where individual psychotherapy by mental health professionals had been the dominant model. Individual therapy in many instances is quite useful, particularly when people are resistant or cannot tolerate drug treatment, or as an adjunct to drug treatment. But such psychotherapy should be brief and focused. Traditional long-term therapy may have great value as an educational exploration of oneself and relations with others, but long-term psychotherapy is not a cost-effective way of treating psychiatric disorders. Psychiatric drugs bring relief more quickly and in a more cost-effective way, although some additional supportive and goal-directed brief psychotherapy can help produce good outcomes. From a social policy perspective, insuring for extended psychotherapy is an inefficient way of using limited mental health resources. Although persons in the population attuned to traditional psychotherapies may wish to buy such services on their own, it is a poor policy choice to allow insurance to subsidize this service beyond some modest level without tough determination of its appropriateness and need.

Capitating mental health care within the context of HMOs offers a better potential for organizing services according to the epidemiology of mental health need than simply extending traditional insurance approaches. Doing this successfully depends on HMOs improving their mental health services capacities through their own efforts or through carve-outs. HMOs provide a structure, but much depends on the quality of service providers, the incentives that affect their behavior, and the quality assurance processes in place. As managed care grows as a force in mental health services, it will be important to monitor performance closely over time and particularly in regard to subgroups of the population who are most vulnerable, either because of the nature and quality of their disorders or their social disadvantage.

The situation is somewhat different for persons with the most serious and persistent mental illnesses who have been a public responsibility for more than a century. It is an illusion to believe, given the character of the U.S. health care system, that our system of medical care or the private mental health sector will give such patients high priority unless they are specifically contracted to do so and are held closely accountable. Even if the public mental health sector downsizes as a direct provider of services, and this should happen only very slowly and carefully, it will have to be a significant partner in establishing the definitions of appropriate mental health services and standards for their delivery.

Chapter 8

Managed Mental Health Care

Managed care is a general term that refers to a variety of organizational and financial structures, processes, and strategies designed to monitor and influence treatment decisions so as to provide care in the most cost-effective way (Mechanic et al. 1995). As it is used generally, the term is confusing because it covers approaches that vary in their incentives, processes, and effects, and that combine in a multitude of ways. Although there is a great deal of discussion about whether managed care is good or bad for mental health, such debate is not informative because the answer depends on the specific arrangements in place. Many of the complaints about managed care from psychiatrists and other mental health professionals reflect their anxieties about how these new developments will affect their patient flow, incomes, and clinical discretion. Some reflect concern that service changes being put in place are more motivated by cost-reduction than by a desire to improve services and that the changes will have damaging effects on access to care and the quality of service. With growing competition and many more profit-oriented enterprises, there is little trust that managed care approaches will bring benefits to patients or their caretakers.

In considering the impact of managed care on mental health it is useful to remember, as much of this book illustrates, that preexisting structures and patterns of care have had many deficiencies. Patients often lack access to needed services and frequently receive inappropriate care. Patients have traditionally been put into long-term treatment situations, both on an inpatient and outpatient basis, without a clear treatment plan or focused objectives. There have been few clear treatment standards, and treatment has often been determined more by clinicians' preferences than by objective information. Patients have been unnecessarily hospitalized, with the need for care defined by the number of days their insurance covered. Continuity of care between hospital and outpatient care has been poor, particularly for patients with the most severe and persistent illnesses. Such care frequently has involved a "revolving door" between the hospital and the community, and clients with severe and persistent illness have had much difficulty obtaining the range of community services they need. The overall system has been characterized by fragmentation, important gaps in service, and little coordination.

Basic Mechanisms of Managed Care

Four basic mechanisms underly varying types of managed care structures: capitation, incentives and risks, gatekeeping, and utilization management. Since these are combined in varying ways in different structures it is useful to consider them independently.

Capitation is a form of payment involving a fixed, predetermined payment per person for a specified range of services for a fixed period of time (Mechanic and Aiken 1989). The capitation received by a provider organization is the same regardless of how many services the person actually uses or what they cost. Some provision can be made to adjust capitation to take account of differences in age, sex, illness history, or other characteristics, but the basic idea in any case is that such prospective payment induces providers to carefully consider how they use expensive resources. Use of too many expensive services can lead to financial losses and efficient practices can result in higher earnings.

Capitation can occur at varying levels of organization. A private employer or a governmental program purchasing insurance for its employees or recipients can capitate a provider organization for each such enrollee. The provider organization, in turn, depending on how it organizes and delivers services can *subcapitate* specific service providers such as physicians, dentists, or psychologists. Just as the incentive underlying fee-for-service is to encourage use of services under uncertainty and to overutilize services, the incentive underlying capitation is to be conservative in the use of services in uncertain situations, to substitute less costly alternatives for more expensive ones, and to underutilize services. The extent to which these forms of payment actually lead to over- and underutilization depends on professional socialization, the context of practice, other incentives, and the types of quality assurance processes in place.

Underlying capitation is the idea of putting the provider at financial risk for the period the capitation covers. If providers are inefficient, they are at risk of financial losses or even going out of business. If they function efficiently they can increase their earnings. Managed care organizations can choose to assume the full risk themselves, share the risk with individual providers who are subcapitated, or, in some circumstances, share the risk with the purchaser. Sharing of risk may occur in situations where there is uncertainty about the needs of a patient population and the cost of caring adequately for them. This is often the case in attempting to capitate persons with serious and persistent illness or persons with disabilities. Thus, the purchaser—for example, a state mental health department—may agree to share risk with the contracting organization to help protect it against unanticipated costs.

Subcapitation is often combined with various other mechanisms to fine-tune the incentives for providers. These incentives usually come in the form of *withholds* and *bonuses* (Hillman 1987, 1990). For example, primary care physicians may be capitated to provide all necessary primary care services for particular patients. One way such physicians might deal with work demands is to refer many patients to specialists if they are free of risk for the costs of such referrals. Thus, a primary care physician might refer a patient with a moderate depression to mental health specialty services rather than take responsibility for treating the patient directly. To avoid too many referrals, primary care physicians may be put at risk for the costs of referrals when they exceed a certain threshold. In many cases, part of their income is withheld and the amount returned depends on whether they stay within expected targets. Alternatively, doctors who stay within utilization targets may receive bonuses that reflect the extent to which they practice in economical ways. Withholds and bonuses are used more commonly with primary care physicians and less with mental health specialty providers. The latter most typically work under a negotiated fee-for-service arrangement where the contracting managed care organization gets clinicians to accept discounted fees, and then manages their decisions through various utilization management techniques.

Gatekeeping is a process that limits direct access to specialists, hospitals, and expensive procedures. In many managed care organizations, enrollees are required to select a primary care physician who manages everyday care and becomes a gatekeeper for referral to specialists, hospital care, and various procedures. Patients who wish specialty care or other services such as tests and procedures must first consult their primary care physicians and obtain referral through them. The organization usually will not pay for services accessed directly except in emergencies or if the enrollee is in a special point-of-service plan that allows use of outside services (but with larger out-of-pocket costs). The physicians, as just discussed, have incentives to be judicious in making referrals. The basic idea is to reduce the use of more expensive specialty practitioners and medical procedures.

Utilization management consists of a number of mechanisms, including precertification, concurrent review, high-cost-case management, and second opinion programs. Precertification requires a therapist to seek permission from the utilization reviewer before admitting a patient to a hospital or initiating specified expensive diagnostic and treatment practices. Typically, the clinician, or sometimes the patient, must call the managed care company, describe the symptoms and diagnosis, and seek permission for the procedure. The utilization reviewer at this initial stage is typically a nurse who follows various algorithms to decide whether the requested service is appropriate. Most requests for inpatient care are approved initially, but when disapproved an opportunity is provided to appeal the decision to a physician or psychiatrist, who makes a further determination. Higher levels of appeal are also possible, but they involve considerable time, effort, and hassle. We do not really know how often clinicians advocate for their patients when hospitalization or procedures are refused or how often clinicians simply adapt their practices to what they know utilization reviewers will accept. Utilization review is not standardized, and each company that provides such services has its own criteria, operating procedures, supervision practices, and appeals processes.

Concurrent review of inpatient care is a strategy that seeks to reduce the length of stay and encourage the clinician to find less-expensive alternatives to inpatient care. Here the reviewer may authorize a few days of inpatient care at a time, requiring the clinician to justify each extension of stay. Concurrent review can also be used to monitor other courses of treatment, such as the length of psychotherapy. In high-cost-case management, the case manager from the utilization management company works with the clinician to develop a treatment plan for high-cost patients that utilizes less costly alternative care. In indemnity insurance programs that typically use utilization management, the case manager can authorize payment for services that are not covered under the patients' insurance benefits. The basic idea is to develop a flexible, efficient treatment plan for high-cost clients. Second opinion options or requirements are not typically used in mental health, although they are common for surgical services.

Utilization review and management can occur in any type of insurance program, although they are dominant in traditional indemnity insurance programs. Private utilization management companies sell utilization services to private employers and government programs. They may do so on a risk basis, where they are financially liable for high levels of utilization, or, alternatively, on an administrative basis, where they provide utilization management services for a fee. Increasingly, however, it is common for managed care companies to contract to manage mental health services on a risk basis, utilizing a variety of strategies to contain cost (Frank et al. 1995). Mental health services are carved out from the entire array of health benefits, and the company assumes responsibility and risk for managing the mental health care for the defined population covered by the contract.

Types of Managed Care Organizations

Managed care companies offer many combinations from a diverse menu of products, including benefit design, employee assistance programs, networks of preferred providers, health maintenance organizations, and utilization management. They also develop incentive schemes, profile the behavior of physicians and other providers, and put in place quality assurance systems. Since they work with employers and governments that have varied needs and wishes, they customize their products. Thus, they may vary a great deal from one context to another. As the saying in the industry goes, "When you have seen one managed care plan, you have seen one managed care plan." The variability and changing character of these practices are an enormous headache for mental health services researchers.

There are three basic types of health maintenance organizations (HMOs), with variations within each type. But even these distinctions become blurred as HMOs compete for market share, mixing a wide range of strategies (Zelman 1996). The traditional and most-studied HMO type is the *group model,* in which the insurance plan contracts with one or many large multispecialty groups on a capitated basis to provide services exclusively to its insured population. The professional group is responsible for its internal organization and processes and for distributing income within the group, but the insurance plan provides for hospitals or other needed physical facilities. These facilities may be directly owned by the plan, be available through contracts, or both. *Staff model* HMOs are similar to group models in many ways, but physicians are typically salaried and not personally at risk, although there may be financial incentives to help shape their behavior. The insurance organization, however, is capitated and is at risk. Physicians tend to dislike staff models, which make physicians employees, and they commonly convert to group models over time. Well-known group models include such organizations as Kaiser-Permanente and the Health Insurance Plan (HIP). A well-known staff model HMO is the Group Health Cooperative of Puget Sound, the HMO included in the Rand Health Insurance Experiment (Newhouse and the Insurance Experiment Group 1994).

The most rapidly growing form of HMO is the *network/Independent Practice Association (IPA) model,* a type of HMO in which for-profit organizations dominate. In this model an insurance organization typically builds a network of individual physicians or single-specialty physician groups who serve their enrollees. The insurance plan is capitated and also often pays its physicians and physician groups on a capitated basis. The network of providers is not exclusive; doctors and other providers may be in several such HMO organizations, and may also serve fee-for-service patients. The strength of such HMOs is the greater simplicity in developing them, the extensiveness of their networks, and the capacity to offer enrollees in the plan a wide selection of doctors. However, network/IPA physicians who typically practice in their own offices or in small groups with a diverse population of insured patients are less likely to develop the special programs, preventive care services, or professional teams commonly seen in large group and staff HMOs. Group and staff model HMOs more easily utilize nonphysician personnel, offer health education and chronic disease management programs, and develop sophisticated ways of monitoring their patient populations. However, they are probably less adaptive and accommodating than small practices as they become bureaucratized. The flexibility and choice network/IPA HMOs offer, however, helps explain why they are growing at three times the rate of group model HMOs (Freeborn and Pope 1994).

The preferred provider organization (PPO) is a related innovation that is not technically a form of managed care. The PPO is an insurance plan that contracts with providers to serve its enrollees at a discounted price. Enrollees who use preferred providers have little cost-sharing, while those who use outside providers have to pay a larger part of the cost. Various forms of HMOs are increasingly offering point-of-service options that allow enrollees to see any physician they wish and be partially reimbursed. Such plans provide the enrollee the security of knowing that they could go outside the plan, although they have to cost-share to a considerable degree. Point-of-service options increase the competitiveness of HMOs whose attractiveness to enrollees may be limited because of restrictions in physician choice.

Managed care organizations are difficult to study because they combine features in many different ways, and even organizations of the same type may vary significantly on key dimensions (Mechanic 1995b). Some of the early major HMOs were developed by physicians and sponsored by employers, unions, and consumer groups who believed that capitated care serving enrolled populations was the most appropriate way to organize care for communities (Starr 1982), but recent entries are more attracted to the potential for profits. Most of the early large prepaid practices were organized on a nonprofit basis, but more recent entries are large, profit-oriented firms that are publicly held and pay dividends to stockholders. There is much disagreement about the effects of the profit/nonprofit differences among organizations, but it is clear that varying health insurance plans have significantly different operating philosophies. Plans also differ in how they recruit, select, and supervise physicians and other personnel, their management and quality assurance systems, and the quality of the professionals and facilities in their networks. Plans may or may not own and operate their own hospitals and other facilities, may provide care with varying combinations of doctors, nurses, and other health workers, may provide varying financial incentives and evaluate their professionals differently, and may differ in the resources they devote to varying functions. From a consumer viewpoint, they may provide more or less flexibility in ease of access to care, varying degrees of choice for specialty referral, different types of special disease management and health education programs, and varying access to patient representatives and grievance processes. In short, the devil is often in the details, and these have to be acknowledged to fully understand how such organizations function.

Managed Care for Persons with Mental Illness

Since as many as half of the population report a psychiatric disorder at some time in their lives (Kessler et al. 1994), it is inevitable that all types of HMOs will have a significant number of enrollees with such problems. Most HMOs, however, only provide acute mental health benefits to enrollees and seek to avoid persons with severe and persistent mental illness. Such patients not only are expensive and difficult to treat, but also are high utilizers of all types of medical care. HMOs that offer too attractive a mental health benefit might enroll a disproportionate number of patients with serious psychiatric disorders, and none of them want to. Most plans offer a limited number of hospital days and outpatient visits for mental health problems, although some are developing a more flexible benefit package where persons with severe illness receive more services without significant co-payment, while others who are less ill and impaired but want these services have to pay more of the cost themselves (Sabin 1995).

Managed care plans have varying capacities to provide care for persons with mental disorders. Most deal routinely with common psychiatric problems like depression and anxiety, but few have the needed expertise to provide appropriate management for persons with severe and chronic disorders. Even in the case of such problems like depression, primary care physicians fail to recognize about half of such conditions (Wells et al. 1989). When they recognize and treat depressions, they often fail to use the correct drugs; when they select the correct drugs, they commonly select doses incorrectly. Wells and his colleagues (1989) also found that primary care physicians in HMOs perform more poorly in recognizing depression than doctors in fee-for-service practice, although the reasons for this are not well understood. There are initiatives in the United States and in other countries to improve the capabilities of primary care physicians to recognize and properly treat depression and other prevalent psychiatric problems. Such conditions are very common among medical patients, they contribute to high levels of distress and disability, and patients often resist referral to any specialty mental health services. As noted in the previous chapter, much of the everyday treatment of common mental disorders have been and will continue to be provided by primary care practitioners.

All large managed care organizations will also have as enrollees a smaller but significant number of patients with major mental disorders such as schizophrenia, major depression, bipolar affective disorder, and the like who require a great deal more than routine care. These are persons who may have insurance through their employer or who are covered as dependents on spouse or parental insurance policies. Many persons with the most serious and persistent mental illnesses have no such insurance or have completely exhausted their benefits and often are insured through the Medicare and Medicaid programs, depending on their circumstances and eligibility. Such persons may be treated within a particular managed care organization because that is where they receive their general medical care, because they have selected an HMO as their provider under a government program, or because the managed care provider has a contract with a government program to provide care to its mentally ill enrollees.

Managed care organizations handle serious mental illness in many different ways. Some large HMOs have well-developed specialty services and manage most mental illness within the organization, perhaps occasionally using outside providers on a contractual or fee-for-service basis. A common alternative approach is for the HMO to *carve out* the mental health portion of its activity and contract with a mental health managed care firm to manage services for persons with serious mental illness. Such contracts are often on a capitated basis, and the mental health managed care company assumes financial risk (Frank et al. 1995). The managed care company will have or will develop a network of professionals to provide the needed services. How the company develops this network and arranges financial incentives, reimbursement and utilization, and quality review will vary (Gold et al. 1995). Such companies might use subcapitation, negotiated fee schedules, or a combination of reimbursement mechanisms.

Many persons with serious and persistent mental illness are enrollees in Medicaid or in other programs administered by states. In recent years states have moved aggressively to put their Medicaid populations into managed care programs (Essock and Goldman 1995). In the early days they tended to exclude the disabled population from these changes because of the complexities involved in treating appropriately this high-need population, but now several states are also putting the disabled population into managed care. There are a number of alternative ways of doing this, and states are proceeding differently.

One approach is to mainstream the mentally ill population into existing HMOs. Doing so allows integration of general medical care and mental health care, but most HMOs lack the capacity to provide or arrange for the needed comprehensive mental health services. A demonstration program in Minnesota that mainstreamed the mentally ill into existing HMOs had to discontinue their HMO care when the largest provider refused to continue in the program because of adverse selection (Christianson et al. 1992). A second alternative is for states to contract with comprehensive mental health providers such as community mental health centers to take responsibility for the Medicaid mentally ill population on a capitated basis, and several states are doing so. A third alternative is for states to contract with one or more managed care organizations (called behavioral health companies) on a capitated basis to develop and manage a network of mental health providers for Medicaid enrollees. The behavioral health company assumes risk, or shares risk with the state, and then manages all aspects of services provision. In such cases the contracts between the purchasing agency and the behavioral health firms are of great importance in specifying expectations and responsibilities for ensuring appropriate access to a wide range of mental health services, provision of data on expenditures, access, and client satisfaction, quality assurance procedures, complaints processes, consumer involvement, and many other issues.

Typically, purchasing of mental health services is on a carve-out basis, and there are both advantages and disadvantages to such arrangements. One difficult area is establishing the appropriate boundaries between medical care and mental health care when responsibility is divided between two separate organizations. Persons with serious mental illness often receive poor general medical care; dividing responsibilities makes it more difficult to integrate the two types of care successfully. Moreover, achieving reductions in medical utilization by providing good mental health care may be more difficult when these functions are not well integrated with effective communication among involved participants. Carve-outs have advantages, however, because the networks of specialty providers include individuals who are expert in mental health treatments, who are experienced in dealing with serious mental illness, and who probably have more understanding and empathy with these patients than one typically finds in an integrated medical program. Integrated HMO programs may have dedicated mental health professionals, but they are unlikely to cover the entire range of specialized services needed to provide good community care to patients with significant disabilities. In theory, integration is highly desirable, but in practice carve-outs may serve persons with serious mental illness more appropriately.

An integrated mental health HMO is difficult to develop but might be appropriate for some patient subgroups (Mechanic and Aiken 1989). These are mental health organizations like comprehensive community mental health centers that are capitated to provide the entire range of services needed by highly impaired patients if they are to adapt successfully to community life. Thus, the mental health HMO is capitated by the state not only to provide mental health services but also to take responsibility for arranging needed medical services, housing, employment, rehabilitation, and other important services. Here the primary health provider is a mental health specialty organization responsible for and making arrangements for medical as well as mental health care. The logic is that mental health challenges are primary for patients with serious and persistent mental illness, and that the appropriate manager for integrating all needed care is a mental health specialist.

The most ambitious demonstration of this idea was based in Rochester, New York, where a nonprofit, voluntary corporation, called Integrated Mental Health, was established to administer a capitation program for persons with serious mental illness (Babigian and Marshall 1989). The focus of the program was on patients who had been treated recently as inpatients in a state psychiatric facility, although this capitation demonstration also had a program for persons whose treatment had been on an outpatient basis. The most disabled group, called *continuous patients,* included patients who had spent at least 270 days in a state hospital in the past two years. Integrated Mental Health, which contracted with the State of New York, then subcontracted with various mental health centers on a capitated basis to take integrated responsibility for care of these patients. For example, the capitation for continuous patients included all inpatient and outpatient medical, dental, and psychiatric care, medications, and other costs necessary for community living including housing when required. Two other groups of patients were also capitated—intermittents and outpatients—but the range of responsibility was more limited.

Developing such complex arrangements involves considerable managerial efforts in organization, financing, and coordination of services. Since the patients being capitated are all very high users of services, and risks of high costs are thus not spread over large numbers of patients, many of whom will use no services at all, determining the appropriate capitation payment and how to handle risk of unexpectedly high expenditures is a difficult problem. The challenge in capitating the serious mentally ill and other persons with disabilities is the difficulty of predicting with any accuracy their future utilization patterns. Risk adjustment methods that account for resource utilization in psychiatry are primitive and do not correctly adjust for variations in cost among patients. Thus, a mental health provider who is at risk and who gets too many very-high-cost patients may suffer large financial losses. Since many mental health provider organizations are small and can't take advantage of risk distribution over large numbers of patients, they are vulnerable. Moreover, mental health organizations who are recognized as doing an excellent job with the most severely disabled may attract patients who have the greatest needs and who are most expensive to treat. Thus, they are in danger of being penalized for their excellence. There are a variety of mechanisms for managing such risks in capitated systems, but working out the specific arrangements can be complex.

It should be noted here that the motivation for using capitation for persons with serious mental illness may be different than its use in the general medical sector. In the latter it is assumed that patient utilization and costs will vary a good deal, but in any given year most patients will incur low costs. Thus, costs of expensive cases are spread among a large population. Capitation in this context is primarily a way of inducing clinicians to be more prudent in their decision making and to think carefully about how they allocate resources. In contrast, many more persons among the disabled population will be high-cost cases. Important functions of capitation in this context are to integrate funding and clinical responsibility, to better coordinate services, to allow flexible trade-offs in decision making between alternative services rather than to be held to specific reimbursable benefits as in indemnity insurance, and to hold mental health providers accountable for each specific patient who is capitated. This is a departure from traditional mental health approaches, where providers have been budgeted to provide services to particular catchment areas but were not held accountable for the care of any specific individual. Although cost containment has been an issue for some years, early efforts in mental health capitation were more concerned with improving the organization of services than with reducing cost. The emphasis in the Medicaid program is now tilting more toward cost-containment objectives.

Opportunities and Special Problems in Managed Mental Health Care

I have already noted the lack of clear, agreed-upon standards in much mental health practice, the large variability in professional behavior, and the chaotic nature of much that goes on. Mental health practice, and private psychiatry in particular, has been fiercely individualistic and insistent on the autonomy of the therapist. There is great variability in all medical practice, but the boundaries of mental health practice are particularly inclusive. Managed care provides an organized framework in which clinicians and patients can be better educated about standards for appropriate treatment and management. It provides an opportunity for improved communication about appropriate standards of care and practice norms by making practitioners more conscious and thoughtful about their decisions, by the application of quality assurance processes, and by the review and use of practice standards for treating different conditions now being developed by professional associations and government agencies. The issue is not to impose these standards in a rigid way, but rather, to induce clinicians to examine their assumptions and practices and to encourage a more evidence-based orientation.

Another area that makes mental illness somewhat different from many other medical illnesses is the extent to which mental illnesses, and particularly psychotic illnesses, are stigmatized. High levels of stigma make it more difficult for mental patients to be seen as individuals within large bureaucratically organized systems, to receive appropriate priority relative to other patients, and to be able to advocate for their interests. Stigma is one of the reasons that persons with serious mental illness might not fare well when mainstreamed into general HMOs where clinicians are under heavy work pressures and may not be particularly knowledgeable about their special problems. Indeed, health professionals who have had little experience with the mentally ill might share some of the same stereotypes as the general public about mental illness and might therefore further contribute to stigmatization. Stigma could be as disabling as the condition itself. The presence of stigma makes patients particularly motivated to continue care with clinicians with whom they have developed good relationships and makes them concerned about the confidentiality of what they tell their therapist. Each of these areas may be challenged in managed care as contracts change and networks are modified, requiring changes in therapist. Also, managed care requires sharing confidential information among more people for managerial purposes. Managed care organizations have to be especially sensitive to these issues as they affect stigmatized conditions.

Serious mental illness also involves, more than most other illnesses, social costs for families, the community, and the legal system. Medical studies typically ignore these types of costs. With deinstitutionalization, many responsibilities of the mental health system were redirected to families, neighbors, landlords, the police, and others. New public policies often contributed to satisfactions both for clients and their families, but they sometimes put great burdens on family members and community life. Thus, decisions about when to authorize treatment, in what settings, and for how long affect not only clients but many others. The costs of withholding services can be shifted very easily to other involved persons and agencies in the community. Because these costs are widely distributed, and typically not measured, they are easily underestimated. It is even difficult for clinicians to understand and take these costs into appropriate consideration in treatment decisions. Evaluation of the impact of managed care not only must focus on high-risk subgroups who are especially vulnerable, but must examine costs broadly, considering the added burdens on family members, employers, the criminal justice system, and so on.

Performance of Managed Care

The complexities of managed care strategies, the many ways of combining them, and the different populations studied make it difficult to reach conclusions that are easily generalizable. Research is helpful in identifying particularly useful or damaging strategies, and when findings are reasonably consistent across settings and populations, we can have more confidence in them. Most studies of managed care simply compare some form of managed care organization with some form of traditional care and measure various outcomes such as utilization, costs, rehospitalizations, and functional status. These studies typically treat the managed care structures and strategies as a "black box" with little indication of the variations in the quality and experience of clinicians, operational procedures, financial incentives, risk arrangements, network size and complexity, or whatever. These variations, however, are of crucial importance and must be studied thoroughly.

Currently we know a great deal more about the prepaid group practice type of HMO than any other because this model has been a focus of study for many years. Experience with this type of HMO initially made HMOs attractive to policy makers because of the repeated finding that they provided services comparable to traditional fee-for-service practice at significantly less cost (Luft, 1981; Miller and Luft 1994). This was achieved by reducing hospital use and the rate of surgical interventions. In the mental health area, HMOs achieve economies by reducing hospital use and substituting less-expensive interventions for more-expensive patterns of care. HMOs typically achieve these economies by reducing the number of mental health visits, substituting less-expensive therapists for psychiatrists and psychologists, and providing services in group versus individual settings (Wells et al. 1986, 1987).

Until the Rand Health Insurance Experiment (HIE) there was much controversy as to whether the observed savings were a result of managed care strategies or because HMOs typically attracted healthier populations who needed less expensive care. The HIE randomized patients into the Group Health Cooperative of Puget Sound and compared them to fee-for-service patients who were not required to pay for their care at the point of service, an economically equivalent group. They found the same savings as those typically found in nonexperimental studies, indicating that the savings were a result of different management practice and not social selection (Newhouse and the Health Insurance Group, 1994). No one any longer seriously debates the fact that managed care practices can reduce costs, but there continues to be concern that HMOs seek out and attract healthier enrollees, particularly among the elderly population. This is of great concern, because a small proportion of sick patients account for much of the costs, and an organization that is successful in getting a disproportionate number of healthy enrollees can make very large profits. Such advantages encourage organizations to select the good risks and to try to avoid the bad ones, in contrast to competing on cost, access, and quality of care.

HMOs of both the prepaid practice and network/IPA variety reduce mental health costs for the general population (Miller and Luft 1994). In the Rand HIE, which measured mental health outcomes, patients did as well in the HMO as in fee-for-service practice (Wells et al. 1990), but this study covered few persons with serious mental illness and the range of outcomes measured was limited. The results suggest, however, that HMOs are capable of providing appropriate mental health care to the general population. What is less clear is whether these organizations have the capacity or willingness to effectively treat persons with more serious and persistent illness. Some important findings come from the Medical Outcomes Study (MOS), which examined how practice type affected treatment and outcomes for depressive illness. For the most part, this study found relatively few differences (Rogers et al. 1993). Patients in fee-for-service versus HMOs who were treated by all types of mental health therapists (other than psychiatrists) had comparable outcomes. Psychiatrists, however, typically treat more patients who are very ill, and here the investigators found that those treated in HMOs were less likely to have continuity of medication and had poorer functional outcomes over time than those treated by psychiatrists in fee-for-service settings. This effect was only statistically significant among psychiatrists in IPAs, and was not consistent across all sites, again suggesting the importance of getting beyond the "black box" and understanding internal variations within HMOs better. But this study also provides an important cautionary note about possible harmful effects of managed care that may be difficult to discern because they affect only some patients, treated in only some settings, by particular types of clinicians.

Patients who are most severely and persistently ill are more typically in Medicaid and other government programs, but managed care experiences with this population are too new to provide any clear conclusions about the performance of managed care. There are data on each of a variety of managed care arrangements, including mainstreaming (Christianson et al. 1992), capitation contracting with community mental health centers (Christianson et al. 1995; Manning et al. 1995), capitation with behavioral health companies to develop and manage mental health networks (Callahan et al. 1995), and specialized mental health HMOs (Babigian et al. 1992). All of these approaches successfully reduce costs for the purchaser but not necessarily for patients, their families, or others in the community. For example, in a mainstreaming demonstration in Minnesota, patterns of utilization were comparable among the mentally ill in HMOs and fee-for-service, but patients in the HMOs were more likely to receive services from public sector agencies that were not reimbursed (Christianson et al. 1992). This is, in effect, a form of cost-shifting to the public sector (Mechanic 1992). In capitation studies in both New York State (Monroe County) and in Utah, as well as in the Minnesota study, savings were achieved by reduction in the number of hospital days either by shorter lengths of stay or the prevention of hospital admissions. In the Utah study it is not clear that there were significant financial savings over three and a half years for patients with schizophrenia (Manning et al. 1995). Although budgeted community programs in assertive community treatment technically are not managed care programs as I have defined them, many studies of these quasi-capitation approaches find large reductions in number of inpatient days as well (Olfson 1990).

Data on quality of care and outcomes under managed care are more limited. Despite the significant reduction of hospital use in capitation studies, there is little overall evidence of lower quality of care or poorer outcomes. Existing data, however, also suggest three important cautions. First, they indicate that while overall performance is comparable, patients who are most vulnerable may do less well in managed care settings where a fixed amount of services may be allocated among many severely ill patients. In these situations, patients with schizophrenia who had been high utilizers seem to get less services under capitation and appear to do less well (Manning et al. 1995). This reinforces the need for carefully monitoring the experiences of varying vulnerable subgroups. Second, the adverse effects sometimes observed under capitation seem to increase over time (Lurie et al. 1992; Manning et al. 1995; Ware et al. 1996; Rogers et al. 1993). This should alert us to the need for long-term studies. Patients with such conditions as schizophrenia have a fluctuating course of illness. Patterns of change can only be observed effectively over longer time periods, but most studies only provide data for six months or a year. Third, although the data are more limited than for mental illness, managed care studies on substance abuse present a more negative picture (Mechanic et al. 1995). Substance abuse services are especially problematic because the behaviors being treated are highly stigmatized, are sometimes illegal, and norms of appropriate treatment are less well defined. Consequently, there is a tendency to undertreat. Studies of managed care of substance abuse find, for example, that hospital use is reduced but without compensating increases in outpatient services (Ellis 1992); and that detoxification is substituted for treatment (Thompson et al. 1992), despite the fact that this approach is inconsistent with good treatment standards (Gerstein and Harwood 1990). The directions for future monitoring and evaluation are reasonably clear.

Despite the ubiquity of utilization review, we have less firm knowledge about its effects. It is clear, however, that utilization review successfully reduces costs for the purchaser (employer) by a significant amount (Hodgkin 1992). Although there are few formal studies, data from individual corporations tell a similar story. These employers, however, are not a random sample. The employers on which we have data who were motivated to engage utilization review companies were those who initially had relatively high mental health care costs. The data indicate that it is possible to significantly reduce these costs by using utilization review strategies (Mechanic et al. 1995). Savings occur in two ways. First, the fact of review itself serves as a deterrent and makes clinicians more thoughtful and careful about their resource use decisions. Also, as clinicians learn how utilization reviewers define treatment norms, they may accommodate their practices to these norms to avoid the wasted time, hassle, and frustration in appeal and advocacy efforts. Such accommodation may not be desirable, but it is the likely reality. Second, savings also occur through the decisions made by utilization reviewers not to authorize certain services or to authorize them for shorter periods.

One innovative study in a New York City fee-for-service health insurance plan with utilization management subjected half their enrollees to sham utilization review where all requested care was automatically approved, while the other half received the usual form of utilization management (Rosenberg et al. 1995). Since everyone believed they were under utilization management, this study does not allow assessment of the magnitude of the deterrent effect. It does, however, illustrate the second effect. In this situation the researchers demonstrated a modest but statistically significant reduction in procedures in doctors' offices and in outpatient departments that were true reductions and not simply delays in treatment until the subsequent year. However, there were no significant differences in patient admissions in general or for psychiatric or substance abuse, nor were there differences in length of stay. The reductions achieved by utilization review in this study seem very modest. This may be due to the particular insurance program studied or to the fact that the most significant reductions came through the deterrent effect.

The quality of utilization review is only as good as the quality of the criteria used and the experience and judgment of the reviewers themselves. Companies that offer these services have different operating procedures, have reviewers who may vary in training and experience, and supervise these reviewers in different ways. Some depend on carefully worked-out algorithms; others depend to a greater extent on the professional judgments of their reviewers. Some are more easily accessible for appeals and advocacy than others, and the programs may vary in time, hassle, and paperwork required to get decisions approved. Clinicians may also develop relationships with reviewers over time and learn to work together cooperatively. When reviewers trust the clinician, they may be less intrusive and more willing to accept clinical judgments, concentrating their efforts on clinicians they regard as less trustworthy. Large utilization review companies often have their reviewers and case managers at major hospitals and medical centers who can work directly with clinicians. The National Alliance for the Mentally Ill has begun issuing report cards on the performance of managed care organizations (Hall et al. 1997). In the first such report card, they rate various behavioral health companies on how they deal with the following components: treatment guidelines and practice protocols; inpatient treatment; intensive case management; medication access; response to suicide attempts; involvement of consumer and family members; outcome measures and management; rehabilitation; and housing. They assert that the industry "fails on the basic elements of care that people with serious brain disorders need to survive" (Hall et al. 1997).

Some Unresolved Issues in Managed Care

As managed care is extended to cover more of the U.S. population it will change in many ways. We are just at the beginning of this trajectory, and it is difficult to anticipate all of the significant modifications. However, many key issues are already clear. In this section I briefly review some of the challenges to be faced in this managed care future.

Managed care, whether in the form of capitation or utilization review, requires a very different way of practicing than has been typical in fee-for-service. Most clinicians have been trained to do whatever they believe might be useful for patients regardless of the costs and however little the benefit that might result, and it was assumed that these expenditures would be covered. Managed care significantly changes the decision calculus and requires provider organizations and clinicians to think much more carefully about how to organize services. It encourages more dependence on research evidence and considerations of the cost-effectiveness of alternative treatment strategies. Clinicians, in the future, will more commonly use practice standards as guides to treatment and have their decisions reviewed by others. Medical and professional education will have to adapt to this new practice environment and train student clinicians how to effectively work within these constraints. Managed care interests will also change many of the priorities of professional training and research. More emphasis will inevitably be put on common diseases and disabilities that are high-cost areas for managed care organizations and on ways of preventing disabilities and high-cost episodes. Professional training and research will be slower to change than many other features of the health care environment, but the cost pressures put on major medical centers by managed care is already having a transformative effect.

In the future, clients will have more opportunity to choose from among alternative health plans and will have more, and often bewildering amounts of, information to guide their choices. Much effort is now being put into development of meaningful report cards that provide the public with comparable information on the performance of health plans, including such information as patients' perceptions of access and satisfaction and preventive care screening rates. Although it is useful to have such information, much of it is too general to help persons with significant disabilities choose meaningfully among possible care alternatives. People are primarily interested in the performance of particular clinicians, but most information deals with perceptions of the aggregate performance of health care plans. Thus far, such report cards provide little information on the performance of specialized services such as ease of referral to mental health specialty providers, the availability of day treatment, residential care and other supervised arrangements, or the quality and range of mental health staff and programs. The quality and reliability of such information is likely to improve in future years, but it will probably be of greater use to relatively healthy enrollees than to persons or families with special problems.

Public agencies and mental health advocacy groups will have to play a significant role in assessing the available range of services and service performance as they affect those with the most severe and persistent illnesses. In situations where public programs purchase services for enrollees, great attention has to be given to the accountability of provider organizations, whether they be for-profit behavioral health companies or nonprofit community mental health centers. Specifications must clearly define the range of expected services, including availability of assertive community treatment, assistance with problems of everyday living such as housing and obtaining entitlements, and psychosocial rehabilitation, as well as access to care and quality of performance. Responsibility for providing timely data on such items as expenditures, access, and referrals to varying services must be clear so that performance can be monitored and problems corrected. Mental health advocacy groups, like the National Alliance for the Mentally Ill, must become involved in the contracting and purchasing process at the state and local levels to make the needs of their constituencies known and to influence the provision of services in constructive ways. They must be alert to abuses such as deceptive representations and marketing and efforts to discourage high-risk persons from enrolling. They also must be *watchdogs,* calling to public attention significant deficiencies in care and ways of improving services.

Many technical problems are yet to be resolved, but there are no clear solutions. Risk selection occurs even within subcategories of disabled persons, putting the potentially highest quality and most conscientious provider agencies and clinicians at financial risk. As long as providers can successfully play the risk selection game they have a disincentive to offer a level of comprehensiveness and quality of care that will attract particularly needy and expensive clients. We need much better ways of adjusting capitation to take account of varying complexity of need, and in the absence of such adjustments we require good models for making financial risk manageable. Alternative approaches include stop-loss protection that holds the provider harmless for costs beyond a certain level and blended systems that combine capitation with fee-for-service as a way of moderating the risk. Some states use a gradual process of shifting risk to providers over a period of several years as both the state and the provider gain more experience in the contracting process.

As managed care becomes more dominant in both private and public health insurance, and as profit becomes a more central motivation in health affairs, maintaining the public's trust becomes a challenge. Many states are now developing new approaches to regulating managed care. Advocates of competition resist regulation, believing that in the long run the market will drive out substandard programs. But the complexity of the medical care market, the difficulties of ascertaining quality of care, inadequacies of information, and the opportunities for abuse lead many people to believe that states should provide strong regulatory guidance (Rodwin 1993). To the extent that good non-governmental accreditation processes develop, as in the HMO sector where the National Committee for Quality Assurance (NCQA) is developing useful standards in its accreditation of plans, some relief from regulation can be given to organizations that achieve such accreditation. Although the NCQA is making progress in developing performance standards, this organization is just beginning to engage such specialized issues as mental health, and its mental health measures are limited and not sufficiently predictive (Druss and Rosenbeck 1997).

The extent of appropriate state regulation of managed care remains uncertain, and the HMO sector is critical of efforts to put greater demands on them than on fee-for-service practice. They rightly argue that fee-for-service medicine involves potential abuses such as the provision of unnecessary treatment, and they object to the assumption that their practices are any more suspect. The fact is, however, that the public is more concerned about potential undertreatment than overutilization, and is more suspicious of the management of large insurance organizations that are distant from them than small fee-for-service practices with which they are likely to have a personal relationship.

The question remains as to the appropriate range of regulation of HMOs, utilization management firms, behavioral health companies, and the like. No one really questions regulations that ensure that health insurance programs have sufficient financial reserves to meet their obligations to their enrollees, nor are there major objections to efforts to control misleading marketing, lack of access to care, or refusals to meet contractual obligations. There is more disagreement as to the extent of required disclosure and public reporting, requirements to systematically collect and report data on access, satisfaction, and other performance measures, mandates to provide particular types of grievance and complaints processes, and regulation of the types of incentives plans used with physicians and other providers, such as withholds and bonuses. Some states are also seeking to protect clinicians from reprisals when they appeal review decisions or criticize managed care arrangements. A particular issue has been alleged *gag rules* that contractually limit what clinicians can tell patients about the review process, and several states forbid such contractual clauses. In the case of utilization review companies, states are developing requirements for the timeliness of phone response to minimize clinician hassle, the qualifications of utilization reviewers, and the availability and accessibility of appropriate appeals processes. Some proposals require that only persons with medical training be allowed to disapprove authorization for a particular treatment. Several states and the federal government now regulate *drive-through deliveries,* requiring that new mothers have the option of at least two days in the hospital. Having legislatures micromanage managed care is probably an undesirable practice, but some of these legislative measures reflect public and professional dissatisfaction with what they view as extreme practices, and a breakdown in trust (Mechanic 1997).

U.S. health care is an enormous industry with expenditures exceeding a trillion dollars a year. Its particular structures, and its irrationalities as well as its strengths, reflect our economic and social philosophies and the interest group politics that affect how decisions are made. Despite many of the forceful changes that have occurred in recent years, health care provision remains extremely varied. The managed care strategies we see today may simply be a stage in the development of new structures and strategies to use our resources more wisely and more efficiently. Managed care is a new industry, and a great deal of sorting out is still necessary.

Managed mental health care is even less experienced and more uncertain, and performance data for the most part are unavailable. It is important to be vigilant about potential underservice and other abuses. But it is also important to see managed care as an opportunity to define mental health needs more sharply, to develop broader and better integrated systems of mental health management, to define treatment norms clearly and link them to a stronger evidential basis, and to develop performance indicators and better track the provision of services. Managed care also provides opportunities to train and use different types of mental health personnel and to direct them to tasks that were badly neglected within traditional mental health services. It has the potential of organizing services that were typically fragmented. We must remain alert to abuses of new managerial systems, but at the same time use this opportunity to guide change in constructive ways. Managed care is inevitable, and simply railing against it has little point. The challenge is to shape managed care and its various strategies so that we achieve the best possible outcomes for persons with mental illness and other disabilities.

Chapter *9*

===========================

Central Perspectives in Formulating Mental Health Policies

The future of mental health services in the United States and elsewhere depends on the resolution of many basic scientific and practical issues. Significant scientific advances are being made in the neurosciences and genetics, the behavioral sciences, and other areas, but we still substantially lack understanding of most serious mental disorders and the basic processes through which they occur. Some major advances have been made in pharmacological therapies, but while these drugs alleviate or control painful and disruptive symptoms, they are not curative, and they often have serious and bothersome side effects. Major disagreements continue as to the best way to characterize disorders, meaningful boundaries between mental disorders and social problems, and the means to best prevent, cure, or ameliorate the suffering and disabilities associated with these disorders. Whatever the state of our knowledge at any point in time, we must decide at the practical level whom, when, and where to treat, the appropriate scope of clinical practice and acceptable practitioners, and how to pay for services. In this chapter I explore some key issues that are important in formulating and dealing with mental health policy questions.

Concepts of Severe and Persistent Mental Illness

There is no agreed-on definition of *severe and persistent mental illness* (SPMI), but the term is usually intended to convey a history of serious acute episodes, continuing residual disability, and high levels of medical and psychosocial need. Such patients typically have serious problems in many facets of daily living including work, social relations, and family life. They are commonly unmarried or divorced, isolated from family, unemployed, and on varying forms of public assistance. Operationally, SPMI is often defined by extended or frequent psychiatric hospitalizations and a history of repeated contact with psychiatric services and social agencies (Freedman and Moran 1984). But some in the SPMI population resist or cannot access services and come to our attention primarily through the intervention of police and the criminal justice system.

The concept of SPMI refers to the time frame of illness experience in terms of duration and recurrence. As typically used in the mental health field, it conveys a sense of persistence and intractability, although we know from the studies already reviewed that patients with serious mental disorders such as schizophrenia may have very different trajectories of illness and levels of handicap. Shepherd (1987), for example, in a five-year follow-up of a representative cohort of 121 patients in an English community, assessed with standardized social and clinical measures, described four trajectories: 13 percent had one episode but no impairment; 30 percent had several episodes but with little or no impairment; 10 percent developed impairments after the first episode and had occasional exacerbations of symptoms and no full return to normality; and 47 percent had increasing impairment with subsequent exacerbations of symptoms. Depending on arbitrary definition and the relative emphasis given to symptoms and impairments, the proportion viewed as SPMI might vary from 47 to 87 percent.

In developing the national plan for the chronically mentally ill, the Department of Health and Human Services adopted a definition of chronicity based on diagnosis, disability and duration.

> *The chronically mentally ill population encompasses persons who suffer certain mental or emotional disorders (organic brain syndrome, schizophrenia, recurrent depressive and manic-depressive disorders, and paranoid and other psychoses, plus other disorders that may become chronic) that erode or prevent the development of the functional capacities in relation to three or more primary aspects of daily life—personal hygiene and self-care, self-direction, interpersonal relationships, social transactions, learning, and recreation—and that erode or prevent the development of their economic self-sufficiency.*
>
> *Most such individuals have required institutional care of extended duration, including intermediate-term hospitalization (90 days to 365 days in a single year), long-term hospitalization (one year or longer in the preceding five years), or nursing home placement because of a diagnosed mental condition or a diagnosis of senility without psychosis. Some such individuals have required short-term hospitalization (less than 90 days); others have received treatment from a medical or mental health professional solely on an outpatient basis, or—despite their needs—have received no treatment in the professional service system. Thus included in the target population are persons who are or were formerly residents of institutions (public and private psychiatric hospitals and nursing homes) and persons who are at high risk of institutionalization because of persistent mental disability (Tessler and Goldman 1982, p. 5).*

The notion of chronicity (or its more recent designation, severe and persistent) speaks to the trajectory of the condition and not the diagnosis, and, thus, it is difficult to obtain accurate estimates of this population. While diagnoses such as schizophrenia encompass large proportions of patients with SPMI, the diagnosis itself is not a true measure of chronicity, with course of the disorder and level of function varying a great deal. Typically, for public policy purposes, estimates are made of this population based on duration of illness or treatment or by disability as measured by welfare eligibility, inability to work, or reports of lack of capacity to carry out activities of daily living. Estimates are crude, such as the 2 to 3 percent figure used by the National Mental Health Advisory Council (1993).

In 1989 the National Institute of Mental Health funded a mental health supplement to the Household Interview Survey, a continuing survey of the U.S. household population. Although the survey is representative, it is based on reports of highly stigmatized conditions and, thus, provides conservative estimates. The survey found that 2.1 to 2.6 percent of the household adult population had a serious mental disorder that significantly interfered with one or more functions (Barker et al. 1992). The researchers also estimated that outside households there were 200,000 homeless persons with serious mental illness, more than a million in nursing homes, approximately 50,000 in mental hospitals, and another 50,000 in state prisons. These numbers are all relatively "soft," but they suggest the magnitude of the problem and the various settings in which persons with serious mental illness are typically found. The proportions of persons with serious and persistent mental illness may be small, but this still constitutes many millions of people, the 1989 estimate being 4 million to 5 million (Barker et al. 1992). It is important to keep in mind that persons with severe and persistent mental illness are a heterogeneous population with very different needs. A single number conveys something about the magnitude of the problem, and is helpful in giving the problem visibility and gaining public support, but it can be misleading. There are worlds of difference between the elder with dementia in a nursing home and a young homeless person with schizophrenia on the streets. Good public policy requires careful attention to each of the many subgroups that constitute the population with severe illnesses.

Criteria for Evaluation

Indices of cure have an unhappy history in the mental health field. As in many other areas, such indices have been distorted for administrative and propaganda purposes (Deutsch 1949). Discreditation of earlier treatment results was a source of discouragement and disillusionment in the early twentieth century, but retrospective study has shown that such debunking, like the earlier statistics, was exaggerated unnecessarily, contributing to a sense of hopelessness (Bockoven 1972). Past experience teaches that intelligent assessment of the effects of varying mental health policies must depend less on gross statistics that are easily manipulated administratively, and more on careful study of clinical and social indicators that characterize in specific terms the outcomes for patients and the community. In the last several decades, we have witnessed an enormous social change in the ways in which psychiatric patients are treated and in the contexts of care. Extreme statements—of optimism and gloom—are made on every side of the issue without detailed examination of actual outcomes for varying types of patients, their loved ones, and the community. Although detail always reveals a more ambiguous situation, social policy must arise from such ambiguity and not from idealized characterizations of reality.

The effects of varying mental health policies can be characterized and evaluated in at least three ways: (1) we can measure the subjective response of patients to various kinds of policies—whether they feel they have been helped, or whether they feel they have fewer symptoms and are more able to cope; (2) we can attempt to measure objectively their performance and the quality of their lives and those of others in the community after exposure to varying public policies; or (3) we can attempt to assess the consequences of various policies in terms of economic and administrative costs—does one policy lead to an equivalent outcome at less cost than another? All these forms of evaluation are important and compatible.

The most striking treatment change has been in the decline of long-term hospitalization and the growth of psychiatric treatment in ambulatory care settings. Although admissions are frequent, most patients remain in the hospital only briefly, and most of their care and maintenance occur in the community. Judged solely from this perspective, current practice fits quite clearly the aspirations of the Joint Commission on Mental Illness and Health (1961) and the legislation that followed.

> *The objective of modern treatment of persons with major mental illness is to enable the patient to maintain himself in the community in a normal manner. To do so, it is necessary (1) to save the patient from the debilitating effects of institutionalism as much as possible, (2) if the patient requires hospitalization, to return him to home and community life as soon as possible, and (3) thereafter to maintain him in the community as long as possible. Therefore, aftercare and rehabilitation are essential parts of all service to mental patients, and the various methods of achieving rehabilitation should be integrated in all forms of services, among them day hospitals, night hospitals, aftercare clinics, public health nursing services, foster family care, convalescent nursing homes, rehabilitation centers, work services, and ex-patient groups. We recommend that demonstration programs for day and night hospitals and the more flexible use of mental hospital facilities, in the treatment of both the acute and the chronic patient, be encouraged and augmented through institutional, program, and project grants. (Joint Commission on Mental Illness and Health 1961, p. xviii)*

Subsequently, we have learned what we should have known but missed in our enthusiasm for change. Community life is no panacea unless the patient's suffering is alleviated and social functioning improves. We have learned that community life, without adequate services and supports, could be as dehumanizing and debilitating as the poor mental hospital. We have learned that if the patient is sufficiently disturbed and disoriented, as many schizophrenic patients are, residence in the home or community can cause innumerable difficulties for family and others and may result in a general outcome inferior to good institutional care. We must understand more thoroughly what happens to the mental patient outside the hospital—the extent to which difficulties occur and the way they are handled. Intelligent planning of community services depends on a firm understanding of the true consequences of various policies.

An initial classic study was an experimental investigation of the prevention of hospitalization (Pasamanick, Scarpitti, and Dinitz 1967). The major intent of the study was to determine the relative value of hospital versus home treatment for schizophrenic patients under varying circumstances. The investigators randomized 152 schizophrenic patients referred to a state hospital into three groups: a drug home-care group; a placebo home-care group; and a hospital control group. Patients treated at home were visited regularly by public health nurses and were seen less frequently by a staff psychologist, a social worker, and a psychiatrist for evaluation purposes. The study compared hospital treatment and home-care treatment by public health nurses and also compared home-care patients receiving drugs and those not receiving drugs.

Patients were involved in the study from six to thirty months. The investigators found that over 77 percent of the drug home-care patients remained at home throughout the study period in contrast to 34 percent of those receiving placebos. They estimated, using the hospital control group as a base, that the fifty-seven home patients, receiving drugs saved over 4,800 days of hospitalization and that the forty-one patients in the placebo group saved over 1,150 inpatient days. They also observed that members of the control group treated in the hospital required rehospitalization more frequently after they returned to the community than did the patients who were treated at home on drugs from the very start. The authors came to the following conclusion:

> *This carefully designed experimental study confirmed our original hypothesis that home care for schizophrenic patients is* feasible, *that the combination of drug therapy and public health nurses' home visitations is* effective *in preventing hospitalization, and that home care is at least as good a method of treatment as hospitalization by any or all criteria, and probably superior by most. (Pasamanick Scarpitti, and Dinitz 1967, p. ix)*

One aspect of the study raised some question as to whether remaining at home is an adequate measure of rehabilitation. The investigators selected patients for the study when they were referred to the state hospital for treatment. The relatives of the patients randomly selected for home treatment were informed that hospital treatment was unnecessary and that home care was more appropriate; "a due amount of persuasion" (p. 40) was used to convince the relatives to accept the patient at home. The design of the study had two consequences that differentiated those treated in the hospital from those treated at home. First, the hospital defined itself as a less appropriate context for treating the symptoms and the conditions of some patients and may have served to define different frames of reference as to what symptoms justify hospitalization among relatives of home-care and hospital-care cases. Second, by resisting the hospitalization of patients in the home-care cases, the hospital may have communicated a greater lack or willingness to help the relatives of those in the home-care group during periods of crisis than to help relatives of those in the hospital-care group. It is not unreasonable to expect that, once people are refused help of a particular sort, they are less likely to request it on the second occasion, and this tendency may explain the greater use of the hospital on subsequent occasions by patients in the hospital-treatment group. We must evaluate rehabilitation on other grounds than the frequency of hospitalization.

The investigators provided various data that reflect the psychiatric and social functioning of the patients after six, eighteen, and twenty-four months. These data generally show considerable improvements in all groups by the sixth month, with rather little improvement thereafter. One form of treatment did not have clearly superior results in comparison to the results of others. Using the criterion of social functioning, we have little justification for choosing one form of care over another.

Finally, we should inquire into the social costs of retaining patients in the community. We can assess these costs to some extent by using data on various burdensome kinds of behavior. The investigators demonstrated that these difficult behaviors decreased substantially by the sixth month, although they occurred frequently during the initial study period. At the beginning of the study, all three groups showed an equivalent level of family and community disturbance. When the patient was removed to the hospital, the family and the community were relieved of these difficulties; when the patient stayed home, these problems continued, although they decreased through time. The data from this study did not allow assessment of how quickly the initial symptoms decreased. It was clear, however, that disturbing and troubling behavior was relieved more quickly than inadequate role performance. It should be emphasized, however, that these data on schizophrenic patients described perhaps the most disabled type of patient and cannot be readily generalized to other populations.

These data suggest that there may be considerable social cost in maintaining the patient in the community during the earliest phase of an acute episode. One alternative is to use the hospital during periods of greatest strain early in the illness episode, followed by an expeditious release. The other alternative is to provide intensive community services for patients and those who relate to them during the period when social and family costs are high. Experience in a variety of settings suggests that professional views of what families should and can do to care for disordered patients are powerful influences on behavior. It is possible to persuade families and the community to avoid hospitalization, but such a policy requires aggressive professional support for those who must cope with the social and psychological costs of such policies. In any given instance, the choice of appropriate policy depends on individual circumstances, the services available to relieve and aid in home-care situations, and, if a family setting is not appropriate, the availability of other suitable community settings.

The impact of mental illness on the family and on the psychological development of children and the resulting burden are no small matters (Kreisman and Joy 1974, Feldman et al. 1987, Reinhard and Horwitz 1996, Tessler and Gamache 1994). The psychological developmental theories dominant in the decades of the 1960s and 1970s commonly concentrated on family factors in contributing to mental illness and unfairly, and with little evidence, blamed families for the mental illnesses suffered by their members. Instead of using the family as a resource, therapists often isolated the family and induced feelings of guilt, often in an unconstructive way. There was far too little concern with the real difficulties of living with a seriously mentally ill person, ways of relieving the stress and burden on family members, and the necessary steps for providing community resource systems that would make community care an effective option. Some of the early studies carried out in England clearly pointed to some of the issues that had to be addressed.

An English five-year follow-up study of 339 schizophrenic hospital patients who returned to the community (Brown et al. 1966), for example, examined the behavior of patients and the impact of their behavior on relatives and the community. This study suggests that community care for schizophrenic patients involves considerable social cost. The investigators found that in the six-month period prior to the interview, 14 percent of first admissions and 27 percent of previously admitted patients showed violent, threatening, or destructive behavior. Thirty-one percent of first admissions and 49 percent of readmissions had delusions and hallucinations. Twenty-eight percent and 45 percent, respectively, had other symptoms of schizophrenia, such as marked social withdrawal, slowness, posturing, and odd behavior. Finally, 41 percent of first admissions and 47 percent of previous admissions had other symptoms, such as headaches, phobias, and depression. A significant proportion of relatives of these patients reported that the patient's illnesses were harmful to their health, affected the children adversely, created financial difficulties, and resulted in restriction of leisure activities and of the ability to have persons outside the family visit their homes. Despite these problems, approximately three-quarters of whose who were living with a patient seemed to welcome the person at home, and another 15 percent were acceptant and tolerant.

One of the intentions of the investigators was to evaluate the effect of different hospital policies on patient care and functioning. They compared three hospitals, one of them known for its community care policies, and found that the functioning of patients was much the same in all three. Patients spent less time in the hospital oriented toward community care, but because they were released from the hospital before complete remission of their symptoms, they were more likely to be unemployed when they were in the community, and they experienced difficulties that led to more frequent readmissions to the hospital. Relatives of patients in the community-oriented hospital reported more problems than did relatives of patients in other hospitals.

We must view these data in perspective. Because they pertain to the most disabled category of patients, we cannot generalize the results to other psychiatric patients characterized by less social disturbance. The adequacy of community care program depends on the adequacy of the services available outside the hospital, and in the community studied such services were not fully adequate to the task, although they were probably as good as those found more generally. This investigation does demonstrate, however, that policy changes must be evaluated in terms of their behavioral consequences and problems and not only in terms of administrative statistics.

In a related study, Grad and Sainsbury (1966) tried to compare and evaluate the effects on families of a community care service and of a hospital-centered service. They were able to evaluate outcomes in two relatively comparable communities that had these different services. The investigators measured the amount of burden incurred by relatives both on referral and three to five weeks later. Approximately two-thirds of the families with severe burdens showed some relief from the original problem regardless of the nature of the service. Among patients presenting a less severe burden, improvement was somewhat higher in the hospital-centered service (36 percent versus 24 percent). In general, the investigators found little relationship between psychiatric symptoms and the extent to which burden was relieved in the two services. They did find, however, that patients with depression caused more hardship if treated in a community service rather than in a hospital service. There were other gains in having a hospital-based service. One such gain was that the closest relative felt less anxiety and suffered less interference with social and leisure activities.

In a two-year follow-up study of the same patients, Grad (1968) found that the hospital-based service was more effective in reducing anxiety and distress among patients' relatives and created fewer financial difficulties and other problems for the family. Young men treated in the community service were much more likely than those in the hospital-based service to remain unemployed for the entire two-year period. Differences in social outcome are of large magnitude and raise important questions concerning the philosophy underlying a community-based service. After further investigation the researchers reported that patients in the community-based service were treated more superficially than were those in the hospital-based service. Grad noted the following problems in community-based services.

> *Many social problems, especially those of a more subtle nature, were missed by the psychiatrists. First, their home visits were usually necessarily brief because of pressure of work; second, their interviews in accordance with their training and responsibilities and the families' expectations were patient-focused; third, the high social esteem in which doctors are held meant that family members would often either not presume to detain them by talking about their own troubles or feel relaxed enough in their presence to discuss those family trivia which often reveal social conflicts and stresses. (Grad p. 447)*

Other investigations support the observation by Grad and Sainsbury (1966) that the burden of mental illness on the family is not exclusive to psychotic conditions but, indeed, may be greater in what are regarded as moderate conditions. Hoenig and Hamilton (1967), in their study of burden on the household, found that patients with personality disorders and psychogenic but nonpsychotic conditions caused a considerable amount of objective burden. Rutter (1966), in his study of the effects of mental illness on the health of children in the family, observed that the manner in which symptoms affect family interaction is more important than the nature of the symptoms themselves. While psychotic delusions and hallucinations may not have grave effects on the family if the patient is otherwise considerate and kind, neurotic conditions may lead to destructive and treacherous behavior that disrupts family life and has a profound impact on the psychological state of others in the family.

> *Parental mental disorder is most likely to be followed by behavioral disturbance in the children when the parent exhibits long-standing abnormalities of personality. The "seriousness" of the illness in terms of neurosis or psychosis is probably not important, but the involvement of the child in the symptoms of parental illness does seem to be crucial. For example, delusions per se do not matter particularly but if the delusions directly involve the child and affect the parental care, it seems that the child is more likely to develop a psychiatric disorder. If the psychiatrist is to be on the alert for those disorders which are likely to have a harmful effect on other members of the family, he must inquire not only about the symptoms but also about the impact of the symptoms on other people. (Rutter p. 107)*

The studies by Grad and Sainsbury (1966) and other investigators should have alerted us to the fact that changing administrative policies and modifying psychiatric procedures to a limited extent are not enough to launch a successful community care program (also Hoenig and Hamilton 1967). Grad and Sainsbury believe that the essential ingredient in relieving burden is to assure relatives that help is available and that something can be done;

this is a reasonable goal within either kind of service. This sense of control, which Grad and Sainsbury imply, has been recognized in other areas of investigation as an important factor in mediating stress response in difficult circumstances (Lazarus 1966, Rodin 1986). The investigators further suggest that for certain types of patients in particular social circumstances, home care may leave the family with many more problems than an alternative residential placement. However, because psychiatric patients are not a homogeneous group, we must study in far greater detail which social and psychological circumstances will enable patients to flourish with home care.

In recent years, as more patients with serious mental illness have been treated in community settings, the issue of burden has received more attention, and research in the area is increasingly sophisticated in theory and measurement. Researchers differentiate between objective and subjective burden in relation to the extent of caregiving, where the patient resides, the connection to the client (whether parent and sibling), and the extent to which services are received to reduce burden. Studies consistently find significant problems that families must try and deal with. For example, in a study of family burden in Ohio in relation to a Robert Wood Johnson Foundation demonstration of care for severe illness in large cities, Tessler and Gamache (1994) found that common problems that families tried to control were attention-seeking behaviors (24 percent), night disturbances (18 percent), embarrassing behavior (18 percent), alcohol use (12 percent), suicide (11 percent), drug use (10 percent), and violence (9 percent). Half or more of family caretakers worried a lot about health, safety, services, and social life, and almost half worried a lot about living arrangements. In a New Jersey study, Reinhard and Horwitz (1996) found that two-fifths to three-quarters of parents caring for a mentally ill adult child were distracted from activities, had their household routine upset, experienced family frictions and reduced leisure time, and had financial strain and reduced social contacts. More than a quarter also reported missing work, neglecting other family members, and friction with others. Reinhard and Horwitz also found many subjective burdens, most prominent a worry about what would happen to their child in the future. Many studies report that caretaker burden results in high levels of distress, but Gallagher and Mechanic (1996) also found that living in a household with a seriously mentally ill client is associated with worse physical health as well.

The extent of burden and how well caretakers cope is related to how involved they are with the client and the availability of formal and informal assistance. Tessler and Gamache (1994) found that parents living with a mentally ill adult child provided more help and had to take more measures to control the child's behavior, but the more interesting point is the modest size of this relationship and the fact that even when the adult child is resident elsewhere parental worry and burden is high. The extent of burden parents experience depends in part on the amount of help they provide (Reinhard and Horwitz 1996) either in dealing with disruptive behaviors or in providing instrumental and emotional support and the extent to which they get professional assistance and support (Reinhard 1994). A significant policy challenge is to determine more specifically the types of psychoeducational interventions that help reduce caretaker burden and stress. In an intriguing study and analysis Horwitz and his colleagues (1996) found that the amount of support a caregiver gives to a mentally ill client is in part a mutual exchange. The more support and help a mentally ill family member gave parents and siblings, the more they received. This suggests simple interventions in which clients are taught to be less dependent and more proactive in expressing caring and appreciation, in helping with chores, and providing support such as acknowledging birthdays and other special events.

With the growth of research, and strong advocacy of the National Alliance for the Mentally Ill, caretaker burden has become a more visible issue. Professional services are now much more likely to work cooperatively with families to improve coping and social support. This is a significant advance from earlier periods when families were excluded from the treatment process, given little information, and often defined as part of the problem. Many programs, however, provide inadequate support, information, and instruction, and fail to make use of opportunities to mobilize families as part of treatment planning (Walkup 1997). Many therapists still endorse a strong ideology of patient independence and contribute to tensions between the family and an impaired mentally ill member who may be highly dependent on other family members. The issues are not always clear-cut or easy, but there seems to be little doubt that traditional therapeutic ideologies contributed more to blaming families than to encourage working with them constructively to deal with extremely difficult management issues.

Families of individuals with severe and persistent mental illness are frequently puzzled and angry about their interactions with the mental health system and mental health professionals. In situations where they have received little constructive support but are left with most of the burden, it is understandable that some have argued for slowing the deinstitutionalization process and providing more public mental hospital beds (Isaac and Armat 1990). Studies demonstrate, however, that families as well as patients are much more satisfied with community care than with hospital-oriented care when there is a coherent and well-organized system of community services with a clear focus of responsibility for individual patients (New South Wales Department of Health 1983; Stein and Test 1985; Marks et al. 1994; Leff et al. 1996).

Family concerns are represented by the increasingly influential National Alliance for the Mentally Ill (NAMI), formally established in 1980. This organization has grown rapidly in membership, visibility, and political presence (Hatfield 1987). NAMI represents families of the severely mentally ill who have differing points of view and no single ideology, but some particular ideas come out very strongly. First, the organization focuses on those most ill and has disdain for vague mental health ideologies dealing with the promotion of mental health that divert resources away from those who have profound needs. As two members note, "Bumper-sticker admonitions to 'hug your kid' and dance therapy classes are not of the appropriate caliber" (Howe and Howe 1987). Most NAMI members believe that severe mental illness is substantially biological in nature and strongly support the expansion of biomedical research. Many are angry at mental health professionals who blame families, but they are not hostile to mental health treatment. Most NAMI members support better systems of community care and seek to reduce stigmatization of the mentally ill. NAMI and other newly emerging groups fill an important void in advocacy in the mental health field, an issue to which we will return later in the chapter.

The Processes of Deinstitutionalization

In the discussion of the history of mental health policy, some issues relating to deinstitutionalization were raised. Here I review with greater specificity some of the forces that resulted in the reduction of public mental hospital patients from 560,000 to the small number who reside in such hospitals today (approximately 77,000 in 1996). The intent of this discussion is to define the major forces that resulted in change. Through such understanding we have a better opportunity to define points of leverage for significant improvements in the years ahead.

Deinstitutionalization had been ambiguously defined and includes a variety of different processes (Bachrach 1976). Beginning in about 1955, and particularly in the period 1965–1980, there was a transfer of patients from traditional mental hospitals to such settings as board-and-care facilities, nursing homes, and a variety of other community living arrangements. In some instances, such release policies led to charges of patient "dumping" and efforts on behalf of particular communities to exclude patients through restrictive zoning ordinances. In other instances impaired patients were placed in the community without adequate support and service, only to be victimized and preyed upon by unsavory elements. Various studies have demonstrated a range of patient outcomes and levels of social functioning depending on the community, the nursing home, and the living facility involved, and on the nature of the local mental health policies. It is clear that generalizations do not suffice; community mental health is as diverse as communities themselves and the implementation of local mental health policies. In some settings chronic patients receive superb community treatment and lead lives very much enriched compared with those possible in the best mental hospitals. In other contexts patients in need are neglected and exploited in an appalling fashion, function at low levels, and receive inferior or no services. Deinstitutionalization is decentralization and encompasses a wide range of experiences that result from the use of diversified settings.

The incentives for deinstitutionalization came from many quarters and had a forceful impact on social policy. The preventive and community ideology emerging from post–World War II experience established the general context, drugs provided an important and useful technology, and welfare expansion made the retention of patients in the community possible. The growing economic problems faced by the states in retaining large numbers of patients in mental hospitals were particularly important, and the expansion of the welfare system provided some relief of this growing cost burden on state budgets.

Consider the factors that were operative in the period 1955–1965. Neuroleptic drugs were widely used and were extraordinarily helpful in blunting patients' most bizarre symptoms and giving professionals, administrators, family members, and the community more confidence that patients' most troublesome and frightening symptoms could be contained. This facilitated unlocking hospital wards, allowed more patient movement within the hospital, and aided discharge to the community. There are documented instances in some localities of such changes without the use of antipsychotic drugs (Scull 1977), but it is unlikely that significant reductions in hospital populations, facilitated by a combination of social forces, could have been sustained without drugs.

The phenothiazines were particularly welcomed in large public hospitals that were overcrowded and understaffed and in which hospital personnel lacked confidence in their ability to manage patients or to communicate to families or the community that such patients were controllable. The drugs changed attitudes and encouraged administrative flexibility.

The shift away from hospitals was also facilitated by a social science ideology and a body of research that supported an antihospital orientation. But the key point to note is that despite the ideological environment, the emphasis on community care, the critique of hospitals, and the widespread use of drugs, the reduction of public hospital populations proceeded only slowly, approximately 1.5 percent per year between 1955 and 1965 (Gronfein 1985).

The explanation for the modest reduction of public hospital patients was the lack of an economic support base for returning patients to the community. Hospital staff had no difficulty identifying patients who could be sent to other settings but had many problems in identifying appropriate housing or assuring adequate subsistence. With the passage of Medicare and Medicaid in 1965, the introduction of SSI and the expansion of SSDI (the federal welfare disability programs) in the 1970s, and other initiatives for the poor, a stronger economic and residential base for deinstitutionalization came into being. The 1970s was also a period of social and legal activism on behalf of the civil liberties of persons with mental illness, which made it difficult to involuntarily hospitalize patients who resisted treatment unless they were imminently dangerous. In this period many different incentives were coming together, all contributing to pushing patients out of public hospitals:

- motivation to reduce state costs and shift as many costs as possible to the federal government
- a welfare safety net that supported patient subsistence in the community
- social ideologies championing personal freedom to control one's own life and independence from bureaucratic interference
- civil liberties litigation that made it more difficult to hospitalize patients or keep them there

The number of public hospital patients fell rapidly during this period, dropping from 370,000 in 1969 to 140,000 ten years later, an average reduction of approximately 6 percent a year (Gronfein 1985).

Beginning in 1965, the passage of Medicare stimulated the rapid expansion of nursing home beds, which provided a custodial alternative for elderly patients with dementias and, at the time, a new option for many younger psychotic patients as well. Under the Medicaid program, such patients when treated in state hospitals were fully a state responsibility, but once transferred to nursing homes the federal government paid half or more of the costs. This process of moving patients from one institution to another was called *transinstitutionalization,* and it was a significant part of the larger deinstitutionalization process.

Although the aggregate deinstitutionalization trends were impressive, deinstitutionalization was a disjointed process that proceeded unevenly in varying geographic localities. Many factors affected the different trajectories of states, including the size and configurations of their public hospital populations, fiscal arrangements between state and local government, the power of the hospital bureaucracy to resist downsizing, the vigor of community ideologies and advocacy, the economic position of states and pressures to reduce their budgets, the availability of alternative facilities, and the bureaucratic skills and ideologies of state officials in relation to shifting costs and making the most of federal opportunities. Between 1967 and 1973, five states reduced their inpatient populations by 20 percent or less, twenty-two states by 21 to 40 percent, and five by 61 to 80 percent

(Mechanic and Rochefort 1992). In the period 1973–1983, three states made no reductions or increased their patient populations, while thirty-five states decreased their inpatient populations from 41 to more than 80 percent.

As noted earlier, the social science community and public interest lawyers committed to civil rights and civil liberties provided the ideology that justified the retention of mental patients in the community. Both civil libertarians and social scientists were responding to the evidence of damaging consequences of long-term custodial hospitalization and the means by which people were involuntarily detained. We now turn to an examination of the way such environments affected patients.

Environmental Factors Promoting Effective Performance

The realization that mental hospitalization could produce profound disabilities in patients above and beyond those characteristic of the condition itself was a major stimulus to the community care movement. Different investigators have described these disabilities as institutional neuroses, institutionalism, and so on (Zusman 1966). There are many indices of this syndrome, but generally it can be recognized by apathy, loss of interest and initiative, lack of reaction to the environment or future possibilities, and deterioration in personal habits. Patients who have been in custodial mental hospitals for a long time tend to be apathetic about leaving the hospitals and returning to a normal life and to lose interest in self-maintenance. They lack simple skills such as using a telephone or being able to get from one place to another on their own. For a long time observers believed that this apathy and loss of interest were entirely consequences of psychiatric illness rather than the results of long-term residence in an institutional environment characterized by apathy and dullness. Mental hospitals, of course, are a much less important arena of care than they used to be. It is worth reviewing this informative literature, however, because the same disabilities caused by mental hospitals in the past are now caused by restricted lives in some nursing homes, board and care facilities and other community living contexts.

Erving Goffman (1961) provided one of the most provocative analysis of institutional influences on patients. In Goffman's terms, the mental hospital was a total institution, and its key characteristic was "the handling of many human needs by the bureaucratic organization of whole blocks of people" (p. 6). The central feature of total institutions is the bringing together of groups of coparticipants who live in one place—thus breaking down the barriers usually separating different spheres of life—and under one authority, which organizes the different features of life within an overall plan. People are treated not as individuals but as groups and are required to do the same things together. Activities are tightly scheduled, with the sequence officially imposed from above. The various enforced activities come under a single rational plan designed to fulfill the official aims of the institution.

In depicting the atmosphere of the overcrowded Saint Elizabeth's Hospital, Goffman described the plight of mental patients in vivid terms. From his perspective, hospitalization in a mental institution leads to betrayal of the patients, deprecates their self-image, undermines their sense of autonomy, and abuses their privacy. Hospital life requires the patients to adapt in a manner detrimental to their further readjustment to community life, and their careers as mental patients are irreparably harmful to their future reputation. Goffman was sensitive to many of the deprivations of hospital life and to some of the abuses of the large mental hospital. But the view he presented was one-sided and very much organized from a middle-class perspective. Many of the deprivations Goffman points to were not experienced by all or even most mental patients.

Many patients find their hospitalization experience a relief. The community situation from which they come is often characterized by extreme difficulty and extraordinary personal distress. Their living conditions are poor, the conflicts in their life are uncontrollable, and their physical and mental states have deteriorated. Such patients are frequently capable of harming themselves or others, or at least of damaging their lives in irreparable ways. Many patients in mental hospitals report that hospital restrictions do not bother them, that they appreciate the physical care they are receiving, and that the hospital—despite its restrictions—enhances their freedom rather than restricts it (Linn 1968; Weinstein 1979, 1983).

Although Goffman made us aware of many aspects of total institutions that can be harmful to patients, we must recognize that total institutions can have good or deleterious effects depending on a variety of factors. Total institutions—hospitals, monasteries, schools—are organizations for changing people and their identities. If clients share the goals and aspirations of the organization, their experiences in it may be worthwhile and desirable. If clients are involuntarily admitted and reject the identity the institution assigns them, residence in such an organization may be extremely stressful and lead to profound disabilities in functioning. Hospitalized patients who feel they should not be in the hospital and who resent the regimen imposed upon them find hospitalization a stressful experience. But there are many cooperative patients, and it is incorrect to assume that the effect of the hospital on them is damaging.

Total institutions vary widely in character. They differ in their size, their staffing patterns, the organization of life within them, the pathways by which their clients arrive, and their expenditures of money, time, and effort. Goffman, in building a general model of total institutions, attributed to them all characteristics that may be specific to the hospital he studied, such as its size or staffing pattern. We have evidence that small hospitals with high personnel-patient ratios and large budgets performed their tasks better than those with the opposite characteristics (Ullmann 1967). Some mental hospitals have had deleterious effects on patients for a variety of reasons:

1. Patients may have been involuntarily incarcerated in order to protect the community from them, but once they were in the hospital little of a constructive nature may have been done for them.
2. The hospital may not have made sufficient efforts to maintain the patient's interpersonal associations and skills when removed from the community, although these may deteriorate if the patient remains in the hospital for a significant period of time.
3. Hospitalization may lead to the stigmatization of the patient.
4. The hospital may require adaptations for adjustment to the ward, but such adaptations may be inconsistent with the patterns of behavior necessary to make proper adjustment to the community.

In some hospitals, for example, patients are rewarded for remaining unobtrusive and docile, or they are punished if they attempt to exercise too much initiative. Unwillingness to take initiative, however, may handicap patients when they return to the community. Not all total institutions respond in this way, and the ward staff often views the participation and the initiative of patients as signs of improving health. Our attention should focus not on whether a hospital fits the model of a total institution but rather on specifying those aspects of such institutions that affect their performance.

There are many performance variables by which hospitals may be judged. Traditionally, the major concern has been whether they protected the public and those patients in danger of harming themselves. Early studies of large mental hospitals concentrated on such issues as how hospitals with many patients can be operated by small staffs and few professional personnel. Ivan Belknap (1956) devoted considerable attention to the work system of a large hospital and to the manner in which aides in the hospital developed a reward system for the purpose of maintaining a viable patient work force. Later researchers evaluated the hospital in terms of its effects on the patients' work performance, community participation, self-esteem, sense of initiative, responsibility in performing social roles, reduction of symptoms, and understanding of themselves and their illnesses. Studies of smaller, private hospitals gave greater attention to interaction among patients and staff, communication problems, and administrative conflicts and their effects upon patients (Stanton and Schwartz 1954; Caudill 1958; Coser 1979; and for a review of this literature, see Perrow 1965).

Many investigators have observed that patients with long histories of residence in traditional mental hospitals have disability syndromes that result from apathy and lack of participation rather than from the illness condition. One term used to describe this disability syndrome is *institutionalism*. Even those who adhere to a psychiatric disease theory do not find it easy to separate the effects of the condition from those of the environment because they believe that these interact in an intricate fashion. To evaluate the nature of the institutionalism syndrome, we must look at some of the research on it.

Wing (1962), a researcher studying institutional effects on patients, argued that institutionalism was influenced by three factors: (1) the pattern of susceptibility or resistance to various institutional pressures that the individual possesses when he or she is first admitted; (2) the social pressures to which an individual is exposed after admission to an institution; and (3) the length of time the patient is exposed to these institutional pressures. To test these ideas, Wing measured the extent to which hospitalized schizophrenics were impaired and then attempted to evaluate how length of hospital stay affected institutionalism among patients with comparable degrees of impairment. He found that patient groups with longer lengths of stay showed a progressive increase in the proportion of those who appeared apathetic about life outside the hospital. Although marked symptom change did not occur over time, hopefulness and willingness to cope with life deteriorated. In such studies, of course, there is always the danger that the patient's sense of apathy affects whether he or she is released from the hospital, and thus the results may be a product of the selection process. But alongside other findings, these results support the idea that hospitals can produce a sense of apathy and hopelessness among patients. Wing and Brown (1961), in a study of three British mental hospitals, showed that different hospital environments encourage institutionalism in varying degrees. The outcome of residence depends not only on the patient's susceptibility to hospital influences and the length of exposure to such pressures but also on the nature of such influences, which may vary widely from one hospital to another.

Wing (1967) maintained that patients who were long-term residents of hospitals were selected not only on the basis of their illnesses but also on the basis of their social characteristics. They often did not have strong ties with the community, family, or work, and were vulnerable because of their age, poverty, and lack of social interests and ties. Wing noted that these patients often were not concerned with the problems of personal liberty and restrictions, and might have found the hospital environment far preferable to community residence because this environment met their needs and made minimal demands on them (also see Linn 1968).

A second aspect of institutionalism, Wing argued, was the inherent unfolding of the disease process itself.

> *The bowed head and shoulders, the shuffling gait, the apathetic faces, the social withdrawal and disinterest, the loss of spontaneity, initiative and individuality described so graphically by Barton may be seen in patients who have never been in an institution in their lives. Studies of intellectual performance seem to show that the damage is often relatively sudden in onset, rather than gradual in development as would be the case if it were the result of imposed social isolation. There is little evidence either of gradual clinical deterioration. This is not to say, of course, that the social surroundings do not affect clinical state; indeed, there is evidence to the contrary. (Wing 1967, p. 8)*

The third component of institutionalism described by Wing is the influence of the institution itself, which gradually affects the patient over many years. This aspect of the syndrome is characterized by increasing dependence on institutional life and an inability to adapt to any other living situation. As Wing pointed out, these effects could be observed even on patients "whose premorbid personality was lively and sociable and in whom the disease has not run a severe course" (p. 9). Many studies found that a large proportion of patients in mental hospitals in the United States and other countries had no serious disturbance of behavior and were kept in the hospital for largely social reasons (Brown 1959; Scheff 1963; Ullman 1967). Cross and his colleagues (1957), in a survey of a large mental hospital, found that most of the patients had been under care for a long time and that a majority required only routine supervision. Cooper and Early (1961) also concluded, on the basis of their survey of more than 1,000 long-term patients, that most did not require custodial care and that a majority could work. Many of the traditional practices of mental hospitals failed to encourage patients to take initiative and responsibility and contributed to the institutionalism syndrome.

Many investigators have been impressed with the importance of the atmosphere of the ward on the functioning and attitudes of mental patients (Stanton and Schwartz 1954; Kellam et al. 1966), and concern with the influence of environmental atmospheres extends also to other organizations, such as schools and universities. The basic idea is that the emotional tone, tensions, attitudes, and feelings dominant on a ward affect the interactions among the patients, between patients and staff, and even among staff. This interaction, in turn, affects the patient's motivation, attitudes, and emotional state. For many years the investigation of these ideas had been largely impressionistic because of the difficulty of measuring different ward environments and correlating these to various performance and symptom measures. Significant progress had been made in the measurement problem by Rudolf Moos.

Moos (1974, 1997) developed a Ward Atmosphere Scale that depicts the effect of the climate of ward life on relationships, treatment, and administrative structure or system maintenance dimensions. The relationships include involvements of patients on the ward, support among patients and staff, and the degree of open expression and spontaneity. Treatment dimensions include autonomy, practical orientation, personal problem orientation, and expression of anger and aggression. Administrative structure variables include order and organization, staff control, and program clarity. Moos used these scales to study many hospital wards in the United States and England, and profiles of ward atmosphere can be used to examine treatment outcomes and patient adjustment. Moos found that programs that keep patients out in the community the longest have high scores on open expression of feelings in a context emphasizing a practical orientation, order and organization, staff control, and autonomy and independence. In contrast, programs with high dropout rates tend to have little emphasis on involving patients, few social activities, and poor planning of patients' activities. Patients in such programs have little interaction and little guidance, and staff are unresponsive to criticisms or patients' suggestions.

Clearly, in acknowledging the detrimental effects of institutions on people, we should not assume that such institutional environments have not produced rehabilitative effects as well. Mental hospitals have traditionally offered patients impoverished environments and have done little to stimulate them, but this does not reflect the changes that have taken place in hospital environments and many current efforts to develop personal skills and resources. Mental health workers have too frequently made the naive assumption that community life is always constructive, although particular family and community environments might have the same adverse effects on the patient's functioning and skills as a poor mental hospital does. The issue is not so much whether patients are resident in a hospital as it is whether the environment to which they are exposed is a stimulating and useful one for minimizing incapacities resulting from their illnesses and for maximizing their potential for living a life of reasonable quality.

As already noted, inpatient care continues to be a major component of management of persons with mental illness. Discharges for psychiatric care in general hospitals have been increasing over time (Mechanic and McAlpine 1997). There were 1.9 million such discharges from community general hospitals in 1994, and the type of patients being cared for are increasingly more severely ill as the capacity of public mental hospitals is much reduced. Thus patterns of inpatient care and their links with subsequent aftercare services are of great importance. Unfortunately, we know too little about the effects of varying inpatient interventions on the quality of patient outcomes.

My colleagues and I have been studying this issue in hospitals in New York State for a number of years (Mechanic 1997). Based on the literature (Olfson et al. 1993) we identified seven dimensions of care likely to have a positive effect on how well patients with schizophrenia do following hospital care: linkage of inpatient care to external services; medication education; medication management; illness education; family involvement;

substance abuse treatment; and psychosocial rehabilitation. We surveyed 178 specialized psychiatric units in general hospitals, virtually all of such units in the state, and found large variations in the extent to which staff reported giving attention to each of the seven dimensions. We found that units that devote efforts to mobilize family attention and resources also give greater attention to linkage which is crucial to a pattern of continuing care. Patients who had schizophrenia and also used drugs were most likely to fail to maintain their medication and to become homeless, indicating that this is a population that needs especially targeted efforts for compliance and for linkage with aftercare services.

Relatively few studies have examined the community contexts and environments that stimulate the patient's functioning and sense of hope and those that bring a morbid response. In an intriguing study referred to in an earlier discussion, Brown and his colleagues (1962) followed a group of schizophrenic men released from the hospital. They assessed the severity of the symptoms of these patients just before discharge and saw the patients at home with their relatives two weeks after discharge. During this home interview, they measured the amount of expressed emotion in the family. The researchers found that patients returning to a relative who showed high emotional involvement (based on measurement of expressed emotion, hostility, and dominance) deteriorated more frequently than did patients returning to a relative who showed low emotional involvement. This finding had been replicated in a variety of settings (Brown et al. 1972; Vaughn and Leff 1976; Leff and Vaughn, 1985). Earlier I noted various theoretical explanations for links between stress and schizophrenic breakdown, and it remains possible that schizophrenics cannot tolerate intense emotions of any kind. We still know too little about the types of environments that best promote control over symptoms and a reasonable level of social functioning. We do know, however, that disabled patients require incentives for activity and involvement, reinforcement for initiative and successful performance, and protection against an environment that is too demanding and too stimulating. The wide range of contexts for community care of schizophrenic patients yields a great diversity of treatment environments. Work is proceeding to describe these environments and their effects in greater detail.

One such study by Segal and Aviram (1978) examined patients and proprietors of sheltered care in California. Compared to the population, sheltered care residents studied were disproportionately in the age group fifty to sixty-five, had low education and low involvement in employment, and almost all had either never been married or had come from broken marriages (95 percent). Almost all such patients were supported by welfare, with three-quarters receiving Supplemental Security Income. Although this group was only moderately symptomatic and not particularly troublesome to the community, this population constituted a highly disabled group from a social point of view and was very much dependent on the community for its support.

Segal and Aviram examined the correlates of both *external* and *internal integration* in sheltered care. They first measured the relationship of the patient to the community in terms of access and participation, the latter involved the extent to which the patient is involved in the sheltered facility and the extent to which the operator assumes responsibility for mediating the patient's needs and relationships with the community. In the sample studied, the researchers found much more internal than external integration. By far the most important factor in external integration was neighbor response, and the most important individual factor was the patient's available spending money, which could facilitate community participation. Environments high on what Moos (1974) would call "involvement" and those with a practical orientation facilitated internal integration. Positive neighbor response as reflected in their reaching out to residents also facilitated internal cohesion. In short, community social support and involvement with clients facilitated constructive participation both within the facility and in the community as a whole.

Implications of Community Institutional Placement

Deinstitutionalization has not only resulted in the return of most patients to the community, but has also involved major transfers of patients from traditional facilities to other community contexts, including nursing homes and intermediate care facilities. From a public policy perspective, it should be apparent that providing an effective environment for mental patients is not simply a matter of whether they reside in hospitals or other types of institutions but, more importantly, what quality of life is achieved. We know with some certainty that inactivity, lack of participation, and dependence have an erosive effect on social functioning. Uninvolvement and excessive dependence contribute to diminished coping skills, loss of effort, and a sense of helplessness. The first requirement of any program for the long-term care of mental patients is to use the potential of patients to contribute to their own needs, to assume some responsibility for their lives, and to participate socially in a meaningful way.

Patients now reside in a wide variety of community settings. Board and care residences, group homes, and supervised apartments provide a common source of housing for persons with persistent illness in a variety of age groups, while nursing homes are a primary source of care for elderly persons with mental illness. These institutions sometimes provide superb care, but too often the care is primarily custodial, keeping patients as quiet as possible to minimize supervision requirements. Patients in such settings were often on heavy doses of drugs and were kept in constraints more for the convenience of the institution than for the welfare of the clients.

Following a study by the Institute of Medicine of the National Academy of Sciences, the U.S. government developed regulations requiring institutions receiving funds from Medicare and Medicaid to meet certain care standards, including the provision of mental health services to patients who were in such institutions by virtue of mental illness. Regulations also required that facilities providing nursing, medical and rehabilitative care to Medicare and Medicaid beneficiaries carry out comprehensive, standardized assessments of each resident's functional capacity to assist staff in thinking about care planning and treatment decisions. Considerable progress has been made in reducing some of the worst practices such as the use of constraints, but continued monitoring and improvement is needed, and great variability in quality of care persists. Patients in these settings are often overdosed on drugs and sit passively many hours each day in front of television sets staring into space, discouraged from activities that might require a larger supervisory investment from the facility. Such practices contribute to an apathy syndrome and client deterioration. A tour through various nursing homes will reveal variations from the situation described here; in some places staff actively engage patients in activities that help maintain cognitive and physical functioning and provide some meaning and control over one's daily life.

The conditions in hospitals and other facilities that affect the function and quality of their residents' lives suggest also the requirements for high-quality client care in the community. The risks of withdrawal, inactivity, apathy, and victimization can be as large or even greater in the community than in residential institutions, despite the fact that the community offers more opportunity for a higher quality of life. Thoughtful residential placements, however, can enhance the lives of even the most impaired patients. Leff and his colleagues (1996) have followed a cohort of 737 long-stay patients who returned to the community with the closing of two London mental hospitals. Although there was very little improvement in patients' psychiatric symptoms and social behavior, the community residential settings where these patients were resettled gave them increased freedom, which they valued, and they reported making more friends. Within these staffed housing arrangements there was little problem with crime, and only seven patients, who were lost to follow-up, were presumed to have become homeless. One unexpected consequence was a decrease in contact with relatives following discharge.

Appropriate housing is, of course, only one component of successful community living for persons with severe and persistent illnesses and disabilities. Some excellent models of community care have been developed, providing the groundwork for considering the policy initiatives that make for a good system of community services. Let us now examine some of these programs and their performance evaluations.

Models for Community Care

In recent years a variety of creative settings and programs have been developed for the care of highly impaired patients in the community, including supervised housing, foster care, innovative board-and-care facilities, halfway houses, and patient communities. One of the most innovative of such demonstrations was a Wisconsin experiment based on a training program in community living in which an educational coping model was compared with a progressive hospital care unit (Stein et al. 1975; Stein and Test 1980a, b). An unselected group of patients seeking admission to a mental hospital was randomly assigned to experimental and control groups. Subsequent analysis found no differences on significant variables between these two groups, indicating that successful randomization had occurred. The control group received hospital treatment linked with community after-care services. The experimental group was assisted in developing an independent living situation in the community, given social support, and taught simple living skills such as budgeting, job seeking, and use of transportation. Patients in both groups were evaluated at various intervals by independent researchers. The findings indicated that it was possible for patients who were highly impaired to be cared for almost exclusively in the community. Compared with control patients, patients in the experimental group made a more adequate community adjustment as evidenced by higher earnings from work, involvement in more social activities, more contact with friends, and more satisfaction with their life situation. Experimental patients at follow-up had fewer symptoms than the controls. This experiment demonstrated that a logically organized and aggressive community program can effectively treat even highly impaired patients in the community.

Wisconsin has had a unique mental health system for many years and Dane County, the area where Stein and Test carried out their work, is not necessarily representative of the range of community obstacles to care evident in other communities. The program, however, has been adopted in part or in its totality in other areas of the country with reports of equally promising outcomes. There has been a considerable range of successful experience with chronic patients in small and moderately sized communities, but the problems of such care in large urban areas seem especially formidable. It is in this context that the replication of the Stein and Test experiment in Sydney, Australia, is of particular interest.

In the period 1979–1981, psychiatrist John Hoult and his colleagues adopted the Wisconsin model in this large urban Australian area using a randomized controlled experiment. They obtained very similar patient care and cost-effectiveness outcomes (New South Wales Department of Health 1983). Particularly notable, and consistent with the Wisconsin experience, was the extent to which patients and their families preferred the community care option. For example, at twelve-month follow-up, almost two-thirds of the experimental patients were very satisfied with treatment, in contrast to less than one-third of the controls. Similarly, 83 percent of relatives of project patients with whom they lived were very satisfied with treatment in contrast to 26 percent of the controls (New South Wales Department of Health 1983).

One issue the Wisconsin experiment does not speak to is the intensity of staffing essential to carry out the types of aggressive and continuing care necessary to the program. A persistent problem in many areas is the limited resources available, and the viability of the community-care model depends on a reasonable minimum of staffing. Assessing what would be an acceptable range of staffing intensity is, thus, of importance. It is notable that the Australian replication had very favorable outcomes despite a lower level of staffing than in Dane County. The demonstration was so successful that the state of New South Wales in 1983 reorganized mental health services throughout the state using the Wisconsin model (Hoult 1987).

The Stein and Test approach, generally known as the Program of Assertive Community Treatment (PACT), is now widely used all over the world. These are not exact replications, but in each case most or some of the PACT elements are used in designing community treatment. Overall, studies of PACT-like models, although sustaining the findings of reduced hospitalization and high levels of patient and family satisfaction in comparison to more conventional care, show variation in the extent of positive improvement (Olfson 1990; Santos et al. 1995). When such variations occur it remains uncertain whether they are due to different populations of patients, variations in medication adherence, differences in local ecology, or variations in implementation of the program. Such programs can also be influenced by specific events and local professional politics.

For example, the PACT program was replicated in a district in South London in England as a randomized trial between 1987 and 1992. In the first phase of this trial assertive treatment was compared with existing inpatient and outpatient care (Marks et al. 1994). For the initial twenty months, the researchers found in comparison with conventional care small improvements in symptoms and social adjustment and relatively high satisfaction among patients and relatives. Inpatient days in the PACT-like group were much reduced and costs were significantly lower (Knapp et al. 1994). However, media attention given to the murder of a child by a member of the PACT-like group, fourteen months after it occurred, created political turmoil and resulted in transfer of authority for inpatient decisions from the program to a hospital ward team, undermining authority over care and demoralizing staff. In the subsequent period, most gains from the program with the exception of patient and family satisfaction were not sustained (Audini et al. 1994). Although the later results cannot be attributed to the PACT approach, since decision-making authority was no longer in place, it is important to note that even initially improvements in symptoms were small. Like some other studies, the English study showed that a comparable quality of care could be provided in the community at less cost, at least initially, and with high client and family satisfaction, but that one must be realistic about the magnitude of sustained improvement that can be achieved among highly impaired patient populations. Nevertheless, PACT programs offer the best approaches available for providing cost-effective community care, and many states have adopted PACT teams as a central component of their community care strategies. It remains to be seen how PACT-like programs are integrated into the managed care (behavioral health) sector.

Family-oriented rehabilitation models based on similar principles and on the clinical research on expressed emotions have also yielded promising results in both England (Leff et al. 1982) and the United States (Falloon et al. 1984, 1985). In a controlled social intervention trial in London, schizophrenic patients having intense contact with relatives and demonstrating high expressed emotion were randomly assigned to either routine outpatient care or an intervention program for patients and their families emphasizing education about schizophrenia and the role of expressed emotion in exacerbations of patients' symptoms (Leff 1982). The intervention also included family sessions in the home and relatives' groups. All patients were maintained on psychotropic drugs. After nine months, half of the twenty-four control patients relapsed, but only 9 percent in the experimental group did so. There were no relapses in the 73 percent of the experimental families where the aims of the intervention were achieved.

A similar experimental trial was carried out in California, where family members of schizophrenics were taught about the condition and instructed in problem-solving techniques, and efforts were made to reduce family tensions (Falloon et al. 1984). Follow-up at nine months found that patients in families receiving such interventions had a much lower rate of exacerbations than those in a control group receiving clinic-based individual supportive care. Only one patient in the intervention group (6 percent) was judged to have a relapse, in contrast to eight (44 percent) in the control group (Falloon et al. 1982). A less systematic and intense follow-up after two years found that the reduction in exacerbations was maintained over the longer period (Falloon et al. 1985).

Various studies confirm that a psychoeducational approach with families of schizophrenic patients with high expressed emotion reduce or delay relapses. In a sophisticated randomized study Hogarty and his colleagues (1991) randomly assigned patients with schizophrenia who were expected to return to families exhibiting high expressed emotion to four groups, all whom received medication: (1) family psychoeducation/management (FT); (2) social skills training (SST); (3) a combination of FT and SST; and (4) a control group receiving medications and social support. In the first year they found that the proportion of patients relapsing in the experimental groups was only half that of the control group. No patient with combined treatment relapsed in the first year. By the end of the second year, about a quarter of those in the groups receiving family treatment relapsed, while half of those only receiving skills training relapsed, and three-fifths of the control group relapsed. At the end of the second year, skills training did not add to improving the effect of family psychoeducation, which remained effective in preventing or delaying relapse. Such studies have helped make family psychoeducation a significant aspect of treatment.

In a somewhat different twist on this theme, McFarlane and his colleagues (1995) randomized patients with schizophrenia into either single or multiple family psychoeducational groups at six New York public hospitals and studied relapses over a two-year period. Patients treated in family groups were less likely to relapse (16 percent) than those treated in single family groups (27 percent). The differences were even larger among patients who were at high risk of relapse. Although it is difficult to know for sure, providing services for patients and their families in groups may provide greater social support, enhance social networks, and provide opportunities to learn from the experiences of other families. The group setting may also affect how emotions and tensions are managed. The researchers also report that over-involved family members seem to become more functional as they develop relationships with other family members.

Some of the studies described above are just a small sample from a much larger literature showing the value of community care and psychoeducational approaches (Stein and Test 1978; Kiesler 1982; Gudeman and Shore 1984; Kiesler and Sibulkin 1987). A wide variety of experimental studies have shown that alternative care is often more effective than hospitalization across a wide range of populations and treatment strategies (Kiesler and Sibulkin 1987).

Common to much community care and treatment programs is developing and reinforcing important living skills. The emphasis on social learning has been carried to the extreme in experimental work by Paul and Lentz (1977), who have successfully used this model to resocialize patients with long histories of chronic mental illness and inappropriate behavior. Using a highly controlled treatment environment in which all staff adopt responses consistent with learning principles, concerted and continued efforts are made to shape patients' behavior so as to condition more normal responses. The approach uses instruction, direction, and reinforcements through reward and punishment. The researchers have reported dramatic behavioral improvements and demonstrate quite convincingly that even the most regressed patterns of response can be modified.

Elements of the social learning approach are used in almost all community care and social rehabilitation programs. Community care programs can never have the level of control over patients that characterizes a total institution, and our concepts of appropriate care, civil liberties and respect for the preferences of patients make it unlikely that such intensive approaches will be used extensively. These and other reasons explain the inattention given to this successful experimental program, but it is clear that social learning approaches are now an important part of the types of efforts in community care already described.

Programs for community care for chronic mental illness have not suffered from lack of innovation or evaluation. The major difficulty had been the lack of a public policy framework that facilitates the development of necessary organizational entities, allows the essential service elements and funding to be brought together, provides reimbursement for the many service components and mental health providers, and contains incentives for balancing trade-offs between traditional medical and hospital services and a broader range of social services needed by chronic patients with large rehabilitative needs (Stein and Ganser 1983, Mechanic 1985, Talbott 1985, Mechanic and Aiken 1987). Good rehabilitation treats acute psychiatric episodes, ensures appropriate medication monitoring, maintains nutrition and health more generally, makes provision for shelter and reasonable levels of activity and participation, provides crisis support, and builds on patients' personal capacities through continuing educational efforts.

Community care involves medical and social challenges and is not inexpensive if costs are seriously assessed (Wolff et al. 1995). A careful economic cost-benefit analysis of the Wisconsin experiment, taking into account a wide range of hidden as well as explicit costs, such as welfare payments and supervised residency costs, suggests that although such programs yield a net benefit, they are not less expensive than more conventional approaches (Weisbrod et al. 1980). Also there are social costs in maintaining patients in the community as compared with hospital care during the more acute phases of disorder as reflected in law violations and assaultive behavior (Stein and Test 1980a, b). The prevalence of such behavior was low, but it was not inconsequential. This experiment also shows—as does experience elsewhere—that if an aggressive program does not continue, patients do not maintain the high level of functioning demonstrated (Stein and Test 1980a, b). A five-year-follow-up of the original experiment by Pasamanick and his associates (1967) also found a regression of patient functioning following the termination of the experiment (Davis et al. 1972). These studies suggest that treatment of chronic mental patients cannot be based on a short-term commitment but requires an intensive continuing effort. These programs, however, do not become institutionalized, not only because they are difficult to administer and model in relation to more conventional hospital care but also because current financing of mental health services in most communities provides no basis for stability of funding for such programs.

Long-term therapy for chronic schizophrenic patients is further complicated by the fact that antipsychotic medication, which is an important component of care, often has unpleasant side effects and long-term adverse biological effects. Although antipsychotic medication is extremely helpful in controlling delusions, hallucinations, severe excitement, or withdrawal and odd behavior, it occasionally produces extrapyramidal motor reactions and, with prolonged use, tardive dyskinesia (Berger 1978). The extrapyramidal symptoms include uncontrollable restlessness, muscle spasms, and other symptoms resembling Parkinson's disease. These can be controlled by anticholingeric drugs used for treating Parkinson's disease. Tardive dyskinesia, which consists of involuntary movements of the lips, tongue, face, and other upper extremities is less reversible, more dangerous, and stigmatizing. It constitutes a serious risk for chronic patients on long-term maintenance antipsychotics. These findings on side effects complicate the treatment of chronic schizophrenic patients, particularly in community settings. First, the side effects lead patients to discontinue medication, often resulting in a relapse of their bizarre behavior. Second, both problems of patient cooperation and the real dangers of these powerful drugs require close medical supervision and monitoring of such patients. This constitutes a more strategic problem in a community than on a hospital ward and requires an aggressive and sustained administrative effort to ensure appropriate medical and rehabilitative care.

The development of new neuroleptic drugs, and alternative modes of administration, may contribute to addressing three difficult areas in medicating patients: lack of response to treatment, disturbing side effects, and failure to take medication. As noted earlier, clozapine appears helpful with patients refractory to other neuroleptic drugs and has fewer extra-pyramidal side effects. But because of clozapine's other life-threatening potential side effects, patients on this drug regimen must have their blood closely monitored. Also, the cost of using this drug is high. A new atypical antipsychotic, risperidone, seems to be effective in treating both positive and negative symptoms of schizophrenia and appears to reduce the risk of extra-pyramidal side effects, but longer experience with this drug is needed to assess it. One way of dealing with low-compliant patients is to use depot preparations of neuroleptic drugs, medications given by intramuscular injection. Depending on how they are prepared, medication levels in the blood can be maintained from three days to a month. Thus, depot medications can be particularly useful when discharging low-compliant patients from inpatient care to the community where there is high risk of non-compliance. One difficulty is that such patients are less informed about their medication and are not likely to have their medication dose adjusted when they sense an increase in florid symptoms. Psychosocial programs increasingly give attention to educating patients about their symptoms and their medications, improving their ability to recognize when their symptoms are returning or getting worse, and making them more aware of when their medication dosage may need adjustment.

In recent years community care for persons with severe and persistent mental illness has developed substantially in two previous neglected areas: housing and employment. In the 1980s the capacities of mental illness programs were limited by lack of access to housing, and many patients were homeless. Program managers understood the need to have access to suitable housing, and many began developing their own housing programs and working with government housing authorities to locate and develop suitable housing opportunities. In the Robert Wood Johnson Foundation Program on Chronic Mental Illness in large cities, housing was one of the key features, and the provision of Section 8 housing certificates to mental health authorities in demonstration cities helped some patients return to independent living (Newman et al. 1994).

The increased concern over housing has focused attention on what constitutes appropriate housing for persons with serious and persistent illness, and this area is marked by strong ideological positions. At one extreme are those who strongly support supervised residential living and at the other are those who advocate normalization and scattered site independent living. All would agree, however, that different patients have varying needs and that a spectrum of housing alternatives are needed that range in the degree of supervision or independence. Initially, it was believed that patients should be moved through a continuum of housing from more to less supervised housing over time as their capacities for independent living increased. Such policies were highly disruptive to patients, however, because they could not establish stability or permanence in their housing arrangements, and frequent moves were themselves stressful. It is now commonly believed that the best strategy is to find a relatively permanent suitable housing situation, and one that the client also prefers, and then provide the level of supervision that best fits the client's needs (Carling 1993). Most clients want to live in their own residences, but there are circumstances (such as in the case of substance abuse comorbidities) where this may not be an optimal alternative (Schutt and Goldfinger 1996). In any case, the dominant idea is to wrap services around the client in a setting they find most preferable, if this can be achieved. As clients cope more independently, supervision is relaxed. Some clients, of course, require high levels of long-term supervision. Mental health services are now oriented by a strong consumer empowerment philosophy. Research in the area linking mental status, choice, and outcomes is still relatively primitive, and we have a great deal to learn about the most suitable types of arrangements for different types of patients.

The consumer empowerment philosophy is also playing out in the area of employment, with seemingly positive results. Work plays a particularly meaningful role in life, and one of the areas where persons with serious mental illness particularly want more help is in finding and maintaining employment. One problem many patients with persistent illness face is simply keeping busy in some meaningful way, avoiding the boredom and sameness of every day, and having some role that provides some sense of productivity. Mental health programs have often provided sheltered work outside competitive settings, but such work does not necessarily transfer to competitive employment. In addition, the work itself, typically some form of assembly task, is often below the capacities and education of the client. One form of available help has been vocational rehabilitation, but many clients have not found such services responsive to their needs or particularly helpful in finding suitable employment.

As with housing, there have been strong ideologies about how to prepare persons with serious mental illness for employment. A traditional view was that clients had to be introduced to employment slowly by prevocational training, practice in sheltered work situations, and graduated introduction into more competitive work situations. The supported work model, in contrast, seeks to place the client directly into competitive work situations, providing whatever support is needed. Job coaches commonly assist the client in job counseling, in dealing with whatever work problems occur, and in providing encouragement and support. The basic idea of supported employment is that clients become regular employees in usual work settings at the prevailing wage rate rather than in some artificial work setting. Bond and his colleagues (1997) have identified six elements common to most supported employment programs: a goal of a permanent competitive job; minimal screening for employability; individualized placement; avoidance of prevocational programs; consideration of client preferences; and continuing support as needed with no time limits. Supported employment has been found to be far more successful in achieving competitive employment than traditional vocational services (Bond et al. 1997; Drake and Becker 1996).

Many of the jobs typically available to clients are not particularly desirable, such as janitorial work, food service, dishwashing, and laundering, and some of these jobs can be very stressful. This may help explain why work experience is unrelated to quality of life, improvements in self-esteem, and reduction in symptoms. However, there is no evidence that such competitive work leads to negative outcomes such as increased relapse rates. Client preference in selecting jobs is important, and such preferences are generally realistic. Clients who obtain competitive employment in preferred areas of work are more likely to stay in such jobs and are more satisfied with them. Becker and her colleagues (1996) found that at six-month follow-up of patients in supported employment, those who were working in preferred areas had twice as many weeks in their jobs as those who did not.

Possible reasons for the success of supported employment are the difficulty of predicting beforehand who will do well in competitive employment and the importance of preparing clients in real employment conditions, rather than in the artificial conditions that characterize many prevocational programs. Despite the successes reported, it is necessary to recognize that many patients with severe and persistent illnesses will be unable to work, or can only work part time, and that many of those who do work are marginalized in some of the least attractive employment conditions. The Americans With Disabilities Act, which requires employers to make reasonable accommodation, may assist in moving more clients into employment, but this legislation is more likely to protect those already in jobs than new job seekers. Many important research questions remain on how to place clients in a broader range of jobs beyond entry level and unskilled occupations, how to prevent attrition, and the cost-effectiveness of varying approaches.

Points of Leverage

Key elements in building appropriate and effective sources of community mental health care are the organizational and financing systems and policy decisions concerning the populations and services to be covered and the types of institutions and therapists who will provide services. It is with such decisions that public policy most vitally impacts the shape of the mental health arena. Without stable funding, no innovation, however effective, is likely to be sustained for very long. Financing decisions are crucial. Such decisions must be made with sensitivity to the problems and needs of varying types of patients, understanding of services alternatives, and appreciation of the ambiguities of mental health concepts.

Mental health funds come from four major sources: third-party insurance programs; state and local appropriations for mental health institutions and services; Medicaid and Medicare; and welfare benefits such as SSDI and SSI. Since third-party insurance is typically linked with stable employment, in the absence of a national insurance system it is unlikely that the extension of such insurance, however worthy, would address the special needs of the most chronic patients. Improvements in community mental health care for the most chronic patients thus depend on reforms in state mental health policy, Medicaid, and the Social Security disability programs.

Modifying State Mental Health Systems

Traditionally, mental illness has been a state responsibility and constitutes a significant part of state expenditures. States were invested substantially in their mental institutions, and with reduction of public inpatients many have improved their hospitals and treatment and rehabilitation programs. The vast majority of seriously mentally ill are in the community, but most states continue to be focused institutionally because of their commitments to maintain hospital improvements in a context of increased court scrutiny, because of the pressures of hospital employees and communities that depend on the financing of hospitals, and because states are reluctant to take on large new community obligations within a context of fiscal constraint.

The problem of getting services to follow the patient is inherently more difficult in states having well-established hospital systems, communities economically dependent on hospitals, and well-organized and unionized employees. Such systems require transition plans that allow funds to follow the patient on a graduated basis, that guarantee the stability of the hospital system over some period of time, and that facilitate working closely with unions and employees in programs of scheduled attrition and retraining to the extent feasible. Concomitantly, structures need to be developed for diversion of inappropriate admissions to community programs and for intensive discharge planning commencing soon after a patient is admitted to a hospital.

Because of the barriers in many states to a community-based system, phasing in such programs initially requires enhanced funding to build community care structures while maintaining some redundant hospital support. To the extent that such financing allows the initiation of a more rational care process, it is a wise long-term investment, although it may require considerable persuasion before state legislatures, facing resource constraints, see the wisdom of this course. One innovative approach to this problem was the New York State Community Mental Health Reinvestment Act, passed in 1993. The act reallocated an estimated $210 million over five years, 1994–1999, contingent on the decline in New York's psychiatric hospital census (Swidler and Tauriello 1995). Funds saved from hospital expenditures were earmarked to purchase services for persons with the most severe illnesses, special populations such as children, the homeless, persons with comorbid substance abuse, and other hard-to-serve populations, as well as other defined needs. Politicians generally dislike formula reallocations that limit their future budgetary discretion, and passage of the act was contentious and difficult. When the Pataki administration took control of state government in 1994, there were efforts to rescind the act but despite political opposition the reallocation approach has been sustained.

Medicaid Reform

As already described, Medicaid is the single largest and most important medical program affecting persons with severe and persistent mental illness. In addition, it is used by those who are disabled, elderly or poor. Medicaid involves fifty-three separate programs, and while there is some uniformity prescribed by federal law, states have considerable latitude to define the scope, amount, and duration of services, and there is little uniformity. Until recently, states controlled their Medicaid expenditures by the way they reimbursed institutions and providers; in many states payments to professionals were so low that caregivers refused to treat enrollees in the program. Instead, states used Medicaid as a way to subsidize public providers and to reconfigure their public mental health systems. Using Medicaid as a base, some states have very wisely built a community support system for persons with mental illness that is attentive to a wide range of needs such as housing and rehabilitation. More recently, however, most states are aggressively moving toward managed mental health care, viewing this both as a means to control expenditures and as an approach to integrating mental health services.

As of 1997, states have rapidly been moving their Medicaid enrollees into various types of managed care arrangements, which we reviewed in the previous chapter. Initially, the focus was on the nondisabled population, but now states are also bringing disabled enrollees into managed care as well. Because of the many vulnerabilities of this population, and the extent to which cost-containment objectives are motivating these changes, advocates are greatly concerned. Managed care has potential to integrate needed services and to achieve more effective use of resources, but there are also major risks of underservice and a narrow definition of responsibility that does not extend to housing, employment, and other important quality-of-life issues. States must proceed carefully in developing contracts with managed care organizations if the mental health safety net is to be preserved.

States are currently taking two major approaches in extending Medicaid managed care to the disabled population. On the one hand, state mental health authorities are contracting with existing providers of mental health services such as community mental health centers on a capitated basis to provide the range of covered services to their Medicaid enrollees. Often these are the same organizations that were previously providing services on a negotiated fee-for-service basis or through a budget. Thus, the big difference is the movement to capitation payment, where the mental health organization is at financial risk because they are now being paid a fixed amount per person for all necessary care. Capitation payment provides potential for the state program to reduce its expenditures and establish beforehand what its expenditures will be. It is assumed that capitation provides an incentive for mental health organizations to organize services efficiently and function more effectively. But we have no good evidence that long-term costs for persons with serious mental illness are significantly less or that the quality of care will be maintained.

Alternatively, states are contracting with behavioral health companies on a financial risk basis (usually through capitation) to organize a services network for persons with serious mental illness and to manage care through selection of appropriate providers, financial arrangements with providers, utilization management and review, and quality assurance processes. Although there are many such managed care companies, a small number of large private companies dominate the marketplace. These companies are developing extensive care networks and a great deal of expertise, but many experts and advocates worry whether the mental health "dollar" is sufficiently large to allow cost savings for the states and profits to the investors in these private corporations and still provide responsive and high-quality care. Developments in this area are moving far more rapidly than our ability to monitor them, and in some sense we are flying blind. On an anecdotal basis, it is easy to identify examples of outstanding management of care, but also examples of very shoddy practices (Hall et al. 1997). What we don't know is the distribution of such performance, how it is changing over time, or how it compares with prior patterns of care. Vulnerable populations should be a focus of sustained attention because we know that damaging consequences are not immediately observable, and often poor outcomes will not become evident until two or three years have passed. This argues for states involving consumers and their advocates closely in services planning and evaluation, since they are often the first groups to understand when things are going badly and that they are not getting needed services.

In sum, traditional Medicaid is rapidly fading from the scene. As we approach a new century, Medicaid will be very differently organized, with very different financing methods, ways of organizing providers, and standards of care. In all likelihood, the program will continue to have different shapes in varying localities as states retain and increase their discretion in the use of federal Medicaid funds. Medicaid changes will not only affect clients but also have profound effects on mental health delivery systems and the varying mental health professions. As we go forward it will be important for consumers and experts to insist on broad measures of effectiveness that have become more central in the past decade. Such measures should reflect not only the amount of care given but also patients' function and quality of life, family burden, patient and family satisfaction, and the absence of client victimization, arrest, and imprisonment. If these later indicators show deterioration, they should alert us to potential problems in community care and the community support system under managed care.

Improving Disability Determination

The disability program, as it affects the mentally ill, is instructive. Based on a concept of permanent and total disability, eligibility criteria are believed to reinforce a sense of personal defeat and to be a disincentive to rehabilitation. Many mental health professionals feel ambivalent in encouraging clients to enter the disability system (Estroff et al. 1997). Viable community care, however, depends on such support, since many severely mentally ill cannot maintain employment, are too disoriented, or behave too bizarrely to be acceptable to employers. By the mid-1970s there had been a major expansion of numbers of disabled persons receiving disability insurance, among whom the mentally ill were a major subgroup. Estimates suggest that by the late 1970s there were more than a half million mentally ill receiving either SSI or SSDI (National Institute of Mental Health 1987).

The growth in disability costs led to the 1980 amendments to the Social Security Act in which Congress required that states review all awards at least every three years. These reviews resulted in the loss of benefits by large numbers of severely mentally ill, among others, and subsequently to much litigation in the federal courts. It became apparent that the application of existing disability criteria seriously underestimated the incapacities of many chronic patients to work in a sustained way and stripped significant numbers of their benefits. Between 1981 and 1983 the benefits of a half million people, many of them mentally ill, were terminated. Eventually, some 290,000 of those terminated were reinstated (Osterweis et al. 1987). New psychiatric criteria based on an integrated functional assessment were developed, which have supported the reinstatement of many patients excised from the disability rolls.

Persons with mental illness were targeted for removal from the disability rolls for a variety of reasons. Such persons were generally much younger than persons with more traditional and common medical disabilities such as heart disease, and in targeting the young the Social Security Administration saw opportunities to achieve large financial savings by removing persons who were likely to remain on the disability rolls for many years. Also, unlike many medical conditions, psychiatric symptoms are not well correlated with functional capacities. Moreover, the symptoms of persons with severe psychiatric illness can fluctuate, and persons who seem superficially capable of work may decompensate under realistic work demands. Thus, evaluating work capacity requires a functional assessment of how such persons could work in a competitive workplace environment. In response to much criticism and a study by the General Accounting Office, the Congress passed a number of administrative reforms that included new medical impairment standards.

Allowances for mental health impairments peaked after the new regulations were put in place, and although they dropped in 1987, they resumed a steady upward course into the 1990s. Since the change in regulations, such mental health allowances have accounted for approximately one-quarter of new entrants into the SSDI and SSI programs, in part as a result of aggressive efforts of mental health professionals to get their clients into the program so that they have income support while living in the community. Surprisingly, the most rapid increases have been among persons with affective disorders, who by 1993 were the largest group of persons in the program by reason of mental impairments.

The number of children in the SSI program increased rapidly following the 1991 Supreme Court decision in *Sullivan v. Zebley,* and revised child disability criteria were introduced a few months earlier. These new regulations required functional as well as medical criteria for evaluating disability, and for the first time included as criteria for disability such disputed categories as attention deficit hyperactivity disorder of children and developmental and emotional disorders for children less than one year of age. In *Zebley* the Supreme Court found that the assessment process did not comply with the law's requirement that a child be defined as disabled if "he suffers from a medically determinable physical or mental impairment of comparable severity" to one that would grant disability status to an adult. Between the end of 1989 and 1993, the number of children covered by SSI increased from 300,000 to 770,000 (National Academy of Social Insurance 1994). In 1996, the Congress passed legislation intended to cut back the numbers of children on SSI, as well as adults with substance abuse disorders.

Expeditious attainment of disability benefits is important in order to stabilize the chronic patients' life situations and plan appropriate care. Barriers include the common delays in awarding benefits and the contradictory eligibility criteria for such benefits and access to vocational rehabilitation services. We need a better way of providing the chronic patient essential subsistence while not discouraging rehabilitation. In some localities, mental health personnel and state agencies administering disability determinations locate government workers in mental health service facilities to make the disability filing process more simple and accessible. But if the potential of this system is to be better realized, the disability system must be linked to stronger incentives for rehabilitation. This requires reconciling contradictory assumptions and eligibility requirements in these program areas (Mashaw and Reno 1996).

Many provisions within the Social Security disability system speak to rehabilitation, but they clash with the requirement that recipients prove that they cannot work because of a long-lasting medical impairment. To become eligible for rehabilitation, the disabled have had to prove their work potential and their ability to benefit. Moreover, there had been little motivation for state vocational rehabilitation agencies to serve most mentally ill clients, because the Social Security Administration only paid for these services when the recipient returned to work for a continuous period of nine months (Osterweis 1987, pp. 70–71); but these patients involve a high risk of rehabilitation failure. It is thus no surprise that the rehabilitation provisions of the act are rarely used.

In 1986, the Congress extended the Vocational Rehabilitation Act. For the first time, supported work activities were permitted under the act, including transitional employment for persons with chronic mental illness. The legislation specifically includes community mental health centers among agencies encouraged to collaborate with departments of vocational rehabilitation. But vocational rehabilitation among the millions of mentally ill is still a highly underdeveloped service, and consumers with mental illness often report that it serves them poorly.

The Case-Management Approach

As communities view the challenge of developing appropriate care for the most disabled, they embrace the case management concept. The concept has varied meanings in different contexts, but even in its legislative context involving the Medicaid program it is poorly defined. One survey of case management concepts within Medicaid concluded, "In concept and in practice, case management appears to be an ill-defined process that lacks substance" (Spitz 1987, p. 69).

Case management has a long tradition in social work, where the case worker helped identify and mobilize a variety of community services on behalf of a client. Many of the case management approaches used in social work for decades—such as street teams, crisis intervention, and brokering community services—have been adapted to a variety of mental health functions. These functions include such assertive team efforts as in the PACT programs described earlier, in less intensive programs in which case managers coordinate services, within managed care organizations where case managers work with clinicians to develop more efficient treatment plans, and in a wide variety of community programs with younger persons with severe and persistent illness and the homeless mentally ill who commonly are suspicious of the mental health system and traditional service approaches.

Case managers, thus, come in many varieties and have little in common but their name. They range from masters-trained nurses, social workers, and psychologists to people with no specialized training. Some case managers have clinical responsibilities as well as acquiring services for clients such as housing, disability insurance, psychosocial rehabilitation, family psychoeducation, and the like. Others are simply brokers with sole responsibility to link services to people, but they have no control over resources and little clout with the professionals whose services they must enlist. Some case managers control independent resources they can use to enhance already existing services and entitlements, as in the New York State Intensive Case Management Program (Surles et al. 1992), whereas others depend solely on exhortation. Intensive case management programs might have professional case managers with no more than ten clients per manager, whereas other programs might have as many as forty or fifty, or even a hundred or more. Some case-management programs, such as the New York program, are freestanding, focusing on particularly high and expensive utilizers of the existing system of services; others, such as the PACT case-management teams, are part of systems of integrated care. Some case managers function primarily as advocates for the patient, whereas others play dual roles in working for clients but also allocating scarce resources within a context of bureaucratic pressures to stay within budget.

Case management is loosely thought of as a solution to a wide variety of difficult problems. But the responsibilities it is expected to bear are often unrealistic in the context of the realities of system disorganization and the types of personnel given these tasks. Thinking about case management in the more restricted medical context, the case manager is the primary care physician who serves as the doctor of first contact, provides the necessary continuing care and supervision, and makes appropriate referral for specialized medical and other services. The integrity of this role requires high-level and broad-scope clinical judgment, linkage with the needed specialized services, and authority with other doctors and professionals and with the patient. What is more important, it requires the authority under reimbursement programs or existing financial arrangements to provide or prescribe necessary services (Lewis et al. 1976).

Case management for persons with severe and persistent disorders is inherently more complex. It not only requires appreciation of general medical and psychiatric needs and care, but sophistication about such varied issues as housing, disability and welfare benefits, psychosocial rehabilitation, sheltered and competitive work programs, and issues relating to the legal and criminal justice systems. The scope of case-management functions, the typical caseload, the level of expected training and experience, and the authority of the case manager vary enormously, both within and among systems of care. Thus, it is essential to carefully look within the *black box* that is labeled as case management. For example, in one systematic study of case management, 417 chronically mentally ill in Texas were randomly assigned to experimental and control groups. Each patient had two or more admissions to state and/or country mental hospitals in approximately a two-year period. Although the control group could receive any but case-management services, the experimental group were assigned to a case management unit staffed by a supervisor and seven case managers with undergraduate or graduate degrees in the social sciences and an average of about four years of experience working with the mentally ill. During the study they spent about half their time providing non-clinical services to clients and two-fifths of their time brokering services. After twelve months it was clear that the case management group received more services, were admitted to mental hospitals more often, and incurred higher costs. Although there were tendencies in favor of the experimental group on quality of life measures, they were small and not statistically significant (Franklin et al. 1987). Concepts that sound appealing in theory often do not achieve their goals in practice. There are large and significant differences between case management as practiced in the Texas study and case management in the PACT program.

The concept of the case manager has intuitive appeal, but it remains unclear whether it is appropriate or realistic to assign such varied and complex functions to individuals in contrast to more complex teams or subsystems of care. First, there must be a clear definition of continuing responsibility; few professionals other than physicians have traditionally taken such roles. Second, given the diverse and complex functions necessary, specialization is more likely to lead to effective service. Third, case management of these patients is clearly a longitudinal process, but the "half-life" of case managers is short and attrition is high. Case managers typically do not have the training and experience, control over resources, or professional standing to command resources from other organizations or even to be persuasive with them. Thus, case management, to be effective, must be embedded in an organizational plan that defines clearly who is responsible and accountable for the care of the most highly disabled patients, has in place the necessary service elements to provide the full spectrum of needed services, and can coordinate and control diverse resources that flow into the system so that balanced decisions can be made about the expenditure of limited resources.

Organizational Barriers

In the hospital we take shelter, activity, and basic medical supervision for granted, but each poses serious challenges for community programs of care. The closed character of hospitals allowed staff to monitor patient activities carefully, to ensure medication regulation and compliance, and to induce appropriate behavior through a system of rewards. In the community, each of these areas becomes problematic and presents organizational challenges. Even approximations of these responsibilities require a level of organization and coordination absent in most community mental health service programs. Scarce resources, fragmentation of funding and service elements, lack of clear definition of responsibility, and poorly developed career structures for the mental health professions in community care pose significant obstacles.

The Absence of a Clear Focus of Responsibility and Authority

In most of the nation's urban areas, responsibility for serving the mentally ill is fragmented among varying levels of government and categorical service agencies. There is typically little coordination among governmental sectors and providers of service, resulting in inefficiencies, duplication, poor use of resources, and failure to serve clients in need. Hospital units might be poorly or not at all linked with outpatient psychiatric care or psychosocial services. Admission to and discharge from inpatient units often occurs without relation to an ongoing system of community services, or careful long-term planning of patients' needs. Agencies serving the homeless, the substance abuser, or the retarded maintain separate service systems, making it particularly difficult to help patients with multiple problems, and inpatient care under Medicaid and local medical assistance program often function independently of outpatient care or psychosocial rehabilitation services in the community.

The precise shape of the necessary administrative structures remains unclear; different structures will fit varying political, legal, and service delivery environments. Although establishment of mental health authorities implies centralization, an administrative authority could promote local diversity and program innovation. Concentration, however, can lead to less flexibility, innovation, and public support. In one city, for example, the director of a functioning authority for most of the chronic patients in that community made the strategic decision not to take over a number of smaller agencies serving some of these patients. The rationale was that each of these agencies had an enthusiastic board who served as advocate for improved care and such advocacy outweighed the advantages of his taking direct control over these agencies.

The relative merits of organizing mental health services through government agencies, special boards designated by statute, managed behavioral health companies, nonprofit voluntary groups, or some hybrid of these forms remain unclear. Nor is it obvious to what degree such entities should be direct-service providers as well as planning, financing, and administrative bodies, or whether they should restrict themselves to limited administrative and regulatory functions in relation to contracting providers. These assessments cannot be made in the abstract, but must be weighed in relation to the organization and effectiveness of existing service providers, statutory requirements, and the political culture of the locality. In theory, performance contracting and the competition it implies seem advantageous to publicly organized services, but in practice the funders often become dependent on their contractees and may have few real options (Dorwart et al. 1986).

Efforts to develop stronger public mental health authorities in various cities in the late 1980s contributed to thoughtful consideration of how services fragmentation might be reduced and resulted in improving the continuity of care in some of these localities, but there was no evidence that they produced substantial improvements in patient outcomes. One major change during this period was the extent to which mental health authorities began to see housing as part of their responsibilities. They increased their efforts in many localities to develop new housing options or to work with public housing authorities cooperatively. Although the efforts to develop stronger public mental health authorities did not live up to their promises, they were helpful in keeping mental health issues on the public agenda during a period in which the U.S. public and policy makers were demanding tax relief and losing interest in public programs to help the disadvantaged.

Interest in public mental health authorities has diminished as the public sector now increasingly seeks to contract out more of its care responsibilities to the private and non-profit sectors. Such contracting is commonly seen as a way of dealing with programs that often have become bureaucratic, self-protective, risk-aversive, and resistant to innovation. One advantage of the private sector is that it is much less vulnerable to the political power of unions, professional associations, and communities, and, thus, may have greater flexibility in reducing redundant and unproductive components of the service system. States have a great deal of difficulty in closing institutions, replacing civil service employees, and changing work practices. The private sector in building service networks might, over time, be more successful in challenging many of the entrenched institutional and professional forces. The opportunity, however, involves the danger of diminishing some essential institutions that are better prepared to manage severe and persistent illness than many private-sector providers. Thus, state and mental health authorities still have essential planning, financing, monitoring, and regulatory roles.

Chapter 10

Innovations in Mental Health Services

Historically, one of the largest problems in providing mental health services for patients with severe disorders was the absence of a reasonable range of alternatives to match diverse conditions or varying levels of disability. With the development of community mental health care and a growing emphasis on treating patients within the least restrictive alternative (Chambers 1978), there is a continuing search for good community models of care for chronic patients. We have already reviewed some examples of innovative programs. Here we focus on some of the difficulties of developing and sustaining them.

There is wide recognition of the need for solutions that provide more protection and support than is typical in outpatient therapy but do not involve the dependency or isolation characteristic of hospitalization. Although many patients can remain in the community, they are not prepared to participate fully in community activities and require considerable supervision and support. Early developments in community care were in the use of transitional communities for the social resettlement of prisoners of war in the civilian community at the end of World War II (Wilson et al. 1952). The British used transitional communities for the social resettlement of prisoners of war in the civilian community at the end of World War II (Wilson et al. 1952). They found that the readjustment of such men was difficult, and they decided to institute a program to help refit them for civilian life. They developed Civil Resettlement Units as transitional communities that facilitated the resumption of a civilian role. The purpose was to attempt to neutralize the suspicions of these men toward authority, to allow them to develop role-taking skills appropriate to civilian life but within the supportive environment of the unit, to reestablish their relationships with the home society, and to help them structure their personal goals. Men who went through the program made a better adjustment than did men with comparable experiences who did not.

The halfway house and the community hostel are transitional communities used in the care of the mentally ill. Halfway houses, located within the community, are relatively small units housing five to twenty persons. Patients share a common situation and provide emotional support for one another; additional supervisory personnel are usually available. The halfway house is an intermediate solution in that patients who are not prepared to return home or to their jobs or who are too insecure to make their own living arrangements can live in a supportive environment with others who understand their problems, who are tolerant of their difficulties, and who provide emotional support. Hostels, frequently used in European countries for housing former mental patients, provide similar support. Both halfway houses and hostels facilitate the relocation in the community of patients who have no relatives or friends willing to assume responsibility for their care. Similarly, they provide therapeutic personnel with an option if they feel that family living arrangements are inappropriate for the patient. These transitional communities also facilitate a later readjustment in which ex-patients may try to live completely on their own.

Partial hospitalization refers most frequently to night and day hospitals. Day hospitals provide a program for mental patients who live at home or at some other lodging but who spend their days at the hospital. Such institutions relieve the burden on the family and also provide programs that keep patients active and involved while providing them with support and other therapeutic services. They allow the patient to retain ties with the community, but they also reduce the psychological and social costs for the community and the patient. When day hospitals began in the United States, they were used as halfway institutions for patients who had been hospitalized. They are now used largely in lieu of hospitalization. There are a number of impressive studies documenting some of the advantages of day treatment relative to more traditional inpatient care. Creed and colleagues (1997), for example, randomized 179 patients with acute psychiatric illness referred for hospital admission to inpatient care or a day treatment program. Assessments over a twelve-month period included patient psychopathology, social behavior, burden on caretakers, and costs. There were no significant differences in psychopathology or social behavior, although at twelve months caretakers in the day treatment program reported somewhat greater burden. Day treatment was found to be 30 to 40 percent cheaper than inpatient care, and it was estimated that 30 to 40 percent of the potential admissions could be treated in this way. Night hospitals are for patients capable of fulfilling work responsibilities but requiring a treatment and support program. Through the night hospital, patients maintain productive functioning in the community at the same time that they are able to take advantage of a hospital program.

Studies of partial hospitalization suggest that it is a relatively effective treatment modality. However, while it is less costly than round-the-clock hospitalization it is still an expensive treatment modality, and insurers have not favored it. Some believe that managed care might invigorate partial hospitalization as a substitute for traditional hospital care, but it is more likely that the emphasis will be on finding alternative community care that is much less expensive. With the exception of some public contracts, mental health insurers and managed care organizations are not responsible for housing, so treating patients outside of health institutions is financially advantageous to them.

Intermediate programs have been organized in many ways. Some have been associated with public mental hospitals, some with Veterans Administration hospitals, and others with private psychiatric hospitals or psychiatry departments in general hospitals. Some of these institutions stand alone, but most are integrated with a variety of community and social services for clients. Among the more important of such services are sheltered workshops, programs in psychosocial rehabilitation, various case-management programs, clubhouses, and self-help consumer-run services. Sheltered workshops provide work opportunities and work learning experiences under supervision but do not expose patients to the competitive situation of a normal job. Their purpose is to give clients an opportunity to develop confidence so that they can undertake employment in the community, although more recent research indicates that it is more effective to directly place clients in competitive employment (Bond et al. 1997). Sheltered workshops, however, might succeed with clients who would otherwise be unemployed or without any useful activity. Often, however, the work is boring and repetitive, and patients sometimes complain of being mixed with people with visible disabilities, such as persons with developmental disabilities.

After-care services provide treatment monitoring and other services and programs needed by many persons with disabilities in the community. Clients are often faced with loneliness, isolation, a lack of activities, and other social and psychological difficulties. Many programs now provide clients with opportunities for participation, teach them necessary living skills, and provide psychological and social support. Some clubhouses specializing in psychosocial rehabilitation have a strong empowerment philosophy—they define clients as members and expect them to take an interest in and responsibility for carrying out essential tasks in maintaining clubhouse activities. There is some evidence that a sense of empowerment contributes to clients' perceived quality of life. Consumer self-help programs perform some of the same functions, giving persons the support of other ex-patients and helping to alleviate the isolation of many persons with serious psychiatric disabilities.

There are numerous examples of viable and creative community alternatives for chronic patients. Fairweather and his colleagues (1969) established a community group living situation for chronic post–hospital patients that included the organization of a janitorial service that responded to community needs for such services. As the project continued, supervision over patients was relaxed, and the patients took more responsibility. In comparing this program with traditional after-care, the investigators found patients in this program to have greater productivity without loss in the area of psychosocial adjustment, and even during periods of maximum supervision the experimental programs were considerably less expensive than the traditional services. The Fairweather Lodge program has been adopted in various contexts. In Austin, Texas, for example, chronic patients in a lodge have responsibility for cleaning the Texas legislature facilities, and even severely ill patients have been self-supporting. Several innovative community service programs have been developed in Denver, Colorado (Polak 1978), in which hospitalization is avoided and problems are dealt with through home visits and systems intervention. During periods of crisis or when no adequate permanent home is available, patients are placed in carefully selected families and are supported by clinical supervision, instruction of home sponsors, and clinical home visits. Families taking such patients receive a per diem payment for room, board, and client care. Other programs train and use community members to assist chronic patients in daily life activities (Weinman and Kleiner 1978). Communities have established patient apartment complexes, clubs, drop-in centers, information centers, and other resources for persons with persistent illness (Stein and Test 1978; Stein and Hollingsworth 1995; Breakey 1996).

Maintenance of Patients with Persistent Disorders

Much of the treatment of patients with mental illness in the past was based on a view of people as sponges—absorbing developmental and environmental stimuli—rather than as active agents molding and affecting, to some extent, the conditions to which they are exposed. In fact, much of our psychological vocabulary is phrased in terms of intrapsychic responses to environmental stress rather than in terms of active strivings and social performance. Although all scientific activity must ultimately be based on a deterministic model of some form, social activity is a product of the manipulation and arrangement of symbols. The scope of the symbolic environment is so vast and so rich that people have considerable opportunity to affect the direction of their lives. We can, therefore, gain some advantage by conceptually specifying for psychiatric purposes the active problem-solving aspects of human adaptation, their relationship to the social structure, and their bearing on the rehabilitation of chronic patients.

In considering the meaning of the concept of social and psychological *stress,* we realize that this term refers to neither stimuli nor reactions in themselves, but rather to a discrepancy between a problem or challenge and an individual's capacity to deal with or to adapt to it. This definition makes clear the importance of skill and performance components as well as of psychological defenses. *Coping* is the instrumental behavior and problem-solving capacity of a person to meet demands and goals. It involves the application of acquired skills, techniques, and knowledge. The extent to which a person experiences discomfort in the first place is often a product of the inadequacy of such skill repertoires. In contrast to coping, *defense* (as I am using the term) is the manner in which a person manages his or her emotional and affective states when discomfort is aroused or anticipated. Most psychodynamic and psychological work deals with defense and not with coping.

Many clinicians who work with persons with psychiatric disabilities emphasized psychological barriers and techniques and gave too little attention to the strategies and techniques people use to deal with tasks and other people. This emphasis has been implicit in their psychological bias. Instead of exploring the nature of the patient's difficulties that lead him or her to seek care or others to insist upon removal from the social situation, clinicians frequently emphasized early development and relationships. Too often clinicians undertake therapy designed to change patients without carefully considering the situation and problems to which patients must return, the skills they will require, and their significant others' attitudes and feelings about their disabilities. Although many problems in accomplishing difficult tasks or in dealing with the social environment may not realistically be amenable to intervention, mental health workers can help improve patients' coping effectiveness either by changing or modifying their level of instrumental efforts or by helping to alter the social conditions under which they live so that their skills are more adequate and their problems less of a handicap.

Irrespective of whether psychiatric conditions are a consequence of neurological, psychological, genetic, or other problems, various social factors can affect the course of a disability. Rehabilitation, in contrast to treatment, is frequently concerned with manipulating and regulating the context of the illness rather than the illness itself to achieve the best possible outcome, given the practical limits of the nature of the condition and the situational contingencies. Rehabilitation is well advanced in physical medicine; experts have developed ingenious devices that allow persons with serious disabilities to overcome them and to live useful lives. In comparison, the mental health area offers a more difficult and uncertain situation, and experts continue to grope for a feasible model by which rehabilitation may be furthered (Watts and Bennett 1983; Shepherd 1984).

A rehabilitation approach is based on the premise that the person's injury, defect, or condition is irreversible because of the current state of knowledge and medical technology. The basic concern, then, is to provide techniques for changing living situations so that the condition, injury, or defect results in the least possible disability. Devices that change some aspect of the people and provide them with new skills include artificial hands, seeing eye dogs, and artificial talking devices for those who have cancer of the larynx and can no longer speak. These new tools help overcome the disability, and a period of training allows patients to adapt to their use. Disability can also be contained by controlling the environment in various ways. People who have disabling conditions can continue to meet role expectations through the use of special equipment that allows them to continue to do their jobs. A homemaker confined to a wheelchair can use kitchen appliances of different height and construction. The operating principle of such rehabilitation attempts is to change the skills and environment of a person so that an irreversible physical condition results in the least possible disability and disruption of patterns of living.

Rehabilitation does not imply that it is desirable to contain disability in contrast to reversing illness conditions. Unfortunately, in many areas we lack the necessary knowledge and the technology to do this, and under such conditions it is important to help people cope within the limits of their condition. Until we have a better understanding of the etiology, course, and treatment of most mental illnesses, it may be more reasonable to attempt to contain disability in this area than to pursue cures without any real knowledge of the ways they are to be achieved.

Because there is little agreement on approaches for community care programs, the decision to provide a program in no sense specifies what is to be undertaken. At one extreme stand those who visualize community care as nothing more than the extension of the various forms of psychotherapy to new categories of people. More commonly, community care is visualized as a form of social work in which a trained practitioner helps the patient and the family weather crises by applying some knowledge of group and psychodynamic functioning or by the practitioner serving as an ombudsman, helping to bail the patient and the family out of difficulty with official agencies. I suspect that all these approaches supply a certain degree of support and help that mental patients do not ordinarily receive. But they do not necessarily either correspond to the magnitude of the disability these patients often experience or encourage patients to strive more actively to improve their capacities to cope with their environment. I do not want to belittle any support and sustenance offered to these patients because the most elementary forms of such help are so frequently absent from their lives, and we know that even contact with unskilled but sympathetic workers can do much to keep them functioning in the community. If we are to meet our responsibility to the mentally ill and their families, however, we must aspire to achieve and accomplish much more than this.

As we consider various alternatives for rehabilitation programs, an educational approach often seems better fitted to the needs of community care than do traditional medical approaches. Successful functioning results in large part from the way people learn to approach problems and to the practice they obtain through experience and training. Patients frequently lack information, skills, and abilities that are important in satisfactorily adapting to community life. Although improving the patient's capacity to make a satisfactory adjustment to the community is in no way a cure, the acquisition of new and relevant skills can inspire hope and confidence and can increase involvement in other aspects of a treatment program as well. An educational approach focuses more attention and emphasis on the patient's current level of social functioning and less on his or her past, and it encourages detailed and careful assessment of the way the patient behaves in a variety of non-hospital contexts.

Successful social functioning depends on a person's ability to mobilize effort when such effort is necessary, on the manner of organizing and applying such efforts, on psychological and instrumental skills and abilities, and on supports in the social environment. Although social support is well developed within most community care programs, the other facets of social functioning have been relatively neglected.

The mobilization of effort, assuming some level of involvement, may be facilitated by developing personal and social controls that reinforce and encourage good work habits. Traditionally in the care of the mentally ill in the United States, patients defined as sufficiently sick to require institutional care were defined as too deteriorated to perform in work roles. Instead, they were frequently allowed to sink into an apathetic stupor while their work skills atrophied. Although the attitude toward the work of mental patients has become more reasonable, such persons are often regarded as too sick to pursue meaningful tasks, and a very limited scope of such activity is available to the patient in many treatment contexts. The assumption that mental illness is totally incapacitating is reinforced by programs that fail to keep active those sustainable aspects of social functioning. Yet, the ability to continue performing meaningful tasks while under treatment can do much to raise patients' confidence in themselves and to encourage persistence in coping efforts.

Organization of effort involves:

- the way persons anticipate situations
- the way they seek information about them
- the extent to which they plan, prepare, and rehearse them in a psychological and social sense
- the way they test problem solutions
- the way they consider and prepare alternative courses of action should the situation require it
- the way they allocate time and effort

When one begins to look at this problem in the case of persons with severe and persistent disabilities, it is astonishing how poorly their efforts are organized. In general psychiatric practice, the ineffectual organization of effort is often seen as a byproduct of the patient's condition and not as a basic component of it. Although such ineffectual performance may be an attribute of the illness, improvement in functioning may be valuable for the patient's self-confidence and mental state generally.

One of the difficulties all psychiatric programs face is the inability to obtain a comprehensive view of the way the patient behaves in a variety of meaningful social contexts. Because it is usually impractical for mental health workers to follow the patient closely within the community, they must depend either on informants or on information gleaned from observations of the patient's behavior in the clinical context. The clinical context is a highly artificial one, however, and may produce coping problems that are unrelated to those that confront the patient in the community. As clinical contexts are constructed so that they are more characteristic of actual living conditions, more accurate assessment of patients and the provision of programs fitted to their needs become possible. To return to the work example, it is valuable to focus on real competitive work whenever possible, and this helps explain why placing patients in competitive work situations is more successful than sheltered work for subsequent success.

In one sense a mental health program is a school in which the educational program, like a good tutorial program, takes into account the social, educational, and psychological needs of the student. From at least one perspective, mental patients suffer from inadequate and misguided socialization experiences; they have failed to acquire the psychological and coping skills necessary for reasonable social adjustment. Such failures may be the product of inherited capacities, brain damage, impoverished childhood circumstances, inadequate training for dealing with stress, or a variety of other causes. The source of the difficulty, however, may not be as important as the question of whether it can be remedied with appropriate rehabilitation.

One can visualize various advantages in using an educational model in contrast to a medical one. Successful social functioning requires some ability to act as one's own agent, and one of the disadvantages of the medical model is the tremendous dependence the chronic patient develops on physicians, nurses, social workers and other mental health workers, and on the institution as a physical entity. An educational model is likely to encourage higher expectations concerning personal responsibility and initiative, and its goals are specific.

A Further Note on Employment

In the past, traditional public mental hospitals were run substantially by patients who often maintained the grounds, farmed, prepared food, worked in the laundry, and performed many other vital functions. Indeed, hospitals were sometimes reluctant to discharge key workers who they had come to depend on for carrying out important work functions in underfinanced and understaffed institutions. There is a considerable history of research on industrial rehabilitation of patients, particularly in England (Wing 1967). Various studies showed that persons with chronic schizophrenia who wanted to leave the hospital could be trained successfully for industrial work. Even older patients who were more resistant to rehabilitation showed some benefits from work rehabilitation programs. Hospitals that prepared patients for industrial work did better than those that did not. Such industrial rehabilitation units provided conditions difficult to devise in mental hospitals, such as a realistic industrial setting, a majority of noninstitutionalized workers, and specific training in work habits appropriate to real work conditions.

In our society high value is placed on independent competitive employment, and this is a realistic goal for many but not all persons with serious mental illness. For many years mental health workers believed that it is necessary to move impaired patients along a continuum from highly sheltered work situations to competitive work, and a variety of approaches have been developed that protect the patient from the usual stresses of competitive work. More recent studies suggest that it is difficult to predict who will do well in competitive work, and that directly mainstreaming patients into the work force is often more effective than a more gradual approach, particularly if the jobs are reasonably consistent with patient preferences. But varying approaches are still needed for patients who lack the confidence and organization to maintain a competitive job.

Patients working within sheltered work do not encounter the same situations as those working regular jobs. Ideally, a sheltered situation is a temporary expedient until the patients' psychological states improve and they develop the confidence to take a regular job. Other patients, if they are to work at all, require long-term work insulated from common work stresses. The relative balance between these approaches depends on contingencies such as the competitiveness of the job market and disincentives in disability insurance for taking on a regular job and risking the loss of income and medical benefits. When the labor market is tight, employers are more tolerant of the peculiarities and special needs of persons with mental illness than when labor is in abundant supply. Although the Americans with Disabilities Act in theory protects patients with mental illness against employment discrimination and requires employers to make "reasonable accommodation" to their disabilities, there is little indication that the act, thus far, has contributed substantially to improving employment prospects. It is extremely difficult to monitor employment practices and assess when employers are unreasonably discriminatory. Progress is understandably slow because it requires cultural change, but increasing numbers of employers are cooperating in employment programs for people with mental illness and are discovering that they are often reliable and excellent employees.

Some community programs, for example, contract with employers to provide a certain number of jobs for clients in the program who are able to work. The care system makes a commitment that workers will come to work and perform at a reasonable level and that in emergencies staff members will fill the jobs to meet the commitment. In well-run programs, employers learn that many patients with psychiatric illness are more reliable and perform better than recruits from the labor pool employers typically rely on, and employers find such arrangements in their interest. Initially, employers are insecure about the mentally ill. It is important that they feel they can get immediate help when a mental health problem develops at the workplace.

As discussed before, a major difficulty is that many of the jobs for patients are in service industries that offer poor working conditions, such as kitchens, laundries, and restaurants. Many psychiatric patients are well educated and have a high level of skill but suffer great insecurities in the work context. It is more difficult to return these patients to suitable work since most programs concentrate on less educated and less skilled workers, who are the more typical clients. Expectations are higher in higher level jobs and employer tolerance is lower because employers typically recruit from a more stable labor force than in work demanding few skills.

It is worth noting that mental symptoms are often independent of work skills, and many handicapped patients are good and reliable workers. Some of the most handicapped patients, even during periods of acute symptoms, can work in some settings, as experience in Fairweather Lodges have demonstrated. These work settings typically do not involve direct contact with the public, and thus social reactions do not become a barrier to allowing the patient to continue working. Much more can be accomplished in work settings with the mentally ill, but work rehabilitation funding is essential to organize and carry out these programs. Program barriers to rehabilitation embedded in the incentives in the Social Security system discussed earlier need to be addressed.

The education model, in contrast to the medical model, may also be useful in that it makes the problems of patients appear more reasonable to the uninformed, and it may help minimize the stigma attached to the patients' difficulties. Despite a vast educational campaign, the concept of mental illness still carries the connotation of insanity. By emphasizing the normal potentialities of the mental patient, the educational approach may decrease social distance between treatment personnel and patients and between mental health and community contexts.

In the long run, of course, little is achieved by changing the labels we use without changing our practices. The proper organization of an educationally oriented rehabilitation program depends on the attitudes and approaches of mental health workers. To the extent that they nurture patients' dependency responses, encourage sick-role reactions, and serve patients rather than motivate them to serve themselves, educational efforts are limited. An educational approach must start with the assumption that most people with mental illness either have or can develop the capacities to meet their own needs. Through sympathetic attention and good medication management, encouragement of motivation, and scheduling and reinforcement of mastery experience, we may be able to set the stage for patients' improvement in social and psychological functioning.

The foregoing considerations of an educational approach in dealing with patients with disabilities are based on the assumption—by no means proved—that a significant part of the psychological discomfort people experience results from failures in social functioning and not solely from an endogenous disorder. If skills and mastery can be developed so that they respond appropriately to difficult events in their environment, the experience of successful performance and mastery may in itself help resolve some of the suffering of many persons with mental illness.

Problems in the Diffusion of Mental Health Innovations

As some of the examples suggest, there have been many innovative developments in community mental health care. Such new ideas face considerable resistance in becoming widely accepted and used, and these programs often face problems in finding stable funding even in areas where they do develop. Such new service programs are frequently outside existing reimbursement schemes. In order to become established, these programs must attract special developmental funds from federal or state government or must receive financial backing from local government. Because local government is reluctant to increase expenditures for what might become an expensive program attracting new clients, achieving financial stability is an uphill battle. It remains to be seen whether managed care providers will be expected to organize and provide such services to clients who can benefit.

Effective community care requires a shift from traditional bureaucratic procedures. Such programs must be attentive to community acceptance, the employment market, the welfare and social services system, housing, relationships with police and other community agencies, and intraprofessional relationships and rivalries. The professional working in community care has a less formal role than in an institution. Such a person must be a facilitator, coordinator, and integrator. These professionals must be tolerant of more fluid roles and relationships and must be able to work on a more equal basis with a wide range of other mental health professionals and community participants. Individuals must engage in definition and redefinition of tasks as they deal with others in related programs in the network of services. The professional, in a sense, becomes a broker who must negotiate among varying interests and agencies, and effectiveness resides in the ability to get things done and not in a traditional authority structure or special degrees.

It is not too difficult to understand why successful innovations are not readily replicated. Funding arrangements are often difficult. Unusual leadership is often necessary. The excitement and rewards in being an innovator are not as great for those who copy what has been done elsewhere and require giving up the security of defined roles and relationships and the comfort that comes from achieving certainty and control over the work environment. There is a great inertia in the existing pattern of professional services. A change in direction requires a leader who can communicate to others the sense of excitement in a new venture and who has the organizational skills to bring the necessary people and organizations together. In the absence of a strong incentive—such as available funding—it is extraordinarily difficult to build the necessary momentum.

Even in innovative programs that become established, maintaining momentum is a difficult challenge. The patients to be cared for are chronic and difficult. While something new generates excitement and enthusiasm, people eventually get tired. They seek to regularize their work patterns and control uncertainties in their environment. Even new roles tend to become bureaucratized with attempts to define responsibilities and turfs more precisely. Over time, unless leadership is very strong, personnel tend to become more cynical, more smug about their failures, less sensitive to their clients, and less committed to their jobs. In the jargon of the professional world, they *burn out*. Moreover, the leaders who develop these programs—being innovators—move on to other challenges leaving a gap in administration. If such a program is lucky enough to attract a talented administrator who can help institutionalize its innovativeness, it may have a good prognosis, but often the most talented personnel drift away to other programs as their talents and successes are recognized.

In sum, the diffusion of innovation in service patterns is a difficult challenge and one not easily achieved. New types of services and organizational arrangements are highly fragile and unstable and require a great deal of community support. While traditional services, such as hospitals, outpatient clinics, and nursing homes, are integrated into community organizational and financial arrangements, new care programs must sell their care, convincing community leaders that they are effective, efficient, and worthy of support. Such new community programs not only require public relations but face competition from conventional services that are reluctant to give up existing funding or community support. Developing effective programs requires not only initiative and technical competence but also a good sense of community politics.

Innovations in Housing

Housing the severely mentally ill in large cities, while typically not thought of as a mental health issue, is one of the most critical problems faced by mental health services. It is unreasonable to anticipate that community care programs can provide adequate mental health services to patients living on the street, in large shelters for the homeless, or in dangerous and unsuitable housing. Housing is not a formal responsibility of the mental health sector, but the sector neglects this problem at its peril.

Causes of homelessness among the mentally ill have already been reviewed. Much of the difficulty is the scarcity of housing and the competition among needy groups for the available housing units. Other problems include fear and prejudice toward the mentally ill in many neighborhoods, community resistance to group homes and other sheltered housing arrangements, and a profound lack of understanding about mental illness among those typically responsible for housing development and assignment.

Federal efforts to create new housing opportunities have diminished and the emphasis is away from public housing to private-sector development. Public housing support is thus concentrated in helping eligible clients pay rent in the community housing marketplace. These subsidies, however, are far too few to meet the necessary demand, and many eligible mental patients who have the capacity to live independently in dwellings scattered throughout the community find it impossible to get the necessary assistance.

But even if such assistance were available, scattered-site independent housing is not suitable for some severely mentally ill patients who require help and supervision. Thus, good community care requires a broad spectrum of housing opportunities ranging from those with varying levels supervision to independence. In many communities there is strong community resistance to the establishment of group homes, board and care facilities, supervised apartments, and other special projects directed to housing the mentally ill. Gaining community support presents some difficult dilemmas (Dear and Taylor 1982). On the one hand, a mental health program can inform a neighborhood that it plans to locate a group house in their vicinity and seek to gain cooperation. Such prior information provides an opportunity for opponents to mobilize political resistance (Hogan 1986a, b), which can end the project. On the other hand, the strategy of quietly establishing the facility without the neighborhood's awareness can result in bitter confrontations and isolation of the facility from the neighborhood. Often, however, the quiet establishment of a facility has so little effect that when neighbors learn of its existence, they accept it. Problems arise when patients with bizarre mannerisms wander on others' property or make their presence obvious. Resistance is much less in urban commercial zones where residents are much less involved in neighborhoods. Such locations may be advantageous if they are close to services and facilities patients need, but too often these sites are chosen as paths of least resistance, independent of any advantages of the location.

In recent years many mental health professionals with expertise in housing issues and mental health programs now routinely view housing as an essential part of the needs assessment and treatment planning process. They have learned to work cooperatively with landlords to gain their acceptance and support while providing assurance that they will be available as a resource to deal with crises or special problems that may occur. A variety of self-help and group-support mechanisms encourage ex-patients to help one another, as in the independent living movement. Perhaps the biggest change in recent years has been the shift from moving patients along a continuum of care from less to more independence to one of locating clients in stable housing situations and bringing them the services they need to adapt to community living in a satisfactory way. As more localities develop ser-

vices that move away from clinics to more assertive community treatments and crisis services they gain the types of flexibility that facilitate greater client choice in living arrangements. We have learned that client participation in the choice of their housing is an important facilitator of successful residential arrangements.

Changing Roles of the Mental Health Professions

Community mental health has changed opportunities and roles in carrying out mental
health activities. Modifications result from the different tasks required, changes within the
knowledge base and professional organization of each of the mental health professions,
and changes in reimbursement policies. Professionals are not only responsive to their work
situation but also attuned to issues of prestige, autonomy, and position within their own
professional structures. The relations among the professions are always in flux to some
degree, but managed care is likely to have even larger impact on the future in defining
dominant providers of various tasks.

Community care provides opportunities for new and expanded roles in administration
of teams and programs, in various case-management functions, in psychosocial rehabilitation, in discharge planning and linkage, and in housing and employment. As with psychotherapy, any of these functions can, in theory, be performed by any of the mental health
professions including psychiatry, psychology, social work, or nursing, as well as a range
of others with background or training in rehabilitation, counseling, or special education,
for instance. Psychiatry and medicine have retained their dominance by exclusive control
over prescribing medications. Psychology over the years has established its standing by
legal recognition in most states as independent providers of psychological services and by
recognition in most instances as a reimbursable provider. Although psychologists from
time to time make the case that their role ought to include prescription of psychoactive
drugs, the profession itself is divided on this issue and there seems little indication that this
is likely in the foreseeable future. Social work is making some progress in being recognized as a reimbursable provider, but social workers continue largely to be located in public and nonprofit agencies where they are remunerated by salary. Because social workers
tend to be less expensive providers than other mental health professionals providing
psychotherapeutic services it is likely that their role will increase as managed care firms
rachet down fees. Nursing has largely been centered in institutional settings, but psychiatric nurses are playing an increasingly important role in utilization review and case-
management functions.

Although various types of mental health professionals often work successfully in
teams, competition for political recognition and legitimation remains a salient aspect of
their relationships. This was seen clearly in the debates over benefit design in the Clinton
health care plan in the early 1990s, where psychologists fought vigorously against limits
on coverage for psychotherapy visits, which would have threatened their incomes more
than that of psychiatrists who focus more on inpatient care, medication treatment, and
more seriously ill subgroups of clients. The well-known observation of Freidson (1970)
that professional control resides with those groups that can gain public acceptance of their
special and unique competence and contribution still rings true.

In recent years new developments in mental health care other than in the area of drug treatment have come substantially from nonmedical disciplines. Behavior therapy and its applications are largely based on psychological research, and its practical use was primarily stimulated by psychologists. Crisis intervention techniques have a long history in social work, and the practical management of patients now so relevant for community care has been a traditional concern among social work agencies. As behavioral and social techniques have come to be used increasingly in patient management, such professions as psychology can claim special expertise more credibly, and the growing strength of clinical psychology derives not only from good politics but also from the growing acceptance of behavioral and cognitive therapies in the treatment of mental disorders.

Future Trends in Innovative Mental Health Services

Developing innovative services and allowing them to take root require both a mechanism for financing them and incentives that bring about an efficient and effective mix of these important new activities. Managed care can provide both financing and incentives for new ways of using and integrating various service providers. Managed care, however, if it is to give attention to the various broad needs of clients, will have to be carried out within a benefit design framework that requires attention to housing, rehabilitation, safety, and quality of life.

As states move into managed care arrangements for Medicaid clients and other vulnerable populations, they can contract on a capitated basis either with managed behavioral health companies who organize and manage a network of services or more directly with community providers such as community mental health centers. Contracts can be carefully specified to require provision and coordination of a comprehensive pattern of care. Organizations providing or managing the entire range of mental health, medical, and social services could be given incentives to integrate services in a way that substitutes less expensive staff and services when appropriate for more expensive inpatient and professional services. Such substitution alarms some observers because of the potential to provide too few or inappropriate alternatives, but such tendencies can be monitored. Although it is important to be prudent in designing incentives to reduce care, we should recognize that the traditional system gave too little attention to organizing care efficiently and often had incentives that encouraged expensive and not particularly optimal patterns of service.

Health care providers required to work with fixed budgets have strong incentives to seek economies and reasonable substitutions. They also have disincentives to encourage client dependency on care in areas where it may be constructive for the client to take more responsibility. Mental health care involves a long history of viewing patients as lacking the capacity to make decisions and choices about their lives and of highly paternalistic approaches. Capitation approaches encourage organizations to give more consideration to the value of support groups, self-help efforts, and treatment in group settings. But as the research we reviewed on family psychoeducational programs indicates, treatment in group settings need not be lesser care, and can be more efficacious than individual treatment. We should not assume that less expensive care is necessarily worse care. We must be vigilant, however, against inclinations to withhold needed services or to provide less than adequate services for economic or budgetary reasons.

In sum, developing innovative approaches has not been a major problem in the mental health arena. It has frequently been difficult to obtain careful evaluation of varying innovations and to distinguish between those that were truly effective as compared with those that were mere fads. Once particular approaches have been found to be superior to conventional services, it has often been difficult to achieve their widespread adoption because of reimbursement rules, conflicting interests between traditional programs and new innovations, and the pattern of traditionally organized professional relationships. Innovation requires more than having a good idea. It necessitates understanding of financial aspects of care and the political organization of service agencies and professional relationships. It also requires those with the good idea to attract people to new roles and tasks and to stimulate their motivation and commitment.

Chapter *11*

The Social Context of Mental Health Practice

Foundations of Trust

Mental health practice is more sensitive to issues of trust than many other aspects of health care because mental illness is seen to involve the entire personality and identity of individuals and to threaten stigmatization and discrimination. Moreover, psychotherapy often involves private and intimate material, what one thoughtful psychiatrist refers to as a *confessional model* of psychiatry (Sabin 1997). Thus, patients and their families are rightly concerned that their caretakers act on their behalf and as their agents, that they advocate for their needs, and that they rigorously protect confidential information. Mental health practice depends substantially on using interpersonal processes to relieve distress and achieve personal change, whether in psychotherapy or in rehabilitation, and, thus, the quality of relationships and their continuity take on even greater importance than they do in other types of care.

To say we trust mental health professionals is to say that we anticipate that they will perform their responsibilities competently, that they will act in our interest, and that they will be able to exercise appropriate control over the course of our treatment (Mechanic 1996; Mechanic and Schlesinger 1996). Historically, mental health practice often deviated from such trust conditions because mental health professionals often functioned within organizations that served the community and social control needs as much as they served individual patients, and much care was provided on an involuntary basis. In more contemporary situations, involuntary care is used more sparingly. Other challenges to trust derive from the changing organization of care and management by behavioral health care companies and utilization reviewers. It is common for third parties to become involved in the details of the patient's problems and treatment and for sensitive information about the patient to be shared widely among therapeutic, managerial, and administrative personnel. Beyond the good or bad influences that managed care might have, to the extent that managed care practices challenge the patient's trust they reduce the likelihood that patients will seek mental health care, that they will reveal sensitive and intimate information, or that they will adhere to therapeutic advice or otherwise cooperate in treatment. Achieving and maintaining trust, thus, is a major responsibility of effective mental health practice.

All mental health professionals are influenced in their activities and judgments by the sociocultural context, by their social and personal biographies, by the perspectives, theories and scientific conceptions of their respective disciplines and professions, and by the economic and organizational constraints of their particular roles and practice settings. Mental health practice involves varied and sometimes competing roles. A social worker as therapist functions differently and assumes different perspectives and responsibilities than a social worker as utilization reviewer whose responsibilities include cost containment. Although mental health workers may select themselves into certain roles and not others, it is common for them to have multiple professional roles with no clear demarcation among them. Much of professional practice still has important social control functions, and mental health practitioners are in part political actors.

In the discussion that follows I will commonly refer to psychiatrists, although most of the points equally refer to other mental health professionals such as social workers, psychologists, and nurses. Unfortunately, most of the studies have focused on doctors and psychiatrists, and we have much less systematic evidence on professional practice in other mental health areas. Increasingly, however, psychiatrists are limiting their efforts to medication and treatment supervision, and more of the interpersonal therapies and rehabilitation efforts are being performed by social workers, nurses, psychologists, and other mental health workers.

Freidson (1970) in an influential analysis noted the distinction between scientists and practitioners. The goal of the physician is treatment and not knowledge. The physician believes in what he or she is doing, and this can be functional for both doctor and patient. Skeptical detachment so necessary in science, when it becomes too much part of the practice role, may discourage the patient and erode the suggestive power of the therapeutic relationship. If therapists truly believe in what they are doing, and communicate their confidence and hope to patients, this becomes a powerful ingredient in the treatment situation. While the scientist seeks to develop a coherent theory, the clinician is a pragmatist, depending heavily on subjective experience and trial and error in situations of uncertainty. While the scientist seeks to determine regularity of behavior in relation to abstract principles, the clinician is more subjective and suspicious of the abstract. The responsibilities of clinical work make it difficult to suspend action, to remain detached, and to lack faith that one is helping patients.

The differences between the objectives of science and practice suggest different ways of proceeding in the two roles. The researcher in psychiatry must be concerned with precise and reliable diagnosis. Only through effective distinctions among varying clinical entities can knowledge of etiology, course, and effective treatment be acquired (Mechanic 1978). Although such efforts in making finer distinctions or in identifying new conditions may be uncertain and yield no benefits for the patient, they may serve the development of scientific inquiry and understanding. Such diagnostic orientations used in a clinical context, however, may be of little use or even be dysfunctional. The labeling of questionable conditions may induce anxiety in the patient, may be stigmatizing, and may divert efforts from taking constructive action on behalf of the patient. As suggested in earlier chapters, the professionalization of psychiatry in the late nineteenth century in the United States, and the growing assumption that mental disorders were biological in origin and required organic interventions, undermined the useful activities of social reformers who gave attention to the social context of treatment (Grob 1966). If mental disease was an unfolding of biological propensities, why worry about the social environment? The irony, of course, was that the new conception had little to offer patients and undermined helpful and constructive interventions.

Mental health professionals in their capacity as clinicians have a social role that extends beyond their technical knowledge. The scope of their activities might be constrained by their conceptions of appropriate mental health activities, but they have limited control in defining the types of patients that seek their help. They have a social responsibility to do what they can to help patients who are suffering and seek assistance, and thus cannot be constrained merely by the state of established knowledge. Clinicians work in part on the basis of scientific knowledge and clinical experience and in part on the basis of their social judgment of what is appropriate for the situation. As the problems faced become more uncertain and are less resolvable through existing expertise, the professional's social biography and values have a larger impact on decision making.

Because psychiatry deals with deviance in feeling states and behavior, its conceptions run parallel to societal conceptions of social behavior, personal worth, and morality. Behavior can be viewed from competing vantage points, and thus is amenable to varying professional stances. In the absence of clear evidence on etiology or treatment, personal disturbance can be alternatively viewed as biological in nature, as a result of developmental failures, as a moral crisis, or as a consequence of socioeconomic, social, or structural constraints. Remedies may be seen in terms of biological restoration, moral realignment, social conditioning, or societal change. Although all of these elements might be present in the same situation, the one that the clinician emphasizes has both moral and practical implications. There is no completely neutral stance. Diagnostic and therapeutic judgments have political and social implications (Halleck 1971).

In this context it is of great importance whom the therapist represents. To the extent that the therapist acts exclusively as the patient's representative and in the patient's interest as far as this can be known, the situation is relatively simple. The patient suffers and seeks assistance, and the role of the therapist is to do whatever possible to define the options available for the patient and to proceed in an agreed-upon manner. Such intervention may be at the biological, psychological, or social level or within a medical, psychodynamic, or educational model. The definition of the endeavor, however, is in terms of the patient's interests and needs. In real situations, failure to define options is common, and the clinician's values and ideologies or practice orientations may intervene, resulting in deviations from the ideal. Indeed, clinicians may not be conscious of their own ideologies and orientations because they are so entrenched in their own world view. Or they may proceed against the patient's wishes because they assume greater knowledge of the patient's interests. Despite these complexities, the approach is distinctive in that actions taken are for the sake of the patient and no other.

The ethic that the physician's responsibility is to the patient and no other is itself a value, as are other norms of practice such as confidentiality. Increasingly, clinicians are expected to be allocators as well as advocates, balancing the needs of individual patients against the needs of the collectivity. In the People's Republic of China, psychiatric practice is a public function with primary commitment to the interests of the state and not the individual (Kleinman and Mechanic 1979). Psychiatric practice takes place openly in consultation with family members and with community leaders. The way the patient will be handled is a public issue, and information concerning the patient's problems and management is shared with officials and work supervisors. Although the basic content of psychiatry is seen as primarily biological, the social consequences of psychiatric advice are recognized. Professional practice cannot be divorced from existing forms of social organization.

China may seem far from U.S. psychiatric concerns, but the issues of whom the clinician represents and the proper scope of confidentiality are critical issues in the care of the chronically mentally ill. Many families of mental patients have expressed bitterness against mental health professionals, who they feel left them uninformed and provided little help in dealing with the burden of a severely ill child or spouse. Many families have been dissatisfied with the information they receive, feeling that communication is almost exclusively with the patient, isolating them from the treatment process (Hatfield 1987; Tessler et al. 1987). Effective care of chronic patients often requires communication with landlords, police, employers, and others that pushes against the ethic of confidentiality that traditionally defines patient–therapist relationships.

In Western societies, psychiatrists may work as agents of individual patients or as agents of collectivities or organizations, such as families, schools, industries, courts, and the armed services (Szasz 1970). Under some circumstances, mental health professionals may retain autonomous roles in which they continue to act as agents for patients, but their organizational auspices make such roles more uncertain and more susceptible to encroachment (Halleck and Miller 1963). Couples therapy or therapy involving parents and children inevitably involves a clash of wills and interests, and the therapist is forced to take sides, though this may be reflected only in the most subtle ways. Although such therapies may involve sufficient common interest among the parties to sustain the encounter, the therapist must walk a difficult line. Therapists in such situations often see themselves as playing an autonomous role; such a role may become more tenuous as the power of the institution employing the therapist intrudes on the relationship.

When clinicians work for organizations other than the patient, their loyalties are split. Although conflict of loyalties may not be a major issue in routine everyday practice, it may at any time become problematic whenever the organization and the patient have competing needs or interests. The most dramatic examples of such forms of bureaucratic practice are found in totalitarian countries in which psychiatrists are state bureaucrats and may perform social control functions for the state, or in the military in which psychiatrists serve as agents of the organization. Similar pressures exist, however, whenever the psychiatrist represents some collectivity, whether it be a court, prison, school, or industrial organization. In all but the most crass cases, the psychiatrist as double agent is sufficiently ambiguous that the professional can experience feelings of neutrality and participation in the public interest. It is this comforting sense of lack of partiality that is most dangerous because it diverts attention from the dilemmas in resolving conflicts between involved parties. The use of psychiatry to discredit political dissenters or innovators is reasonably evident, even if disputed. It is the subtle social influences on psychiatric work that are more difficult to bring into the open.

Social Influences on Psychiatric Judgment

In most instances in which psychiatric judgments are made, there are no reliable independent tests to confirm or contest them. While psychiatric diagnosis focuses on disordered thought and functioning and not deviant behavior per se (Lewis 1953), judgments of disorder must be tied to social contexts and the clinician's understanding of them based not only on clinical experience but also normal life experience. Most lay persons can recognize the bizarre symptoms associated with psychosis; it is the borderline areas that are more at issue, and at these borders it becomes more difficult to disentangle subculture, illness behavior, and psychopathology. As the subcultural situation is further from the psychiatrist's firsthand experience, the likelihood increases that inappropriate contextual norms will be applied. To the extent that the patient comes to the therapist voluntarily and seeks relief from suffering, the lack of precision in making such contextual judgments is less of a concern than when the psychiatrist acts on behalf of some other interest. Even in the former situation, however, the prestige of the therapist reinforces considerable personal power in the encounter with the patient and may reinforce one of the alternative views of the nature of the patient's problem.

The absence of procedures or laboratory tests to establish diagnoses independent of the therapist's contextual judgment makes it relatively easy for critics to insist that psychiatrists label patients on the basis of social, ethical, or legal norms and not on clearly established evidence of psychopathology (Szasz 1960; Rosenhan 1973). Although such criticisms cannot really speak to the scientific validity of the application of a disease model to the patient's suffering or deviant behavior (Spitzer 1976; Mechanic 1978), they apply to the role of psychiatrist as clinician or bureaucrat in dealing with social problems and psychological disorder. The psychiatrist who mediates conflicts between husband and wife, between parent and child, between employer and employee, and between citizens and official agencies inevitably must mix social judgments with assessments of psychopathology. When the psychiatrist acts as an agent to excuse failures at work, to obtain special preference for housing or other benefits, to obtain disability payments, to excuse deviant behavior, or in a wide variety of other arenas, he or she typically parades social judgments and personal decisions as psychiatric practice. It is therefore essential to know something about the social orientations and world views of psychiatrists and other clinicians who make such judgments.

Personal and Social Biographies

Psychiatrists have gone through a variety of selective screenings involving entry into medical school, into psychiatry, and into particular types of psychiatric functions, such as individual psychotherapy, hospital work, or administration. This selective process involves not only academic performance and interests but also social background, values and ideologies, and individual aspirations. Various studies show that physicians selecting psychiatry differ from students in other specialties, such as surgery or family practice, on social background, attitudes, and political orientations (Christie and Geis 1970; Colombotos et al. 1975). In their classic book, *Social Class and Mental Illness,* Hollingshead and Redlich

(1958) reviewed the dramatically varying social biographies of psychiatrists in New Haven who pursued analytic–psychological orientations as compared with those who were more directive in their approaches and depended more on organic therapies. Despite an obvious convergence in therapeutic practice, with many psychiatrists using a combination of therapies and drugs, there continued to be a distinctive selection process of mental health professionals into psychotherapy.

Therapists engaged in office-based psychotherapy were both distinctive and relatively homogeneous in their social characteristics.

> *Careers terminating in the private practice of psychotherapy are populated, to a very large extent, by practitioners of highly similar cultural and social backgrounds. They come from a highly circumscribed sector of the social world, representing a special combination of social marginality in ethnic, religious, political, and social-class terms. (Henry, Sims, and Spray 1973, p. 3)*

Psychotherapists coming from psychiatry, clinical psychology, and social work are more similar in social background and practice orientations to one another than to psychiatrists who are more medically inclined (Henry, Sims, and Spray 1971, 1973). Persons who become therapists, regardless of profession, perform similar activities, having comparable work styles, share many viewpoints, and have strikingly similar developmental experiences.

The implications of similarities of development and perspective among therapists are not obvious but very suggestive. Certainly it is reasonable to assume that therapists who are upwardly mobile, socially marginal, nonreligious, divorced, and politically liberal will see social and moral issues differently from more socially integrated and conventional persons, and they will communicate quite different judgments. Because therapists' personalities and orientations are important aspects of therapy, and because psychotherapy is largely an influence process (Frank 1974), the encounter inevitably involves the transmission of values. Therapists may wish to minimize personal biases, however, but they cannot help but transmit what they stand for. To the extent that this is explicit to the patient, it is less of a problem than when masked behind a professional mystique.

Greenley, Kepecs, and Henry (1979) provide data collected in 1973 from psychiatrists practicing in Chicago, some of whom were also studied in a 1962 survey (Henry, Sims, and Spray 1971). These data indicate that at least in Chicago there was strong persistence of a dominant Freudian-analytic orientation and office-based private practice. Although more psychiatrists reported having an eclectic orientation, the enthusiasm of the early 1960s for social and community psychiatry had receded. It was noted as the orientation of only some 15 percent of respondents in 1973. If this study was repeated today, it would probably show the growing dominance of biological psychiatry.

There is some evidence from this survey that the social characteristics of both psychiatrists and their patients are becoming more like those of the general population, although large differences still exist. The growth of psychodynamic therapy in the United States can be viewed as a social movement, developing first among particular practitioners and patients facing certain existential dilemmas (Mechanic 1975). Psychodynamic therapies developed their roots in urban areas, with many practitioners of urban, middle-class, Jewish origins. This therapy initially attracted persons with social inclinations and characteristics similar to those of the therapists. As the movement grew, however, and therapy became more widely accepted in the culture, one would have anticipated that it would become more heterogeneous in geographic distribution and in the characteristics of both therapists and patients. The indications were that such heterogeneity was developing as psychotherapy became institutionalized, and Greenley, Kepecs, and Henry's (1979) Chicago data illustrate this trend. Comparing cohorts of psychiatrists completing residencies in different periods from before 1950 to the time of the survey, they observe a steep decline in the proportion of those with immigrant fathers, those who were Jewish, and those who were raised in a large city. Psychiatrists in 1973, as compared with 1966, reported having more women, blacks, Catholics, and poor persons as patients, and somewhat fewer Jewish patients.

The Chicago data, as well as other experience, indicate that psychiatric practice has become more varied and complex (Redlich and Kellert 1978, Olfson and Pincus 1996). This should allow greater opportunity for patients to locate therapists who have orientations and perspectives closer to their own and should promote a healthy diversity within psychiatry itself concerning the relationship between mental health concerns and values.

The Sociocultural Context

The sociocultural context in which young psychiatrists develop and mature and within which they practice has a dramatic influence on their world views as well as their professional activities. Varying periods of historical time and specific cultural contexts provide different images of the nature of man, the boundaries of deviance, and the professional role of social and psychiatric intervention. In Europe, psychiatry remained closer to general medical practice than in the United States, where psychodynamic therapies were viewed by psychiatrists as more prestigeful than taking care of severely disturbed or chronic patients. In the post-World War II period, psychodynamic ideas came to dominate residency programs in psychiatry and had a major effect on the way psychiatrists perceived their roles and practiced their craft. Why the United States and not Europe was the more fertile ground for psychoanalytic ideas is amenable to many interpretations; nevertheless, the fact is that it was and it resulted in a dramatic influence on views of psychopathology and treatment of patients.

During the 1960s there was great ferment in U.S. society, characterized by social activism and an ideology that government could effectively attack social problems. This ideology had a broad sweep, and it also came to encompass conceptions of the social causes of and remedies for mental illness. Psychiatrists caught up in the ethos of the time began making grandiose claims of the potentialities for a community psychiatry. Such advocacy was not grounded in improving programming for chronic mental patients who were increasingly being returned to communities, but in claims for special societal expertise. In the words of one such advocate, "The psychiatrist must truly be a political personage in the best sense of the word. He must play a role in *controlling* the environment which man has created" (Duhl 1963, p. 73).

A major component of this new ideology was the notion that psychiatry could engage in primary prevention to limit the occurrence of mental illness. Caplan (1964) maintained that such efforts involved identifying harmful influences, encouraging environmental forces that support individuals in resisting them, and increasing the resistance of the population to future illness. The program he offered under the guise of psychiatric expertise was simply a form of social and political action. As Caplan saw it,

> *The mental health specialist offers consultation to legislators and administrators and collaborates with other citizens in influencing governmental agencies to change laws and regulations. Social action includes efforts to modify general attitudes and behavior of community members by communication through the educational system, the mass media, and through interaction between the professional and lay communities. (Caplan 1964, p. 56)*

Clearly Caplan wished psychiatrists to become involved in matters such as morality and values on which there were many views and differences of opinion. Caplan even went so far as to speculate that a psychiatrist might "exercise surveillance over key people in the community and . . . intervene in those cases where he identifies disturbed relationships in order to offer treatment or recommend dismissal" (p. 79). However, he rejected this role not because of lack of ability or knowledge on the part of psychiatrists but because it would be a distasteful role for most psychiatrists and because of political and social complications.

Some of the concepts implicit in early preventive psychiatry were unfortunate not only because they were grandiose, naive, and an obvious projection of political values, but also because they continued to divert attention from making many of the remedial efforts more consistent with existing knowledge and expertise. Preventive care during pregnancy and adequate postnatal care, still not fully available to the poor, are important in preventing mental retardation, prematurity, brain damage, and a variety of other difficulties. Family planning services and facilities for families with handicapped children are often difficult to find. The system of services in the community for chronic mental patients is at best fragmentary. By what set of values do we divert attention from these issues to pursue illusory goals? The greatest weakness of preventive psychiatry in the 1960s was the substitution of vague ideals for tangible action and a failure to specify in any clear way how psychiatric expertise could lead to the laudable goals being advocated.

The extraordinary range of roles played by psychiatrists is reflected in the work of a Harvard psychiatrist as a consultant for the Boston Patriots football team. Among his tasks were teaching techniques "to program the mind to achieve peak athletic performance" and "meeting with team members before a game to help prepare them psychologically for a competition" (Nicholi 1987). Other functions included individual therapy, drug-use prevention efforts, helping resolve conflicts among team members, and improving relations between coach and players. The prestigious *New England Journal of Medicine,* which publishes little on chronic mental illness and rations its space in the most parsimonious way devoted more than five pages to psychiatric consultation in football.

It is essential from an ethical perspective to differentiate among varying psychiatric roles. From the role of psychiatrist as researcher, it is fully appropriate to examine the value of interpersonal interventions. Caplan (1964) maintained that various crises and transitional periods in the life span, such as entering school, having a child, going to the hospital for surgery, or moving to a new environment, pose severe stresses that may burden a person's coping capacities and entail a high risk of social breakdown. He asserted that during such periods persons had a heightened desire for help and were more responsive to it. He argued that community psychiatrists should seek out situations in which persons feel vulnerable and provide supportive help and new coping techniques. The theory argued that social breakdowns could be prevented either by intervening in the lives of people and their families during crises or by working through various professionals, such as doctors, nurses, teachers, and administrators, who naturally come into contact with people during such crises. Among the contexts Caplan suggested for such crises intervention were prenatal and surgical wards, divorce courts, and colleges. The basic hypothesis, and one legitimate and worthy of detailed inquiry, is that it is possible to give people anticipatory guidance and emotional inoculation that help them cope with threatening events (Mrazek and Haggarty 1994).

When the psychiatric role moves from investigation to practice, the hypothesis of crisis intervention involves major ethical dilemmas. First, although aspects of the theory are promising, it is based on a vague conceptualization that environmental trauma and the lack of coping abilities cause mental illness, a conception for which the evidence is incomplete and far from secure. Second, although such efforts may be made with laudable goals in mind, the evaluation literature attests to the fact that such programming often not only fails to achieve desired objectives, but also makes matters worse (Robins 1979a). Third, there is really very little evidence that the types of trouble-shooting preventive psychiatrists advocated although perhaps valuable in reducing distress, have any real impact on the occurrence of mental illness or are directed at those who are likely to become mentally ill if untreated. Despite these ethical concerns, the psychiatrist could justifiably engage in such programs with interested community groups to the extent that they understand the limitations and elect to participate voluntarily. Such interventions may be viewed as any other uncertain therapy, with possible positive and adverse effects that must be balanced.

Preventive psychiatry intuitively seems enticing. After all, isn't it better to prevent illness than treat it after it occurs? Moreover, the proponents of prevention typically argue that it saves vast amounts of money, since treating severe illness is much more expensive than initial preventive care. But as we have learned so well in the area of general medical care, this argument is simplistic and often incorrect (Russell 1986, 1987). The success of prevention and potential cost savings depend on the ability to target individuals who will become more seriously ill without treatment and the cost and effectiveness of the preventive intervention. But even when we have interventions that we believe to be efficacious and that are not too costly, preventive efforts may still be a bad bargain unless we have the knowledge to target precisely. The number of people who become seriously mentally ill is a small proportion of the population. In contrast, the number of people who can be potential targets of preventive intervention is very large. Even a relatively inexpensive intervention averaged over large numbers of people can result in large aggregate costs. But many of these people get better without formal intervention. The ECA project estimated that 30 million people had a DIS-DSM III disorder and that many more millions have high levels of distress and dysfunction without such disorder. If we add additional vulnerable individuals including those under high stress, those experiencing bereavement or divorce, the unemployed, and so on, we can readily identify a target population of 100 million people. Thus, an intervention costing $100, not a particularly expensive one by psychiatric standards, would in the aggregate cost $10 billion. Think of what even a small fraction of this could do for the severely mentally ill.

Preventive psychiatry is particularly on shaky ground when mental health professionals are functioning in bureaucratic roles, providing services to those neither seeking nor desiring their services. In such cases the mental health worker is not the patient's agent. The imposition of such interventions in schools, divorce courts, welfare agencies and the like, supported by the coercive authority of the organization, can be a serious imposition on privacy and the right of persons to refuse treatment. Even if preventive interventions were more certain and more efficacious, involuntary applications or services offered under the threat of coercion would raise serious ethical questions.

As the optimism of the 1960s receded, preventive psychiatry lost much of its luster, and in the 1970s and 1980s psychiatry moved closer to medicine and more restricted biological foci, but preventive work remained an important stream of professional activity. A 1986 survey of a sample of psychiatric residents and faculty at UCLA found that more than half believed that preventive interventions in psychiatry are almost always appropriate, and almost four-fifths reported that preventive psychiatric interventions are generally worth the amount of time they take. But some skepticism was also apparent. Almost two-fifths believed or thought it possible that while preventive psychiatry sounds good in concept, there is little evidence in reality that preventive interventions are effective (Linn et al. 1988). Preventive mental health practice is more modest and realistic in the 1990s than in the optimism of the 1960s, and psychiatric training now gives primary attention to biological bases of behavior and more particularly to brain processes, behavior genetics and molecular biology. Psychodynamic, and even psychoanalytic, views are still common but the field of practice is increasingly heterogeneous with training focused on a more rigorous attitude.

In an earlier section of the book I discussed some current efforts in preventive mental health, building on our increased understanding of vulnerability and the importance of social support and coping. These ideas have been incorporated into much of the therapeutic work undertaken by psychologists and social workers, who are now major providers of psychotherapy and rehabilitation services. These ideas have also penetrated fields such as health education, and there are many programs to improve decision making, teach parenting skills, develop coping skills, and give participants a greater sense of personal efficacy in their lives. The value of many of these programs remains uncertain, but the scientific literature provides some promise of reducing distress and improving personal effectiveness (Mrazek and Haggarty 1994). There is little evidence, however, that primary prevention has promise in most areas of major mental illness.

The particular attitudes and ideologies of mental health professionals reflect their prior socialization, the state of research in mental health, and dominant professional views as reflected in training programs, social ideas about the possibilities of intervention, and opportunities and constraints characteristic of practice opportunities. All of these factors change over time, and we go through cycles of optimism and pessimism. From 1955–1975, for example, mental health practice was characterized by great optimism about the potentials of social reform and professional activism. Practice opportunities were expanding and funding for interventions was available. Since 1980 the field has become far more pessimistic about affecting mental illness through social interventions and professional practice has turned sharply toward biological conceptions, medical approaches, and care based on more restricted concepts of medical necessity. Yet at any given point, the views of mental health workers reflect their respective professions and the ideologies dominant during their formative development. Although views and practices change over time, each cohort tends to retain aspects of the value conceptions characteristic of its unique educational history.

Constraints of Practice Organization and Settings

Professional practice is influenced by the social context of practice organization and the manner in which payment for services is made. The influence of the purchaser on professional decisions is now widely recognized as utilization review and capitated practice have become dominant forces in mental health practice.

We are still in a period of transformation, and traditional practices continue alongside new managed care arrangements. In these traditional forms, the mental health practitioner is a private office-based professional contracting with patients to provide care on a fee-for-service basis. Although practice has been eclectic, involving medication visits, brief psychotherapy, group therapy and other variants, the focus is on more conventional psychotherapy. Traditional psychotherapy patients typically have some insurance for such coverage or are sufficiently affluent to pay for these services with their own funds. Such therapy is organized in time units of forty-five to fifty minutes as often as every day or a couple of times a week, and therapy often extends for long periods of time, sometimes years. Therapists view themselves as solely responsible to their patients and not to insurance programs or abstract notions of community need. The form of payment used—fee-for-service per session—creates an incentive for the professional to see the patient often and to continue therapy beyond any point that such intervention would be cost-effective.

In contrast, community mental health centers and health maintenance organizations are theoretically responsible for a defined population who receive services from the organization. Clinicians in such organizations, unlike fee-for-service therapists, have a dual role of caring for each patient, and also reasonably allocating resources among all the patients who need care. Because mental health services in these contexts cannot be made available to everyone who wants them, or who might benefit from them, and because plans must consider the economic viability of how they distribute care, rationing decisions must be made as to who in the population most need specialized mental health services and to what extent.

Rationing can occur in many different ways. In traditional indemnity insurance, the major approach to rationing is through benefit design, in which there are strict limits on the amount and types of care available and there is high patient cost sharing. Typically, insurance programs limit the number of psychotherapy visits and impose high patient cost sharing, greater than for most other medical services. In HMOs, rationing often occurs by requiring a formal referral from a primary care physician in the plan to a mental health therapist. When such a referral is made, HMOs typically keep consultations brief and provide only short-term therapy, substitute less-expensive practitioners for more expensive psychiatrists, and are more likely to treat people in groups than individually. There are many other ways to limit service demand such as by making it difficult to schedule appointments, increase waiting time, and by strict utilization monitoring and review. In the early stages of managed care mental health practitioners, who disliked working under these kinds of organizational arrangements, chose to practice independently and in more traditional ways, but as managed care becomes the predominant form of service provision, therapists may find it more difficult to sustain an independent practice. On accepting membership in such organizations they must yield some of their practice autonomy and accept more external influence over the scope and character of the services they provide.

Similar types of constraints operate in psychiatric inpatient care or even in community care programs. What can be done for patients depends on the resources and personnel available and the number of clients requiring care. Services are often stretched thinly or are inadequate because demand exceeds capacity. Since inpatient care is particularly expensive care, utilization management is increasingly rigorous in seeking to avoid hospitalization whenever possible and reducing average length of hospital stays. Thus, hospitals commonly have to cope with a sicker group of patients, evaluate and treat them, and make appropriate discharge treatment plans in shorter periods of time. Moreover, as patients' hospital care is increasingly covered by capitation contracts or by discounted payments, hospitals have less resources and seek economies through reduced staffing. Often the first groups to be downsized are social workers and nurses, and thus fewer staff are available to carry out the daily essential tasks. It is difficult to define the point at which increasing efficiency ends and inadequate service begins. This is a major issue and requires careful monitoring and evaluation of patient outcomes.

Competition in the Allocation of Care

It is typical for mental health professionals to bemoan inadequate mental health financing, but it is unlikely that sufficient mental health resources will ever be available to serve all those who might benefit from them. There are no easy ways out of the dilemma posed by the need to ration, and it is clear that however we ration, we must do so in a way that is trusted by the public and those who use mental health services. Mental health practitioners have an ethical obligation to evaluate their techniques and approaches in relation to benefits and costs so that the resources available can be used in cost-effective ways.

In allocating mental health treatments, two major but highly controversial issues concern the services that should be covered and the types of clients who should receive service priority. Mental health practitioners have a large investment in psychotherapeutic services, but there is little compelling evidence that psychotherapies add much value beyond drug treatment for many people with treatable disorders. Some patients can do as well with psychotherapy as with medications, but such treatment takes longer. Some studies suggest that patients do best with a combination of medication and psychotherapy, but there is little justification for public financing of unfocused and long-term psychotherapies. The growth of managed care puts great pressure on therapists to have a focused and time-limited treatment plan. Nevertheless, tensions continue around the issue of how much psychotherapy to reimburse and for what patients.

A second contentious issue concerns the definition of what clients should have priority for mental health specialty care. Epidemiological studies that we have reviewed indicate that as much as a third of the population will have a disorder in any given year, but most will receive no treatment from any source. Many of these people might not need treatment, others who need it might not be aware of their needs or how to get care, and others might not want it. Public attitudes about treatment vary a great deal. Public policy should focus on those who have the most serious mental disorders and associated disabilities and the least ability to take care of themselves.

Although in principle it is relatively easy to agree that services should be distributed in relation to need and that practice should focus on what is cost-effective, the lack of evidence on cost-effectiveness and the ambiguity of the concept of need provides much to disagree about. Moreover, need and cost-effectiveness may be in conflict. For example, some preventive interventions or treatment of people with minor disorders might yield impressive results, while more intensive and expensive interventions among those with the largest disabilities might improve outcomes only modestly or not at all. But values also play an important part, since caring for people with serious disorders in a humane way and offering them hope, even when no effective therapy exists, is a recognized and important goal. Allocating limited resources fairly and intelligently is a challenging task, and one that will occupy our attention over many years.

There is much acrimony in the mental health arena, characterized by the varying perspectives of different advocacy groups. Mental health constituencies have different views, depending on the illness populations they represent (more severe versus less severe disorders), age groups (children, adults and the elderly), the professional group involved (psychiatry versus psychology), and interest in particular types of services (prevention versus treatment; inpatient care versus outpatient treatment; medications versus psychotherapy; treatment versus rehabilitation). Groups representing these various interests compete actively and sometimes in a destructive way. Involved groups have different interests and needs, and the lack of trust makes it difficult to develop strategies and approaches that maximize mental health advocacy or that help resolve competing interests or the ideological and value conflicts involved. It also makes it more difficult to make considered determinations of how to allocate mental health resources among different care priorities. Yet it is apparent that interest group politics is not the best way to resolve difficult treatment and allocation issues.

A Note on the Care of Chronically Impaired Patients

Deinstitutionalization and community mental health care are as much a social ideology as were earlier conceptions of the care of the mentally ill. The ideology consists of beliefs that it is desirable that individuals, to the extent possible, live independently, assume responsibility, and show a desire to adjust in some fashion to community living. The involuntary hospitalization of patients constituted a violation of cherished beliefs about individual rights, and the abuses associated with such involuntary commitment have become widely known, making it more difficult to justify civil commitment. Perhaps less widely appreciated are the pressures now placed on patients and their families to have the patient in the community and the growing tendency to refuse a hospital refuge to some highly impaired patients (Morrissey, Tessler, and Farrin 1979).

The extent to which the community should allow such refuge, and at what point, is very much tied to economic factors and the social ethos. The issue of the extent to which coercive therapies should be used to stimulate and maintain appropriate functioning does not easily yield to a consensus, and practices vary a great deal from one context to another depending on the values and commitments of professionals working with such patients. With the development of aversive techniques of control, "token economies," and other forms of behavior modification, profound questions were raised about the limits of coercion and treatment.

In sum, every aspect of psychiatric conceptualization, research, and practice is shaped by social ideologies and assumptions. Concepts of deviance, boundaries between mental disorders and other types of problems, modes of intervention, and selection of clients all vary by time and place, by the character of social structure, and by dominant social perspectives. The biography of mental health professionals and their practices are culturally shaped, and the economic system poses alternative opportunities and constraints. Because mental health professionals must work with social models and because such models have broad ethical implications for every aspect of their craft, there is no way of escaping the fact that psychiatric practice is as much a moral as a medical endeavor.

Chapter *12*

Mental Illness, the Community, and the Law

Mental disorder creates a variety of problems for the community, as well as for families of the mentally ill. Persons with severe mental illness may be a nuisance in the community and may disrupt normal social activities. They may be frightening and dangerous or so disoriented or neglectful of themselves that their lives are in danger. Suicide is a serious threat and a common problem in the care of patients with serious and disabling mental disorders. How to deal with problems of care and danger among persons who appear to lack control over their welfare and who are of concern to the community has been a longstanding issue (Shah and Sales 1991). Concerns about cost and the growth of managed care is likely to change how we think about some of these issues.

Involuntary hospitalization of the mentally ill has been a source of debate and litigation over many years. The tensions for several decades have been between those who wanted to involuntarily remove persons with serious mental illness from the community for purposes of care, treatment, and social control and patients themselves or their advocates who wanted persons with mental illness to be left alone to live their lives as they saw fit. The cost of treatment was rarely an issue in decisions to hospitalize and, indeed, the threshold to do so was rather low. Now, in contrast, the costs of hospitalization are viewed with great concern, and neither the state nor those who manage insurance benefits look with favor on discretionary hospital admissions and particularly on extended lengths of stay. Thus, it is far more common to keep patients with florid psychoses in community settings, and when involuntary treatment occurs it tends to be relatively brief. The state and community agents are still motivated to detain dangerous persons, but concepts of danger and the threshold for involuntary commitment have changed. Although the impetus for these changes developed out of civil liberty concerns and the protection of individual rights, current policies are reinforced by a desire to deal with mental illness in the least restrictive setting for reasons of economics as well as individual rights. Given the strength of economic considerations, it seems plausible to anticipate increased attention to outpatient civil commitment in coming years, although there are some serious objections to it. To understand current circumstances, it is important to review the history of involuntary care and its evolution in recent years.

Involuntary Hospitalization

Civil commitment has four goals: (1) protecting society from dangerous mental patients; (2) protecting the mentally ill from harming themselves; (3) providing mental health care to those who need it but may not appreciate the need; and (4) relieving families and communities from persons who might not be dangerous but who are bizarre and troublesome and disrupt everyday life.

The battles over involuntary hospitalization have been tugs-of-war between those seeking to protect individual liberties and those viewing the state as parent (*parens patriae*) in ensuring that persons with mental illness be hospitalized if necessary and receive treatment. Legal activism in mental health developed out of the civil rights movement of the 1960s, and for two decades mental health law was in active ferment. Civil libertarians argued that individual freedom was the highest good and must be protected even against those with the most benevolent of motives. Thus, it mattered little whether diagnosis was reliable, treatment effective, or decisions sensible. The value of liberty was foremost, not any empirical fact about psychiatry. Others attacked involuntary commitment because of the unreliability of psychiatric diagnosis and predictions of danger, the large inconsistencies between commitment criteria and their implementation, and selective outcomes from one jurisdiction to another (Miller 1976). Many patient rights lawyers believed that mental patients facing involuntary confinement, depriving them of their liberties, ought to have the same procedural rights as those available to criminal defendants.

Concerns about civil commitment go back more than one hundred years. Institutionalization of persons with mental illness was informally administered until the middle of the nineteenth century, although the State of Virginia enacted a law for involuntary commitment of mental patients as early as 1806. By mid-century, however, there was much concern about unjustified hospitalization of sane persons in mental institutions, and in 1845 Chief Justice Lemuel Shaw of the Massachusetts Supreme Court established the precedent that individuals could be restrained only if dangerous to themselves or others and only if restraint would be conducive to their restoration. This principle became the foundation for most state statutes. Although intended to protect the rights of sane individuals, these statutes ultimately became vehicles to deprive patients with psychiatric disorders of their civil liberties when they were little threat to themselves or the community. It was the routine abuse of these statutes that attracted the attention and energy of civil liberties lawyers in the 1960s and 1970s.

It should not be difficult to understand the motivation of relatives and others in the community who often demand that persons with mental illness be hospitalized and treated against their will. Such concerns derive from fear and intolerance of disruptive behavior, as well as real concern that the person with mental illness cannot understand the need for treatment and resists it. The behavior of persons with active psychotic disorders can be dangerous and highly disruptive. Although most simply annoy others by their presence and inappropriate behavior, others pose serious threats of suicide or violence, engage in destructive behavior, or demonstrate grossly bizarre and disturbing symptoms.

Two landmarks occurred in civil commitment with the Lanterman–Petris–Short Act passed in California in 1969 and the *Lessard* decision in Wisconsin in 1972. The California act was purposely designed to create obstacles to discourage commitment and, particularly, long periods of confinement (Segal and Aviram 1978). The law made criteria for involuntary commitment more stringent and created financial incentives to stimulate local government to provide alternative care to the large California state institutions. The legislation established a series of graduated categories that required more evidence of impairment or danger to justify longer periods of involuntary hospitalization. Continuing review of such decisions was also required, making it difficult to follow the past practice of committing patients indefinitely.

In the *Lessard* decision the court found that mental patients faced with civil commitment have rights to timely notice of the charges, notice of right to a jury trial, aid of counsel, protection against self-incrimination, and assurance that the evidence on which a claim of dangerousness is made be established "beyond a reasonable doubt." The California and Wisconsin developments had a pervasive effect on many other jurisdictions and helped make the criteria for civil commitment more specific, requiring some combination of mental illness and either dangerousness or incapacity to care for oneself. In addition, duration of commitment was specified and made more brief, and due process guarantees used in criminal cases were extended to civil commitment procedures (Lamb and Mills 1986).

Although practices from one area to another were variable, the use of civil commitment declined. As Stone noted:

> *Psychiatrists who once committed people because it was the easiest thing to do are increasingly diffident. Courts are apt to be more scrupulous in reaching their decisions; lawyers are more frequently involved in preventing confinement; and hospitals are more fastidious about their own role. (Stone 1975, p. 43)*

Many psychiatrists vigorously opposed such changes, arguing that they left the community inadequately protected and left patients "to die with their rights on" (Treffert 1973). These critics alleged that existing procedures were unduly restrictive, denied needed care to many individuals, and contributed to the criminalization of mental illness and to the homeless mentally ill wandering our streets (Issac and Armat 1990). As one critic argued, "The right to liberty has become an excuse for failing to address, even failing to recognize, the needs of thousands of abandoned men and women we sweep by in our streets, in our parks, and in the train and bus stations where they gather for warmth." (Appelbaum 1987)

Critics' claims were exaggerated and supported more by occasional anecdotes and emotionalism than by evidence, but they pointed to important issues and the fact that legal changes do not solve deep human problems. New statutes were successful in reducing the amount and duration of involuntary hospitalization, but many patients did not get adequate community care services and others were pushed into jails and prisons. Although new legislation and court decisions made it more difficult to deprive people of their freedom because of mental illness and vague assertions of danger, they did little to create support for the painstaking work of developing well-organized systems of community services.

The tensions between different perspectives received widespread publicity in the case of Joyce Brown, a homeless woman who was picked up by New York City workers in 1987 under a policy announced by the then-mayor, Ed Koch, to remove seriously disturbed homeless people from the street. Miss Brown lived on the sidewalk in front of a hot air vent in Manhattan. When Miss Brown was brought to the hospital, it was alleged that she defecated on herself, burned and cut up paper money, ran into traffic, shouted obscenities at passers-by, and wore inadequate clothes for winter. City psychiatrists maintained that she was a person with schizophrenia, although psychiatrists for the New York Civil Liberties Union that came to her defense contested this diagnosis. In a decision that enraged some observers, the judge hearing the case concluded:

Freedom, constitutionally guaranteed, is the right of all, no less of those who are mentally ill. Whether Joyce Brown is or is not mentally ill, it is my finding after careful assessment of all the evidence, that she is not unable to care for her essential needs. I am aware her mode of existence does not conform to conventional standards, that it is an offense to esthetic senses. It is my hope that the plight she represents will also offend moral conscience and rouse it to action. There must be some civilized alternatives other than involuntary hospitalization or the streets. (Barbanel 1987; New York Times 1987).

The judge's decision was based on the fact that the psychiatrists substantially disagreed in their testimony, that there were plausible explanations for some of Joyce Brown's seemingly strange behaviors, that she had already survived a winter on the streets without apparent difficulty, and that in court she was logical and coherent. Thus, she did not meet the criteria for involuntary treatment.

Is, then, civil commitment or involuntary treatment ever justified in the absence of imminent physical danger? Improving due process encourages a more responsible stance from both physicians and the courts, but it hardly solves the problem of coping with many difficult dilemmas that some mentally ill persons present for themselves, their families, and community members. Although there is strong rhetoric supporting management of disturbing patients within the context of the criminal law, this is neither in the patient's interest nor consistent with humanitarian concerns. The grounds for commitment should be narrow, the protections for the alleged mentally ill rigorous, and the use of less restrictive alternatives exhausted. There are, however, patients who fail to recognize a problem and cause great pain and anguish for others and damage to themselves. If they are sufficiently disturbing, they will be dealt with by the community in one way or another. What we really seek is not a sense of righteousness that may come from knowing that we have avoided the use of police powers, but some sense that we have found a constructive response to a painful problem, one that protects the future life chances of the disturbed patient.

One can argue that a certain amount of suffering is a price we must pay to protect our liberties and that many mental patients should be handled within the context of criminal law. But as one get closer to the human dilemmas that highly symptomatic and disoriented persons can cause for families and communities, one appreciates the need for continuing to explore the humane alternatives that allow intervention without threatening the rights of most mentally ill persons, who need no such forceful interference in their lives. The difficulty lies in knowing where to draw the line and establishing uniform criteria in which the community can have confidence.

Stone (1975) suggested a five-step procedure through which assessments could be made as to the appropriateness of civil commitment: (1) reliable diagnosis of a severe mental illness, (2) assessment as to whether the person's immediate prognosis involves major distress, (3) availability of treatment, (4) the possibility that the illness impaired the person's ability to make a decision as to whether he or she was willing to accept treatment, and (5) assessment as to whether a reasonable person would accept or reject such treatment. Stone argued that involuntary confinement was justified when there was convincing evidence of a serious illness causing suffering for which treatment is available, where the patient's refusal of treatment is irrational, and where a reasonable person in possession of all faculties under the circumstances would accept such treatment. He called this the Thank You Theory, implying that patients looking back on the experience would be grateful for state intervention.

> *This is the Thank You Theory of Civil Commitment: it asks the psychiatrist to focus his inquiry on illness and treatment, and it asks the law to guarantee the treatment before it intervenes in the name of parens patriae. It is radical in the sense that it insists that society fulfill its promise of benefit when it trenches on human freedom. It is also radical in that it divests civil commitment of a police function; dangerous behavior is returned to the province of criminal law. Only someone who is irrational, treatable, and incidentally dangerous would be confined in the mental health system. (Stone 1975, p. 70)*

Although Stone's Thank You Theory is appealing, it depends on trust in the integrity and reliability of psychiatric assessment and treatment, areas of continuing controversy. Many people weigh the values involved differently and would not want to trade off some patients' civil liberties for treatment that psychiatrists contended was valuable. Those who favor civil commitment primarily as a means to get dangerous and troublesome people off the street find Stone's approach disturbing, in that it separates the social control function from civil commitment. Stone's approach, however, is valuable because its main intent is to assist patients who may not appreciate their own needs rather than to assist the community. The Thank You Theory attempts to struggle with the central dilemmas underlying commitment rather than simply to take an ideological position.

In 1983, the American Psychiatric Association suggested a model state law on civil commitment (Stromberg and Stone, 1983) substantially influenced by the thinking underlying the Thank You Theory. A central part of the proposal was to extend the *parens patriae* grounds for commitment to cover cases where the person is likely to suffer substantial mental and physical deterioration and lacks the capacity to make an informed decision. A commitment would occur if a severely mentally ill person would be likely to suffer or continue to suffer severe and abnormal mental, emotional, or physical distress associated with substantial deterioration of prior ability to function independently. While the intent of the drafters was to bring into treatment many of the mentally ill now languishing on the streets, the criteria were sufficiently ambiguous to be successfully applied to other populations of patients, and in the words of one of its critics is "extremely broad and ultimately incoherent" (Rubenstein 1985). As with so many other attempts, such language as "substantial deterioration" is difficult to apply clearly and consistently (for a useful debate on the issues, see Appelbaum 1985).

The language of commitment statutes is not unimportant, and litigation and court decisions are an important part of defining and improving our procedures, but it is a mistake to depend too substantially on them. Many wise people have addressed the language of civil commitment procedures, but no language, however astutely drafted, can compensate for the deficiencies of mental health care. Almost all of the existing statutes have language sufficiently broad to allow judges to commit patients they believe should be hospitalized. Dangerousness is open to varying interpretations, as is the notion of grave disablement, both common features of many state laws. The problem is less in the specification of legal criteria and more in the conflicting views among psychiatrists, lawyers, the mentally ill and society at large, and the overall inadequacy of mental health services. No language games can adjudicate these real conflicts. Moreover, while the courts may establish reasonable principles, the inadequacies of both the mental health and criminal justice systems result in a large gap between theory and reality (Warren 1982). As one very experienced forensic psychiatrist noted:

> *My experience suggests that no matter how clear or detailed a law is, judges, police, attorneys, and bureaucrats often ignore or have no knowledge of its fine points. These officials, especially judges, who are often not accountable to anyone, routinely do what they think is best for the patient or what they think the law intends without regard to what the law really says. (Zusman 1985, p. 978)*

Civil commitment is part of a larger structure of mental health care, and changes in procedures, without concomitant changes in other areas, are likely to have unanticipated consequences. A study of such legal changes following the murder of an elderly couple in Seattle by a twenty-three-year-old neighbor, who earlier in the day had been denied voluntary admission to a state hospital, illustrates the issue (Pierce et al. 1986). Like every other state, Washington had tightened its civil commitment procedures in the period following *Lessard* in Wisconsin. But in 1979, the legislature, in response to public pressure, revised its criteria for commitment to expand the definition of grave disability and allow commitment of persons noncompliant with medication regimens and at risk of severe deterioration. The act also added "danger to property" as a danger criterion. Admissions increased substantially in response to the murder in the locality where it had occurred even before the law was changed, suggesting the robustness of the earlier criteria. In another part of the state less affected by the murder publicity, admissions dramatically increased but only following the legal changes. Thus, it seems that strong public opinion and legal changes can have their independent effects. But the effects were not what policy makers intended or anticipated. In both instances, hospital capacity did not increase, and the involuntary commitments displaced those seeking voluntary admission. This is particularly ironic in the light of the fact that the murderer who activated public opinion on this issue had sought to enter the hospital voluntarily but had been refused.

In reviewing the struggles over the civil commitment of the mentally ill, certain conclusions seem inescapable. The legal process itself reflects the need of society to deal with troublesome issues and demands from the community that something be done. However legal terms are defined, courts and mental health professionals will still respond to strong public opinion and economic and political pressures. The problems themselves cannot be defined away. Judges may conscientiously try to apply formal definitions and procedural guidelines, but application of these procedures in concrete cases under prevailing time constraints can be enormously difficult and often impossible. Some judges don't even seriously try, and simply apply their own common-sense perceptions to the decision-making process. Even with the best of legal intentions there remains a large gap between legal theories and civil commitment realities (Warren 1982).

Commitment of the mentally ill is part of a larger social process that the law has little control over. To the extent that the legal system tightens opportunities for civil commitment, other mechanisms may be used more frequently to deal with troublesome persons, such as arrests for minor legal infractions, and many people with mental illness now find themselves jailed. Many of the pressures for mental health beds for the elderly, to take a different but important example, were relieved through the expansion of nursing home beds that provided an alternative, but not necessarily superior, residence. The key point is that the community pressures that encourage commitment of the mentally ill do not disappear simply because legal procedures have been tightened. If hospitalization is difficult to achieve, some other alternative will be used, such as jails or homeless shelters, where vulnerable persons are in danger of victimization.

It is not surprising, thus, that over time the allegedly revolutionary changes that legal activism brought to the area of civil commitment and related areas—such as the right to refuse treatment—were reinterpreted in their implementation, and that mental health professionals, judges, and even lawyers representing the mentally ill, often accepted the redefinition of terms to allow involuntary treatment when truly needed. There are, of course, exceptions, and it is the exceptions such as the case of Joyce Brown that reaffirm sharply the nature of the tensions between libertarian and treatment interests. But looking back, as Appelbaum (1994) convincingly observes, neither the hopes of the most ardent libertarians nor the fears of many mental health professionals have been realized. In fact, a common-sense approach prevails, whereby decisions are based on the specific facts and circumstances that surround particular cases. This does not suggest that all is well, or that attention to legal process is without merit. It does suggest, however, that what happens to persons with mental illness transcends the legal system and cannot easily be contained by it. As Appelbaum notes:

> *The studies are nearly unanimous in indicating that, when the law goes against the grain of popular opinion concerning the legitimate scope of commitment, the law gives way. Persons in need of treatment are called "dangerous" by clinicians in the absence of clear evidence that they are. Judges accept the characterization of patients as "gravely disabled" when what they really believe is that these persons are suffering and would be better off receiving care. Lawyers who claim to be advocates for mentally ill respondents at commitment hearings provide them with inadequate assistance or actually work against their expressed wishes. (Appelbaum 1994, p. 56)*

Outpatient Commitment

Outpatient commitment is an available legal mechanism to deal with many of the problems and dilemmas we have reviewed, but it has not been commonly used. This might change in coming years as managed care programs act vigorously to avoid and minimize inpatient care and provide effective mental health care in the community. The reasons for resistance to widespread use of outpatient commitment are not trivial, but if it achieves professional and community acceptance, it fits well with the ideology of managed community mental health care and integrated service delivery, and it does so in the least restrictive and most economical treatment settings. But outpatient commitment also opens again the everlasting tensions between liberty and treatment interests.

Many states have made provision for commitment in a less restrictive environment (Miller 1985; Torrey and Kaplan 1995). Clinicians seem to have little knowledge about the conditions under which such procedures should be used, and there is little evidence of close collaboration between clinicians and representatives of the legal system. There seems to be much confusion about the necessary conditions for outpatient commitment, the responsibilities of the mental health system in these cases, the applicability of patient rights honored in the hospital context, and the powers and discretion of judges when they use this mechanism. The best research studies depict experience in the state of North Carolina, an innovating state in outpatient commitment, and they illustrate both the potential and complexity of implementing this legal mechanism successfully. Much depends on the attitudes and cooperation of mental health professionals and the quality of mental health and social services in the community. When the mental health system is receptive, this new mechanism can work well (Hiday and Goodman 1982; Hiday and Scheid-Cook 1987b).

Other legal alternatives for protecting persons who lack the capacity to care for themselves include guardianship and conservatorship arrangements, but such mechanisms are poorly understood and rarely used. California specifically provides a conservatorship arrangement for individuals gravely disabled as a consequence of mental illness, and the court assigns a conservator for one-year renewable periods. The conservator has the legal power to manage the person's affairs including hospitalizing the individual when required, deciding on living arrangements, and managing the individual's money. Two highly experienced professionals familiar with this mechanism in California view it as an important therapeutic instrument when the conservators have appropriate backgrounds relevant to understanding chronic mental illness (Lamb and Mills 1986).

In 1994 Torrey and Kaplan (1995) surveyed states on use of outpatient commitment. Although thirty-five states and the District of Columbia had laws allowing such commitments, they were not often used. Many noted that mental health centers had little interest in treating this population, a longstanding problem; without their willing cooperation, outpatient commitment is not feasible, as experience in North Carolina has demonstrated. Other reasons for not using such commitments were concerns about civil liberties, potential liability of mental health facilities should a patient under their supervision act in a way that harms others, and economic concerns. Acceptance of community responsibility would in some instances shift the costs of commitment from states (who pay for inpatient commitment) to the locality that would have to share in the cost of treatment under outpatient commitment arrangements. Other complicating difficulties were overly stringent commitment criteria, the failure of laws to specify what was to happen if the patient did not cooperate with the treatment plan, and lack of information and uncertainty about the process itself.

Outpatient commitment raises the traditional issue of the grounds for depriving individuals of their liberties, and laws vary a great deal on who can be committed and under what circumstances. Many mental health professionals would accept outpatient commitment as an incentive for compliance before patients reach the stage where they are disruptive and dangerous but are reluctant to take responsibility once patients reach this point. However, civil libertarians question the appropriateness of using the coercive powers of the state under circumstances where patients' symptoms have not reached the critical point of danger or grave impairment, and the commitment is simply a convenience to force patients to accept treatment. Civil commitment has promise as an approach to keep patients with severe and persistent mental illness in treatment and compliant with medication, but we have a great deal to learn about what benefits and problems it potentially offers, for what types of patient groups it is most suitable, and how to meaningfully deal with some of the fiscal, liability, and service issues involved. The research in this area is provocative but not systematic or rigorous, and controlled randomized trials of involuntary outpatient commitment is needed in a variety of settings (Swartz et al. 1995). Such studies are now beginning to take place, and the impetus of managed care is likely to encourage such work and move it along.

Outpatient commitment—or any other such mechanism—cannot prosper in an impoverished and fragmented community care system. The abuses in the use of civil commitment in earlier periods were in part motivated by a desire to take action when there were few decent community alternatives for mentally ill people. With changes in mental health policies and more stringent criteria for civil commitment, many patients who would have been hospitalized remain in the community. Most are probably better off, but others continue to suffer seriously from their problems and to lead unhappy and pitiful lives. The potentialities exist for developing a wide variety of alternatives for assisting the patient without unduly disrupting whatever positive ties remain in the community. We have done poorly in developing needed assistance, particularly for the long-term chronic patient—the type of patient who is a prime candidate for civil commitment. Without alternatives, the community will find some way of dealing with the mentally ill who are difficult, disturbing, and frightening that will often not be in the interests of the patient. If civil commitment presents an affront to the concept of individual freedom and personal integrity, less restrictive but more effective alternatives must be developed and encouraged, in addition to improvements in due process.

A Note on Dangerousness and the Relationship between Mental Illness and Violence

As we have seen, the potential for danger is important, but the concept remains fuzzy, discussion is often influenced more by ideology than evidence, and research on the topic is difficult. Lay people in making such judgments often focus on bizarre and inexplicable behavior that frightens them, but such behavior is not necessarily associated with violence and harm. Psychiatrists in evaluating danger have typically focused on a past history of danger, explicit threats of violence, and various psychological assessments such as repression of normal aggression, the presence of deep feelings of rage, a sense of helplessness and feeling trapped, the presence of paranoid delusions and hallucinations (especially when these imply violence), and patients' reports that they find it difficult to control their antisocial urges. Psychiatrists have also commonly maintained that aggression, particularly associated with the excessive use of alcohol and drugs, is very dangerous. Others have given attention to subcultural factors such as the readiness to express aggression (Rappeport 1967). While predictions of danger based on such criteria are often wrong, there is now increasing evidence that alcohol and drug abuse and mental illness, particularly active psychotic symptoms, are associated with increased risk of violence (Monahan 1992; Link et al. 1992; Swanson et al. 1990; Marzuk 1996).

Danger and violence are culturally specific to a considerable degree, and acts of violence vary manyfold among nations, depending on social and situational circumstances. They are also substantially associated with age, sex, education, and socioeconomic circumstances, and such differences are commonly larger than those between persons with and without mental illness. Moreover, dangerousness and violence are often specific to particular social situations and are not simply an attribute of personality. The same person may have varying risks for violence depending on the situational context. Fortunately, violence is a relatively uncommon event even among those with a greater inclination toward such behavior. But efforts to predict it typically result in large numbers of false positives (Stone 1975).

It should be clear from this discussion that the concept of danger refers to an expectation of physical attacks on persons and property and not to broader concepts of harm to others that might result from careless driving or white-collar criminality such as knowingly manufacturing and selling defective and harmful products. Although we recognize the harm in these activities, such behaviors are more easily understandable to us within our assumptions about motivation and the context of our commercial and materialistic culture. What particularly frightens the public about violent acts committed by persons with mental illness is the seeming irrationality and unpredictability of these behaviors.

Pescosolido and her colleagues (1997) examined the public's views of mental illness and the need for coercion using data from the General Social Survey, a representative sample of the U.S. population. In the survey, respondents were given descriptions of persons with various mental illness conditions constructed on the basis of criteria in DSM-IV. The descriptions were of persons with schizophrenia, major depression, drug abuse, and alcohol dependence. An additional description of a troubled person who did not meet clinical criteria for a DSM disorder was also included. The respondents were asked various questions about the people in these descriptions.

In general, the public was more concerned about and less sympathetic with persons who were described as meeting the criteria for drug abuse. When asked about the competence of persons with varying diagnoses to make treatment decisions, persons with schizophrenia, drug abuse, and alcohol dependence were seen as less competent. However, two thirds of respondents thought persons with major depression were competent to make decisions, and almost everyone ascribed competence to the troubled person. A similar pattern of attributions were made for money management. Comparable results were evident in respondent's views of danger to others and self, with drug abusers and persons with alcohol dependence seen as most dangerous, and persons with schizophrenia in an intermediate position. More than two thirds of respondents did not view persons with major depression as dangerous to others, but many more were likely to see such persons as dangerous to themselves. The public was much more receptive to coercion in dealing with persons with drug problems and schizophrenia than with the other types of cases, with persons with alcohol problems being in the middle among the five types of cases.

Recent research indicates that persons with mental disorder report more violent acts than persons without such disorders (for good reviews, see Monahan 1992, 1997 and Marzuk 1996), although highest risk is associated with substance abuse disorders and persons with florid psychotic symptoms. Two studies among many have been particularly important in helping understand the issue (Swanson et al. 1990; Link, Andrews and Cullen, 1992). The first used data from the ECA study, described in an earlier chapter, and examined the relationship between having DSM disorders and self-reported violent behavior in the previous year (Swanson et al. 1990). These behaviors included items like hitting or throwing things at your spouse (partner), fights with others that came to swapping blows, use of a weapon like a stick, knife, or gun in a fight, and physical fights while drinking. The researchers found that while only 2 percent of those with no DSM disorder reported such behaviors in the past year, 25 percent of those with alcohol abuse or dependence and 35 percent of those with other drug abuse or dependence reported such instances of violence in the prior twelve months. Most other major diagnoses fell in the middle: schizophrenia (13 percent); major depression (12 percent); mania or bipolar disorder (12 percent), etc. Persons with multiple disorders reported higher rates of violent behavior, and when a major mental disorder occurred together with a substance abuse disorder, there was a significantly higher propensity to engage in violent behavior.

These findings need to be seen in perspective. One major limitation of the study is that it depends on reports from individuals both of their symptoms and of violent acts. The size of relationships can easily be inflated by the fact that individuals more willing to report socially undesirable symptoms are also more likely to report socially stigmatized acts. Also, as previously noted, rates of such acts also occur commonly in subgroups in the population such as young males (16 percent) and young females (9 percent) in the lowest socioeconomic group, and these rates are comparable to the rates found among most subgroups of persons with mental illness. Finally, the items used to measure violence, while reflecting undesirable behavior, characterize incidents varying greatly in severity and danger. Perhaps most important is the fact that even among persons with severe mental illness, such as persons with schizophrenia, the vast majority (87 percent) do not report any violent behavior. Thus, while some of these individuals may be more dangerous than members of the general public, identifying them reliably is extremely difficult.

Abuse of alcohol and drugs is commonly connected with occurrences of violence and pose more danger than psychotic symptoms. For example, Tiihonen and his colleagues (1997) in Finland prospectively studied a 1966 birth cohort of more than 12,000 individuals over 26 years and assessed the relationship between mental disorder and criminal behavior. Data on crimes came from files maintained by the Ministry of Justice and covered offenses of persons between ages 15 and 25. Psychiatric diagnostic data came from hospital records and outpatient registers. As in other studies, substance abuse is especially linked with criminal behavior. Offenses were highest among males with alcohol induced psychoses and males with schizophrenia and co-existing alcohol abuse. In the cohort studied, 128 individuals had at least one registered violent crime and the vast majority of such violators (117 persons) had no record of mental illness. However, persons with mood disorders with psychotic features and persons with schizophrenia had an adjusted odds ratio of criminal behavior relative to those without disorders of 10.4 and 7.2.

In the very best study in the area, thus far, Bruce Link, Howard Andrews, and Francis Cullen (1992) compared mental patients and comparable community residents who never received any mental health treatment on several measures of violent and illegal conduct based on both official records and self-reports. They applied sophisticated multivariate controls reflecting sociodemographic differences and differences in social context, as well as one for social desirability response bias, a problem noted in reviewing the ECA study. Consistent with the earlier study, they found that patients with a history of mental treatment reported more violent behavior and also had higher arrest rates for violent crimes. They also included in their study a measure of psychotic symptoms, including such items as feeling that thoughts were put in your head that were not your own, that you were possessed by a spirit or devil, and that your mind was dominated by forces beyond your control. Such reports are relatively rare in a normal community sample. Link and his colleagues were able to demonstrate that these psychotic symptoms accounted for all the differences in levels of violent and illegal behavior between patients and the never treated community sample that were not already explained by other sociodemographic and contextual effects. They conclude that: ". . . the excess risk of violence posed by mental patients is modest compared to the effects of other factors. Moreover, only patients with current psychotic symptoms have elevated rates of violent behavior and it may be that inappropriate reactions by others to psychotic symptoms are involved in producing the violent/illegal behavior" (Link et al. 1992, p. 290).

In an extension of this study, Link and Stueve (1994) attempted to define more precisely the types of symptoms that best explained the relationship between mental illness and violence. They found three psychotic survey items that most successfully predicted future violent behavior (During the past year how often have you felt that your mind was dominated by forces outside your control?; How often have you felt that thoughts were put into your head that were not your own?; How often have you felt that there were people who wished to do you harm?). The authors suggest that these are "threat/control override symptoms" in which irrational thoughts are accepted as real, and internal controls on concern about irrational thoughts are undermined. These results were also replicated using data from the ECA study (Swanson et al. 1996).

Research on dangerousness of patients with mental illness, thus, takes us only a small way in understanding how to identify the small minority of persons who are likely to seriously threaten the public. Certainly some patients are dangerous. Link and his colleagues have successfully identified some psychotic symptoms that begin to refine distinctions, but we still have much work to do to isolate other important indicators that reduce the number of false positives that commonly result from psychiatric assessments. Yet, predictions of dangerousness will always be an uncertain activity because so much depends on situation and context. As Link and his colleagues note, even the dangerous behavior they identified may be a response to the way people react to persons exhibiting bizarre psychotic symptoms. It has been commonly observed in the past, for example, that some of the violent and aggressive behavior seen in persons with schizophrenia seemed more a product of the harsh and rejecting social response than of the illness itself. Much of the research we have reviewed on expressed emotion also supports the notion that it is not solely the illness that brings on difficult events but the way characteristics of the illness respond to the reactions of family and others. We need to isolate as clearly as possible the conditions, symptoms, stages of illness and circumstances that are most likely to trigger violent behavior.

One consequence of the efforts to tighten commitment laws has been the attempt to be more explicit in defining danger. The *Lessard* decision, for example, required that such a finding be based on a "recent act, attempt, or threat to do substantial harm." As Brooks (1978) has noted, even this effort to clarify language begs the question of what type of act and with what recency, as well as what constitutes an attempt or threat. In practice, psychiatrists and judges read into these definitions whatever they wish, and there is a failure to distinguish between real menace and substantial nuisance and imposition. How should judges deal, as Brooks (1978) asks, with a manic person who depletes family resources and exposes them to financial hardship, or a hysterical person who continually calls others on the phone in the middle of the night, night after night? It appears that what judges and psychiatrists do is less determined by precise legal definitions and more by the state of community opinion and pressures at the time. When a psychotic man killed two persons in New York City following the Statue of Liberty celebration, psychiatrists began to detain more patients and psychiatric emergency rooms and hospitals filled to capacity. The law did not change to make detention easier, but public opinion changed, making psychiatrists feel that they would be held responsible for releasing dangerous mentally ill persons. Thus, they became much more cautious. This phenomenon was illustrated by the experience in the state of Washington discussed earlier (Pierce et al. 1986).

In areas other than the law, our society needs assessments of whether persons are reliable or whether there is a considerable risk that they may engage in dangerous behavior. The armed forces must have some assurance that the handling of nuclear weapons and other dangerous tasks are not allocated to unstable persons. Businesses and industrial firms are concerned that persons in positions of considerable responsibility are able to perform their tasks without endangering others or the company. A pilot with schizophrenia is probably too inattentive to fly an airplane safely, and, indeed, such inattentiveness may risk the lives of a great many people. There are attempts to assess psychologically and psychiatrically the mental stability of potential employees for particular jobs, although the adequacy of these screening programs is in doubt. Concern even extends to the threat that high public officials who are psychiatrically disabled may harm the public because of their illness, but as yet no one has found an adequate way to balance these risks against the political risk of surveillance of mental health and the risks inherent in the imprecise character of psychiatric selection procedures. Much more research and conceptual sophistication are needed in these areas, but it seems unlikely that we can ever fully resolve the fundamental dilemmas.

The Right to Treatment

The significance of right to treatment concepts depends substantially on application to persons who are involuntarily hospitalized. Initially, right to treatment approaches were directed at remedying the horrendous conditions common in many public institutions but public interest lawyers were ambitious to expand the concept more widely. The Donaldson case was brought as a right to treatment suit to the Supreme Court, but the case was decided narrowly by the Court which elected to ignore the broad right to treatment claim. Instead the Court ruled that the state could not continue to confine involuntarily a mentally ill person who was not dangerous to himself or others, was not receiving treatment, and who was capable of surviving safely outside the hospital (Stone 1984). The case involved Kenneth Donaldson, a patient in Chatahoochee State Hospital in Florida from 1957 to 1972, who had refused medication and electroshock treatment, claiming at times to be a Christian Scientist, but who received no other treatment. Donaldson had been diagnosed as a chronic paranoid schizophrenic, and his efforts to gain release and his assertion that he would write a book about his confinement were interpreted as part of his paranoia (see his book, Donaldson 1976). Hospital officials took neither his efforts nor those of other caretakers in the community to gain his release seriously. They confined him to a ward for the criminally insane and denied him ground privileges despite lack of evidence of dangerous behavior. Ultimately, a jury awarded Donaldson $38,500 in compensatory and punitive damages, deciding against two hospital doctors who had confined him involuntarily.

With deinstitutionalization, improvements in many public hospitals, and the reluctance of the Supreme Court to accept the legal theory that patients enjoy a constitutional right to treatment, momentum in right to treatment efforts has been lost, but as I will illustrate there are unanticipated problems with devising a remedy applicable to only involuntary hospital care.

Although there were early precedents in right-to-treatment decisions (Stone 1975, pp. 83–96), a major breakthrough came in 1971 in *Wyatt v. Stickney,* in which the federal district court in Alabama held that involuntarily committed patients "unquestionably have a constitutional right to receive such individual treatment as will give each of them a realistic opportunity to be cured or to improve his or her mental condition" (Mechanic 1974, p. 233). The court found that the defendant's treatment program was deficient because it failed to provide a humane psychological and physical environment and a qualified staff in sufficient number to administer adequate treatment and individualized treatment plans. In the judgment of the court, "to deprive any citizen of his or her liberty upon the altruistic theory that the confinement is for humane therapeutic reasons and then fail to provide adequate treatment violates the very fundamentals of due process" (Mechanic 1974, p. 233).

On the arguing of litigants, the court established a large number of standards, which it defined as "medical and constitutional minimums," mandating changes in staffing, physical resources, and treatment processes. If the implementation of such standards alleviates the horrible conditions that were documented as prevalent, they obviously contribute to fairness and decency. It is not clear, however, that the standards promulgated were particularly wise in achieving the best outcomes in relation to cost that would be possible if such resources were used as part of an overall mental health strategy, including both inpatient and community care of the mentally ill. The nature of legal advocacy required an approach that focused on the involuntary hospital patient because the "handle" was the argument that the deprivation of liberty for humane therapeutic reasons without the provision of treatment was a violation of due process of law. This need for a strategy required the litigants to view the mental health system narrowly and to focus their attention on only one aspect of care, allowing the possibility of displacement of the problem to other parts of the mental health system not so easily addressed by litigation.

The hospital standards promulgated had a variety of limitations. They tended to reinforce a medical model of treatment and highly stratified roles among health professionals at the same time that health experts were increasingly becoming aware of the limitations of professional dominance and rigidly enforced roles. They encouraged the allocation of resources to hospital care in contrast to a network of community facilities more appropriately fitted to the management of mental health problems in the community. They demanded that extensive and scarce medical resources be devoted to the parts of the mental health system in which they may be least effective in treatment and thus yield a low benefit-cost outcome. Perhaps most dangerous of all is that such standards encouraged an indiscriminate dumping of patients in the community without providing an adequate network of community care that facilitated social functioning and alleviated the social costs for families and community members of having highly disabled persons residing in the community.

There are no definitive data on the full consequences of the right-to-treatment decisions, even in Alabama where such major court rulings were applied on a large scale. There is evidence, however, that large numbers of patients were released from Alabama hospitals following these decisions. The number of releases were larger than would have been expected on the basis of existing trends in adjacent states (Leaf 1978a, b). Right-to-treatment decisions assisted, if they did not affect directly, efforts to increase Alabama's mental health budget and the staffing patterns in psychiatric institutions. It is difficult to come to any conclusion other than that the *Wyatt* decision contributed to a climate that brought greater support and investment for mental health facilities and programs in Alabama. Although we have only modest knowledge about the fate of patients who were released to either the community or nursing homes, indications are that they had varying experiences, some not conducive to a high quality of social functioning. Many remained institutionalized in the community or in nursing homes, but, on balance, the result seems positive (Leaf 1978a). Because of the middle-class bias of public interest lawyers, it is almost inconceivable to them that any patients could be better off in hospitals given institutional inadequacies. Study of the situation of some chronic mental patients, however, suggests that lower-status and highly disabled patients sometimes find it more comforting to have residence in institutions than in the community (Ludwig and Farrelly 1966). Once patients are released to the community, they are no longer protected by right-to-treatment decisions, and they are at the mercy of prevailing conditions and resources in the community, which are often minimal and may be more inadequate than those available in a hospital program.

The right-to-treatment theory supported by Judge Frank Johnson in Alabama received little support in *Donaldson*. It was clear that the majority of the Supreme Court was not ready to support the theory of a constitutional right to treatment. While Chief Justice Burger in his concurring opinion made clear his strong opposition to the assertion of a new right, his opinion has apparently not deterred judges in lower courts from proceeding on this theoretical basis (Stone 1984, p. 117). Some judges, in response to public interest lawyers' litigation, have even extended this right to community care, but it is now clear to what degree activist courts can direct state governments on how to establish priorities and allocate limited public resources.

It seems clear that there is at least an accepted constitutional right to minimal standards for the mentally retarded. In *Youngberg and Romeo,* the Supreme Court established that committed retarded patients had a right to "conditions of reasonable care and safety, reasonable nonrestrictive confinement conditions, and such training as may be required by these interests." Federal courts have extended the concept of minimum rights to include treatment to prevent clinical deterioration among committed patients, but it is unclear that these legal theories can be successfully extended (Lamb and Mills 1986).

In many localities impaired patients have been dumped in communities without adequate financial, social, or treatment resources. Many live with other deviants in "welfare hotels" in disorganized areas, frequently find themselves in substandard facilities in the community run for profit by operators who provide few treatment resources, or are without homes at all. Given the poor conditions to which they are exposed, these patients frequently experience an exacerbation of symptoms and insecurities and, given their limited coping capacities, face horrendous life problems. In the case of schizophrenic patients, it is recognized that aggressive care is required if they are not to regress (Davis et al. 1972), but under most community circumstances, such care is not available and former patients simply become lost in the community.

Establishing a right to treatment cannot be seen independently of these other trends. If we do not consider the mental health system as a whole, we may find that by putting pressure on one aspect of the system, we create more intense problems in other areas. A major limitation of the litigation approach is the difficulty of viewing the system as a whole in contrast to seeking particular constitutional remedies.

Thus, it is difficult to be confident about the benefits gained through right-to-treatment decisions. Fair and effective rehabilitation for mental patients depends on the entire framework of medical and mental health care and decisions made through the legislative process. The publicity accompanying right-to-treatment litigation helped make inadequate conditions of mental health care more salient to legislators and aroused the sympathies of the public. It also contributed to eliminating some obvious abuses of institutional care. The concept of right to treatment really means adequate or acceptable treatment and not all that science or knowledge allows. To the extent that this legal approach focused attention on the lack of treatment or unacceptable care, it is a justified strategy. Beyond this, we need a means to examine treatment in all contexts, not only the hospital, so that we can use our resources most beneficially for all patients wherever they are.

Right to Refuse Treatment

Malpractice standards based on the common law encompass the illegality of a physician treating patients without their consent, except under conditions where consent cannot be reasonably expected, as in medical emergencies. This is an important principle, but the courts have traditionally allowed mental hospitals to treat mental patients involuntarily. In pursuing right-to-refuse-treatment litigation in mental hospitals, lawyers have adopted a constitutional rather than a malpractice approach (Stone 1981).

Right-to-refuse-treatment efforts began in the 1970s with measures to protect involuntary patients in quasi-criminal institutions from experimental drug treatment and psychosurgery (Brooks 1979; Stone 1984), but it was only later that these suits were extended to medications where much of the controversy has focused. Two major cases, *Rennie* in New Jersey and *Rogers* in Massachusetts, accounted for much of the contentious debate over the regulation of psychiatric treatment.

As Stone (1981) has conceded, whatever the theory, it is clear that there must be a right to refuse treatment from a legal perspective, but the real issue is "how it can be implemented in a way that takes into account both the rights of patients and their needs" (p. 360). An additional question is how to achieve an appropriate balance between regulatory efforts and the use of limited psychiatric resources in an efficient and meaningful way.

The declaration of a right to refuse treatment has no substantial statistical effect. Relatively few patients actually refuse treatment, and the protracted litigation has direct influence on a limited number of cases. But the assertion of the right contributes to communication and negotiation with patients about their treatment regimen and induces psychiatrists in institutions to be more respectful of patients' concerns about their treatment (Lamb and Mills 1986; Appelbaum 1994). An alleged cost of such regulation is its effect on the morale and perspectives of psychiatrists, who are said to view such requirements as intrusions on their ability to care for patients appropriately and, as a result, become apathetic about providing proper treatment (Stone 1981). The difficulty appears to be less in the principle itself and more in the way psychiatrists may define the situation and limit their own efforts to treat.

In *Rennie,* the federal district court in New Jersey accepted the view that involuntary medication with neuroleptic drugs was an invasion of constitutionally protected privacy. Later, the circuit court of appeals changed the constitutional rationale to "protection from harm." The Massachusetts federal district court accepted the further theory, based on the First Amendment guaranteeing free speech and thought, that the administration of neuroleptic drugs alters the mind and thus interferes with the constitutionally protected right. The Massachusetts decision was viewed by psychiatrists as particularly offensive and nonsensical and as an affront to the necessary discretion of clinicians (Stone 1981). There is no basis in the belief that neuroleptic drugs affect the mind in the sense accepted in the *Rogers* decision. This view was later rejected by the circuit court of appeals.

While these decisions have instituted some checkpoints on psychiatric discretion, they do not prevent psychiatrists from administering medications in emergencies (Appelbaum 1994). In a later decision in a Wisconsin case (*Stensvad v. Reivitz*), the United States district court upheld a Wisconsin provision allowing an involuntarily committed patient in a criminal commitment to be medicated without consent (Lamb and Mills 1986). Considerable discretion remains, and hospital practice is believed not to have been much affected. To the extent that these cases have motivated more thoughtfulness in the use of medication, better communication with patients, and greater awareness of how particular medications and dosage may be particularly troublesome for the patient, they probably contribute to better patient care and the type of consideration one would expect in any decent medical encounter.

These cases and the court judgments reflect the fact that many medications have serious adverse effects and may cause permanent disability, as in the case of tardive dyskinesia with the use of neuroleptics. Mental hospitals neither attract the best clinicians nor represent the ideal context for a sensitive therapeutic relationship. There is no indication that the formal procedures prescribed by the courts are frequently used, leading some psychiatrists to argue that this is all a "tempest in a teapot." In contrast, others believe that the assertion of a right to refuse treatment and establishing procedures to review refusals serves as a deterrent to arbitrary and insensitive care and indirectly contributes to a more humane treatment context. The evidence remains unclear, but the basic point is not. Treatment should always take place so as to give credence to the patient's wishes and reactions. Good care requires not only prescribing the right medication, but calibrating and scheduling it so that it interferes to the smallest possible extent with the patient's sense of well-being. Indeed, there may be possibilities for selecting among different drugs, varying means of administration, and alternative schedules. Moderating the arbitrariness of care thus moves us in the right direction, unless there is contrary evidence that the regulatory process has either resulted in inability to treat patients who need care or diverted significant resources from patient care to support regulatory mechanisms.

The right to refuse treatment still remains a highly contentious issue. In making sense of the debate, Appelbaum (1994) distinguishes between those who have a quarantine concept of civil commitment versus those who have a treatment orientation. A quarantine concept would be that the state has a responsibility to protect against danger but should intrude as little as possible once the threat has been addressed. Those who support a treatment view see little sense in involuntarily detaining people in a hospital but then allowing them to refuse the treatment that might bring them to a more normal state. Appelbaum argues that what makes mental illness different from other dangerous behavior is that we target such behavior prospectively because we believe that the behavior derives from an illness that can be treated both for the benefit of the patient and society. He argues: "Quarantine is not enough to justify confinement indefinitely, even when harm to others alone motivates commitment. Treatment must also be provided. To fail to treat committed persons, when the treatment is essential for them to regain their liberty, undercuts the rationale that legitimizes civil commitment." (p. 148)

Appelbaum (1994) accepts the research findings that show that most patients eventually agree to medications, that judges and review panels authorize most emergency requests for involuntary medication, and that right to refuse treatment often leads to a more thoughtful treatment plan. But he also reviews evidence that suggests that inpatient units with fewer patients medicated are more dangerous places for staff and other patients and that large administrative resources are devoted to the administrative review process. Instead he suggests as an alternative a quality review process in which treatment plans are carefully reviewed by attending and outside specialists for their suitability and appropriateness as occurs in other areas of medical care. Such views seem sensible but they are unlikely to be persuasive to those whose largest concern is maintenance of individual liberties and limiting the coercive authority of the state.

The Social Context of Legal Reform in Mental Health

In the last couple of decades of legal activism many other aspects of mental illness received sustained attention, including issues related to incompetency to stand trial, the insanity defense, and the preventive detention of sexual offenders. Each are complicated and important areas, but have less to do with mental health services than the areas I have reviewed. However, one area deserving explicit notice is the *Tarasoff* decision on the duty to warn and its subsequent modifications creating a duty to protect. This duty, now adopted in many jurisdictions, requires therapists who determine that a patient presents a serious danger of violence to another person to take whatever steps are reasonably needed to protect the intended victim.

There probably has been no set of legal decisions that has more upset mental health professionals than this duty, because it was seen as a threat to confidentiality and a deterrent to patients' openness with their therapists. Psychiatrists alleged that these decisions would destroy the doctor–patient relationship and thought up countless difficulties that would harm patients, mental health professionals, and even future victims. There were widespread predictions of catastrophe, but in fact little harm resulted. Studies showed that therapists were already taking steps prior to *Tarasoff* to warn victims that they feared were in danger, that informing patients of these responsibilities had less negative effect than anticipated and sometimes were seen in a positive light, and that the courts themselves were attentive to the needs and concerns of clinicians in interpreting and revising the relevant statutes. As Appelbaum (1994) concludes after an extensive review of the relevant literature, "The duty to protect has complicated life for some clinicians, but it may have made life safer for some potential victims; and it has by no means been the disaster some authorities feared." (p. 99)

A broad view of the complex relations between the mental health field and the law suggests the importance of social context and the extent to which the economic and social realities of life constrain and modify what may first appear as momentous legal changes. Law and the courts never function in a vacuum. They are responsive to changing public opinion, economic problems and budgetary limits, and the need to maintain the stability of community life. Legal reform can, of course, be a force for meaningful changes and redressing abuses, but the courts are mindful of the obligations they put on government and other community institutions. Furthermore, the law functions on an important symbolic level, but it would be a mistake to confuse legal decisions with what really goes on in the courts. As we have seen repeatedly, judges often do not follow the letter of the law in dealing with difficult mental health dilemmas, but rather, they adopt common-sense solutions that seem to work in context. As in the general administration of the criminal law, courts do not operate in practice as they do in theory. Talented psychiatrists and lawyers seek to avoid such proceedings, and the courts deal with cases in a hurried fashion. Careful legal procedures under such conditions are often disregarded.

Civil commitment, right to treatment, and right to refuse treatment are examples of a large number of complex legal issues affecting the fate of the mentally ill. As treatment procedures change, as our concept of rights change, and as we become more aware of less visible abuses, a history of litigation develops in neglected areas, sometimes resulting in the development of new standards. The questions are often complex; they require research and understanding that is often lacking; and they involve professional judgments that remain uncertain. Often they raise issues of balancing the welfare of the individual with that of society and the needs of present with those of future generations.

We are increasingly sensitive about research carried out with patients, particularly those who are in institutions or other coercive situations and where there are questions about their ability to give informed consent. We face ticklish problems about a patient's right to refuse treatment, particularly when the patient is psychotic and out of touch and when failure to provide treatment creates a range of problems and costs for the facilities involved and perhaps other patients. Does a patient have rights to insist on more expensive as compared with less expensive treatment approaches, and, if so, does the state have a responsibility to pay when the patient is indigent? How does one deal with refusal of treatment when the treatment itself is built into the institutional environment as with token economies, therapeutic communities, and education for community living?

It is foolish to consider any of these issues as simple or clear-cut. Certain principles, however, are helpful in examining them and in reaching pragmatic decisions. First, whenever possible, it seems desirable to maximize the individual's right to avoid coercion. This principle is best achieved by offering choices and options. Second, when there is a conflict between the needs of individuals and the needs of an organization or society, preference should always be given to the needs of the individual unless the reasons not to are very compelling. The individual as compared with society is weak; large organizations or the community can absorb costs in uncertain situations more readily than individuals. Preference must, I believe, be given to individual needs. Last, but perhaps most essential, is the value of providing good and humane alternatives. To the extent that we do so, the requirement even to consider legal coercion is minimized.

References

Allen, Priscilla. "A Consumer's View of California's Mental Health Care System." *Psychiatric Quarterly* 48 (1974): 1–13.

American Psychiatric Association. *Diagnostic and Statistical Manual of Mental Disorders: Fourth Edition (DSM-IV)*. Washington, D.C., 1994.

Andersen, Ronald, et al. "Psychologically Related Illness and Health Services Utilization." *Medical Care* 15 (1977 supplement): 59–73.

Angrist, Shirley, et al. "Tolerance of Deviant Behaviour, Posthospital Performance Levels, and Rehospitalization." *Proceedings of the Third World Congress of Psychiatry* 1 (Montreal 1961): 237–241.

Anthony, James C., et al. "Comparison of the Lay Diagnostic Interview Schedule and a Standardized Psychiatric Diagnosis." *Archives of General Psychiatry* 42 (1985): 667–675.

Appelbaum, Paul S. "Special Section on APA's Model Commitment Law." *Hospital and Community Psychiatry* 36 (1985): 966–989.

———. *Almost a Revolution: Mental Health Law and the Limits of Change*. New York: Oxford University Press, 1994.

———. "Crazy in the Streets." *Commentary* 83 (1987): 34–39.

Audini, B., et al. "Home-Based versus Outpatient/Inpatient Care for People with Serious Mental Illness." *British Journal of Psychiatry* 165 (1994): 204–210.

Avnet, Helen Hershfield. *Psychiatric Insurance: Financing Short-Term Ambulatory Treatment*. New York: Group Health Insurance, 1962.

Babigian, Harouton M., and Phyllis Marshall. "Rochester: A Comprehensive Capitation Experiment." In *Paying for Services: Promises and Pitfalls of Capitation*, edited by David Mechanic and Linda Aiken, pp. 43–54. New Directions for Mental Health Services Number 43. San Francisco: Jossey-Bass, 1989.

Babigian, Harouton, M., et al. "A Mental Health Capitation Experiment: Evaluating the Monroe-Livingston Experience." In *Economics and Mental Health*, edited by Richard Frank and Willard Manning, pp. 307–331. Baltimore: Johns Hopkins Press, 1992.

Bachrach, Leona L. *Deinstitutionalization: An Analytical Review and Sociological Perspective*. Division of Biometry and Epidemiology, Series D, No. 4, DHEW Publication No. (ADM) 76–351. Washington, D.C.: U.S. Government Printing Office, 1976.

———. "The State of the State Mental Hospital in 1996." *Psychiatric Services* 47 (1996): 1071–1078.

Back, Kurt W. *Beyond Words: The Story of Sensitivity Training and the Encounter Movement*. New York: Russell Sage Foundation, 1972.

Bandura, Albert. *Principles of Behavior Modification*. New York: Holt, Rinehart and Winston, 1969.

Barbanel, Josh. "Homeless Woman Sent to Hospital under Koch Plan Is Ordered Freed." *New York Times* November 13, 1987, pp. A1, B2.

Barker, Peggy R., et al. "Serious Mental Illness and Disability in the Adult Household Population: United States, 1989." In Center for Mental Health

Services and National Institute of Mental Health, *Mental Health, United States,* 1992, edited by Ronald W. Manderscheid and M. A. Sonnenschein, pp. 255–268. DHHS Pub. No. (SMA) 92–1942. Washington, D.C.: U.S. Government Printing Office, 1992.

Bart, Pauline B. "Social Structure and Vocabularies of Discomfort: What Happened to Female Hysteria?" *Journal of Health and Social Behavior* 9 (1968): 188–193.

Bassuk, Ellen L., et al. "The Characteristics and Needs of Sheltered Homeless and Low-Income Housed Mothers." *Journal of the American Medical Association* 276 (1996): 640–646.

Bassuk, Ellen et al. "The Homeless Problem." *Scientific American* 251 (1984a): 40–45.

Bassuk, Ellen et al. "Is Homelessness a Mental Health Problem?" *American Journal of Psychiatry* 141 (1984b): 1546–1549.

Bateson, Gregory, et al. "Toward a Theory of Schizophrenia." *Behavioral Science* 1 (1956): 251–264.

Baxter, Raymond and Robert E. Mechanic, "The Status of Local Health Care Safety Nets." *Health Affairs* 16 (1997): 7–23.

Bayer, Ronald, and Robert L. Spitzer. "Neurosis, Psychodynamics, and DSM-III: A History of the Controversy." *Archives of General Psychiatry* 42 (1985): 187–196.

Beck, Aaron T. *Cognitive Therapy and the Emotional Disorders.* New York: International Universities Press, 1976.

Becker, Deborah R., et al. "Job Preferences of Clients with Severe Psychiatric Disorders Participating in Supported Employment Programs." *Psychiatric Services* 47 (1996): 1223–1226.

Becker, Howard S. *Outsiders: Studies in the Sociology of Deviance.* New York: Free Press, 1963.

Belknap, Ivan. *Human Problems of a State Mental Hospital.* New York: McGraw-Hill, 1956.

Berger, Douglas, and Isao Fukunishi. "Psychiatric Drug Development in Japan." *Science* 273 (1996): 318–319.

Berger, Philip A. "Medical Treatment of Mental Illness." *Science* 200 (1978), 974–981.

Bickman, Leonard, ed. "Special Issue: The Fort Bragg Experiment." *The Journal of Mental Health Administration* 23 (1996): entire issue.

Bleuler, Manfred. *The Schizophrenic Disorders: Long-Term Patient and Family Studies,* translated by S. M. Clemens. New Haven, Conn.: Yale University Press, 1978.

Bockoven, J. Sanbourne. "Some Relationships between Cultural Attitudes toward Individuality and Care of the Mentally Ill: An Historical Study." In *The Patient and the Mental Hospital: Contributions of Research in the Science of Social Behavior,* edited by Milton Greenblatt, Daniel J. Levinson, and Richard H. Williams, pp. 517–526. New York: The Free Press, 1957.

———. *Moral Treatment in Community Mental Health.* New York: Springer-Verlag, 1972.

Bond, Gary R., et al. "An Update on Supported Employment for People with Severe Mental Illness." *Psychiatric Services* 48 (1997): 335–346.

Borus, Jonathan F., et al. "The Offset Effect of Mental Health Treatment on Ambulatory Medical Care Utilization and Charges: Month-by-Month and Grouped-Month Analyses of a Five-Year Study." *Archives of General Psychiatry* 42 (1985): 573–580.

Breakey, William R., ed. *Integrated Mental Health Services: Modern Community Psychiatry.* New York: Oxford University Press, 1996.

Breier, Alan, and John Strauss. "Self-Control in Psychotic Disorders." *Archives of General Psychiatry* 40 (1983): 1141–1145.

Brenner, Harvey M. *Mental Illness and the Economy.* Cambridge: Harvard University Press, 1973.

Brooks, Alexander D. "Notes on Defining the 'Dangerousness' of the Mentally Ill." In *Dangerous Behavior: A Problem in Law and Mental Health,* edited by C. Frederick, pp. 37–59. Rockville, Md.: National Institute of Mental Health, 1978.

———. "The Impact of Law on Psychiatric Hospitalization: Onslaught or Imperative Reform." *New Directions for Mental Health Services* 4 (1979): 13–35.

Brown, Bertram S. "The Federal Government and Psychiatric Education: Progress, Problems, and Prospects." New Dimensions in Mental Health. DHEW Pub. No. (ADM) 77-511, Alcohol, Drug Abuse, and Mental Health Administration. Washington, D.C.: U.S. Government Printing Office, 1977.

Brown, George W. "Social Factors Influencing Length of Hospital Stay of Schizophrenic Patients." *British Medical Journal* 2 (1959): 1300–1302.

———. "Mental Illness." In *Applications of Social Science to Clinical Medicine and Health Policy,* edited by Linda H. Aiken and David Mechanic, pp. 175–203. New Brunswick, N.J.: Rutgers University Press, 1986.

Brown, George W., et al. "Influence of Family Life on the Course of Schizophrenic Illness." *British Journal of Preventive and Social Medicine* 16 (1962): 55–68.

Brown, George W., et al. *Schizophrenia and Social Care: A Comparative Follow-up Study of 339 Schizophrenic Patients.* New York: Oxford University Press, 1966.

Brown, George W., and James L. T. Birley. "Crisis and Life Changes and the Onset of Schizophrenia." *Journal of Health and Social Behavior* 9 (1968): 203–214.

Brown, George W., James L. T. Birley, and John K. Wing. "Influence of Family Life on the Course of Schizophrenic Disorders: A Replication." *The British Journal of Psychiatry* 121 (1972): 241–258.

Brown, George W., T. K. J. Craig, and Tirril O. Harris. "Depression: Distress or Disease? Some Epidemiological Considerations." *British Journal of Psychiatry* 147 (1985): 612–622.

Brown, George W., and Tirril O. Harris. *Social Origins of Depression: A Study of Psychiatric Disorders in Women.* New York: The Free Press, 1978.

Brown, George W., and Tirril O. Harris, eds. *Life Events and Illness.* New York: Guilford Press, 1989.

Brown, George W., Tirril O. Harris, and Catherine Hepworth. "Loss, Humiliation, and Entrapment Among Women Developing Depression: A Patient and Non-Patient Comparison." *Psychological Medicine* 25 (1995): 7–21.

Callahan, James J., et al. "Mental Health/Substance Abuse Treatment in Managed Care: The Massachusetts Medicaid Experience." *Health Affairs* 14 (1995): 173–184.

Caplan, Gerald. *Principles of Preventive Psychiatry.* New York: Basic Books, 1964.

Carling, Paul J. "Housing and Supports for Persons With Mental Illness: Emerging Approaches to Research and Practice." *Hospital and Community Psychiatry* 44 (1993): 439–449.

Carstairs, George M. "The Social Limits of Eccentricity: An English Study." In *Culture and Mental Health: Cross-Cultural Studies,* edited by Marvin K. Opler, pp. 373–389. New York: The Macmillian Company, 1959.

Caudill, William. *The Psychiatric Hospital as a Small Society.* Cambridge, Mass.: Harvard University Press, 1958.

Center for Mental Health Services. *Mental Health United States, 1996,* edited by R. W. Manderscheid and M. A. Sonnenschein. DHHS Publication No. (SMA)96–3098. Washington, D.C.: Government Printing Office, 1996.

Chambers, David L. "Community-Based Treatment and the Constitution: The Principle of the Least Restrictive Alternative." In *Alternatives to Mental Hospital Treatment,* edited by Leonard I. Stein and Mary Ann Test, pp. 23–39. New York: Plenum Press, 1978.

Chartock, Lee R., and Anquing Shin. "Psychiatrists' Hours by Work Setting." *Psychiatric Services* 47 (1996): 133.

Cheung, Fanny M., and Bernard W. K. Lau. "Situational Variations of Help-Seeking Behavior Among Chinese Patients." *Comprehensive Psychiatry* 23 (1982): 252–262.

Christianson, Jon. B., et al. "Use of Community-Based Mental Health Programs by HMOs: Evidence From a Medicaid Demonstration." *American Journal of Public Health* 82 (1992): 790–796.

Christianson, Jon B., et al. "Utah's Prepaid Mental Health Plan: The First Year." *Health Affairs* 14 (1995): 160–172.

Christie, Richard, and Florence L. Geis. *Studies of Machiavellianism.* New York: Academic Press, 1970.

Chu, Franklin D., and Sharland Trotter. *The Madness Establishment.* New York: Grossman, 1974.

Ciompi, Luc. "Natural History of Schizophrenia in the Long Term." *British Journal of Psychiatry* 136 (1980): 413–420.

Clausen, John A. "Mental Disorders," In *Contemporary Social Problems: An Introduction to the Sociology of Deviant Behavior and Social Disorganization,* edited by Robert K. Merton and Robert A. Nisbet, pp. 127–180. New York: Harcourt, Brace, and World, 1961.

Clausen, John A. "Mental Disorder." In *Handbook of Medical Sociology,* edited by Howard E. Freeman, Sol Levine, and Leo G. Reeder, 3rd ed., pp. 97–112. Englewood Cliffs, N.J.: Prentice-Hall, 1979.

Clausen, John A. "Stigma and Mental Disorder: Phenomena and Terminology." *Psychiatry* 44 (1981): 287–296.

Clausen, John A., and Carol L. Huffine. "Sociocultural and Sociopsychological Factors Affecting Social Responses to Mental Disorder." *Journal of Health and Social Behavior* 16 (1975): 405–420.

Clausen, John, Nancy Pfeffer, and Carol L. Huffine. "Help-Seeking in Severe Mental Illness." In *Symptoms, Illness Behavior, and Help-Seeking,* edited by David Mechanic, pp. 135–155. New Brunswick, N.J.: Rutgers University Press, 1982.

Clausen, John A., and Marian R. Yarrow, eds. "The Impact of Mental Illness on the Family." *Journal of Social Issues* 11 (1955): entire issue.

Cleary, Paul, and David Mechanic. "Sex Differences in Psychological Distress among Married People." *Journal of Health and Social Behavior* 24 (1983): 111–121.

Cloninger, C. Robert, et al. "The Principles of Genetics in Relation to Psychiatry." In *Handbook of Psychiatry 5: The Scientific Foundations of Psychiatry,* edited by M. Shepherd, pp. 34–66. New York: Cambridge University Press, 1985.

Coleman, Jules V., and Donald L. Patrick. "Psychiatry and General Health Care." *American Journal of Public Health* 68 (1978): 451–457.

Colombotos, John, Corinne Kirchner, and Michael Millman. "Physicians View National Insurance: A National Study." *Medical Care* 13 (1975): 369–396.

Conte, Hope R., et al. "Combined Psychotherapy and Pharmacotherapy for Depression." *Archives of General Psychiatry* 43 (1986): 471–479.

Cooper, A. B., and D. F. Early. "Evolution in the Mental Hospital: Review of a Hospital Population." *The British Medical Journal* 1 (1961): 1600–1603, 1961.

Corney, Roslyn H. "The Effectiveness of Attached Social Workers in the Management of Depressed Female Patients in General Practice." *Psychological Medicine* (1984): monograph supplement 6.

Coser, Rose Laub. *Training in Ambiguity: Learning through Doing in a Mental Hospital.* New York: The Free Press, 1979.

Crandell, Dewitt L., and Bruce P. Dohrenwend. "Some Relations Among Psychiatric Symptoms, Organic Illness, and Social Class." *The American Journal of Psychiatry* 123 (1967): 1527–1538.

Creed, Francis et al. "Cost Effectiveness of Day and Inpatient Psychiatric Treatment: Results of a Randomized Controlled Trial." *British Medical Journal* 314 (1997): 1381–1385.

Cross, K. W. et al. "A Survey of Chronic Patients in a Mental Hospital." *British Journal of Psychiatry* 103 (1957): 146–171.

Cummings, Nicholas A., and William T. Follette. "Psychiatric Services and Medical Utilization in a Prepaid Health Plan Setting: Part II." *Medical Care* 6 (1968): 31–41.

Curtis, Rick. "The Role of State Government in Assuring Access to Care." *Inquiry* 23 (1986): 277–285.

Cutting Edge. "Change Is the Only Constant for MCO Rankings." *Open Minds* 10 (1996): 9.

Davis, Anne E., Simon Dinitz, and Benjamin Pasamanick. "The Prevention of Hospitalization in Schizophrenia: Five Years After an Experimental Program." *American Journal of Orthopsychiatry* 42 (1972): 375–388.

Davis, Anne E., Benjamin Pasamanick, and Simon Dinitz. *Schizophrenics in the New Custodial Community: Five Years after the Experiment.* Columbus: Ohio State University, 1974.

Davis, James A. *Education for Positive Mental Health: A Review of Existing Research and Recommendations for Future Studies.* Chicago: Aldine Publishing Co., 1965.

Dear, Michael J., and S. M. Taylor. *Not on Our Street.* London: Pion, 1982.

Dennison, Charles F. "1984 Summary: National Discharge Survey." *Advanced Data From Vital and Health Statistics* 112 (1985).

Deutsch, Albert. *The Mentally Ill in America: A History of Their Care and Treatment from Colonial Times,* 2nd ed. New York: Columbia University Press, 1949.

Dial, Thomas H. "Training of Mental Health Providers." In *Mental Health, United States, 1992.* Edited by R.W. Manderscheid and M.A. Sonnenschein. DHHS Publication No. (SMA) 92–1942. Washington, D.C.: U.S. Government Printing Office, 1992.

Dickey, Barbara, et al. "Managing the Care of Schizophrenia: Lessons from a 4-year Massachusetts Medicaid Study." *Archives of General Psychiatry* 53 (1996): 945–952.

DiMasi, Joseph A., and Louis Lasagna. "The Economics of Psychotropic Drug Development." In *Psychopharmacology: The Fourth Generation of Progress,* edited by Floyd E. Bloom and David J. Kupfer, pp. 1883–1896. New York: Raven Press, 1995.

Dohrenwend, Barbara Snell, and Bruce P. Dohrenwend. eds. *Stressful Life Events: Their Nature and Effects.* New York: Wiley-Interscience, 1974.

———. *Stressful Life Events and Their Contexts.* New Brunswick, N.J.: Rutgers University Press, 1981.

Dohrenwend, Bruce P. "Sociocultural and Social-Psychological Factors in the Genesis of Mental Disorders." *Journal of Health and Social Behavior* 16 (1975): 365–392.

———. "Some Issues in the Definition and Measurement of Psychiatric Disorders in General Populations." In *Proceedings of the 14th National Meeting of the Public Health Conference on Records and Statistics,* pp. 480–489. Washington, D.C.: National Center for Health Statistics, Health Resources Administration, 1973.

Dohrenwend, Bruce P., and Barbara Snell Dohrenwend. *Social Status and Psychological Disorder: A Causal Inquiry.* New York: Wiley-Interscience, 1969.

———. "Psychiatric Disorders in Urban Settings." In *American Handbook of Psychiatry,* 2nd ed., vol. 2, edited by Silvano Arieti, pp. 424–447. New York: Basic Books, 1974a.

———. "Social and Cultural Influences on Psychopathology." *Annual Review of Psychology,* vol. 25, pp. 417–452. Palo Alto, Calif.: Annual Reviews, Inc., 1974b.

Dohrenwend, Bruce P., et al. "What Psychiatric Screening Scales Measure in the General Population, Part I: Jerome Frank's Concept of Demoralization." Unpublished manuscript, 1979.

Dohrenwend, Bruce P., et al. *Mental Illness in the United States: Epidemiological Estimates.* New York: Praeger, 1980.

Dohrenwend, Bruce P., et al. "Socioeconomic Status and Psychiatric Disorders: The Causation-Selection Issue." *Science* 255 (1992): 946–952.

Dolan, Lawrence W. *Recent Trends in the Evolution of State Psychiatric Hospital Systems.* New Brunswick, N.J.: The Rutgers–Princeton Program in Mental Health Research, 1986.

Dollard, John, and Neal E. Miller. *Personality and Psychotherapy: An Analysis in Terms of Learning, Thinking, and Culture.* New York: McGraw-Hill Book Co., 1950.

Donaldson, Kenneth. *Insanity Inside Out.* New York: Crown Publishers, 1976.

Dorwart, Robert A., Mark Schlesinger, and Richard T. Pulice. "The Promise and Pitfalls of Purchase-of-Service Contracts." *Hospital and Community Psychiatry* 37 (1986): 875–878.

Dorwart, Robert A., et al. "A National Study of Psychiatrists' Professional Activities." *American Journal of Psychiatry* 149 (1992): 1499–1505.

Drake, Robert E., and Deborah R. Becker. "The Individual Placement and Support Model of Supported Employment." *Psychiatric Services* 47 (1996): 473–475.

Druss, Benjamin, and Robert Rosenheck. "Evaluation of the HEDIS Measure of Behavioral Health Care Quality." *Psychiatric Services* 48 (1997): 71–75.

Duhl, Leonard J. *The Urban Condition: People and Policy in the Metropolis.* New York: Basic Books, 1963.

Eaton, William W., and Larry G. Kessler. *Epidemiologic Field Methods in Psychiatry: The NIMH Epidemiologic Catchment Area Program.* Orlando, Fla.: Academic Press, 1985.

Elder, Glen H., Jr. *Children of the Great Depression: Social Change in Life Experience.* Chicago: The University of Chicago Press, 1974.

Ellis, Randall P., and Thomas G. McGuire. *Cost-Sharing and Demand for Ambulatory Mental Health Services: Interpreting the Results of the Rand Health Insurance Study.* Boston, Mass.: Boston University, Department of Economics, 1984.

———. "Cost-Sharing and Patterns of Mental Health Care Utilization." *The Journal of Human Resources* 21 (1986): 359–379.

Ellis, Randall P. "Employers Tackle Treatment Costs." *Substance Abuse Issues* 3 (1992): 1–3.

English, Joseph T., et al. "Diagnosis-Related Groups and General Hospital Psychiatry: The APA Study." *American Journal of Psychiatry* 143 (1986): 131–139.

Ennis, Bruce J. *Prisoners of Psychiatry: Mental Patients, Psychiatrists, and the Law.* New York: Harcourt Brace Jovanovich, 1972.

Erickson, Kai T. *Wayward Puritans: A Study in the Sociology of Deviance.* New York: John Wiley and Sons, 1966.

Essen-Möeller, E. "Individual Traits and Morbidity in a Swedish Rural Population." *Acta Psychiatrica et Neurologica Scandinavica* 100 (1956): supplement.

Essock, Susan M., and Howard H. Goldman. "Embrace of Managed Mental Health Care." *Health Affairs* 14 (1995): 34–44.

Essock, Susan M., et al. "Clozapine Eligibility among State Hospital Patients." *Schizophrenia Bulletin* 22 (1996): 15–25.

Estroff, Sue E. *Making It Crazy: An Ethnography of Psychiatric Clients in an American Community.* Berkeley and Los Angeles: University of California Press, 1981.

Estroff, Sue E. et al. "No Other Way to Go": Pathways to Disability Income Application Among Persons with Severe, Persistent Mental Illness. In *Mental Disorder, Work Disability, and the Law.* Edited by R. J. Bonnie and J. Monahan. Chicago: University of Chicago Press, 1997.

Fairweather, George W., et al. *Community Life for the Mentally Ill: An Alternative to Institutional Care.* Chicago: Aldine, 1969.

Falloon, Ian R. H., et al. "Family Management in the Prevention of Exacerbations of Schizophrenia: A Controlled Study." *New England Journal of Medicine* 306 (1982): 1437–1440.

Falloon, Ian R. H., Jeffrey L. Boyd, and Christine W. McGill. *Family Care of Schizophrenia.* New York: Guilford Press, 1984.

Falloon, Ian R. H., et al. "Family Management in the Prevention of Morbidity of Schizophrenia." *Archives of General Psychiatry* 42 (1985): 887–897.

Feldman, Ronald, Arlene Rubin Stiffman, and Kenneth G. Jung. *Children at Risk: In the Web of Parental Mental Illness.* New Brunswick, N.J.: Rutgers University Press, 1987.

Felix, Robert H. *Mental Illness: Progress and Prospects.* New York: Columbia University Press, 1967.

Foley, Henry A., and Steven Sharfstein. *Madness and Government: Who Cares for the Mentally Ill?* Washington, D.C.: American Psychiatric Press, 1983.

Follette, William, and Nicholas A. Cummings. "Psychiatric Services and Medical Utilization in a Prepaid Health Plan Setting." *Medical Care* 5 (1967): 25–35.

Follman, Joseph F., Jr. *Insurance Coverage for Mental Illness.* New York: American Management Associations, Inc., 1970.

Frances, Allen, Michael B. First, and Harold Alan Pincus. *DSM-IV Guidebook.* Washington, D.C.: American Psychiatric Association, 1995.

Frank, George H. "The Role of the Family in the Development of Psychopathology." *Psychological Bulletin* 64 (1965): 191–205.

Frank, Jerome D. *Persuasion and Healing: A Comparative Study of Psychotherapy,* rev. ed. New York: Shocken Books, 1974.

Frank, Richard G., and Thomas G. McGuire. "A Review of Studies of the Impact of Insurance on the Demand and Utilization of Specialty Mental Health Services." *Health Services Research* 21 (1986): 241–265.

Frank, Richard G., Thomas G. McGuire, and Joseph P. Newhouse. "Risk Contracts in Managed Mental Health Care." *Health Affairs* 14 (1995): 50–64.

Frank, Richard G., et al. "Some Economics of Mental Health 'Carve-Outs.'" *Archives of General Psychiatry* 53 (1996): 933–937.

Franklin, Jack L., et al. "An Evaluation of Case Management." *American Journal of Public Health* 77 (1987): 674–678.

Freeborn, Donald K., and Clyde R. Pope. *Promise and Performance in Managed Care: The Prepaid Group Practice Model.* Baltimore: Johns Hopkins Press, 1994.

Freedman, Ruth I., and Ann Moran. "Wanderers in a Promised Land: The Chronically Mentally Ill and Deinstitutionalization." *Medical Care* 22 (1984 supplement): 12.

Freeman, Howard E., and Ozzie G. Simmons. *The Mental Patient Comes Home.* New York: John Wiley, 1963.

Freeman, R. B., and B. Hall. "Permanent Homelessness in America?" Cambridge, Mass.: National Bureau of Economic Research, Working Paper No. 2013, unpublished, 1986.

Freidson, Eliot. *Professional Dominance: The Social Structure of Medical Care.* New York: Atherton, 1970.

Fried, Marc. "Effects of Social Change on Mental Health." *American Journal of Orthopsychiatry* 34 (1964): 3–28.

Friedman, Meyer, and Ray H. Rosenman. *Type A Behavior and Your Heart.* New York: Alfred A. Knopf, 1974.

Friedman, Robert M., and Barbara J. Burns. "The Evaluation of the Fort Bragg Demonstration Project: An Alternative Interpretation of the Findings." *The Journal of Mental Health Administration* 23 (1996): 128–136.

Fromm, Erich. *The Sane Society.* New York: Rinehart and Co., 1955.

Fullerton, Donald T., Francis N. Lohrenz, and Gregory R. Nycz. "Utilization of Prepaid Services by Patients with Psychiatric Diagnoses." *The American Journal of Psychiatry* 133 (1976): 1057–1060.

Gallagher, Sally, and David Mechanic. "Living with the Mentally Ill: Effects on the Health and Functioning of Other Household Members." *Social Science and Medicine* 42 (1996): 1691–1701.

Gerstein, Dean R., and Henrick J. Harwood, eds. *Treating Drug Problems.* Washington, D.C.: National Academy Press, 1990.

Gibelman, Margaret, and Philip Schervish. "Practice Areas and Settings of Social Workers in Mental Health." *Psychiatric Services* 46 (1995): 1237.

Ginsberg, Susannah M., and George W. Brown. "No Time for Depression: A Study of Help-Seeking among Mothers of Preschool Children." In *Symptoms, Illness Behavior and Help-Seeking,* edited by David Mechanic, pp. 87–114. New Brunswick, N.J.: Rutgers University Press, 1982.

Ginzberg, Eli, et al. *The Ineffective Soldier: Lessons for Management and the Nation,* 3 vols. New York: Columbia University Press, 1959.

Glass, Albert J. "Psychotherapy in the Combat Zone." In *Symposium on Stress,* pp. 284–294. Graduate School, Walter Reed Army Medical Hospital. Washington, D.C.: Army Medical Service, 1953.

———. "Observations upon the Epidemiology of Mental Illness in Troops during Warfare." In *Symposium on Preventive and Social Psychiatry,* pp. 185–198. Washington, D.C.: Walter-Reed Army Research, Government Printing Office, 1958.

Goffman, Erving. *Asylums: Essays on the Social Situation of Mental Patients and Other Inmates.* Garden City, N.Y.: Doubleday, Anchor, 1961.

Gold, Marsha R., et al. "A National Survey of the Arrangements Managed Care Plans Make with Physicians." *New England Journal of Medicine* 333 (1995): 1678–1683.

Goldberg, David. *The Detection of Psychiatric Illness by Questionnaire.* London: Oxford University Press (Maudsley Monograph No. 21), 1972.

Goldberg, David, and Peter Huxley. *Mental Illness in the Community: The Pathways to Psychiatric Care.* New York: Tavistock Publications, 1980.

Goldberg, Irving D., Goldie Krantz, and Ben Z. Locke. "Effect of a Short-Term Outpatient Psychiatric Therapy Benefit on the Utilization of Medical Services in a Prepaid Group Practice Medical Program." *Medical Care* 8 (1970): 419–428.

Goldberger, Leo, and Schlomo Breznitz, eds. *Handbook of Stress: Theoretical and Clinical Aspects.* New York: Free Press, 1982.

Goldhamer, Herbert, and Andrew W. Marshall. *Psychosis and Civilization: Two Studies in the Frequency of Mental Disease.* Glencoe, Ill.: The Free Press, 1953.

Goldman, Howard H., Judith Feder, and William Scanlon. "Chronic Mental Patients in Nursing Homes: Re-examining Data from the National Nursing Home Survey." *Hospital and Community Psychiatry* 37 (1986): 269–272.

Goldsmith, Harold F. et al. "The Ecology of Mental Health Facilities in Metropolitan and Nonmetropolitan Counties." In *Mental Health, United States, 1994.* Edited by Manderscheid, R.W. and Sonnenschein, M.A. DHHS Publication No. (SMA) 94–3000. Washington, D.C.: U.S. Government Printing Office, 1994.

Gottesman, Irving I. "Schizophrenia and Genetics: Where Are You? Are You Sure?" In *The Nature of Schizophrenia: New Approaches to Research and Treatment,* edited by L. Wynne, et al., pp. 59–69. New York: John Wiley and Sons, 1978.

Gottesman, Irving I., and James Shields. *Schizophrenia: The Epigenetic Puzzle.* New York: Cambridge University Press, 1982.

Grad, Jacqueline C. "A Two-Year Follow-up." In *Community Mental Health: An International Perspective,* edited by Richard H. Williams and Lucy D. Ozarin, pp. 429–454. San Francisco: Jossey-Bass, 1968.

Grad, Jacqueline C., and Peter Sainsbury. "Evaluating the Community Psychiatric Service in Chichester: Results." *The Milbank Memorial Fund Quarterly* 44 (1966): 246–278.

Graves, E. J. 1993 Summary: National Hospital Discharge Survey. *Advance Data from Vital and Health Statistics,* No. 264. Hyattsville, Md.: National Center for Health Statistics, 1995.

Greenley, James R. "Social Control and Expressed Emotion." *Journal of Nervous and Mental Disease* 174 (1986): 24–30.

Greenley, James R., Joseph G. Kepecs, and William H. Henry. "A Comparison of Psychiatric Practice in Chicago in 1962 and 1973." Unpublished manuscript, Dept. of Psychiatry, University of Wisconsin–Madison, 1979.

Greenley, James R., and David Mechanic. "Social Selection in Seeking Help for Psychological Problems." *Journal of Health and Social Behavior* 17 (1976): 249–262.

Greenley, James R., David Mechanic, and Paul D. Cleary. "Seeking Help for Psychological Problems: A Replication and Extension." *Medical Care* 25 (1987): 1113–1128.

Grob, Gerald N. *The State and the Mentally Ill: A History of Worcester State Hospital in Massachusetts, 1830–1920.* Chapel Hill: The University of North Carolina Press, 1966.

———. *Mental Institutions in America: Social Policy to 1875.* New York: The Free Press, 1973.

———. "Rediscovering Asylums: The Unhistorical History of the Mental Hospital." *The Hastings Center Report* 7 (1977): 33–41.

———. *Mental Illness and American Society. 1875–1940.* Princeton, N.J.: Princeton University Press, 1983.

———. "The Forging of Mental Health Policy in America: World War II to New Frontier." *Journal of the History of Medicine and Allied Sciences* 42 (1987): 410–46.

———. *The Mad among Us: A History of the Care of America's Mentally Ill.* New York: Free Press, 1994.

Gronfein, William. "Incentives and Intentions in Mental Health Policy: A Comparison of the Medicaid and Community Mental Health Program." *Journal of Health and Social Behavior* 26 (1985): 192–206.

Group for the Advancement of Psychiatry. "Preventive Psychiatry in the Armed Forces: With Some Implications for Civilian Use." Report No. 47. New York: Group for the Advancement of Psychiatry, 1960.

Gudeman, John E., and Miles F. Shore. "Beyond Deinstitutionalization: A New Class of Facilities for the Mentally Ill." *The New England Journal of Medicine* 311 (1984): 832–836.

Gurin, Gerald, Joseph Veroff, and Sheila D. Feld. *Americans View Their Mental Health.* New York: Basic Books, 1960.

Hagnell, Olle. *A Prospective Study of the Incidence of Mental Disorder.* Stockholm: Svenska Bokförlaget Norstedts-Bonniers, 1966.

Hall, Laura L. et al. *Stand and Deliver: Action Call to a Failing Industry.* Arlington, Virginia: NAMI, 1997.

Halleck, Seymour L. *The Politics of Therapy.* New York: Science House, 1971.

———. *The Treatment of Emotional Disorders.* New York: Aronson, 1978.

Halleck, Seymour L., and Milton H. Miller. "The Psychiatric Consultation: Questionable Social Precedents of Some Current Practices." *The American Journal of Psychiatry* 120 (1963): 164–169.

Hamburg, David A., et al. "Clinical Importance of Emotional Problems in the Care of Patients with Burns." *The New England Journal of Medicine* 248 (1953): 355–359.

Harding, Courtenay M., et al. "The Vermont Longitudinal Study of Persons with Severe Mental Illness: I. Methodology, Study Sample, and Overall Current Status." *American Journal of Psychiatry* 144 (1987): 718–726.

Harding, Courtenay M., et al. "The Vermont Longitudinal Study: II. Long-Term Outcome of Subjects who Retrospectively Met the Criteria for DSM-III Schizophrenia." *American Journal of Psychiatry* 144 (1987): 727–735.

Harding, Courtenay M., Joseph Zubin, and John S. Strauss. "Chronicity in Schizophrenia: Fact, Partial Fact or Artifact?" *Hospital and Community Psychiatry* 38 (1987): 477–486.

Harrington, Charlene et al. "The Effect of Certificate of Need and Moratoria Policy on Change in Nursing Home Beds in the United States." *Medical Care* 35 (1997): 574–588.

Harris, Tirril O., George Brown, and Antonia Bifulco. "Loss of Parent in Childhood and Adult Psychiatric Disorder: The Role of Social Class Position and Premarital Pregnancy." *Psychological Medicine* 17 (1987): 163–183.

Hatfield, Agnes, ed. *Families of the Mentally Ill: Meeting the Challenges.* New Directions for Mental Health Services, No. 34. San Francisco: Jossey-Bass, 1987.

Health Care Financing Administration. "Medical and Medicaid Statistical Supplement." *Health Care Financing Review.* Baltimore, Md.: U.S. Department of Health and Human Services, 1996.

Henry, William E., John H. Sims, and S. Lee Spray. *The Fifth Profession: Becoming a Psychotherapist.* San Francisco: Jossey-Bass, 1971.

———. *Public and Private Lives of Psychotherapists.* San Francisco: Jossey-Bass, 1973.

Heston, Leonard L. "Psychiatric Disorders in Foster Home Reared Children of Schizophrenic Mothers." *The British Journal of Psychiatry* 112 (1966): 819–825.

Hiday, Virginia, and Rodney Goodman. "The Least Restrictive Alternative to Involuntary Hospitalization, Outpatient Commitment: Its Use and Effectiveness." *Journal of Psychiatry and Law* 10 (1982): 81–96.

Hiday, Virginia, and Teresa Scheid-Cook. "The North Carolina Experience with Outpatient Commitment: A Critical Appraisal." Paper presented at the International Congress of Law and Psychiatry, Montreal, 1986.

Hillman, Alan L. "Financial Incentives for Physicians in HMOs: Is There a Conflict of Interest?" *New England Journal of Medicine* 317 (1987): 1743–1748.

———. "Health Maintenance Organizations, Financial Incentives, and Physicians' Payments." *Annals of Internal Medicine* 112 (1990): 891–893.

Hodgkin, Dominic. "The Impact of Private Utilization Management on Psychiatric Care: A Review of the Literature." *Journal of Mental Health Administration* 19 (1992): 143–157.

Hoenig, Julius, and Marian W. Hamilton. "The Burden on the Household in an Extramural Psychiatric Service." In *New Aspects of the Mental Health Services,* edited by Hugh Freeman and James Farndale, pp. 612–635. Elmsford, N.Y.: Pergamon Press, 1967.

Hogan, Richard. "It Can't Happen Here: Community Opposition to Group Homes." *Sociological Focus* 19 (1986): 361–374.

———. "Gaining Community Support for Group Homes." *Community Mental Health Journal* 22 (1986): 117–126.

Hogarty, Gerald E., et al. "Family Psychoeducation, Social Skills Training, and Maintenance Chemotherapy in the Aftercare Treatment of Schizophrenia." *Archives of General Psychiatry* 48 (1991): 340–347.

Hollingshead, August B., and Frederick C. Redlich. Social *Class and Mental Illness: A Community Study.* New York: John Wiley and Sons, 1958.

Hoover Commission. Task Force Report on Federal Medical Services, February 1955.

Horgan, Constance, and Stephen F. Jencks. "Research on Psychiatric Classification and Payment Systems." *Medical Care* 25 (1987): S22–S36.

Horwitz, Allan V., Susan Reinhard, and Sandra Howell-White. "Caregiving as Reciprocal Exchange in Families with Seriously Mentally Ill Members." *Journal of Health and Social Behavior* 37 (1996): 149–162.

Hoult, John. "Replicating the Mendota Model in Australia." *Hospital and Community Psychiatry* 38 (1987): 565.

Howe, Carol, and James Howe. "The National Alliance for the Mentally Ill: History and Ideology." In *Families of the Mentally Ill: Meeting the Challenges,* New Directions for Mental Health Services, No. 34, edited by A. B. Hatfield, pp. 23–33. San Francisco: Jossey-Bass, 1987.

Huber, G., G. Gross, and R. Scheuttler. *Schizophrenia.* Berlin: Springer, 1979.

Institute of Medicine. *Mental Health Services in General Health Care.* A Conference Report. Vol 1. Washington, D.C.: National Academy of Sciences, 1979.

———. *Homelessness, Health, and Human Needs.* Washington, D.C.: National Academy Press, 1988.

Institute for Social Research. Newsletter, pp. 4–5. Ann Arbor: University of Michigan, 1979.

Isaac, Rael J., and Virginia C. Armat. *Madness in the Streets: How Psychiatry and the Law Abandoned the Mentally Ill.* New York: Free Press, 1990.

Jahoda, Marie. *Current Concepts of Positive Mental Health.* New York: Basic Books, 1958.

Jencks, Christopher. *The Homeless.* Cambridge, Mass.: Harvard University Press, 1994.

Jencks, Stephen F., Constance Horgan, and Carl A. Taube. "Evidence on Provider Response to Prospective Payment." *Medical Care* 25 (1987 supplement): 537–541.

Jenkins, Rachel, and Vida Field, eds. *The Primary Care of Schizophrenia,* 2nd ed. London: HMSO, 1996.

Joint Commission on Mental Illness and Health. *Action for Mental Health.* New York: Science Editions, 1961.

Jones, Kenneth R., and Thomas R. Vischi. "Impact of Alcohol, Drug Abuse, and Mental Health Treatment on Medical Care Utilization: A Review of the Research Literature." *Medical Care* 17 (1979 supplement): 12:1–89.

Kadushin, Charles. "Individual Decisions to Undertake Psychotherapy." *Administrative Science Quarterly* 3 (1958): 379–411.

———. "Social Distance between Client and Professional." *American Journal of Sociology* 67 (1962): 517–531.

————. "The Friends and Supporters of Psychotherapy: On Social Circles in Urban Life." *American Sociological Review* 31 (1966): 786–802.

Kallman, Franz J. "The Genetic Theory of Schizophrenia." In *Personality in Nature, Society, and Culture,* 2nd ed., edited by Clyde Kluckhohn and Henry A. Murray, pp. 80–99. New York: Alfred A. Knopf, Inc., 1953.

Katon, Wayne J., and Junius Gonzales. "A Review of Randomized Trials of Psychiatric Consultation-Liaison Studies in Primary Care." *Psychosomatic Medicine* 35 (1994): 268–278.

Keeler, Emmet B., et al. *The Demand for Episodes of Mental Health Services* (R-3432-NIMH). Santa Monica, Calif.: Rand Corporation, 1986.

Kellam, Sheppard G., June L. Schmelzer, and Audrey Berman. "Variation in the Atmosphere of Psychiatric Wards." *Archives of General Psychiatry* 14 (1966): 561–570.

Kendell, Robert E., Ian F. Brockington, and Julian P. Leff. "Prognostic Implications of Six Alternative Definitions of Schizophrenia." *Archives of General Psychiatry* 36 (1979): 25–31.

Kendler, Kenneth S. "Genetic Epidemiology in Psychiatry: Taking Both Genes and Environment Seriously." *Archives of General Psychiatry* 52 (1995): 895–899.

Kessler, Ronald C. "A Disaggregation of the Relationship Between Socioeconomic Status and Psychological Distress." *American Sociological Review* 47 (1982): 752–764.

Kessler, Ronald C., and Harold W. Neighbors. "A New Perspective on the Relationships Among Race, Social Class, and Psychological Distress." *Journal of Health and Social Behavior* 27 (1986): 107–115.

Kessler, Ronald C., et al. "Lifetime and 12-Month Prevalence of DSM-III-R Psychiatric Disorders in the United States: Results from the National Comorbidity Study." *Archives of General Psychiatry* 51 (1994): 8–19.

Kety, Seymour S. "Concluding Comments." In *The Nature of Schizophrenia: New Approaches to Research and Treatment,* edited by L. Wynne et al., pp. 156–157. New York: John Wiley and Sons, 1978.

————. "The Interface Between Neuroscience and Psychiatry." In *Psychiatry and Its Related Disciplines,* edited by R. Rosenberg, F. Schulsinger, and E. Strömgren, pp. 21–28. Copenhagen: World Psychiatric Association, 1986.

Kiesler, Charles A. "Mental Hospitals and Alternative Care." *American Psychologist* 37 (1982): 349–360.

Kiesler, Charles A., and Amy E. Sibulkin. *Mental Hospitalization: Myths and Facts about a National Crisis.* Newbury Park, Calif.: Sage Publications, 1987.

Kiesler, Charles A., and Celeste G. Simpkins. *The Unnoticed Majority in Psychiatric Inpatient Care.* New York: Plenum, 1993.

Kleinman, Arthur M. "Neurasthenia and Depression: A Study of Somatization and Culture in China." *Culture, Medicine and Psychiatry* 2 (1982): 117–190.

————. *Social Origins of Distress and Disease: Depression, Neurasthenia and Pain in Modern China.* New Haven, Conn.: Yale University Press, 1986.

Kleinman, Arthur, and David Mechanic. "Some Observations of Mental Illness and Its Treatment in the People's Republic of China." *Journal of Nervous and Mental Disease* 167 (1979): 267–274.

Klerman, Gerald L., et al. *Manual for Short-Term Interpersonal Psychotherapy (IPT) of Depression.* New York: Basic Books, 1984.

Knapp, M., et al. "Service Use and Costs of Home-based versus Hospital-based Care for People with Serious Mental Illness." *British Journal of Psychiatry* 165 (1994): 195–203.

Kohn, Melvin L. "Social Class and Schizophrenia: A Critical Review and a Reformulation." *Schizophrenia Bulletin* 7 (1973): 60–79.

————. *Class and Conformity: A Study in Values,* 2nd ed. Chicago: University of Chicago Press, 1977.

Kohn, Melvin L., and John A. Clausen. "Social Isolation and Schizophrenia." *American Sociological Review* 20 (1968): 265–273.

Kohout, Jessica L. "Employment Settings of Psychologists." *Pyschiatric Services* 46 (1995): 1115.

Kolb, Lawrence C. *Modern Clinical Psychiatry.* 9th ed. Philadelphia, Pa.: W. B. Saunders, 1977.

Koran, Lorrin M. "Psychiatrists' Patients." *Psychiatric Services* 46 (1995): 873.

Korbasa, Suzanne C. "Stressful Life Events, Personality, and Health: An Inquiry into Hardiness." *Journal of Personality and Social Psychology* 37 (1979): 1–11.

Koyanagi, Chris, and Howard Goldman, eds. *Inching Forward.* Alexandria, Va.: National Mental Health Association, 1991.

Kramer, Morton. *Psychiatric Services and the Changing Institutional Scene, 1950–1985.* National Institute of Mental Health, Series B., No. 12. Washington, D.C.: U.S. Government Printing Office, (ADM) 77–433, 1977.

Kramer, Morton, et al. "General Discussion." In *Psychiatric Epidemiology and Mental Health Planning,* edited by Russell R. Monroe, Gerald D. Klee, and Eugene B. Brody. Psychiatric Research Reports 22 (1967): 357–364.

Kreisman, Dolores E., and Virginia D. Joy. "Family Response to the Mental Illness of a Relative: A Review of the Literature." *Schizophrenia Bulletin* 10 (1974): 34–57.

Kringlen, Einar. "Adult Offspring of Two Psychotic Parents, with Special Reference to Schizophrenia." In *The Nature of Schizophrenia: New Approaches to Research and Treatment,* edited by L. Wynne, et al., pp. 9–24, New York: John Wiley and Sons, 1978.

Kulka, Richard A., Joseph Veroff, and Elizabeth Douvan. "Social Class and the Use of Professional Help for Personal Problems: 1957 and 1976." *Journal of Health and Social Behavior* 20 (1979): 2–17.

————. *Mental Health in America. Patterns of Help-Seeking from 1957 to 1976.* New York: Basic Books, 1981.

Lamb, H. Richard. "The New Asylums in the Community." *Archives of General Psychiatry* 36 (1979): 129–134.

————. ed. *The Homeless Mentally Ill, A Task Force Report of the American Psychiatric Association.* Washington, D.C.: American Psychiatric Association, 1984.

Lamb, H. Richard, and Robert W. Grant. "The Mentally Ill in an Urban County Jail." *Archives of General Psychiatry* 39 (1982): 17–22.

Lamb, H. Richard, and Mark J. Mills. "Needed Changes in Law and Procedure for the Chronically Mentally Ill." *Hospital and Community Psychiatry* 37 (1986): 475–480.

Langner, Thomas S. "A Twenty-Two Item Screening Score of Psychiatric Symptoms Indicating Impairment." *Journal of Health and Human Behavior* 3 (1962): 269–276.

Langner, Thomas S., and Stanley T. Michael. *Life Stress and Mental Health: The Midtown Manhattan Study.* New York: The Free Press of Glencoe, 1963.

Lazarus, Richard S. *Psychological Stress and The Coping Process.* New York: McGraw Hill Book Company, 1966.

Lazarus, Richard S., and Susan Folkman. *Stress, Appraisal and Coping.* New York: Springer, 1984.

Leaf, Philip J. "Legal Intervention into a Mental Health System: The Outcomes of 'Wyatt vs. Stickney'." Unpublished Ph.D. dissertation, Dept. of Sociology, University of Wisconsin, 1978.

————. "The Medical Marketplace and Public Interest Law: Part II. Alabama after Wyatt: PIL Intervention into a Mental Health Services Delivery System." In *Public Interest Law: An Economic and Institutional Analysis,* edited by Burton A. Weisbrod in collaboration with Joel F. Handler and Neil K. Komesar, pp. 374–394. Berkeley: University of California Press, 1978.

Leaf, Philip J., et al. "Contact with Health Professionals for the Treatment of Psychiatric and Emotional Problems." *Medical Care* 23 (1985): 1322–1337.

Leff, Julian. "Social and Psychological Causes of Acute Attack." In *Schizophrenia: Toward a New Synthesis,* edited by John Wing, pp. 139–165. New York: Grune and Stratton, 1978.

Leff, Julian. "Schizophrenia: Aetiology, Prognosis and Course." In *The Primary Care of Schizophrenia,* edited by Rachel Jenkins and Vida Field, 2nd ed., pp. 5–15. London: HMSO, 1996.

Leff, Julian, et al. "A Controlled Trial of Social Intervention in the Families of Schizophrenic Patients." *British Journal of Psychiatry* 141 (1982): 121–134.

Leff, Julian, and Christine Vaughn. *Expressed Emotion in Families.* New York: Guilford Press, 1985.

Leff, Julian, Noam Trieman, and Christopher Gooch. "Team for the Assessment of Psychiatric Services (TAPS) Project 33: Prospective Follow-up Study of Long-Stay Patients Discharged from Two Psychiatric Hospitals." *American Journal of Psychiatry* 153 (1996): 1318–1324.

Leighton, Alexander H. "Is Social Environment a Cause of Psychiatric Disorder?" In *Psychiatric Research Reports,* edited by R. R. Monroe, G. D. Klee, and E. G. Brody, pp. 337–345. Psychiatric Epidemiology and Mental Health Planning, 1967.

Leighton, Dorothea C., et al. *The Character of Danger: Psychiatric Symptoms in Selected Communities.* New York: Basic Books, 1963.

Lemert, Edwin M. *Social Pathology: A Systematic Approach to the Theory of Sociopathic Behavior.* New York: McGraw-Hill Book Company, 1951.

Leventhal, Howard. "Findings and Theory in the Study of Fear Communications." In *Advances in Experimental Social Psychology,* vol. 5, edited by Leonard Berkowitz, pp. 119–186. New York: Academic Press, 1970.

Levit, Katharine R. et al. "National Health Expenditures, 1994." *Health Care Financing Review* 17 (1996): 205–242.

Lewis, Aubrey. "Health as a Social Concept." *British Journal of Sociology* 4 (1953): 109–124.

Lewis, Charles E., Rashi Fein, and David Mechanic. *A Right to Health: The Problem of Access to Primary Medical Care.* New York: Wiley-Interscience, 1976.

Lidz, Theodore. *The Family and Human Adaptation: Three Lectures.* London: The Hogarth Press, 1963.

Link, Bruce G., and Francis T. Cullen. "Contact with the Mentally Ill and Perceptions of How Dangerous They Are." *Journal of Health and Social Behavior* 27 (1986): 289–303.

Link, Bruce G., Howard Andrews, and Francis T. Cullen. "The Violent and Illegal Behavior of Mental Patients Reconsidered." *American Sociological Review* 57 (1992): 275–292.

Link, Bruce G., and Ann Stueve. "Psychotic Symptoms and the Violent\Illegal Behavior of Mental Patients Compared to Community Controls." In *Violence and Mental Disorder: Developments in Risk Assessment,* edited by John Monahan and Henry Stedman. Chicago: University of Chicago Press, 1994.

Linn, Lawrence S. "Social Characteristics and Social Interaction in the Utilization of a Psychiatric Outpatient Clinic." *Journal of Health and Social Behavior* 8 (1967): 3–14.

———. "The Mental Hospital in the Patient's Phenomenal World." Unpublished Ph.D. dissertation, University of Wisconsin, Madison, Dept. of Sociology, 1968.

Linn, Lawrence S., Joel Yager, and Barbara Leake. "Psychiatrists' Attitudes Toward Preventive Intervention in Routine Clinical Practice." *Hospital and Community Psychiatry* 39 (1988): 637–642.

Linn, Margaret W., et al. "Nursing Home Care as an Alternative to Psychiatric Hospitalization." *Archives of General Psychiatry* 42 (1985): 544–551.

Excerpts from decision by Acting Justice Robert D. Lippmann. " 'Though Homeless, She Copes, She Is Fit, She Survives.' " *New York Times* November 13, 1987, pp B2.

Lohr, Kathleen N., et al. *Use of Medical Care in the RAND Health Insurance Experiment: Diagnosis- and Service-Specific Analyses in a Randomized Controlled Trial,* Pub. No. R-3469-HHS, Santa Monica, Calif.: RAND Corporation, 1986.

Ludwig, Arnold M., and Frank Farrelly. "The Code of Chronicity." *Archives of General Psychiatry* 15 (1966): 562–568.

Luft, Harold S. *Health Maintenance Organizations: Dimensions of Performance.* New York: Wiley-Interscience, 1981.

Luft, Harold S. *Health Maintenance Organizations: Dimensions of Performance.* New Brunswick, N.J.: Transactions Publishers, 1987.

Lurie, Nicole, et al. "Does Capitation Affect the Health of the Chronically Mentally Ill?: Results from a Randomized Trial." *Journal of the American Medical Association* 267 (1992): 3300–3304.

Maccoby, Eleanor E. "The Choice of Variables in the Study of Socialization." *Sociometry* 24 (1961): 357–371.

Manis, Jerome G., et al. "Validating a Mental Health Scale." *American Sociological Review* 28 (1963): 108–116.

———. "Estimating the Prevalence of Mental Illness." *American Sociological Review* 29 (1964): 84–89.

Manning, Willard G., et al. "A Controlled Trial of the Effect of a Prepaid Group Practice on Use of Services." *New England Journal of Medicine* 310 (1984): 1505–1510.

Manning, Willard. G., Jr., et al. *Use of Outpatient Mental Health Care: Trial of a Prepaid Group Practice versus Fee-for-Service* (R-3277-NIMH). Santa Monica, Calif.: Rand Corporation, 1986.

Manning, Willard G., Jr., and Kenneth B. Wells. "Preliminary Results of a Controlled Trial of the Effect of a Prepaid Group Practice on the Outpatient Use of Mental Health Services." *Journal of Human Resources* 21 (1986): 292–320.

Manning, Willard G., Jr., et al. "Outcomes for Medicaid Beneficiaries with Schizophrenia in the Utah Prepaid Mental Health Plan." Paper presented at the Annual Meeting of the *Association for Health Services Research,* August 1995.

Marks, Isaac M. *Fears and Phobias.* New York: Academic Press, 1969.

———. "Research in Neurosis: A Selective Review—I. Causes and Courses." *Psychological Medicine* 3 (1973): 436–454.

Marks, Isaac M., et al. "Home-based versus Hospital-based Care for People with Serious Mental Illness." *British Journal of Psychiatry* 165 (1994): 179–194.

Marzuk, Peter M. "Violence, Crime, and Mental Illness: How Strong a Link?" *Archives of General Psychiatry* 53 (1996): 481–486.

Mashaw, Jerry L. *Bureaucratic Justice: Managing Social Security Disability Claims.* New Haven, Conn.: Yale University Press, 1983.

Mashaw, Jerry L., and Virginia P. Reno, eds. *The Environment of Disability Income Policy: Programs, People, History and Context.* Washington: D.C.: National Academy of Social Insurance, 1996.

McCloskey, Amanda H., et al. *Reforming the Health Care System: State Profiles 1996.* Washington, D.C.: American Association of Retired Persons, 1996.

McCord, Joan. "A Thirty-Year Follow-up of Treatment Effects." Paper presented at the meetings of the American Association of Psychiatric Services for Children, 1976.

McDowell, Ian, and Clare Newell. *Measuring Health: A Guide to Rating Scales and Questionnaires.* New York: Oxford University Press, 1987.

McFarlane, William R., et al. "Multiple Family Groups and Psychoeducation in the Treatment of Schizophrenia." *Archives of General Psychiatry* 52 (1995): 679–687.

McFarlane, William R., et al. "A Comparison of Two Levels of Family Aided Assertive Community Treatment." *Psychiatric Services* 47 (1996): 744–750.

McGhie, Andrew, and James Chapman. "Disorders of Attention and Perception in Early Schizophrenia." *British Journal of Medical Psychology* 34 (1961): 103–116.

McGuffin, Peter, Ann E. Farmer, and Irving I. Gottesman. "Modern Diagnostic Criteria and Genetic Studies of Schizophrenia." In *Search for the Causes of Schizophrenia,* edited by H. Hafner, et al., pp. 143–156. Berlin: Springer-Verlag, 1987.

McGuire, Thomas. *Financing Psychotherapy: Costs, Effects, and Public Policy.* Cambridge, Mass.: Ballinger, 1981.

Mechanic, David. "Some Factors in Identifying and Defining Mental Illness." *Mental Hygiene* 46 (1962): 66–74.

———. *Students under Stress: A Study in the Social Psychology of Adaptation.* New York: The Free Press, 1962. (Republished by the University of Wisconsin Press with a new introduction, 1978.)

———. "Social Class and Schizophrenia: Some Requirements for a Plausible Theory of Social Influence." *Social Forces* 50 (1972a): 305–309.

———. "Social Psychologic Factors Affecting the Presentation of Bodily Complaints." *The New England Journal of Medicine* 286 (1972b): 1132–1139.

———. *Politics, Medicine, and Social Science.* New York: Wiley-Interscience, 1974.

———. "Sociocultural and Social-Psychological Factors Affecting Personal Responses to Psychological Disorder." *Journal of Health and Social Behavior* 16 (1975): 393–404.

———. *The Growth of Bureaucratic Medicine: An Inquiry into the Dynamics of Patient Behavior and the Organization of Medical Care.* New York: Wiley-Interscience, 1976.

———. *Medical Sociology,* 2nd ed. New York: The Free Press, 1978.

———. *Future Issues in Health Care: Social Policy and the Rationing of Medical Services.* New York: The Free Press, 1979a.

———. "Development of Psychological Distress Among Young Adults." *Archives of General Psychiatry* 36 (1979b): 1233-1239.

———, ed., *Symptoms, Illness Behavior, and Help-Seeking.* New Brunswick, N.J.: Rutgers University Press, 1982.

———. "Health Care for the Poor: Some Policy Alternatives." *Journal of Family Practice* 22 (1986a): 283-289.

———. *From Advocacy to Allocation: The Evolving American Health Care System.* New York: The Free Press, 1986b.

———. "Treating Mental Illness, Generalist vs. Specialist." *Health Affairs* 9 (1990): 61–75.

———. Editorial: Managed Care for the Seriously Mentally Ill. *American Journal of Public Health* 82 (1992): 788–789.

———. "Can Research on Managed Care Inform Practice and Policy Decisions?" In *Controversies in Managed Mental Health Care,* edited by Arnold

Lazarus, pp. 211–225. Washington, D.C.: American Psychiatric Press, 1996.

———. "Managed Care as a Target of Distrust." *Journal of the American Medical Association* 277 (1997): 1810–1811.

Mechanic, David, ed. *Improving Inpatient Psychiatric Treatment in an Era of Managed Care.* New Directions for Mental Health Services Number 73. San Francisco, CA: Jossey-Bass, 1997.

Mechanic, David, and Linda H. Aiken. "Improving the Care of Patients with Chronic Mental Illness." *New England Journal of Medicine* 317 (1987): 1634–1638.

Mechanic, David, and Linda H. Aiken, eds. *Paying for Services: Promises and Pitfalls of Capitation.* New Directions for Mental Health Services 43. San Francisco: Jossey-Bass, 1989.

Mechanic, David, Ronald Angel, and Lorraine Davies. "Risk and Selection Processes between the General and Specialty Mental Health Sectors." *Journal of Health and Social Behavior* 32 (1991): 49–64.

Mechanic, David, Paul D. Cleary, and James R. Greenley. "Distress Syndromes, Illness Behavior, Access to Care and Medical Utilization in a Defined Population." *Medical Care* 20 (1982): 361–372.

Mechanic, David, and James R. Greenley. "The Prevalence of Psychological Distress and Help-Seeking in a College Student Population." *Social Psychiatry* 11 (1976): 1–14.

Mechanic, David, and Donna D. McAlpine. *Changing Patterns of Inpatient Psychiatric Care in General Hospitals: 1988–1994.* New Brunswick, N.J.: Institute for Health, Health Care Policy and Aging Research, Rutgers University, 1997.

Mechanic, David, and David A. Rochefort. "A Policy of Inclusion for the Mentally Ill." *Health Affairs* 11 (1992): 128–150.

Mechanic, David, and Mark Schlesinger. "The Impact of Managed Care on Patients' Trust in Medical Care and Their Physicians." *Journal of the American Medical Association* 275 (1996): 1693–1697.

Mechanic, David, Mark Schlesinger, and Donna McAlpine. "Management of Mental Health and Substance Abuse Services: State of the Art and Early Results." *Milbank Quarterly* 73 (1995): 19–55.

Mechanic, David, and Richard Surles. "Challenges in State Health Policy and Administration." *Health Affairs* 11 (1992): 34–50.

Merwin, Elizabeth et al. "Certified Psychiatric Nurse Specialists." *Psychiatric Services* 47 (1996): 235.

Miller, Kent S. *Managing Madness: The Case against Civil Commitment.* New York: Free Press, 1976.

Miller, Robert D. "Commitment to Outpatient Treatment: A National Survey." *Hospital and Community Psychiatry* 36 (1985): 265–267.

Miller, Robert H., and Harold S. Luft. "Managed Care Performance Since 1980: A Literature Analysis." *Journal of the American Medical Association* 271 (1994): 1512–1519.

Mischler, Elliot G., and Nancy E. Waxler. "Family Interaction Processes and Schizophrenia: A Review of Current Theories." *Merrill-Palmer Quarterly* 11 (1965): 269–315.

Monahan, John. "Mental Disorder and Violent Behavior: Perceptions and Evidence." *American Psychologist* 47 (1992): 511–521.

Monahan, John. "Clinical and Actuarial Predictions of Violence." In *Modern Scientific Evidence: The Law and Science of Expert Testimony,* edited by David L. Faigman, David H. Kaye, Michael J. Saks, and Joseph Sanders, Vol 1. St. Paul, Minn.: West Publishing Co., 1997.

Moos, Rudolf H. *Evaluating Treatment Environments: A Social Ecological Approach.* New York: Wiley-Interscience, 1974.

Moos, Rudolf H. *Evaluating Treatment Environments: The Quality of Psychiatric and Substance Abuse Programs.* 2nd edition. New Brunswick, N.J.: Transaction Publishers, 1997.

Morrissey, Joseph P., Richard C. Tessler, and Linda L. Farrin. "Being 'Seen But Not Admitted': A Note on Some Neglected Aspects of State Hospital Deinstitutionalization." *American Journal of Orthopsychiatry* 49 (1979): 153–156.

Mrazek, Patricia J., and Robert J. Haggarty. eds. *Reducing the Risks for Mental Disorders: Frontiers for Preventive Intervention Research.* Washington, D.C.: National Academy Press, 1994.

Murphy, George E. "The Physician's Responsibility for Suicide: I. An Error of Commission." *Annals of Internal Medicine* 82 (1975): 301–304.

———. "The Physician's Responsibility for Suicide: II. Errors of Omission." *Annals of Internal Medicine* 82 (1975): 305–309.

Murphy, H. B. M. "Social Change and Mental Health." In *Causes of Mental Disorders: A Review of*

Epidemiological Knowledge, pp. 280–329. New York: The Milbank Memorial Fund, 1961.

Murphy, Jane M. "Psychiatric Labeling in Cross-Cultural Perspective." *Science* 191 (1976): 1019–1028.

Myers, Jerome K., and Lee L. Bean. *A Decade Later: A Follow-up of Social Class and Mental Illness.* New York: John Wiley and Sons, 1968.

Myers, Jerome K., et al. "Six-Month Prevalence of Psychiatric Disorders in Three Communities." *Archives of General Psychiatry* 41 (1984): 959–967.

National Mental Health Advisory Council. "Health Care Reform for Americans with Severe Mental Illness." *American Journal of Psychiatry* 150 (1993): 1447–1465.

National Institute for Mental Health. *Mental Health, United States, 1985.* Washington, D.C.: DHHS Pub. No. (ADM) 85-1378, 1985. U.S. Government Printing Office.

National Institute for Mental Health. *Mental Health, United States, 1987,* edited by Ronald W. Manderscheid, and Sally A. Barrett, DHHS Publication No. (ADM) 87–1518. Washington, D.C.: U.S. Government Printing Office, 1987.

New South Wales Department of Health. *Psychiatric Hospital versus Community Treatment: A Controlled Study.* Sydney, Australia: (HSR 83-046), 1983.

Newhouse, Joseph P. "A Design for a Health Insurance Experiment." *Inquiry* 11 (1974): 5–27.

Newhouse, Joseph P., et al. "Some Interim Results from a Controlled Trial of Cost Sharing in Health Insurance." *New England Journal of Medicine* 395 (1981): 1501–1507.

Newhouse, Joseph P., and the Insurance Experiment Group. *Free for All?: Lessons from the RAND Health Insurance Experiment.* Cambridge, Mass.: Harvard University Press, 1994.

Newman, Sandra J., et al. "The Effects of Independent Living on Persons with Chronic Mental Illness: An Assessment of the Section 8 Certificate Program." *Milbank Quarterly* 72 (1994): 171–198.

Nicholi, Armand M., Jr. "Psychiatric Consultation in Professional Football." *New England Journal of Medicine* 316 (1987): 1095–1100.

Ødegaard, Ø. "Discussion of 'Sociocultural Factors in the Epidemiology of Schizophrenia'." *International Journal of Psychiatry* 1 (1965): 296–297.

Olfson, Mark. "Assertive Community Treatment: An Evaluation of the Experimental Evidence." *Hospital and Community Psychiatry* 41 (1990): 634–641.

Olfson, Mark, and David Mechanic. "Mental Disorders in Public, Private Nonprofit, and Proprietary General Hospitals." *American Journal of Psychiatry* 153 (1996): 1613–1619.

Olfson, Mark, and Harold A. Pincus. "Outpatient Mental Health Care in Nonhospital Settings: Distribution of Patients across Provider Groups." *American Journal of Psychiatry* 153 (1996): 1353–1356.

Olfson, Mark, et al. "Inpatient Treatment of Schizophrenia in General Hospitals." *Hospital and Community Psychiatry* 44 (1993): 40–44.

Olfson, Mark, et al. "Professional Practice Patterns of U.S. Psychiatrists." *American Journal of Psychiatry* 151 (1994): 89–95.

Osterweis, Marian, Arthur Kleinman, and David Mechanic, eds. *Pain and Disability: Clinical, Behavioral, and Public Policy Perspectives.* Washington, D.C.: National Academy Press, 1987.

Pasamanick, Benjamin, Frank R. Scarpitti, and Simon Dinitz. *Schizophrenics in the Community: An Experimental Study in the Prevention of Hospitalization.* New York: Appleton-Century-Crofts, 1967.

Patrick, Donald L., Jeff Eagle, and Jules V. Coleman. "Primary Care Treatment of Emotional Problems in an HMO." *Medical Care* 16 (1978): 47–60.

Paul, Gordan L., and Robert J. Lentz. *Psychosocial Treatment of Chronic Mental Patients.* Cambridge, Mass.: Harvard University Press, 1977.

Pearlin, Leonard I., and Joyce S. Johnson. "Marital Status, Life-Strains, and Depression." *American Sociological Review* 42 (1977): 704–715.

Perrow, Charles. "Hospitals: Technology, Structure, and Goals." In *Handbook of Organizations,* edited by James G. March, pp. 910–971. Chicago: Rand McNally, 1965.

Pescosolido, Bernice A., et al. "Public's View of Individuals with Mental Health Problems: Competence, Dangerousness and the Need for Coercion in Health Care." Presentation at the Annual Meeting of the American Sociological Association, August 1997, Toronto, Canada.

Phillips, Derek L., and Kevin J. Clancy. "Response Biases in Field Studies of Mental Illness." *American Sociological Review* 35 (1970): 503–515.

Pickar, David, and John K. Hsiao. "Clozapine Treatment of Schizophrenia." *Journal of the American Medical Association* 274 (1995): 981–983.

Pierce, Glenn L., et al. "The Impact of Public Policy and Publicity on Admissions to State Mental Health Hospitals." *Journal of Health Politics, Policy, and Law* 11 (1986): 41–66.

Plunkett, Richard J., and John E. Gordon. *Epidemiology and Mental Illness.* New York: Basic Books, 1960.

Polak, Paul R. "A Comprehensive System of Alternatives to Psychiatric Hospitalization." In *Alternatives to Mental Hospital Treatment,* edited by Leonard I. Stein and Mary Ann Test, pp. 115–137. New York: Plenum Press, 1978.

Price, Richard H., Michelle Van Ryn, and Amiram D. Vinokur. "Impact of a Preventive Job Search Intervention on the Likelihood of Depression among the Unemployed." *Journal of Health and Social Behavior* 33 (1992): 158–167.

Quinton, David, and Michael Rutter. "Family Pathology and Child Psychiatric Disorder: A Four-Year Prospective Study." In *Longitudinal Studies in Child Psychology and Psychiatry: Practical Lessons from Research Experience,* edited by R. Nichol. New York: Wiley, 1984.

———. "Parents with Children in Care: Intergenerational Continuities." *Journal of Child Psychology and Psychiatry* 25 (1984): 231–250.

Radloff, Lenore Sawyer. "The CESD Scale: A Self-Report Depression Scale for Research in the General Population." *Applied Psychological Measurement* 1 (1977): 385–401.

Rappeport, Jonas R., ed. *The Clinical Evaluation of the Dangerousness of the Mentally Ill.* Springfield, Ill.: Charles C. Thomas, 1967.

Redlich, Frederick C., and Daniel X. Friedman. *The Theory and Practice of Psychiatry.* New York: Basic Books, 1966.

Redlich, Fritz, and Stephen R. Kellert. "Trends in American Mental Health." *American Journal of Psychiatry* 135 (1978): 22–28.

Regier, Darrel A., et al. "The NIMH Epidemiologic Catchment Area Study." *Archives of General Psychiatry* 41 (1984): 934–941.

Regier, Darrel A., et al. "The de Facto U.S. Mental and Addictive Disorders Service System: Epidemiologic Catchment Area Prospective 1-Year Prevalence Rates of Disorders and Services." *Archives of General Psychiatry* 50 (1993): 85–94.

Reich, Theodore, et al. "Genetics of the Affective Psychoses." In *Handbook of Psychiatry 3: Psychoses of Uncertain Actiology,* edited by John K. Wing and Lorna Wing, pp. 147–159. New York: Cambridge University Press, 1985.

Reid, Donald D. "Precipitating Proximal Factors in the Occurrence of Mental Disorders: Epidemiological Evidence." In *Causes of Mental Disorders: A Review of Epidemiological Knowledge,* pp. 197–216. New York: The Milbank Memorial Fund, 1961.

Reinhard, Susan C. "Perspectives on the Family's Caregiving Experience in Mental Illness." *Image: Journal of Nursing Scholarship* 26 (1994): 70–74.

Reinhard, Susan, and Allan V. Horwitz. "Caregiver Burden: Differentiating the Content and Consequences of Family Caregiving." *Journal of Marriage and the Family* 57 (1996): 741–750.

Robert Wood Johnson Foundation. *Special Report: Update Report on Access to Health Care for the American People.* Princeton, N.J., 1983.

Robins, Lee N. *Deviant Children Grown Up: A Sociological and Psychiatric Study of Sociopathic Personality.* Baltimore: Williams and Wilkins, 1966.

———. "Evaluation of Psychiatric Services for Children in the United States." In *Roots of Evaluation,* edited by J. K. Wing and H. Hafner. London: Oxford University Press, 1973.

———. "Alcoholism and Labeling Theory." In *The Labeling of Deviance: Evaluating a Perspective,* edited by W. R. Gove, pp. 21–33. New York: Halstead Press, 1975.

———. "Longitudinal Methods in the Study of Normal and Pathological Development." In *Psychiatri der Gegenwart,* vol. 1, 2nd ed., edited by Karl Peter Kisker, et al., pp. 627–684. Heidelberg: Springer-Verlag, 1979.

———. "Follow-up Studies of Behavior Disorders in Children." In *Psychopathological Disorders of Childhood,* 2nd ed., edited by H.C. Quay and J. S. Werry. New York: John Wiley and Sons, 1979.

———. "Continuities and Discontinuities in the Psychiatric Disorders of Children." In *Handbook of Health, Health Care, and the Health Professions,* edited by David Mechanic. New York: Free Press, 1983.

———. "Epidemiology: Reflections on Testing the Validity of Psychiatric Interviews." *Archives of General Psychiatry* 42 (1985): 918–924.

Robins, Lee N., et al. "Lifetime Prevalence of Specific Psychiatric Disorders in Three Sites." *Archives of General Psychiatry* 41 (1984): 949–958.

Robins, Lee N., et al. "The Diagnostic Interview Schedule." In *Epidemiologic Field Methods in Psychiatry,* edited by W. W. Eaton and L. G. Kessler, pp. 143–170. New York: Academic Press, 1985.

Robins, Lee N., and Darrel A. Regier, eds. *Psychiatric Disorders in America: The Epidemiological Catchment Area Study.* New York: Free Press, 1991.

Rodin, Judith. "Aging and Health: Effects of Sense of Control." *Science* 233 (1986): 1271–1276.

Rodin, Judith, and Ellen J. Langer. "Long-Term Effects of a Control-Relevant Intervention with the Institutionalized Aged." *Journal of Personality and Social Psychology* 35 (1977): 897–902.

Rodwin, Mark. *Medicine, Money, and Morals: Physicians' Conflicts of Interest.* New York: Oxford University Press, 1993.

Rogers, William H., et al. "Outcomes for Adult Outpatients with Depression under Prepaid or Fee-for-Service Financing." *Archives of General Psychiatry* 50 (1993): 517–525.

Rosenbach, Margo L., and Carol J. Ammering. "Trends in Medicare Part B Mental Health Utilization and Expenditures: 1987–92." *Health Care Financing Review* 18 (1997): 19–42.

Rosenberg, Stephen N., et al. "Effect of Utilization Review in a Fee-for-Service Health Insurance Plan." *New England Journal of Medicine* 333 (1995): 1326–1330.

Rosenhan, David L. "On Being Sane in Insane Places." *Science* 179 (1973): 250–258.

Rosenthal, David. *Genetic Theory and Abnormal Behavior.* New York: McGraw-Hill Book Co., 1970.

Rossi, Peter H. *Down and Out in America: The Origins of Homelessness.* Chicago: University of Chicago Press, 1989.

Rossi, Peter H., and James D. Wright. "The Determinants of Homelessness." *Health Affairs* 6 (1987): 19–32.

Rossi, Peter H., et al. "The Urban Homeless: Estimating Composition and Size." *Science* 235 (1987): 1336–1341.

Roter, Debra L., and Judith A. Hall. *Doctors Talking with Patients/Patients Talking with Doctors: Improving Communication in Medical Visits.* Westport, Conn.: Auburn House, 1992.

Rothman, David J. *The Discovery of the Asylum: Social Order and Disorder in the New Republic.* Boston: Little, Brown, 1971.

Rubenstein, Leonard. "APA's Model Law: Hurting the People It Seeks to Help." *Hospital and Community Psychiatry* 36 (1985): 968–972.

Rubenstein, Mark, and Richard Simons. "The Schizophrenic Disorders." In *Understanding Human Behavior in Health and Illness,* 2nd ed., edited by Richard Simons and Herbert Pardes, pp. 612–625. Baltimore, Md.: Williams and Wilkins, 1981.

Russell, Louise B. *Is Prevention Better than Cure?* Washington, D.C.: The Brookings Institution, 1986.

———. *Evaluating Preventive Care: Report on a Workshop.* Washington, D.C.: The Brookings Institution, 1987.

Rutter, Michael. *Children of Sick Parents: An Environmental and Psychiatric Study.* New York: Oxford University Press, Inc., 1966.

———. "Relationships between Child and Adult Psychiatric Disorders." *Acta Psychiatrica Scandinavia* 48 (1972): 3–21.

Ryder, Norman B. "The Cohort as a Concept in the Study of Social Change." *American Sociological Review* 30 (1965): 843–861.

Sabin, James E. "Organized Psychiatry and Managed Care: Quality Improvement or Holy War?" *Health Affairs* 14 (1995): 32–33.

———. "What Confidentiality Standards Should We Advocate for in Mental Health Care, and How Should We Do It?" *Psychiatric Services* 48 (1997): 35–41.

Sampson, Harold S., Sheldon L. Messinger, and Robert D. Towne. *Schizophrenic Women: Studies in Marital Crisis.* New York: Atherton Press, 1964.

Santos, Alberto B., et al. "Research on Field-Based Services: Models for Reform in the Delivery of Mental Health Care to Populations with Complex Clinical Problems." *American Journal of Psychiatry* 152 (1995): 1111–1123.

Saravay, Stephen M., and James J. Strain. "APM Task Force on Funding Implications of Consultation-Liaison Outcome Studies." *Psychosomatics* 35 (1994): 227–231.

Sartorius, Norman, et al. "Early Manifestations and First-Contact Incidence of Schizophrenia in Different Cultures." *Psychological Medicine* 16 (1986): 909–928.

Schappert, Susan M. "Office Visits to Psychiatrists: United States, 1989–90." *Advance Data from Vital and Health Statistics* 237 (1993).

Scheff, Thomas J. "Legitimate, Transitional, and Illegitimate Mental Patients in a Midwestern State." *American Journal of Psychiatry* 120 (1963): 267–269.

Scheff, Thomas J. "Users and Non-Users of a Student Psychiatric Clinic." *Journal of Health and Human Behavior* 7 (1966): 114–121.

———. *Being Mentally Ill: A Sociological Theory.* Chicago: Aldine, 1966 (2nd edition, 1984).

Schulberg, Herbert C., et al. "Treating Major Depression in Primary Care Practice: Eight-Month Clinical Outcomes." *Archives of General Psychiatry* 53 (1996): 913–919.

Schutt, Russell K., and Stephen M. Goldfinger. "Housing Preferences and Perceptions of Health and Functioning among Homeless Mentally Ill Persons." *Psychiatric Services* 47 (1996): 381–386.

Scull, Andrew T. *Decarceration: Community Treatment and the Deviant.* Englewood Cliffs, N. J.: Prentice Hall, 1977.

Segal, Stephen P., and Uri Aviram. *The Mentally-Ill in Community-Based Sheltered Care: A Study of Community Care and Social Integration.* New York: Wiley-Interscience, 1978.

Seiler, Lauren H. "The 22-Item Scale Used in Field Studies of Mental Illness: A Question of Method, a Question of Substance, and a Question of Theory." *Journal of Health and Social Behavior* 14 (1973): 252–264.

Seligman, Martin E. P. *Helplessness: On Depression, Development, and Death.* San Francisco: W. H. Freeman and Company Publishers, 1975.

Sewell, William H. "Infant Training and the Personality of the Child." *American Journal of Sociology* 58 (1952):150-159.

Shah, Saleem A., and Bruce D. Sales, eds. *Law and Mental Health: Major Developments and Research Needs.* DHHS Publ. No. (ADM)91–1875. Rockville, Md.: National Institute of Mental Health, 1991.

Shapiro, Sam, et al. "Utilization of Health and Mental Health Services: Three Epidemiological Catchment Area Sites." *Archives of General Psychiatry* 41 (1984): 971–978.

Shapiro, Sam, et al. "Measuring Need for Mental Health Services in a General Population." *Medical Care* 23 (1985): 1033–1043.

Shepherd, Geoff. *Institutional Care and Rehabilitation.* London: Longman, 1984.

Shepherd, Michael. "Formulation of New Research Strategies on Schizophrenia." In *Search for the Causes of Schizophrenia,* edited by Heinz Hafner, et al., pp. 29–38. Berlin: Springer-Verlag, 1987.

Shepherd, Michael, A. N. Oppenheim, and Sheila Mitchell. "Childhood Behavior Disorders and the Child-Guidance Clinic: An Epidemiological Study." *Journal of Child Psychology and Psychiatry* 7 (1966): 39–52.

Shepherd, Michael, et al. *Psychiatric Illness in General Practice.* New York: Oxford University Press, 1966.

Simmons, Robert G., Susan D. Klein, and Richard L. Simmons. *Gift of Life: The Social and Psychological Impact of Organ Transplantation.* New York: Wiley-Interscience, 1977.

Skinner, B. F. *Beyond Freedom and Dignity.* New York: Alfred A. Knopf, 1971.

Smith, G. Richard, Jr., Roberta A. Monson, and Debbie C. Ray. "Psychiatric Consultation in Somatization Disorder: A Randomized Controlled Study." *New England Journal of Medicine* 314 (1986): 1407–1413.

Spitz, Bruce. "A National Survey of Medicaid Case-Management Programs." *Health Affairs* 6 (1987): 61–70.

Spitzer, Robert L. "More on Pseudoscience in Science and the Case for Psychiatric Diagnosis." *Archives of General Psychiatry* 33 (1976): 459–470.

Spitzer, Robert L., and Jean Endicott. "Medical and Mental Disorder: Proposed Definition and Criteria." In *Critical Issues in Psychiatric Diagnosis,* edited by Robert L. Spitzer and Donald F. Klein. New York: Raven Press, 1978.

Srole, Leo, et al. *Mental Health in the Metropolis: The Midtown Manhattan Study.* New York: McGraw-Hill, 1962.

Stanton, Alfred H., and Morris S. Schwartz. *The Mental Hospital: A Study of Institutional Participation in Psychiatric Illness and Treatment.* New York: Basic Books, 1954.

Stapp, Joy, et al. "Census of Psychological Personnel: 1983." *American Psychologist* 40 (1985): 1317–1351.

Starr, Paul. *The Social Transformation of American Medicine.* New York: Basic Books, 1982.

Stein, Leonard I., Mary Ann Test, and Arnold J. Marx. "Alternative to the Hospital: A Controlled Study."

American Journal of Psychiatry 132 (1975): 517–522.

Stein, Leonard I., and Leonard J. Ganser. "Wisconsin System for Funding Mental Health Services." In *New Directions for Mental Health Services: Unified Mental Health System,* edited by J. Talbott, pp. 25–32. San Francisco: Jossey-Bass, 1983.

Stein, Leonard I., and Mary Ann Test. "Training in Community Living: One Year Evaluation." *The American Journal of Psychiatry* 133 (1976): 917–918.

———, eds. *Alternatives to Mental Hospital Treatment.* New York: Plenum, 1978.

———. "Alternatives to Mental Hospital Treatment I. Conceptual Model Treatment Program and Clinical Evaluation." *Archives of General Psychiatry* 37 (1980): 392–397.

———. "Alternatives to Mental Hospital Treatment III. Social Cost." *Archives of General Psychiatry* 37 (1980): 409–412.

———, eds. *The Training in Community Living Model: A Decade of Experience.* New Directions for Mental Health Services Number 26. San Francisco: Jossey-Bass, 1985.

Stein, Leonard I., and Ellen J. Hollingsworth, eds. *Maturing Mental Health Systems: New Challenges and Opportunities.* New Directions for Mental Health Services Number 66. San Francisco: Jossey-Bass, 1995.

Stevens, Robert, and Rosemary Stevens. *Welfare Medicine in America: A Case Study of Medicaid.* New York: The Free Press, 1974.

Stone, Alan A. *Mental Health and the Law: A System in Transition.* DHEW Pub. No. (ADM) 75-176. Rockville, Md.: National Institute of Mental Health, Center for Studies of Crime and Delinquency, 1975.

———. "The Right to Refuse Treatment." *Archives of General Psychiatry* 38 (1981): 358–362.

———. *Law, Psychiatry, and Morality.* Washington, D.C.: American Psychiatric Press, 1984.

Stotsky, Bernard A. *The Nursing Home and the Aged Psychiatric Patient.* New York: Appleton-Century-Crofts, 1970.

Strauss, John S. "The Functional Psychoses." In *Psychiatry in General Medical Practice,* edited by Gene Usdin and Jerry Lewis, pp. 279–302. New York: McGraw Hill, 1979.

Strauss, John S., and William T. Carpenter. "Prediction of Outcome in Schizophrenia: III. Five-Year Out-

come and Its Predictors." *Archives of General Psychiatry* 34 (1977): 159–163.

Stromberg, C. D., and Alan Stone. "A Model State Law on Civil Commitment of the Mentally Ill." *Harvard Journal on Legislation* 20 (1983): 275–296.

Styron, William. *Darkness Visible: A Memoir of Madness.* New York: First Vintage Books, 1992.

Sullivan, Harry Stack. *The Interpersonal Theory of Psychiatry.* New York: W. W. Norton & Company, 1953.

Surles, Richard C., et al. "Case-Management Strategies for System Change." *Health Affairs* 11 (1992): 151–152.

Susser, Ezra, Elmer L. Struening, and Sarah Conover. "Psychiatric Problems in Homeless Men." *Archives of General Psychiatry* 46 (1989): 845–859.

Susser, Ezra et al. "Preventing Recurrent Homelessness Among Mentally Ill Men: A "Critical Time" Intervention after Discharge from a Shelter." *American Journal of Public Health* 87 (1997): 256–262.

Sutherland, Norman S. *Breakdown.* New York: Stein and Day, 1977.

Swanson, Jeffrey W., et al. "Violence and Psychiatric Disorder in the Community: Evidence from the Epidemiologic Catchment Area Surveys." *Hospital and Community Psychiatry* 41 (1990): 761–770.

Swanson, Jeffery W. et al. Unpublished manuscript (reviewed in Monahan, 1997, p. 305), 1996.

Swartz, Marvin S., et al. "New Directions in Research on Involuntary Outpatient Commitment." *Psychiatric Services* 46 (1995): 381–385.

Swidler, Robert N., and John V. Tauriello. "New York State's Community Mental Health Reinvestment Act." *Psychiatric Services* 46 (1995): 496–500.

Swindle, Ralph, et al. "Confronting Mental Health Problems: How Americans Experienced and Coped with Mental Health Problems in Three Decades." Presentation at the Annual Meeting of the American Sociological Association, August 1997, Toronto, Canada.

Szasz, Thomas S. "The Myth of Mental Illness." *American Psychologist* 15 (1960): 113–118.

———. *Law, Liberty, and Psychiatry: An Inquiry Into the Social Uses of Mental Health Practices.* New York: Macmillan, 1963.

———. *Ideology and Insanity: Essay on the Psychiatric Dehumanization of Man.* New York: Doubleday-Anchor, 1970.

———. *The Myth of Mental Illness: Foundations of a Theory of Personal Conduct,* rev. ed. New York: Harper and Row, 1974.

Talbott, John A. "The Fate of the Public Psychiatric System." *Hospital and Community Psychiatry* 36 (1985): 46–50.

Tarrier, Nicholas, et al. "Bodily Reactions to People and Events in Schizophrenics." *Archives of General Psychiatry* 36 (1979): 311–315.

Taube, Carl, Eun S. Lee, and Ronald N. Forthofer. "DRGs in Psychiatry: An Empirical Evaluation." *Medical Care* 22 (1984): 597–610.

Taube, Carl, Larry Kessler, and M. Feuerberg. "Utilization and Expenditures for Ambulatory Medical Care during 1980." *National Medical Care Utilization and Expenditure Survey Data Report* No. 5, DHHS Publication No. (PHS) 84–2000, Washington, D.C.: Government Printing Office, 1984.

Tessler, Richard, David Mechanic, and Margaret Dimond. "The Effect of Psychological Distress on Physician Utilization: A Prospective Study." *Journal of Health and Social Behavior* 17 (1976): 353–364.

Tessler, Richard, and David Mechanic. "Psychological Distress and Perceived Health Status." *Journal of Health and Social Behavior* 19 (1978): 254–262.

Tessler, Richard, and Howard H. Goldman. *The Chronically Mentally Ill: Assessing the Community Support Programs.* Cambridge, Mass.: Ballinger Publishing Company, 1982.

Tessler, Richard, and Gail Gamache. "Continuity of Care, Residence, and Family Burden in Ohio." *Milbank Quarterly* 72 (1994): 149–169.

Tessler, Richard, et al. "Stages in Family Response to Mental Illness: An Ideal Type." *Psychosocial Rehabilitation Journal* 10 (1987): 3–16.

Thase, Michael E., and David J. Kupfer. "Recent Developments in the Pharmacotherapy of Mood Disorders." *Journal of Consulting and Clinical Psychology* 64 (1996): 646–659.

Thoits, Peggy A. "Stress, Coping, and Social Support Processes: Where Are We? What Next?" *Journal of Health and Social Behavior.* Extra issue (1995): 53–79.

Thompson, James W., et al. "Initial Level of Care and Clinical Status in a Managed Mental Health Program. " *Hospital and Community Psychiatry* 43 (1992): 599–603.

Tiihonen, Jari et al. "Specific Major Disorders and Criminality: A 26-Year Prospective Study of the 1966 Northern Finland Birth Cohort." *American Journal of Psychiatry* 154 (1997): 840–845.

Torrey, E. Fuller, and Robert J. Kaplan. "A National Survey of the Use of Outpatient Commitment." *Psychiatric Services* 46 (1995): 778–784.

Tousignant, Michael, Guy Denis, and Rejean Lachapelle. "Some Considerations Concerning the Validity and Use of the Health Opinion Survey." *Journal of Health and Social Behavior* 15 (1974): 241–252.

Treffert, Darold A. "Dying with Their Rights On." *American Journal of Psychiatry* 130 (1973): 1041.

Tsuang, Ming T., Robert F. Woolson, and Jerome A. Fleming. "Long-Term Outcome of Major Psychoses: I. Schizophrenia and Affective Disorders Compared with Psychiatrically Symptom-Free Surgical Conditions." *Archives of General Psychiatry* 36 (1979): 1295–1301.

Turner, R. Jay, and Morton O. Wagenfeld. "Occupational Mobility and Schizophrenia: An Assessment of the Social Causation and Social Selection Hypotheses." *American Sociological Review* 32 (1967): 104–113.

Ullmann, Leonard P. *Institution and Outcome: A Comparative Study of Psychiatric Hospitals.* Elmsford, N.Y.: Pergamon Press, 1967.

U.S. Department of Health and Human Services. *Toward a National Plan for the Chronically Mentally Ill. Report to the Secretary—1980.* DHHS Publication No. (ADM 81-1077). Rockville, Md.: Department of Health and Human Services, 1980.

U.S. Department of Housing and Urban Development (HUD). *A Report to the Secretary on the Homeless and Emergency Shelters.* Washington, D.C.: Office of Policy Development and Research, 1984.

U.S. General Accounting Office. *Homelessness: A Complex Problem and the Federal Response.* Washington, D.C.: General Accounting Office, 1985.

U.S. President's Commission on Mental Health. *Report of the Task Panel on the Nature and Scope of the Problems,* Vol. I, Vol. II Appendix. Washington, D.C.: U.S. Government Printing Office, 1978.

Uttaro, Thomas and Mechanic, David. "The NAMI Consumer Survey Analysis of Unmet Needs." *Hospital and Community Psychiatry* 45 (1994): 372–374.

Vaughn, Christine E., and Julian P. Leff. "The Influence of Family and Social Factors on the Course of Psychiatric Illness: A Comparison of Schizophrenic and Depressed Neurotic Patients." *British Journal of Psychiatry* 129 (1976): 125–137.

Vladeck, Bruce. *Unloving Care: The Nursing Home Tragedy.* New York: Basic Books, 1980.

Wakefield, Jerome. "Conceptual Validity of DIS Diagnostic Criteria and ECA Prevalence Estimates." Unpublished paper. Institute for Health, Health Care Policy, and Aging Research, Rutgers University, New Brunswick, N.J., 1997.

Walkup, James. "Family Involvement in General Hospital Inpatient Care." Edited by D. Mechanic, *Improving Psychiatric Treatment in an Era of Managed Care.* New Directions for Mental Health Services Number 73. San Francisco: Jossey-Bass, 1997.

Ware, John E., Jr., et al. "Comparison of Health Outcomes at a Health Maintenance Organization with those of Fee-for-Service Care." *Lancet* 14 (1986): 1017–1022.

Ware, John E., et al. "Differences in 4-Year Health Outcomes for Elderly and Poor, Chronically Ill Patients Treated in HMO and Fee-for-Service Systems: Results from the Medical Outcomes Study." *Journal of the American Medical Association* 276 (1996): 1039–1047.

Warren, Carol. *The Court of Last Resort: Mental Illness and the Law.* Chicago: University of Chicago Press, 1982.

Watts, Fraser N., and Douglas H. Bennett, eds. *Theory and Practice of Psychiatric Rehabilitation.* New York: John Wiley and Sons, 1983.

Waxler, Nancy E. "Is Outcome for Schizophrenia Better in Non-Industrial Societies? The Case of Sri Lanka." *Journal of Nervous and Mental Disease* 167 (1979): 144–158.

Weinman, Bernard, and Robert J. Kleiner. "The Impact of Community Living and Community Member Intervention on the Adjustment of the Chronic Psychotic Patient." In *Alternatives to Mental Hospital Treatment,* edited by Leonard J. Stein and Mary Ann Test, pp. 139–159. New York: Plenum, 1978.

Weinstein, Raymond. "Patient Attitudes toward Mental Hospitalization: A Review of Qualitative Research." *Journal of Health and Social Behavior* 20 (1979): 237–258.

———. "Labeling Theory and the Attitudes of Mental Patients: A Review." *Journal of Health and Social Behavior* 24 (1983): 70–84.

Weisbrod, Burton A., Mary Ann Test, and Leonard I. Stein. "Alternatives to Mental Hospital Treatment II. Economic Benefit–Cost Analysis." *Archives of General Psychiatry* 37 (1980), 400–402.

Weiss, Robert S. *Marital Separation.* New York: Basic Books, 1975.

Weissman, Myrna M., and Eugene S. Paykel. *The Depressed Woman: A Study of Social Relationships.* Chicago: University of Chicago Press, 1974.

Weissman, Myrna M., and Gerald L. Klerman. "Sex Differences and the Epidemiology of Depression." *Archives of General Psychiatry* 34 (1977): 98–111.

Weissman, Myrna M., and Jerome K. Myers. "Affective Disorders in a U.S. Urban Community: The Use of Research Diagnostic Criteria in an Epidemiological Survey." *Archives of General Psychiatry* 35 (1978): 1304–1311.

Weissman, Myrna M., et al. "Cross-National Epidemiology of Major Depression and Bipolar Disorder." *Journal of the American Medical Association* 276 (1996): 293–299.

Wells, Kenneth B., et al. *Cost-Sharing and the Demand for Ambulatory Mental Health Services* (CR-2960-HHS). Santa Monica, Calif.: Rand Corporation, 1982.

Wells, Kenneth B., Willard G. Manning, Jr., and Bernadette Benjamin. "Use of Outpatient Mental Health Services in HMO and Fee-for-Service Plans: Results from a Randomized Controlled Trial." *Health Services Research* 21 (1986): 453–474.

———. "Cost-Sharing and the Use of General Medical Physicians for Outpatient Mental Health Care." *Health Services Research* 22 (1987): 1–17.

———. "Comparison of Use of Outpatient Mental Health Services in an HMO and Fee-for-Service Plans." *Medical Care* 25 (1987): 894–903.

Wells, Kenneth B., et al. "Detection of Depressive Disorder for Patients Receiving Prepaid or Fee-for-Service Care: Results from the Medical Outcomes Study." *Journal of The American Medical Association* 262 (1989): 3298–3302.

Wells, Kenneth B., et al. "The Functioning and Well-Being of Depressed Patients: Results from the Medical Outcomes Study." *Journal of the American Medical Association* 262 (1989): 914–919.

Wells, Kenneth B., Willard G. Manning, Jr., and R. Burciaga Valdez. "The Effects of a Prepaid Group Practice on Mental Health Outcomes." *Health Services Research* 25 (1990): 615–625.

Wells, Kenneth B., et al. *Caring for Depression.* Cambridge, Mass.: Harvard University Press, 1996.

Werner, Emmy E., and Ruth S. Smith. *Overcoming the Odds: High-Risk Children from Birth to Adulthood.* Ithaca, N.Y.: Cornell University Press, 1992.

Wheaton, Blair. "Models for the Stress-Buffering Functions of Coping Resources." *Journal of Health and Social Behavior* 26 (1985): 352–64.

Wheaton, Blair. "The Sociogenesis of Psychological Disorder: Reexamining the Causal Issues with Longitudinal Data." *American Sociological Review* 43 (1978): 383–403.

White, Kerr L. "Evaluation of Medical Education and Health Care." In *Community Medicine: Teaching, Research and Health Care,* edited by Willoughby Lathem and Anne Newbery, pp. 241–270. New York: Appleton-Century-Crofts, 1970.

Wig, N. N., et al. "Expressed Emotion and Schizophrenia in North India." *British Journal of Psychiatry* 151 (1987): 156–173.

Wilson, A. T. M., E. I. Trist, and Adam Curle. "Transitional Communities and Social Reconnection: A Study of the Civil Resettlement of British Prisoners of War." In *Readings in Social Psychology,* rev. ed., edited by Guy E. Swanson, Theodore M. Newcomb, and Eugene L. Hartley, pp. 561–579. New York: Holt, Rhinehart & Winston, 1952.

Wing, John K. "Institutionalism in Mental Hospitals." *British Journal of Social and Clinical Psychology* 1 (1962): 38–51.

———. "Rehabilitation of Psychiatric Patients." *The British Journal of Psychiatry,* 109 (1963): 635–641.

———. "The Modern Management of Schizophrenia." In *New Aspects of the Mental Health Services,* edited by Hugh Freeman and James Farndale, pp. 3–28. Elmsford, N.Y.: Pergamon Press, 1967.

———. *Reasoning about Madness.* Oxford: Oxford University Press, 1978.

Wing, John K., and George W. Brown. "Social Treatment of Chronic Schizophrenia: A Comprehensive Survey of Three Mental Hospitals." *Journal of Mental Science* 107 (1961): 847–861.

———. *Institutionalism and Schizophrenia: A Comparative Study of Three Mental Hospitals, 1960–1968.* Cambridge: Cambridge University Press, 1970.

Wing, John K., et al. "Reliability of a Procedure for Measuring and Classifying 'Present Psychiatric State'". *The British Journal of Psychiatry* 113 (1967): 499–515.

Wing, John K., and Anthea M. Hailey, eds. *Evaluating Community Psychiatric Service: The Camberwell Register, 1964–1971.* London: Oxford University Press, 1972.

Wing, John K., John E. Cooper, and Norman Sartorius. *Measurement and Classification of Psychiatric Symptoms.* Cambridge: Cambridge University Press, 1974.

Wing, Lorna, et al. "The Use of Psychiatric Services in Three Urban Areas: An International Case Register Study." *Social Psychiatry* 2 (1967): 158–167.

Wolff, Nancy, Thomas W. Helminiak, and Ronald J. Diamond. "Estimated Societal Costs of Assertive Community Mental Health Care." *Psychiatric Services* 46 (1995): 898–906.

Wolpe, Joseph. *Psychotherapy by Reciprocal Inhibition.* Stanford, Calif.: Stanford University Press, 1958.

Woodwell, David A. and Susan M. Schappert. "National Ambulatory Medical Care Survey: 1993 Summary." *Advance Data from Vital and Health Statistics* 270 (1995).

World Health Organization. *Report of the International Pilot Study of Schizophrenia,* Vol. 1. Geneva: World Health Organization, 1973.

———. *Schizophrenia: An International Follow-up Study.* Geneva, New York: John Wiley and Sons, 1979.

Wright, James D. *Address Unknown: The Homeless in America.* New York: Aldine de Gruyter, 1989.

Yarrow, Marian Radke, et al. "The Psychological Meaning of Mental Illness in the Family." *The Journal of Social Issues* 11 (1955): 12–24.

Yudofsky, Stuart, Robert E. Hales, and Tom Ferguson. *What You Need to Know about Psychiatric Drugs.* Washington, D.C.: Psychiatric Press, 1991.

Zelman, Walter A. *The Changing Health Care Marketplace: Private Ventures, Public Interests.* San Francisco: Jossey-Bass, 1996.

Zusman, Jack. "Some Explanations of the Changing Appearance of Psychotic Patients: Antecedents of the Social Breakdown Syndrome Concept." *Milbank Memorial Fund Quarterly* 44 (1966, Part 2): 363–394.

———. "APA's Model Commitment Law and the Need for Better Mental Health Services." *Hospital and Community Psychiatry* 36 (1985): 978–980.

Name Index

Subject Index